# THE MĀṆḌŪKYOPANIṢAD

WITH

# GAUḌAPĀDA'S KĀRIKĀ

# THE MĀṆḌŪKYOPANIṢAD

WITH

## GAUḌAPĀDA'S KĀRIKĀ

AND

## ŚAṄKARA'S COMMENTARY


TRANSLATED AND ANNOTATED

*by*

**SWĀMĪ NIKHILĀNANDA**

WITH A FOREWORD BY

V. SUBRAHMANYA IYER



Advaita Ashrama

(Publication House of Ramakrishna Math)

5 Dehi Entally Road • Kolkata 700 014

*Published by*
Swami Shuddhidananda
Adhyaksha, Advaita Ashrama
Mayavati, Champawat, Uttarakhand, India
*from its Publication House, Kolkata*
Email : mail@advaitaashrama.org
Website : www.advaitaashrama.org



Sixth Edition, May 1987
Seventeenth Reprint, August 2023
1M1C

ISBN 978-81-7505-022-8

*Printed in India at*
Trio Process
Kolkata 700 014

## CONTENTS


| | | PAGES |
|---|---|---|
| Foreword | | i–viii |
| Preface | | ix–xxxv |
| Vedic Invocation | | 1-5 |
| Chapter I. | Āgama Prakaraṇa | 7–85 |
| Chapter II. | Illusion | 86–135 |
| Chapter III. | On Advaita | 136–211 |
| Chapter IV. | Quenching of Fire-Brand | 212-313 |
| The Concluding Salutation by Śrī Śaṅkarācārya | | 314-315 |
| Index | | 316–320 |

# PUBLISHER'S NOTE

In 1936, Sri Ramakrishna's first birth centenary was observed all over the world. On that memorable occasion, several centres of the Ramakrishna Order brought out many publications, including translations of the sacred Upaniṣads. One such was this Māṇḍūkyopaniṣad with Gauḍapāda's Kārikā and Śaṅkara's commentary, translated and annotated by the well-known learned monk, Swami Nikhilananda of the Ramakrishna Order, of revered memory, with a scholarly Foreword by the great philosopher, the late V. Subrahmanya Iyer, and published by Sri Ramakrishna Ashrama, Mysore. During this half a century, the book has undergone five editions.

The copyright of the book was made over to Advaita Ashrama, Mayavati, in 1983. We are grateful to Sri Ramakrishna Ashrama, Mysore, for this gesture. It gives us great pleasure now to publish the sixth edition of the book and place it in the hands of the lovers and students of the Upaniṣadic lore. May the incomparable spiritual knowledge and profound philosophy contained in this smallest of the 'major or principal Upaniṣads' spread far and wide is our earnest prayer and wish.

PUBLISHER

Śaṅkara Jayanti
3 May 1987
Advaita Ashrama
Mayavati, Himalayas

# NOTE

The unique feature of *Māṇḍūkya* lies in this that while all the other Upaniṣads deal with the several phases of Vedānta, such as Religion, Theology, Scholasticism, Mysticism, Science, Metaphysics and Philosophy, Māṇḍūkya deals exclusively with *Philosophy*, as defined by *the most modern authorities*. The three fundamental problems of philosophy, according to this special treatise are, (1) the nature of the external (material) and the internal (mental) worlds; (2) the nature of consciousness; and (3) the meaning of causality. Each of these subjects is dealt with in a chapter. The first chapter sums up the whole at the very commencement. There is nothing more for philosophy to do. While it shows how the most advanced modern sciences and modern philosophies are approaching its conclusions, it gives to the world of our own times its central doctrine that partial data give partial truth, whereas the totality of data alone gives perfect truth. The 'Totality' of data we have only when the three states of waking, dream and deep-sleep are co-ordinated for investigation. Endless will be the systems of philosophy, if based on the waking state only. Above all inasmuch as this philosophy holds that mere 'satisfaction' is no criterion of truth, the best preparation for a study of *Vedānta Philosophy* is a training in *scientific method*, but with a determination to get at the very end: 'To stop not till the goal (of Truth) is reached.'

V. S. I.

# FOREWORD

NO one that knows anything of the philosophy of the Upaniṣads can be said to be ignorant of the place that *Māṇḍūkya Upaniṣad* with its *Kārikās* occupies in it. If a man cannot afford to study all the hundred and more Upaniṣads, it will be enough, it is declared in the *Muktikopaniṣad*, if he reads the one Upaniṣad of Māṇḍūkya, since, as Śaṅkara also says, it contains the quintessence of all of them. Thoroughly to grasp the philosophy taught in Māṇḍūkya, one needs a knowledge of the whole field of ancient Indian thought. Such being the nature of this work, one with my limitations of knowledge cannot presume to be able to do any justice to its merits and that in, what is called a 'Foreword'. And yet if I agreed to write a foreword to Swāmī Nikhilānandaji's most valuable publication it was not because I had any thought that this well-known and learned author of the translations of *Vedāntasāra* and *Dṛg-Dṛśya-Viveka* and frequent writer to many leading Indian journals on religion and philosophy needed an introduction to the literary world. Nor did I think that I could add anything of value to his critical and scholarly preface and notes. On the other hand, I consented because I felt that this was an opportunity for me to indicate in some measure the place of Gauḍapāda, not among religionists, theologians, scholastics or mystics but among *philosophers*. In what high regard he is held by the Vedāntins of the past is well known. But the esteem that he commands among distinguished men of our own times has yet to be pointed out. With this object in view and also with an idea of acknowledging my own indebtedness to some of them I have ventured to say a few words. Of two such renowned personages of our day one was my most revered Guru, the late Śrī Saccidānanda Śivābhinava Narasiṁha Bhāratī Swāmī of Sringeri, who introduced me to the study of the *Kārikās*, at whose feet I had the inestimable privilege of sitting as a pupil. Here, a short account of my first lesson in Gauḍapāda may not be considered irrelevant by the reader. The very first day I paid my respects to the Swāmī more than forty years ago, I started thus: 'The follower of every religion thinks that his faith, his scripture or his interpretation of it reveals the highest truth and that they are therefore superior to other faiths, scriptures or interpretations. This notion has contributed not a little to the misfortunes of mankind in this world. The case is not far different with many of those that are called philosophers. Though they have not instigated men to cause bloodshed, as mere religionists have done and are still doing, yet they have made their followers delight rather in their points of *difference* than in those of *agreement*. How then is a Hindu in any way better than a Mahomedan or a Christian? Or, again, if truth or ultimate truth, a something common to all minds, cannot be rationally reached, is not *philosophic* enquiry a wild goose chase, as so many modern and honest thinkers have held? Lastly, as regards truth itself, everyone, even a fool, thinks that what he knows is the truth.' The Swāmī in reply said, 'What you say may be true with regard to mere religion, mysticism, theology or scholasticism which are mistaken for philosophy. It may be so with the early or intermediate stages in philosophy. But Vedānta, particularly its philosophy, is something different. It starts with the very question you ask. It sets before itself the object of finding a truth, "Free from all dispute" and "Not opposed to any school of thought or religion or interpretation of scriptures". Its truth is independent of sect, creed, colour, race, sex, and belief. And it aims at what is "Equally *good* for *all* beings"'. Then, I said, that I would devote the whole of my life to the study of Vedānta, if the Swāmī would be so gracious as to introduce me to a Vedāntin, past or present, that did not or does not claim superiority for his religion over others on the authority of his own scripture, who does not refuse to open the gates of his heaven to those that differ from him, but who seeks only such philosophic *truth* as does not lead to differences among men. Immediately the revered Guru quoted three verses from Gauḍapāda, *Kārikās* II-1, III-17 and IV-2, and explained them, the substance of which has been quoted above. 'If you want', he added, 'truth indisputable by any one and truth beneficent to *all* men, nay, to all *beings*, read and inwardly digest what Śaṅkara's teacher's teacher, Śrī Gauḍapāda says in his *Kārikās*.'

The other eminent personage to whom I owe most of my effort to make a critical study of Gauḍapāda is His Highness the Mahāraja of Mysore, Śrī Kṛṣṇarāja Wadiyar Bahadur IV. His profound and extensive knowledge of philosophy and particularly his high regard for *Māṇḍūkya Upaniṣad* and the *Kārikās*, led to frequent talks on the topics dealt with therein. His Highness who is accustomed to meeting learned scholars, pious religionists, and deep thinkers of all types and of different countries, is a most disinterested critic. This drove me to the necessity of ascertaining how far Gauḍapāda's views are of value from the standpoint of the student of Western science and philosophy and how far the ancient Vedānta could stand the fire of modern criticism, particularly of science, a knowledge of which is so indispensable to the study of philosophy nowadays.

In this connection, I must not forget to mention that my debt is also immense to Mr. K. A. Kṛṣṇasvāmi Iyer, the

Vedāntin of Bangalore, and to those Swāmīs of the Śrī Rāmakṛṣṇa Order, that have devoted their life to the *philosophical* pursuit of truth both from the ancient and from the modern view-points and that have been with me at Mysore.

After studying Gauḍapāda for a time I turned to the Upaniṣad and to *Brahma-Sūtras* as interpreted by Śaṅkara, under the Sringeri Swāmī's invaluable guidance. I have now for more than forty years read and re-read them in the light of the Swāmī's teachings and I find that Vedānta is far in advance, not merely of the most modern Western philosophic thought, but also of scientific thought, so far as its pursuit of knowledge for its own sake is concerned. To refer to an instance or two: Two thousand years ago Gauḍapāda anticipated what science is just beginning to guess in regard to 'causal' relation without a knowledge of which Vedānta can *never* be understood. The meaning of 'Truth' which is still a matter of dispute among many philosophers, has been investigated by him more deeply than has yet been done by other thinkers.

Vedānta in its highest, that is its philosphic, aspect can have no significance to one who has not realized the importance of the *most fundamental* question in philosophy: What is truth, particularly 'Ultimate Truth'? How is it to be tested? It is the Upaniṣads that answer it by declaring that Ultimate Truth is that which admits of no difference of view of any kind, as two plus two are equal to four. Gauḍapāda and Śaṅkara follow this doctrine in all its implications. It assigns to religious faith, theology, scholasticism, mysticism, art and science, their respective places in the one grand edifice of human knowledge, *as a whole*. Gauḍapāda rejects no kind of knowledge or experience. Even the views of his opponents, he welcomes and accepts as parts of the knowledge that leads to the attainment of truth and

Ultimate Truth. His distinction lies in the emphasis he lays on the impossibility of reaching the highest truth unless the *totality* of human experience or knowledge be taken into consideration. Others generally build their systems on the *waking* state alone. But the philosophers of the Upaniṣads hold that unless the three states of waking, dream and deep sleep be co-ordinated, there cannot be adequate data for the enquiry regarding Ultimate Truth. This is a matter still unknown to Europe and America. Nor has the West as yet evaluated *conceptual* knowledge. The relation of mind to its ideas or contents is another problem that has not as yet been even dreamt of in Western Philosophy.

To one desirous of making a scholarly study of Vedānta, the historical side of the evolution of philosophic thought in India is of great value. One can, however, easily obtain this information in any of the modern text-books on Indian Philosophy. But, though Gauḍapāda could be fairly appreciated even without such background, yet, his commentator Śaṅkara and his followers cannot be fully comprehended without a previous acquaintance with the several systems of Indian thought. Swāmī Nikhilānandaji has therefore furnished valuable notes to make such matters clear. One point, however, needs to be referred to here, as it is of special interest to modern thinkers.

The several theories of perception, for instance, are discussed in the *Kārikās*, it being taken for granted that causal relation is an unquestionable fact. Like all true *philosophers*, not mere metaphysicians, he starts with the *perceptual world* and pursues the enquiry. If the word 'real' be confined to percepts, Gauḍapāda is not a realist. If the word 'ideal' be confined to what is known within, apart from the senses, he is not an idealist. But he admits that the concepts, *real* and *ideal*, are of value as steps leading to the *highest truth* which is beyond idealism, or realism, or spiritualism, all of which only refer to waking experience. To him the external world as well as the internal is unreal. But his philosophy does not lead to illusionism, as the goal. The relation between mind and matter, idea and sense objects, or even mind and its contents is a matter of dispute to this day. But Gauḍapāda's explanation may or may not be accepted, to the extent to which it is confined to the waking state. It does not, however, affect in the least his conclusion which is based on the *three* states. He denies the category of relationship, in what is Ultimate Truth. Nor does he admit 'Satisfaction' (*Ānandam*) to be a test of it.

Another important feature is that he is a thinker of the most rational type, which Śaṅkara's interpretation of him, points out. The 'philosophic method' (*prakriyā*) described here clears so many misapprehensions regarding the meaning of *philosophy*, in general.

Philosophy, according to Gauḍapāda and Śaṅkara, is an interpretation of the *totality* of human experience or of the *whole* of life from the standpoint of truth. Philosophy, therefore, is the whole, of which Religion, Mysticism (*Yoga*), Theology, Scholasticism, Speculation, Art and Science are but parts. Such philosophy or Vedānta as ignores any part or parts, is no Vedānta. In fact it employs the scientific method more rigorously than modern science does. Gauḍapāda's and Śaṅkara's view of *philosophy* is being echoed and re-echoed by modern Western thinkers in defining it. These ancient philosophers further declare that all other kinds of experience and knowledge are but several *stages* in the evolution of life and philosophic thought. And the object sought by philosophy, as these two pre-eminent Hindu philosophers say, is the happiness (*Sukham*) and welfare (*Hitam*) of *all* beings (*Sarva Sattva*) in this world (*Ihaiva*).

Gauḍapāda is little known in the West. There is not the least doubt that his work will open new vistas of thought to Western enquiries and will make them turn to the East for more light. Without the slightest fear of exaggeration, it may be said that in no other part of the 'world' has man dared to pursue *truth* with the degree of devotion, and particularly of *determination* with which he has done in India. It is in India alone that one sees the seeker sacrificing not merely all his material belongings as in other countries, but also every feeling, thought, view, or perception to which he may, at the start, be *attached*. Till one makes sure that one's mind has been completely purged of all preconceptions or prejudices which are the offspring of *attachment*, one cannot hope to command the concentration of mind needed for climbing the topmost steps leading to *truth*. One of the greatest characteristics of *philosophy* in India—not Indian theology and the like—is the perfection to which the method of *eliminating preconceptions* is carried. And to do this one must be a *dhīra* (hero).

Much less does the West know of Gauḍapāda's method of complete eradication of 'Ego' or the personal 'self,' a subject, to the supreme importance of which, Western Science—not its Philosophy or speculation which is blissfully ignorant of it—is just becoming alive. Swāmī Vivekānanda says, 'Can anything be attained with any shred of "I" left?' And Śrī Śaṅkara says, 'The root of all obstacles (in the pursuit of Truth) is the first form of ignorance called the "Ego". So long as one has any connection with the "Ego", vile as it is, there cannot be the *least* talk about liberation (from ignorance)."

As has been hinted in the Note also at the beginning, the best modern scientists hold that: 'The Scientific man has *above all things* to strive at *self-elimination*, in his judgments to provide an argument which is *true*....unbiassed by *personal feeling* is characteristic of what may be termed the Scientific frame of mind....'

'The validity of a scientific conclusion depends upon the *elimination* of the *subjective element*....'

'What is *most difficult* of attainment and yet *indispensable* is distrust of our *personal bias* in forming judgments. Our hypothesis must be *depersonalized*....'

—*From J. A. Thomson*

How strongly this discipline is enforced on the seeker after *truth* in India may be gathered from what Śrī Kṛṣṇa says in the *Bhāgavata:*

'One should prostate oneself on the ground before every creature down to....an ass or a dog....so that "egoism" may quickly depart.'

The essence of the teachings of Hindu *Philosophy* here is found in the following prayer of the great Śrī Rāmakṛṣṇa Paramahaṁsa: (Translated). 'One man says this, another man says that. O mother, pray, tell me what the Truth is.'

Many such and other matters of great value are ably dealt with by the Swāmiji in the body of the work. This distinguished and learned author has done a real service to such earnest seekers after truth, as are *determined* to reach the end, wherever English is known, by translating this priceless work of Śrī Gauḍapāda, the first Vedāntic *philosopher*, known to Indian history in what is said to be the post-Upaniṣadic or modern period.

V. SUBRAHMAṆYA IYER.

# PREFACE

THE *Māṇḍūkya Upaniṣad*, like *Muṇḍaka, Praśna* and some minor Upaniṣads, forms part of the *Atharva Veda*. It is one of the shortest of the ten principal Upaniṣads. Gauḍapāda has written two hundred and fifteen verses known as the *Kārikā* to explain the Upaniṣad and Śaṅkara has written a commentary on both the Upaniṣad and the *Kārikā*. Ānandagiri in his *Tīkā* explains at greater length Śaṅkara's commentary.

The *Māṇḍūkya Upaniṣad*, like other Upaniṣads, discusses the problem of Ultimate Reality. The knowledge of Brahman or *Ātman*, the goal of existence, is its theme. Unlike most of the Upaniṣads, it does not relate any anecdote or any imaginary conversations to elucidate the subject-matter. It is also silent about rituals and sacrifices in any form as they are irrelevant to the metaphysical or philosophical discussion of Reality. It goes straight to the subject. The extreme brevity of its statements has been the cause of despair to superficial readers who are unable to understand its real significance.

The well-known method of Vedānta to arrive at Reality is what is known as 'Vicāra'. This Upaniṣad also follows the same method. In the first place *Ātman* is associated with the three states of waking, dream and deep sleep, and, then, these states are shown to merge in *Turīya* or the Ultimate Reality. And in the sequel it is pointed out that the non-dual *Ātman* is identical with the three states and therefore all that exists is Brahman. The nature of the Ultimate Reality has been described in the seventh text of the Upaniṣad.

As the generality of men cannot realize the Ultimate Reality which is beyond all categories of time, space and causation, it is sought to help them to do so by means of a symbol. The symbol selected by the *Māṇḍūkya Upaniṣad* as well as the other Upaniṣads is *Aum*, the word of all words. *Aum* consists of three sound symbols, *viz.*, *A*, *U*, and *M*. These three denoting the gross, the subtle and the casual aspects of Brahman (from the relative standpoint), have been equated with the three states mentioned above, which contain the totality of man's experience. The method adopted by the Upaniṣad and followed by Gauḍapāda for arriving at Reality is to analyse our experience. Through the contemplation of the three sound symbols as the three states, the student, endowed with the mental and moral qualifications required for the understanding of Vedānta, is helped to reach the Ultimate Reality.

The *Kārikā* of Gauḍapāda is divided into four chapters (*prakaraṇas*): (1) *Āgama* (Scripture), (2) *Vaitathya* (the illusoriness of self-experiences), (3) *Advaita* (non-duality), (4) *Alātaśānti* (the quenching of the fire-brand). The first chapter deals with the problem of Reality from the standpoint of the Vedas. The three subsequent chapters demonstrate the same truth by means of reason.

Śaṅkara, who has commented only on Vedāntic works of the most authoritative character, such as *Gītā*, the *Upaniṣads* and the *Sūtras*, has deemed it necessary to write a commentary on Gauḍapāda's *Kārikā*. This indicates the supreme importance and value of this treatise to the philosophy of Advaita Vedānta.

Who was Gauḍapāda? Tradition makes him the teacher of Govinda who was the teacher of Śaṅkara. It is said that Gauḍapāda wrote, besides the *Kārikā* on *Māṇḍūkya Upaniṣad*, commentaries on the *Sāṁkhya* system and *Uttara Gītā*. But there does not exist much evidence to support it. Ānandagiri says in his *Ṭīkā* on Śaṅkara's commentary on the *Kārikā* (4-1) that Gauḍapāda performed great austerities in the Badarikāśrama, in the interior of the Himālayas, in order to propitiate Nārāyaṇa who is worshipped there as the God-Man. Nārāyaṇa being pleased with his devotion revealed to him the secret of the Advaita Vedānta. Gauḍapāda salutes this Nārāyaṇa in the opening verse of the fourth chapter of the *Kārikā*. In the face of the controversy regarding the date of Śaṅkara, the date of Gauḍapāda cannot be definitely fixed. The generally accepted date of Śaṅkara's birth, one agreed to by Bhāṇḍārkar, Pāṭhak and Deussen, 788 A.D. is not free from objections. According to Swāmī Prajñānānanda Sarasvatī and a few other scholars, Śaṅkara flourished before Christ. Some eminent scholars, by an examination of the literary style of Śaṅkara and the historical and other references, push back his date to the second century B.C. Their contention cannot be lightly brushed aside. One fact, however, can be asserted without fear of contradiction that Gauḍapāda is the solitary philosopher, known to us, who, before Śaṅkara, gave a rational explanation of the Advaita Vedānta which is the objective of the Upaniṣadic teachings.

Even the *Sūtras* of Bādarāyaṇa are not free from *a priori* reasoning, that is, reasoning conditioned by the tradition and the authority of the Scriptures. It is only Gauḍapāda that has successfully demonstrated in his *Kārikā* that the non-dual *Ātman* declared in the Upaniṣads as the Ultimate Reality is not a theological dogma, and that it does not depend upon the mystic experiences of the Yogis; but that it is a metaphysical rather a philosophical truth which satisfies the demands of universal tests and which is based upon reason independent of scriptural authority. Gauḍapāda, as already stated, follows, in the first chapter of his book, the traditional method of basing his conclusions on the authority of the Scriptures and demonstrates that the aim of the *Śruti* is to establish the non-dual *Ātman* as the ultimate authority. In the following chapters he re-establishes the same truth through reasoning alone and thus meets the arguments of the Buddhists and other thinkers who do not admit the authority of the Vedas. Śaṅkara refers to this in his commentary on the first verses of the last three chapters of the *Kārikā*.

Here, we deem it necessary to review some of the observations of the latest among well-known authors. Professor S. N. Das Gupta, M.A., Ph.D., in his celebrated work, *A History of Indian Philosophy* (pp. 423–29) regarding Gauḍapāda and his philosophy writes: 'Gauḍapāda thus *flourished after all* great Buddhist teachers Aśvaghoṣa, Nāgārjuna, Asaṅga and Vasubandhu, and I believe that there is *sufficient evidence* in his *Kārikās* for thinking that he was *possibly himself a Buddhist* and considered that the teachings of the *Upaniṣads tallied,* with those of *Buddha.* Thus at the beginning of the fourth chapter of his *Kārikās* he says that he adores that *great man* (*dvipadām varam*) who by knowledge as wide as the sky realized (*sambuddha*)that all appearances (*Dharma*) were like the *vacuous sky* (*gaganopamam*). He thus goes on to say that he adores him who has dictated (*deśita*) that the *touch of the untouch* (*Asparśa Yoga—probably referring to* Nirvāṇa) was the goal that produced happiness to all beings and that he was neither in disagreement with the doctrine nor found any contradiction in it (*avivādaḥ aviruddhaśca*).... In IV. 19 of his *Kārikā*, he again says that the *Buddhas* have shown that there is no coming into being in any way (*sarvathā buddhairajātī paridīpitāḥ*). Again in IV. 4, 2 he says that it was for those realists (*vāstuvādis*), since they found things and could deal with them and were afraid of non-being, that the *Buddha* had spoken of origination (*jāti*). In IV. 90 he refers to

*Agrayāna* which we know to be a name of *Māhāyāna*. Again, in IV. 98 and 99, he says that all *appearances* are 'pure and vacuous' by nature. These the *Buddha*, the emancipated one (*mukta*) and the leaders know. *It was said by Buddha that all appearances were knowledge. He then closes the Kārikās with an adoration which in all probability also refers to the Buddha*.... Gauḍapāda *does not indicate his preference* one way or the other (*i.e.*, regarding the theories of creation), but describes the fourth *state*.... In the third chapter Gauḍapāda says that truth is *like the void* (*Ākāśa*) which is conceived as taking part in birth and death, coming and going and as existing in all bodies, but, however it be conceived, it is all the while non-different from *Ākāśa*.... He should *awaken the mind* (*citta*) *into its final dissolution*.... All the *Dharmas* (appearances) are without death or decay. Gauḍapāda then follows a dialectical form of argument which reminds us of Nāgārjuna.... All experiences (*prajñapti*) are *dependent on reasons*, for otherwise both would vanish.... When we look at all things in a connected manner they seem to be dependent, but when we look at them from the point of view of Reality or truth the *reason ceases to be reason*.... Therefore neither the mind nor the objects seen by it are ever produced. Those who perceive them to suffer production are really *traversing the reason of vacuity* (*Kha*).... *It is so obvious that these doctrines are borrowed* from the *Mādhyamika* doctrines, as found in the *Nāgārjuna Kārikās* and *Vijñānavāda* doctrines as found in *Laṅkāvatāra*, that it is needless to attempt to prove it. Gauḍapāda assimilated all the Buddhist *Śūnyavāda* and *Vijñānavāda* teachings and *thought that these hold good* of the ultimate truth preached by the Upaniṣads. It is immaterial whether he was a Hindu or a Buddhist, *so long as we are sure that he had the highest respect for Buddha* and for his teachings which he believed to be his.... He only incidentally suggested that the great Buddhist truth of indefinable and unspeakable *Vijñāna or vacuity* would hold good of the highest *Ātman* of the Upaniṣads and *thus laid the foundation* of a revival of the Upanishadic studies on Buddhist lines....' (The English words in italics are ours.)

Our interpretation of the passages in the above quotation will be found in the body of the book. Prof. Das Gupta has given his own interpretation of the *Kārikā*, without attaching any value to the commentary of Śaṇkara or the *Ṭīkā* of Ānaṇdagiri and it is clear from the point of view of Prof. Das Gupta that Śaṅkara has failed to understand the sense of the *Kārikā*. This attempt of Prof. Das Gupta to interpret the *Kārikā* according to his own view is no doubt responsible for ascribing to Gauḍapāda the views which, according to us, he never seems even to have dreamt of cherishing. Prof. Das Gupta tries to prove that Gauḍapāda was *possibly* a Buddhist and that his philosophy was borrowed from Buddhism. We shall therefore offer a few words of criticism regarding the views of Prof. Das Gupta.

It has *not* been *settled* that Gauḍapāda flourished after the Buddhist philosophers, Aśvaghoṣa, Nāgārjuna, Asaṅga and Vasubandhu. Some recent researches reveal that he lived long before them. This is, however, a point for the student of history of literature. Further, the *standpoint* and the *conclusion* of Gauḍapāda's philosophy, however, are *fundamentally different* from those of the Buddhist thinkers named above. There is no evidence in his *Kārīkā* to show that Gauḍapāda was *possibly* a *Buddhist*. There is positive proof on the other hand to show that he was not a Buddhist. Gauḍapāda himself states, for instance, in the clearest possible language at the conclusion of the *Kārikā* (IV. 99) that 'This (his own view) is not the view of Buddha'. Śaṅkara in his commentary of this *Kārikā* says that the essence of the Ultimate Reality, which is non-dual and which is free from multiplicity of the perceiver, perception and the perceived, has not been taught by Buddha. In its refutation of the reality of the external objects and in asserting that all objects are mere acts of mind (*manaḥspandanam*), the Buddhist *Vijñānavāda*, no doubt, approaches the non-dual consciousness of the Upaniṣads, but the knowledge of the non-dual *Ātman*, which alone is the Ultimate Reality, can be found in Vedānta alone. We are of opinion that Buddhist metaphysical thought is nearest to Gauḍapāda's *Kārikās*. Further corroboration can be found in Śaṅkara's commentary on *Kārikās* IV. 28 and 83.

Prof. Das Gupta, in order to prove his conclusion, has given his own interpretations. One studying the Upaniṣads and the *Kārikās* in accordance with the six canons (*liṅgam*) of interpretation, *viz.*, the beginning and the conclusion (*upakrama* and *upasaṁhāra*), repetition (*abhyāsa*), originality (*apūrvatā*), result (*phalam*), eulogy (*arthavāda*) and demonstration (*upapatti*), will find that the aims of the Upaniṣads and the *Kārikā* are identical, namely, the establishment of the non-dual self as the Ultimate Reality and this cannot be found in the teachings of the Buddhist philosophers.

At the beginning of the fourth chapter of the *Kārikā* Gauḍapāda does not adore Buddha but Nārāyaṇa who is worshipped in Badarikāśrama through the symbol of *Man*. The word *Dharma* used by Gauḍapāda does not mean *appearance*. '*Dharma*' literally means 'attribute', which is, according to the Vedānta philosophy, non-different from the substance—as the heat and the light are non-different from the sunshine. '*Dharma*' is used by Gauḍapāda to mean *Jīva* which if taken as attribute of Brahman is non-different from it. Gauḍāpāda has admirably proved in his *Kārikā* that all *Dharmas* or *Jīvas* are identical with the non-dual

Brahman and therefore they are ever-pure and ever-illumined. The word '*Dharma*' has been used in the plural sense in view of the multiplicity of the *Jīvas* from the standpoint of empirical experience. Gauḍapāda contends that what others, from their relative standpoint, take to be multiple *Jīvas*, is nothing but non-dual Brahman. The analogy of *Dharma* to *Ākāśa, based upon vacuity,* is far-fetched. The real point of analogy lies in their all-pervasiness, purity and subtle nature. But *Dharma* is not really identical with *Ākāśa* as the latter is known, from the empirical standpoint, to contain the element of insentiency (*jaḍa*). The adoration referred to in IV. 2 is not directed to Buddha, as hinted by Prof. Das Gupta, but to *Nārāyaṇa*.

The translation of the word '*Asparśayoga*' as the 'touch of the untouch' does not convey any meaning. It certainly does not refer to *Nīrvāṇa* as suggested by Prof. Das Gupta, if *Nirvāṇa* means total annihilation. We prefer to translate the word as the *Yoga* which is not related to anything. Apparently there is a contradiction involved in the word. The word '*Asparśa*' meaning freedom from relationship refers to the non-dual Brahman alone. But *Yoga* signifying union indicates quality. Gauḍapāda designates the path of knowledge described in the *Kārikā* and in *Advaita Vedānta* as *Asparśayoga* inasmuch as the word *Yoga* was used in his time also to denote the method of attaining to the Ultimate Reality. In the *Bhagavadgītā*, for instance, *Yoga* is used in different senses. *Yoga* is also used in the broad sense of 'discipline' or 'path'. That this method is free from all relationship has been demonstrated in the *Kārikā*. The Ultimate Reality taught in the *Kārikā* and *Advaita Vedānta* cannot be *Nirvāṇa* if that word means, as is known from the study of some of the Buddhist writers, the total negation of everything. But whether Buddha himself used the word in that sense is doubtful. The non-dual Brahman taught (*vide* Chapter III and II. 23 of *Kārikā*) in the *Advaita Vedānta* is free from hostility and contradiction as according to this philosophy non-dual Brahman alone exists. Hostility and contradiction are inherent in all dualistic systems of thought.

Gauḍapāda has, no doubt, used the word 'Buddha' several times in the *Kārikā*. But the word does not refer to the traditional founder of Buddhism, as Prof. Das Gupta seems to suggest. It only means the knower of Truth. The word '*Agrayāna*' in IV. 90 may be made to indicate '*Mahāyāna*' only by a fanciful resemblance cf words. The word really means '*Prathamataḥ*', *i.e.*, in the first place, otherwise one cannot get any meaning out of the *Kārikā* text in which the word occurs.

Prof. Das Gupta complains that Gauḍapāda 'does not indicate his preference one way or other' regarding the theory of creation. In the *Āgama Prakaraṇa* (*Kārikā*, 7–9) he enumerates several current theories of creation given by those who accept creation as a fact. He calls these theorisers mere speculators on the process of creation (*sṛṣṭicintakāḥ*). Those to whom creation is real are certainly at liberty to advance any theory according to their tastes. But none of these speculators proves the *reality* of creation on rational grounds. Gauḍapāda is not in the least interested in these theories. He questions the reality of the *act* of creation, from the standpoint of the ultimate truth. Creation may be a fact to those who, like children, take empirical knowledge to be ultimate truth. Gauḍapāda, throughout his *Kārikā* and particularly in the fourth chapter, clearly demonstrates that the category of causality cannot be applied to the non-dual *Ātman*. Absolute non-manifestation (*ajāti*) is the only truth. Centuries before Hume and Bradley, Gauḍapāda proved that causality has no basis in fact. Creation indicates an unsatisfied desire on the part of the creator. If the Ultimate Reality be complete or perfect in itself and self-satiated (*āptakāma*), then the *act* of creation can never be predicated of it. Hegel contradicts himself when he says that a logical necessity impels the evolution of the Absolute. Schelling's explanation that the evolution of the Absolute into ego and non-ego can only be understood by an *intellectual intuition*, is mysticism or mystification, but not rational truth. If there be no creation how can one explain the multiplicity of empirical experience in the universe? Gauḍapāda by an inexorable logic proves that this is the *very nature* of the Effulgent Being (*Devasya eṣa svabhāvaḥ*). Whatever one experiences is only non-dual Brahman. All this is verily Brahman. Non-dual Brahman alone is. Diagnosis of the headache of a headless man (*kabandha*) is ludicrous and irrelevant. If the manifested manifold had ever existed, then one would think of its origination or destruction. That we see duality is due to our ignorance of the true nature of Reality which is non-dual Brahman. Again this ignorance (*Māyā*) does not exist from the standpoint of Reality. *Māyā* is only an explanation of creation given by those who *hold* creation to be a *fact*. Therefore Gauḍapāda sums up his philosophy, 'None (is) in bondage, none liberated, this is the ultimate truth' (II. 32). 'No *Jīva* is ever born. Such birth is unreal. This indeed is the highest truth that nothing whatsoever is born' (III. 48).

Gauḍapāda, no doubt, says that *Ātman* is like *Ākāśa* (III. 3). But voidness is not the point of analogy. He intends to convey the idea that *Ātman*, like the *Ākāśa* is subtle, without parts and all-pervading. Gauḍapāda was well aware of the fallacy of Nāgārjuna's reasoning. Void or a negation cannot be the substratum of an illusion. The illusion of the mirage, the snake or the silver must have a positive substratum in the form of the desert, the rope or the mother-o'-pearl. Śaṅkara aptly criticises the position of the Buddhist nihilists as lacking in intelligence, for they, in spite of the very fact of cognition and experience, describe every thing, including their own experience, as mere void. Therefore the Ultimate Reality is not a void or a negation. Without a positive Reality we cannot affirm our empirical experience. But this affirmation is not a *co-relative* of negation. Our relative experiences have the dual predicates of affirmation and negation. The Ultimate Reality is free from affirmation and negation, the inevitable characteristics of the relative.

The translation of the first line of the 44th *Kārikā* of the third chapter as 'He should awaken the "mind" (*citta*) into its final dissolution (*laya*)' does not convey the correct meaning. Gauḍapāda uses the word '*laya*' in the sense of deep sleep or *Yogic Samādhi*. *Samādhi* is the last word of the Yoga mystics. According to Gauḍapāda this is an obstacle to the realistion of truth. The seeking of pleasure in *Samādhi* shows an exhaustion of the inquiring mind. It is because the Yogis look upon mind as separate from *Ātman*, that they seek to control it in *Samādhi*. But Gauḍapāda says that the mind is the non-dual *Ātman*. Therefore there does not arise any question of controlling it. The mind and its activities (*pracāra*, Comp. III. 34) are nothing but non-dual Brahman, ever-pure, ever-free and ever-illumined. It is only due to ignorance that one perceives the duality of the subject-object relationship in the activities of the mind. But a knower of truth perceives everywhere and in all activities only the non-dual Brahman (*Gītā*, IV. 24). Hence Gauḍapāda warns the student against the trap of the *Yogic Samādhi*, as described in the line quoted above (III. 44) which really means that one should awaken the mind from the (inertia of) *laya* (*Samādhi* or deep sleep) by the repeated practice of discrimination. The *Vedāntic Samādhi* does not signify the realisation of Truth with closed eyes. It means the vision of Truth with eyes open on every object. A Vedāntist thus describes the *Samādhi*: 'With the disappearance of the attachment of the body and with the realization of the Supreme Self, to whatever object the mind is directed, one experiences *Samādhi.*'

Nowhere does Gauḍapāda, or Śaṅkara or this Upaniṣad itself say that the 'Fourth' is a 'State' (*Avastha*) as Prof. Das Gupta says.

All *Dharmas* according to Gauḍapāda, are without death or decay (IV. 10). Prof. Das Gupta, as we have already pointed out, wrongly translates *Dharma* as *appearance.* 'Appearance' is certainly attended with disappearance, *i.e.,* death and decay. For, Gauḍapāda rightly defines appearance and illusion as that which does not exist at the beginning or at the end (II. 6). Any appearance is perceived by *Ātman* only so long as that particular condition of his mind which gives rise to the appearance lasts. But *Dharma* can be said to be without decay or death only if it means *Jīva* which is the same as the non-dual Brahman.

We are afraid the translation of the 24th *Kārikā* (Chapter IV) as 'all experience is dependent on reasons' (*sanimittatvam*) is not correct. This *Kārikā* gives the view of the opponent (*Pūrvapakṣa*) who asserts the reality of the external objects. The opponent says that all subjective experiences have their 'cause' (not 'reason') in external objects as otherwise there would exist no variety in experience. Further as no true explanation can be given of the pain and misery we experience, Gauḍapāda refutes the view of the realists with the arguments of the Buddhist idealists in the next *Kārikā*. Gauḍapāda says: If this be the contention of the opponent that external world or objects create subjective idea, we ask, what causes the external world or objects? The realist cannot point out any such cause. Hence the argument of causality based upon such experience fails. The position is summed up in the statement that the argument of so-called external cause (*viz*, the external objects) is not valid. A knower of truth does not see any object other than ideas which, being identical with the mind, are the same as the non-dual Brahman. In IV. 28 Gauḍapāda refutes the Buddhist idealists (*Vijñānavādins*) as well. He quotes the views of the *Vijñānavādins* for the refutation of the realistic theory of consciousness which is, according to that school of thought, momentary, subject to birth and death and full of misery. He says that those who hold mind to be subject to birth and death, etc., are really like those who seek to trace the foot-prints of birds in the sky. The translation of this *Kārikā* (IV. 28) as 'Those who....vacuity' given by Prof. Das Gupta, does not seem to be correct.

As we have already stated, Prof. Das Gupta tries to prove that Gauḍapāda has borrowed his ideas from the Buddhist philosophers. His criticism and estimate of *Kārikā* appear to be prejudiced. Gauḍapāda may have 'assimilated all the Buddhist *Śūnyavāda* and *Vijñānavāda* teachings', but this does not prove that he 'thought that these hold good of the Ultimate Truth preached by the Upaniṣads'. Madhusūdana Sarasvatī and Vācaspati Miśra may have assimilated the entire *Nyāya* system of thought but this does not prove that the *Nyāya* views hold good of the truth established in the *Advaita Siddhi* or *Bhāmatī*. Every philosopher, worth the name, studies contemporary systems of thought. He may even borrow some lines of arguments from others for purposes of explanation. Śaṅkara himself has done so. But it is a travesty of truth to call Saṅkara a crypto-Buddhist (*Praccanna Bauddha*), as some of the dualists have done.

We have not seen anywhere in the *Kārikā* Gauḍapāda saying that he is a believer in Buddha, the founder of Buddhism.

Granting that Gauḍapāda had 'the highest respect for Buddha', every Hindu and every lover of truth cherishes a similar feeling of the highest regard for the Compassionate One. But this does not prove that they necessarily accept all that Buddha or Buddhism teaches. In fact the Hindus recognized centuries ago and even now recognize Buddha as one of the *Avatāras* of *Viṣṇu* like Rāma and Kṛṣṇa. Gauḍapāda does not certainly 'incidentally suggest that the great Buddhist truth of indefinable and unspeakable *Vijñāna* or vacuity would hold good of the highest *Ātman* of the Upaniṣads'. To assert this is to pervert the real import of the *Kārikā*. On the other hand, Gauḍapāda emphatically declares (IV. 28) that he accepts the conclusion of the Buddhist *Vijñānavādins* in order to refute the realist's contention of the reality of the external objects. But neither the *Vijñānavādins* nor the *Śūnyavādins* have got anything to say regarding the non-dual *Ātman*, which can be realized only through the rigorous pursuit of truth which the Advaita system alone does. Gauḍapāda does not let an opportunity pass without criticising the *Mādhyamika* view of absolute nihilism. The estimate of Gauḍapāda and his *Kārikā* as given by Prof. Das Gupta in his *History of Indian Philosophy*, does not indicate the high water-mark of unbiassed judgment.

Prof. Radhakrishnan gives an estimate of Gauḍapāda's philosophy in his well-known *Indian philosophy* (Vol. II. pp. 452-465). He thinks the use of some words in the *Kārikā* is peculiarly Buddhistic. We have answered this point in our criticism of Prof. Das Gupta's remarks. It may be stated here that it is a favourite method of Gauḍapāda and Śaṅkara to put one school of thought against another and ultimately show the untenability of both. Even the conclusions of the

Buddhist philosophers can be found in some place or other of the Upaniṣads. It only proves the fact that at that time certain philosophical terms were the common property of Indian thought in general. One cannot accuse a modern philosopher if he uses the arguments of modern science in order to refute the contentions of his opponents or establish his own position.

Prof. Radhakrishnan says that both 'Bādarāyaṇa and Śaṅkara strongly urge that there is a genuine difference between dream experience and the waking one and that the latter is not independent of existing objects'. According to Gauḍapāda there is no difference between the dream and the waking states from the standpoint of the Ultimate Reality. Thus an attempt is made to point out the difference between Gauḍapāda's system and that of Śaṅkara. Again it is said that 'in Gauḍapāda the negative tendency is more prominent than the positive. In Śaṅkara we have a more balanced outlook'. We disagree with Prof. Radhakrishnan. In his commentary on *Brahma-Sūtras*, Śaṅkara, no doubt, makes a distinction between the waking and the dream states. But that is done from the empirical standpoint. We have not seen Śaṅkara anywhere declaring the reality of both the states, from the standpoint of Ultimate Truth. Gauḍapāda also admits the two states of waking and dream on the empirical plane, in which our experiences are associated with external objects and their absence (IV. 87). But the next *Kārikā* indicates the Ultimate Reality to be that in which there is neither any object, nor the idea of experiencing it. We do not know of any difference between the thoughts of Śaṅkara and Gauḍapāda. Had it been so Śaṅkara would not have written a commentary on the *Kārikā*. Nowhere in his explanation of the *Kārikā* does Śaṅkara point out his disagreement with the views of Gauḍapāda. It cannot be said that the views of Śaṅkara as embodied in the commentary on the *Kārikā* are different from those expounded in the commentaries on the Upaniṣads, the *Brahma-Sūtras* and the *Gītā*. Even the acutest critic of Śaṅkara has not been able to point out any inconsistency in the writings of Śaṅkara.

Sir Radhakrishnan makes the following remarks regarding the philosophy of Gauḍapāda: 'The general idea pervading Gauḍapāda's work, that bondage and liberation, the individual soul and the world, are all unreal, makes the caustic critic observe that the theory which has nothing better to say than that an unreal soul in trying to escape from an unreal bondage in an unreal world to accomplish an unreal supreme good, may itself be an unreality. It is one thing to say that the secret of existence, how the unchangeable reality expresses itself in the changing universe without forfeiting its nature is a mystery, and another to dismiss the whole changing universe, as a mere mirage. If we have to play the game of life, we cannot do so with the conviction that the play is a show and all the prizes in it are mere blanks. No philosophy can consistently hold such a theory and be at rest with itself. The greatest condemnation of such a theory is that we are obliged to occupy ourselves with objects, the existence and value of which we are continually denying in theory. The fact of the world may be mysterious and inexplicable. It only shows that there is something else which includes and transcends the world; but it does not imply that the world is a dream.'

The main difference between the Advaita and other systems of thought is that the former does not find any reason for believing in the *reality* of the process of becoming whereas the latter pin their faith to evolution, creation or manifestation as *real*. Some Advaitic philosophers in order to explain the *fact* of the manifested manifold (which is perceived) adopt their theory of *Vivarta* according to which Brahman *appears* as the world without forfeiting its essential nature. It is like the rope appearing as the snake. Other schools of thought give other explanations of the process of becoming and not one of these explanations can be supported by reason. Gauḍapāda by an irrefutable logic disproves the reality of causation in the fourth chapter of *Kārikā*, and posits the *Ajātavāda* according to which Brahman or Reality *has never become* the universe. No one can ever prove the apparent mystery of one becoming the many, for, the many does never really exist.

Neither Gauḍapāda nor Śaṅkara ignores those who believe in the reality of the external objects or of the manifested manifold on account of their perceiving those objects through the instrumentality of the sense organs or their attachment to the particular avocations of life (IV. 42). They are generous enough to say that any defect that may attach to the belief in the reality of the external objects is not at all serious. If these realists will only pursue truth they will see that to the non-dual *Ātman* causality or duality can never be applied (IV. 42). The generality of mankind bereft of the power of discrimination is, no doubt, satisfied with empirical experience. Let it do so. But it is the aim of the philosopher that is bent upon the discrimination of the real and the unreal to point out the truth, the Ultimate Reality even if it proves the unreality of the tinsels and baubles of sense-perception. The non-discriminating mind no doubt, plunges headlong into the play of life taking every experience to be real and takes the prizes of such experience. But it is only a philosophic mind that sees that the so-called play is but an unreal 'shadow show' and all the prizes are mere blanks. Is that not also the conviction of all sober-minded persons, when they, in their maturity of thought, take a retrospective view of life?

There are two ways of enjoying a theatrical show. Both spectators and those who take part in the show enjoy it. The actors identify themselves with their respective characters and take the show as real. Therefore they cannot be said to enjoy the show in reality. But the spectators on account of their detached outlook, with their knowledge of the unreality of the show, really enjoy it.

The existence of external objects depends upon the belief that they exist (IV. 75). No one has yet been able rationally to demonstrate that things exist independently of the perceiver's mind. Even the thing-in-itself of Kant is a mere hypothesis based upon the *belief* in causality. Kant by making the things-in-themselves which are beyond the categories of time, space and causality, the cause of the phenomena is inconsistent with himself. But, a mere belief in the existence of the external objects does not prove the reality of their existence. Even in common parlance it is said that all that glitters is not gold. The 'hay, wood and stubbles' of the world, when tested by the fire of the philosopher's reasoning, are found to be unreal. It is certainly not irrational in a philosopher to pursue truth and to demonstrate that the game of life which he plays is a mere show and that 'all the prizes in it are mere blanks'. All of us, in a rare moment of discrimination and reflection, realise that 'the world is a dream'. To our utter disillusionment we ultimately discover that we occupy ourselves with objects the existence and value of which must really be no more than those of appearances. A student must be disappointed if he expects Advaita Vedānta to point out to him the means of enjoying pleasures, which depend upon the subject-object relationship, which is based upon duality of existence. The only aim of

Vedānta is to dehypnotise the mind which has been hypnotised into the belief that duality really exists. The only positive satisfaction guaranteed to a Vedāntist is that he will no longer be deluded by ignorance which paints the unreal or the seeming as the real. For, in the language of Śaṅkara, the knowledge of Reality destroys one's hankering after objects which are unreal just as the knowledge of the mother-o'-pearl (mistaken for silver) removes the delusion regarding the silver. This knowledge may be chimerical to those who are still attached to the tinsels and gew-gaws of the world and the prizes it offers; but it is of supreme value to the seeker of Reality.

Sir S. Radhakrishnan seems to suggest that Śaṅkara thinks waking experiences to be more real than the dream ones. This view may be true from the non-philosophical standpoint. The distinction between the reality of the waking and that of the dream experiences is said to depend upon the sense-organs apparently indicating reality. We create a false standard of reality in our relative plane of consciousness and thus hold one set of experiences to be more real than another. But does Śaṅkara say anywhere that waking experiences are real from the standpoint of the Ultimate Truth? All our experiences, whether waking or dream, are possible if we believe the act of creation to be real. What is the view of Śaṅkara regarding creation? When the opponent (*Pūrvapakṣin*) tries to find inconsistencies in the different accounts of creation given in the Vedas, Śaṅkara says in various places, for instance, in the introduction to the fourth chapter of the *Aitareya Upaniṣad* as follows: 'Here (*i.e.*, the theories and stories of creation), the only fact intended to be conveyed is the realization of *Ātman*, the rest is but attractive figure of speech; and this is no fault. It seems to be more reasonable that the Lord, omniscient, omnipotent, did, like a magician, display all this illusion to facilitate explanation or comprehension, inasmuch as stories, although false, are easily understood by all. It is well known that there is no truth to be attained from accounts of creation (as they are false); and it is well established in all the Upaniṣads that the end attained by the conception of the unity of the Real Self is Immortality.' Does it differ from the views expressed by Gauḍapāda regarding creation? He also says: 'Evolution or creation as described by illustrations of earth, iron, sparks of fire, etc., has another meaning, *viz.*, they are only the means to the realization of the unity of Existence. There is nothing like distinction (in it)' (III. 15).

Does Vedānta take away from man his zeal for work? Does Vedānta teach pessimism? Many a Western and Eastern critic of the philosophy of Advaita holds that it makes a man only a dreamer, a sky-gazing spectator. This is a wrong interpretation of Vedānta. Vedānta never teaches one to fly away from the world or to shut himself up in caves and forests. Many a poetic picture has been drawn of the Vedāntic seer living the life of a recluse far away from the maddening crowd of ignoble strife. But this is not true. Śaṅkara, 'the lion of Vedānta', and Swāmī Vivekānanda, 'the paragon of the Vedāntists' (as Prof. James of America characterised him) of modern times, lived in human society and made the mightiest efforts for the uplift of humanity. They dedicated their lives to the amelioration of mankind. Vedānta has nothing to do with pessimism or optimism or any 'ism' for the matter of that. It only teaches Truth. If the realization of Truth stand as an impediment to human progress, then the charge against Vedānta as the enemy of progress may be well justified. Nothing wonderful will happen to the world if the entire mankind be converted to Hinduism, Christianity, Buddhism, or Islam or to any other religion. But assuredly something marvellous will happen if a dozen of men and women pierce the thick walls of the church, temple, synagogue and realize the Truth. Again Truth is no characteristic of a recluse or a misanthrope or a bigoted thinker. The ancient *Ṛṣis* of the Upaniṣads breathed the free air of Truth, sang the song of freedom and enjoyed the truth of life. Many of their highest teachings were imparted in the crowded courts of kings. The message of the *Gītā*, the excellent *vade mecum* of Vedānta, was delivered on the battlefield, where the grimmest realities of life were faced and battles fought. Arjuna after realizing the Vedāntic Truth did not flee away from the world, but girded his loins with fresh vigour and strength to discharge his duty (*svadharma*). After Śrī Kṛṣṇa had delivered his message, Arjuna said, 'Destroyed is my delusion, and I have got back the memory of my real nature through Thy grace, Oh, Kṛṣṇa. I am now firm, my doubts are gone. I will carry out Thy word'. Straightway he plunged into the terrible battle of Kurukṣetra and performed his duty.

Renascence of Indian life, in its various aspects, political, social, material, æsthetic and religious, always followed the restoration of the Truth of Advaita to its pristine glory. The Upaniṣads, the *Gītā*, Buddha, Śaṅkara and Rāmakṛṣṇa stand at the crest of the mighty tidal waves of India's renaissance. And all of them taught the essential truth of Vedānta in different forms.

The greatest tragedy of life is to think that no work is possible without a firm belief in duality and subject-object relationship. Men say that no work is possible without the consciousness of egoism and agency. On the other hand selfishness, sordidness, jealousy, passion, etc., which are manifested in our daily activities, are due to a belief in the reality of the subject-object relationship. The mightiest achievements that have really transformed the fate of humanity have been done by those who have had no thought of their ego. Śrī Kṛṣṇa says in the *Gītā*, 'He who is free from the notion of egoism, whose intelligence is not affected (by good or evil), though he kills these people, he kills them not, nor is bound (by action)'. The artist or the musician shows himself at his best when he feels himself one with his art. Śrī Rāmakṛṣṇa never had the idea of agency in the work of his spiritual ministration. He used to say, 'Perform your work keeping always the knowledge of Advaita in your pocket'.

Is it possible to do any work which always implies the triad of perceiver, perceived and perception, if one be established in non-dual Brahman? The idea may involve a logical or psychological contradiction, but this position can be fully justified from the metaphysical or rather, philosophical standpoint. One pursuing Truth disinterestedly, when once established in Truth, can see this world of multiplicity and at the same time know it to be the non-dual Brahman, pure, free, and ever-illumined. A knower of Truth may move and act in the world like an ordinary man. He feels hungry and thirsty. He goes to sleep when tired. He feels compassion for the misery of others and tries his utmost to alleviate it; but at the same time he sees everywhere the non-dual Brahman alone, ever-free and ever-pure. Śrī Kṛṣṇa also says in the *Gītā*, 'The offering is Brahman, the clarified butter is Brahman, in the fire of Brahman offered by Brahman, by seeing Brahman in actions, he reaches Brahman alone' (*Gītā*, IV. 24). We admit that this position is most difficult to be comprehended by those who are not trained in the pursuit of Ultimate Truth. Truly says Gauḍapāda, 'Those few alone are known in the world as of high intellect who are firm in their conviction of the unborn and undivided Brahman. The ordinary people cannot understand them or their action'

(IV. 95). He himself characterises the teachings of *Kārikā* as very deep (*atigambhīram*) and extremely difficult to be understood (*durdarśam*) (IV. 100).

The superficial critic often asks how it is possible to apply the teachings of Vedānta to our practical everyday life, if we are taught continually to think of the unreality of the world. How can the truth of non-dual Brahman, as taught by Vedānta, help one to work for individual or collective progress? Vedānta certainly does not help us to bring grist to our individual or national mill. It certainly does not tell us how to increase our capacity to enjoy the pleasures derived from material objects. But Vedānta really teaches us how to enjoy the world after realizing its true nature. To embrace or comprehend the universe after realizing it as the non-dual Brahman, gives us peace that passeth all understanding. Says the seer in the *Īśa Upaniṣad*, 'All this—whatsoever moves in the earth—should be realized as permeated by the Lord (*Ātman*). Enjoy (the world) by renunciation (of the illusory names and forms). Covet not anybody's wealth'. Does Vedānta really ask us to negate the world? Does it really teach us to negate the existing objects? A student of the *Kārikā* will at once realize that there is nothing to be negated or added. That which exists can never be non-existent. Brahman alone is existent on account of its persistence in all acts of cognition. Names, forms and relations are illusory on account of their changeability and negatability. Vedānta teaches us to realize the world as Brahman and then be one with it. Vedānta teaches us to see Brahman everywhere even in the so-called illusion. An illusion can never be real and it is perceived on account of our ignorance. A Vedāntist does not negate the world which, being Brahman, can never be negated. It only asks the student to know the real nature of the world. A knower of truth, as we have already stated, does his duty or work in the world. But the knowledge of Truth makes all the difference in his attitude towards the world. Where the ignorant person sees non-Brahman, the *Jñānin* realizes Brahman alone. A *Jñānin* just exercises his understanding, and then uses the same sense-organs in dealing with the same external objects. He sees everywhere the non-dual Brahman.

One often hears in Europe and America that Vedānta is pantheism or idealism. Many foreign critics characterise Vedānta as illusionism. The critics only look at the Vedāntic truth from the relative standpoint. From the standpoint of the Ultimate Truth Vedānta is not idealism, as it does not see, in the Platonic fashion, the duality of illusory external objects and the reality of ideas. Nor does Vedānta teach, like the Buddhist idealists, that ideas, which alone are real, have birth, death and the characteristics of misery. Vedāntic truth is different from Kantian dualism which makes a distinction between noumena and phenomena. Berkley says that all external objects are but ideas in the perceiver's mind and God or the cosmic mind sends these ideas. Vedānta says that God is also an idea and the plurality of ideas and their relationship cannot be proved to be real. Vedānta is not certainly pantheism as it does not recognize any God, independent of the Self, who is the universe. Vedānta denies causality from the highest standpoint and thus invalidates the process of becoming. Vedānta, like Hegel, says that Reality is thought but denies the evolution of the Absolute. Bradley says that time, space, or causal relation cannot apply to the Absolute but at the same time he says that the Absolute '*somehow*' becomes the manifested manifold. Gauḍāpada denies the manifestation, evolution or the becoming of *Ātman*.

The conclusion of Vedānta can be summed up in four words 'All this is Brahman'. Only the non-dual Brahman exists. There is no phenomenal *Jīva* about whom birth and death can be predicated. If one sees such birth etc., it is due to his ignorance of the nature of Reality. Again this ignorance is not real (IV. 58). *Jīvas* are all peace from the very beginning, ever unproduced and indestructible by their very nature, and therefore, eternal and inseparable. All this is unborn and enlightened Brahman (IV. 93). The *Jīvas* are ever free from any obstruction (as obstruction does not exist) being entirely pure by nature. They are all-right and ever-liberated from the beginning (IV. 98). As Brahman alone exists there is nothing which can be accepted nor anything injurious which can be shunned.

The Teachings of Gauḍapāda can benefit only those that are equipped with the *Sādhana-Catuṣṭaya* or the fourfold pre-requisites of philosophical discipline, such as discrimination, non-attachment (renunciation), self-control and an irrepressible hankering after the realization of Truth. Any one who under-takes the study of the *Kārikā* in a dilettante fashion will see in it nothing but confusion and may even be misled. Gauḍapāda has dealt with all the problems of philosophy following the scientific method of the modern times. The careful reader will find in *Kārikā* the solution of such out-standing problems of philosophy as perception, idealism, causality, truth, Reality, etc. Every verse of the *Kārikā* demands profound thinking before it can be understood and appreciated. *But people will rather die than think.* The glory and value of the *Māṇḍūkya Upaniṣad* has been infinitely enhanced by the *Kārikā* of Gauḍapāda.

We are not aware of any other English translation of the *Māṇḍūkya Upaniṣad* with the *Kārikā* and Śaṅkara's commentary than the one by Maṇilāl N. Dvivedī published in

1894. For the most part the translation is reliable and we have looked into it while preparing our translation. We have felt that exhaustive notes are necessary for the average reader to understand the real import of the *Kārikā* and Śaṅkara's commentary. Therefore we have tried to elucidate Gauḍapāda and Śaṅkara with copious notes.

We are profoundly grateful to Mr. V. Subrahmaṇya Iyer, the retired registrar of the Mysore University, for explaining to us the abstruse philosophy of the *Kārikā*. Mr. Iyer, the courageous thinker, taught us that no philosophy can live to-day in anything but a fool's paradise, unless it ventures out into the open but biting air of critical reason as natural science does. Philosophy, like science, is vitally concerned with reasoned or rationally demonstrable truth and must not depend upon mere mystic vision or tradition or authority. The seed which ripens into vision may be a gift of the gods but the labour of cultivating it so that it may bear nourishing fruit is the indispensable function of arduous scientific or rational processes of thought. Mr. Subrahmaṇya Iyer has laid us under an additional debt of obligation by revising the entire book in its manuscript form and agreeing to stand sponsor to it in placing it before the public.

Above all, we cannot adequately express our deep sense of indebtedness to the distinguished Ruler of Mysore, His Highness the Mahārāja, Śrī Kṛṣṇarāja Waḍiyar Bahadūr IV. Not only his philosophic knowledge, but also his philosophic life, has become a household word in the State and throughout India. The days that we spent breathing the spiritual atmosphere created all around by the Temple on the Cāmuṇḍi Hill, at the foot of which is situated His Highness's famous and picturesque capital, were among the happiest. His great devotion to Śrī Rāmakṛṣṇa, the teacher of Universal Love, lends an additional charm to his life. And we felt that the best way in which we could acknowledge all that we owe to Mysore and its famous Ruler would be to bring out a work of this kind, associating it with the name of the royal Vedāntin, who is himself an ardent admirer of Śrī Gauḍapāda.

*Vedānta Society, Providence*
*Rhode Island, U.S.A.*
24*th June*, 1932

Swāmī Nikhilānanda

**Aum Salutation to Brahman**

# THE MĀṆḌŪKYOPANIṢAD

## Vedic Invocation

O Gods (Devāḥ)! Auspicious sounds may we hear with the ears. Auspicious forms may we behold with the eyes. May we, full of praise of the Highest, enjoy, in healthy body with perfect limbs, our allotted years, (may we be) the beloved of the Gods.

Aum Peace! Peace! Peace!

## Invocation by Śaṅkara

I bow to that Brahman that (during the waking state) after having enjoyed (experienced) all gross objects by pervading the entire universe through the omnipresent rays of its immutable consciousness that embraces the entire variety of the movable and the immovable objects; that again, after having digested, as it were—that is to say, experienced within (in the dream state)—all the variety of objects produced by desires and brought into existence by the mind, enjoys bliss in deep sleep and makes us experience through *Māyā*, the bliss; which, further, is designated, in terms of *Māyā*, as the fourth (*Turīya*), and which is supreme, immortal and changeless.

May that *Turīya* that, (through *Māyā*) having identified itself as the entire universe, experiences (in the waking state) the manifold gross objects of enjoyment through ignorance and attachment, that again during the dream state, experiences, being enlightened by its own light, the subtle objects of enjoyment, the objects that are brought into existence by its own internal organ, and which, lastly, in dreamless sleep withdraws all objects (subtle as well as gross) within itself and thus becomes free from all distinctions and differences—(May this *Turīya* that) is ever devoid of all attributes, protect us.

## Śaṅkara's Introduction to the Upaniṣad Commentary

With the word *Aum* etc., begins the treatise, consisting of four[1] chapters, the quintessence[2] of the substance[3] of the import of Vedānta.[4] Hence[5] no separate mention is made of the (mutual) relationship, the subject-matter and the object to be attained (Matters usually stated in an introduction to a study of any Vedāntic treatise). For, that which constitutes the relationship, the subject-matter and the object of the Vedāntic study is evident here. Nevertheless, that one desirous of explaining a *Prakaraṇa* (treatise), should deal with them is the opinion of the scholastic. This treatise must be said to contain a subject-matter on account of its revealing[6] the means (for the realization of *Ātman*) that serves the purpose, or the end to be attained. It therefore possesses, though indirectly, 'specific relationship', 'subject matter' and 'the end to be attained'. What then, is that end[7] in view? It is thus explained: As a man stricken with disease regains his normal[8] state with the removal[9] of (the cause of) the disease, so the self labouring under misapprehension, owing to identification[10] of itself with misery, recovers its normal[11] state with the cessation (of the illusion) of duality, which manifests itself as the phenomenal universe. This realization of non-duality is the end to be attained. This treatise is begun for the purpose of revealing[12] Brahman inasmuch as by knowledge (*Vidyā*) the illusion of duality, caused by ignorance, is destroyed. This is established by such scriptural passages as, 'For where there is, as it were, duality, where there exists, as it were, another, there one sees another, and one knows another. But where all this has, verily, become *Ātman* (for one), how should one see another, how should one know another?'

The first chapter, then, seeks, by dealing specifically with the Vedic texts,[13] to indicate the (traditional) means to the realization of the essential nature of *Ātman* and is devoted to the determination[14] of the meaning of *Aum*. The second chapter seeks rationally[15] to demonstrate the unreality of duality; the illusion (duality) being destroyed, the knowledge of non-duality (becomes evident), as the cessation of the imagination of snake etc., in the rope reveals the real nature of the rope. The third chapter is devoted to the rational demonstration of the truth of non-duality, lest it should, in like manner,[16] be contended to be unreal. The fourth chapter is devoted to the rational refutation of the other schools of thought which are antagonistic to the truth as pointed out in the Vedas and which are opposed to the knowledge of the Advaitic Reality, by pointing out their falsity on account of their own mutual[17] contradiction.

[1] *Four chapters—i.e.,* the *Māṇḍūkyopaniṣad* with the *Kārikā* by Gauḍapāda treated in four chapters: *viz.,* the *Āgama Prakaraṇa,* the *Vaitathya Prakaraṇa,* the *Advaita Prakaraṇa* and the *Alātaśānti Prakaraṇa.* The mere Upaniṣadic portion without the *Kārikā* does not present a full view of the *philosophic* system of Vedānta which seeks to interpret human knowledge as a whole (*vide* Foreword).

[2] *Quintessence*—It is because the *Māṇḍūkya Śruti* confines itself only to the establishment of non-duality without controverting the doctrines of the other systems. *Muktikopaniṣad* aptly describes that *Māṇḍūkya* alone, among the Upaniṣads, is sufficient for liberation (the attainment of truth). *Cf.* माण्डूक्यमेकमेवालं मुमुक्षूणां विमुक्तये.

[3] *Substance*—The doctrine of the non-difference of *Jīva* and *Brahman.*

[4] *Vedānta*—It literally means the *last portion* of the Vedas which is identical with the Upaniṣads. The word also signifies the *essence*

of the Vedas. Vedāntic works usually deal with the following: the fitness of a pupil for the study of *Brahmavidyā*, the qualification of the teacher, the nature of *Jīva* and *Brahman*, and finally the non-difference or non-duality of the two.

[5] *Hence etc.*—Śaṅkara treats the *Māṇḍūkyopaniṣad* and the *Kārikā* not as a *Śāstra* but as a *Prakaraṇa* (treatise). A *Śāstra* though related to a particular end in view deals with varieties of topics. But a *Prakaraṇa* is a short manual which confines itself to some essential topics of a *Śāstra*. All the arguments of the *Māṇḍūkyopaniṣad* with *Kārikā* ultimately point to the establishment of the attributeless Brahman, thus serving the purpose of a *Prakarana* which is defined as follows :

शास्त्रैकदेशसंबन्धं शास्त्रकार्यान्तरे स्थितम् ।
आहु: प्रकरणं नाम ग्रन्थभेदं विपश्चित: ॥

The other Vedāntic texts also establish the truth of non-duality but they incidentally discuss various other philosophical doctrines.

A *Prakaraṇa* (treatise) has four indispensable elements (अनुबन्ध) literally, 'what sticks to another', namely, the determination of the fitness of the student for the study of the treatise (अधिकारी), the subject-matter (विषय), the mutual relationship (संबन्ध) between the treatise and the subject-matter (which is that of the explainer and the explained) and the object to be attained by the study, *i. e.*, its utility (प्रयोजन).

[6] *Revealing etc.*—Though liberation is attained through the knowledge of the non-duality of *Jīva* and *Brahman* and not as a result of the study of scriptures, yet the scriptures indirectly help the attainment of this knowledge by pointing to the illusory character of duality.

[7] *Object*—Is the knowledge something to be produced or is it ever-existent? In the former case, it would be like other effects, impermanent, and in the latter case, the means pursued would be futile. The reply is that though the Knowledge of *Ātman* is eternally existent, yet it is obscured by ignorance in the *Jīva*. The aim of *Sādhanā* is to remove this obstruction. Thus *Sādhanā* serves a useful purpose though it does not make the student attain anything new.

[8] *Normal state*—The sick man thinks that he has lost the normal state during the period of his illness.

[9] *Removal etc.*—This is done by means of medicine, etc.

[10] *Identification etc.*—This suffering is due to the illusion of duality, such as egoism etc., caused by ignorance which does not exist in reality. Otherwise its destruction would be an impossibility.

[11] *Normal state*—This state being in itself perfect, cannot be transcended by any other state.

[12] *Revealing etc.*—This is done by the removal of ignorance which is the cause of the illusion of duality.

[13] *Vedic texts*—The first chapter of the *Māṇḍūkyopaniṣad*, namely, the *Āgama Prakaraṇa*, consists mainly of the Upaniṣadic texts. The doctrines contained therein are established rationally in the following three chapters.

[14] *Determination*—This would enable the student to attain the knowledge of the self, whose real nature is revealed by the demonstration of the unreality of duality which is an illusion. *Ātman* is realized through such knowledge. Therefore the indirect result of the explanation of the real nature of *Aum* leads to the attainment of the *summum bonum*. The rational treatment will follow.

[15] *Rationally*—With the disappearance of the sense of reality with regard to illusions, there spontaneously arises the knowledge of truth. Gauḍapāda in the second, third and fourth chapters of the *Kārikā*, *rationally* presents the truth, presented in the first.

[16] *In like manner*—There may be a doubt regarding the very existence of Reality when duality is removed. The argument followed by the author of the *Kārikā* is that the knowledge of Reality is such that it is never contradicted.

[17] *Mutual contradiction*—The contradictions are pointed out with a view to establishing the truth of non-dualism—a course frequently pursued by both Gauḍapāda and Śaṅkara.

CHAPTER I

# ĀGAMA PRAKARAṆA

## (The Upaniṣadic Chapter)

### I

### Introductory Remarks by Śaṅkara

How does, again, the determination of (the meaning of) *Aum* help the realization of the essential nature of *Ātman*? It is thus[1] explained: The *Śruti*[2] passages such as these declare[3] thus: 'It[4] is *Aum*.' 'This (*Aum*) is the (best)[5] support.' 'Oh, Satyakāma, It[6] is the *Aum* which is also the higher and the lower Brahman.' 'Meditate[7] on the Self as *Aum*.' '*Aum*, this[8] word is Brahman.' 'All[9] this is verily *Aum*.' As the rope etc., which are the substratum of such illusions (misapprehensions) as the snake etc., so is the non-dual *Ātman*, which is the Ultimate Reality, the substratum of such imaginations as the vital[10] breath (*Prāṇa*) etc., which are unreal. Similarly, *Aum* is the substratum of the entire illusion of the world of speech having[11] for its (corresponding) contents such illusory objects as *Prāṇa* etc., imagined in *Ātman*. And *Aum* is verily of the same[12] essential character as the *Ātman*; for it is the name for *Ātman*. All illusions such as *Prāṇa* etc., having *Ātman* for their substratum and denoted by words—which are but modifications[13] of *Aum*—cannot exist[14] without names (which are but the modifications of *Aum*). This is supported by such *Śruti* passages as, 'The modification[15] being only a name arising from speech', 'All this related to It (Brahman) is held[16] together by the cord[17] of speech and strands[18] of (specific) names', 'All these (are rendered possible in experience) by names', etc.

[1] *Thus*—The reason given here chiefly depends upon the scriptural authority, because the first chapter of this work lays emphasis on the scriptural texts.

[2] *Śruti passages*—For detailed explanations of these passages the reader is referred to the respective Upaniṣads in which they occur.

[3] *Declare*—The ultimate relationship between *Aum* and Brahman is thus explained. The phenomena of the world consist of ideas or the mental states. Ideas depend upon words for their expression. The utterance of the word *Aum (A U M)* gives the clue to the pronunciations of all the words or sounds used by human beings. The various parts of the vocal organ used in the utterance of sounds come in contact with each other while pronouncing the word *Aum*. Therefore, *Aum* is the matrix of all sounds which in their diversified forms give rise to words used in the language. The substratum of phenomena is Brahman. The substratum of all sounds, as seen above, is *Aum*. The sounds signifying the phenomena are non-different from the phenomena as both are illusions. When the illusion disappears the substratum alone remains which, being one, admits of no difference. Hence Brahman is *Aum*.

[4] *It is etc.*—*Kaṭhopaniṣad*, 1. 2. 15. When *Aum* is uttered with concentration there arises the consciousness of Brahman in the mind. Therefore *Aum* is the nearest symbol helping the concentration of the mind leading to the realization of Brahman. The principle of this process is known as शाखाचन्द्रन्याय.

[5] *Best*—*Kaṭhopaniṣad*, 1. 2. 17. This is the best symbol of Brahman like an image (प्रतिमा) of Viṣṇu.

[6] *It is etc.*—*Praśnopaniṣad*, 5. 2. 'The knower through the support (of the *Aum*) attains to one or the other. Through the meditation of *Aum* one can realize both the *Para* (attributeless) *Brahman* and the *Apara* (associated with names and forms) Brahman.'

[7] *Meditate*—One, who seeks to realize the Self through 'one-pointed' concentration on *Aum*, feels that the gross universe (symbolised by *A*) is absorbed into the subtle (*U*) and (*U*) into the causal (*M*) and, finally the universe dependent upon causal relation is withdrawn into the transcendental which is known as *Amātrā* and which cannot be designated by any letter or sound.

[8] *This word etc.*—*Taittirīyopaniṣad*, 1. 8. 1. *Aum* indicates that both *Saguṇa* and *Nirguṇa Brahman* have the same substratum which is the *Nirguṇa* (attributeless) *Brahman* or the highest Reality.

[9] *All this is etc.*—Both *i. e., Aum* and *Brahman*, are the support of everything, they form the most universal concept. Therefore the knowledge of *Aum* and Brahman is identical.

[10] *Vital breath*—The non-dual Brahman, being the only existing Reality, does not admit of any other existence. Therefore ***Prāṇa*** etc. and their effects are but mental manifestations which are unreal, having Brahman for their substratum—like the illusion of snake superimposed upon a rope.

[11] *Having etc.—Prāṇa* etc., are merely modifications of speech because they cannot be conceived of without names. As again names are nothing but different manifestations of *Aum*, therefore *Prāṇa* etc., have *Aum* for their substratum.

[12] *Same nature*—The name and the thing indicated by it are identical inasmuch as both are mental (*Kālpanika*).

[13] *Modifications*—All sounds are included in '*A*'—the first letter of the alphabet (*cf.* The *Śruti* passage, अकारो वै सर्वावाक्). '*A*' is the chief constituent of *Aum.* Therefore all mental manifestations (*i. e.,* the objects denoted by them are identical with the sounds associated with them) cannot exist apart from *Aum.*

[14] *Cannot exist etc.*—The purpose of the *Śruti* is to show the identity of the name and the object. This can be understood from the standpoint of mentalism which explains everything as mere idea or a mental state or content.

[15] *Modification—Chānd. Up.*, 6. 1. 4.

[16] *Held with—i. e.,* Pervaded.

[17] *Cord*—It stands for the general (सामान्य).

[18] *Strands*—They denote the particular (विशेष).

Therefore it is said :

हरिः ओम् । ओमित्येतदक्षरमिदं सर्वं तस्योपव्याख्यानं भूतं भवद्भविष्यदिति सर्वमोंकार एव । यच्चान्यत्त्रिकालातीतं तदप्योंकार एव ॥ १ ॥

Harih Aum. *Aum*, the word, is all this. A clear explanation of it (is the following). All that is past, present and future is verily *Aum*. That which is beyond the triple conception of time, is also truly *Aum*.

### Śaṅkara's Commentary

*Aum*, the word, is all this. As all diversified objects that we see around us, indicated by names, are not different[1] from their (corresponding) names, and further as the different names are not different from *Aum*, therefore all this is verily *Aum*. As a thing is known through its name so the highest Brahman is known through *Aum* alone. Therefore the highest Brahman is verily *Aum*. This (treatise) is the explanation of that, *tasya*, that is, of *Aum*, the word, which is of the same nature as the higher as well as the lower Brahman. *Upavyākhyānam* means clear explanation, because *Aum* is the means to the knowledge of Brahman on account of its having the closest proximity to Brahman. The word '*Prastutam*' meaning 'commences' should be supplied to complete the sentence (as otherwise, it is incomplete). That which is conditioned by the triple (conceptions of) time, such as past, present and future is also verily *Aum* for reasons already explained. All that is beyond the three (divisions of) time, *i.e.*, unconditioned by time, and yet known by their effects, which is called '*Avyākṛta*', the unmanifested etc.,—that also[2] is verily *Aum*.

[1] *Not different*—That the name and the object denoted by it are identical is understood from the standpoint of mentalism which explains everything cognized or perceived as only a form of thought.

[2] *Also etc.*—Because the effect is non-different from the cause.

## II

### Introductory Remarks by Śaṅkara

Though the name and the object signified by the name are one and the same, still the explanation[1] has been given (here) by giving prominence[2] to the name (*Aum*). Though in the Upaniṣadic passage—'*Aum*, this word, is all this'—explanation has been furnished by giving prominence[3] to the name (*Aum*), the same thought is again expounded by giving prominence to the thing signified by the name. The object is to realise the knowledge of the oneness of the name and the thing signified by it. Otherwise, (the explanation) that the knowledge of the thing is dependent on the name, might suggest that the oneness of the name and the thing is to be taken only in a figurative[4] sense. The purpose of the knowledge of the unity (of the name and the thing signified by it) is to simultaneously remove, by a single effort, (the illusion of) both the name and the thing and establish (the nature of) Brahman which[5] is other than both. Therefore the *Śruti* says, 'The quarters (*Pādas*) are the letters of *Aum* (*Mātrā*) and the letters are the quarters'.

[1] *Explanation—i. e.*, of what is intended to be taught by the Upaniṣadic text.

[2] *Prominence*—Because *Aum* is the first word of the first Upaniṣad. The purport of the sentence is that *Aum* is the symbol, the most universal, for *all* the phenomena of the world. Therefore prominence is given to *Aum* (अभिधान).

[3] *Prominence*—The second Upaniṣad is 'All this is, truly, Brahman'. Hence the emphasis is on 'All this'—which is the object (अभिधेय) signified by *Aum*.

[4] *Figurative—i. e.*, the mere convention of calling a thing by a particular name.

[5] *Which is etc.*—The knowledge of the attributeless Brahman is possible only when the illusion of both the name and the thing signified by it is removed.

Therefore it says:

सर्वं ह्येतद्ब्रह्मायमात्मा ब्रह्म सोऽयमात्मा चतुष्पात् ॥ २ ॥

All this is verily Brahman. This *Ātman* is Brahman. This *Ātman* has four quarters.

## Śaṅkara's Commentary

All this is verily Brahman. All that has been said to consist merely of *Aum* (in the previous text) is Brahman. That Brahman which has been described[1] (as existing) inferentially[2] is now pointed out, as being directly[3] known, by the passage, 'This Self is Brahman'. The word *this*, meaning that which appears divided into four quarters,[4] is pointed out as the innermost Self, with a gesture[5] (of hand) by the passage, 'This is *Ātman*'. That *Ātman* indicated by *Aum*, signifying both the higher and the lower Brahman, has[6] four quarters (*Pādas*), not indeed, like the four feet (*Pādas*) of a cow,[7] but like the four quarters (*Pādas*) of a coin[8] known as *Kārṣāpaṇa*. The knowledge of the fourth (*Turīya*) is attained by merging the (previous) three, such as *Viśva* etc., in it in[9] the order of the previous one, in the succeeding one. Here[10] the word '*Pāda*' or 'foot' is used in[11] the sense of instrument. The word '*Pāda*' is again used in the sense of an object when the object to be achieved is the fourth (*Turīya*).

[1] *Described*—*i. e.*, by the *Śruti*.

[2] *Inferentially*—*i. e.*, we cannot directly perceive its presence but we can infer it. It is opposed to अपरोक्षज्ञान which refers to the knowledge of a thing that is not directly perceived but about the existence of which one becomes absolutely certain by means of what is known as realization.

[3] *Directly*—The word प्रत्यक्ष, nowadays, is applied, especially in the *Nyāya* Philosophy, to the knowledge of the objects of sense-perception. But occasionally it is used, in the Upaniṣad and the Vedāntic text, in the sense of अपरोक्ष.

[4] *Four quarters*—Namely, *Viśva* (the waking state), *Taijasa* (dream state), *Prājña* (*Suṣupti* or the state of dreamless sleep) and *Turīya* which is same as Brahman or *Ātman*. These four quarters correspond to the three *Mātrās* of *Aum* and the *Amātrā* of *Aum*. *A*, *U* and *M* are the three *Mātrās*. The fourth, which is known as *Amātrā* or without a letter, has no corresponding letter or sound.

This is *silence* or *Ātman* corresponding to *Turīya*. The idea of sound suggests the idea of soundlessness or silence from which sound may be said to proceed.

[5] *Gesture—i.e.,* by placing the hand on the region of the heart which, in popular belief, is the seat of *Ātman.*

[6] *Has etc.*—The four quarters are imagined in *Ātman* to facilitate the understanding of the pupil.

[7] *Cow*—Because cow has actually four feet which are unrelated with one another.

[8] *Coin—Kārṣāpaṇa* is a coin made up of four quarters. A quarter-*Kārṣāpaṇa* is merged in the *half-Kārṣāpaṇa*; the half is merged in the three-fourth-*Kārṣāpaṇa* and the three-quarters ultimately is merged in the full *Kārṣāpana.*

[9] *In the etc.—Viśva* is merged in *Taijasa, Taijasa* in *Prājña* and finally *Prājña* is merged in *Turīya.*

[10] *Here*—It is because the 'fourth' pāda is realized *by means* of merging the three *states* in it.

[11] *In the sense of*—It is because the attention is here drawn to the fourth '*pāda*' which is the *object* of the enquiry.

## III

How[1] four quarters are said to indicate *Ātman* is thus[2] explained:

**जागरितस्थानो बहिष्प्रज्ञः सप्ताङ्ग एकोनविंशतिमुखः**
**स्थूलभुग्वैश्वानरः प्रथमः पादः ॥ ३ ॥**

The first quarter (*Pāda*) is *Vaiśvānara* whose sphere (of activity) is the waking state, who is conscious of external objects, who has seven limbs and nineteen mouths and whose experience consists of gross (material) objects.

### Śaṅkara's Commentary

*Jāgaritasthāna, i.e.,* his sphere[3] (of activity) is the waking state. *Bahiṣprajña, i.e.,* who[4] is aware of objects other than himself. The meaning is that consciousness appears, as it were, related to outward objects on account of *Avidyā*. Similarly *Saptāṅga, i.e.,* he has seven[5] limbs. The *Śruti* says, 'Of that *Vaiśvānara* Self, the effulgent[6] region is his head, the sun his eye, the air his vital breath, the ether (*Ākāśa*) the (middle part of his) body, the water[7] his kidney and the earth his feet'. The *Āhavanīya* fire (one of the three fires of the *Agnihotra* sacrifice) has been described as his mouth in order to complete the imagery of the *Agnihotra* sacrifice. He is called *Saptāṅga* because these are the seven limbs of his body. Similarly he has nineteen mouths. These are the five[8] organs of perception (*Buddhīndriyas*); the five[9] organs of action (*Karmendriyas*); the five[10] aspects of vital breath (*Prāṇa* etc.); the mind (*Manas*); the intellect (*Buddhi*); egoity (*Ahaṁkāra*); mind-stuff (*Citta*). These are, as it were, the mouths, *i.e.,* the instruments by means of which he (*Vaiśvānara*) experiences (objects). He, the *Vaiśvānara*, thus constituted, experiences through the instruments enumerated above, gross objects, such as sound etc. He is called *Vaiśvānara* because he leads all creatures of the universe in diverse ways (to[11] the enjoyment of various objects); or because he comprises all beings. Following the grammatical rules regarding the compound which gives the latter meaning, the word that is formed is *Viśvānara*, which is the same as *Vaiśvānara*. He is the *first quarter* because he is non-different from the totality of gross bodies (known as *Virāṭ*). He is called *first*[12] (quarter) because the subsequent quarters are realized through him (*Vaiśvānara*).

(*Objection*)—While the subject-matter under discussion treats of the innermost Self (*Pratyak Ātman*) as having four quarters—in the text, 'This *Ātman* is Brahman'—how is it that (the external universe consisting of) the effulgent regions etc., have been described as its limbs such as head etc.?

(*Reply*)—This, however, is no[13] mistake; because the object is to describe the entire phenomena, including those of gods (*Adhidaiva*) as having four quarters from[14] the standpoint of this *Ātman* known as the *Virāṭ* (*i.e.*, the totality of the gross universe). And in[15] this way alone is non-duality established by the removal of (the illusion of) the entire[16] phenomena. Further, the one *Ātman* is realized as existing in all beings and all[17] beings are seen as existing in *Ātman*. And, thus alone, the meaning of such *Śruti* passages as, 'Who sees all beings in the Self' etc. can be said to be established. Otherwise,[18] the subjective world will, verily, be, as in the case of such philosophers as the Sāṁkhyas,[19] limited by its (one's) own body. And if that be the case, no room would be left for the Advaita which is the special feature of the *Śruti*. For, in the case of duality, there would be no difference between the Advaita and the Sāṁkhya and other systems. The establishment of the identity of all with *Ātman* is sought by all the Upaniṣads. It is, therefore, quite reasonable to speak of the effulgent regions etc., as seven limbs in connection with the subjective (individual self, *Adhyātma*) associated with the gross body because of its identity with the *Adhidaiva* (comprising the super-physical regions) universe from the standpoint of the *Virāṭ* (the totality of the gross physical universe). This is further known from such characteristic indication (of the *Śruti*), as 'Thy[20] head shall fall' etc.

The identity of *Adhyātma* and *Adhidaiva* from the standpoint of the *Virāṭ* indicates similar identity[21] of the selves known as the *Hiraṇyagarbha* and the *Taijasa*[22] as well as of the Unmanifested[23] (*Iśvara*) and the *Prājña*. It is also stated in the *Madhu-Brāhmaṇa*, 'This bright immortal person in this earth and that bright immortal person in the body (both are *Madhu*)'. It is an established fact that the Self in deep sleep (*Prājña*) is identical with the Unmanifested (*Iśvara*) because[24] of the absence of any distinction between them. Such being the case, it is clearly established that non-duality is realized by the disappearance (of the illusion) of all duality.

[1] *How etc.*—The reason for doubting is that *Ātman* is without parts.

[2] *Thus etc.*—Four quarters are merely *assumed* to facilitate understanding by the unenlightened.

[3] *Sphere etc.*—It is because the Self identifies itself with the experiencer in the waking state.

[4] *Who is aware etc.*—Consciousness *(Prajña)*, really speaking, is identical with Self. It cannot be related to external objects because nothing exists outside consciousness. Owing to *Ajñāna* (ignorance), the *Buddhi Vṛtti* (mental modification) objectifies itself into what are called material entities, ego and non-ego. These material objects do not possess any independent existence. Both the *Vṛtti* and its objects are imagined in *Ātman*. From the standpoint of *Ātman* it does not experience any object external which is totally non-existent.

[5] *Seven*—This assumption is based upon scriptural authority. *Cf. Chānd. Up.*, 5. 18. 2.

[6] *Effulgent etc.*—*i. e., Dyuloka* or the sky with its luminary bodies such as the sun, the moon, the stars, etc.

[7] *Water*—The word '*Rayi*', meaning 'Food' and 'Wealth', also indicates 'Water' by which whatever is 'Food' grows, bringing in its turn 'Wealth'.

[8] *Five organs etc.*—namely, the organ of sight, sound, smell, taste and touch.

[9] *Five organs etc.*—namely, hands, feet and organs of speech, generation and evacuation.

[10] *Five airs or humours etc.*—*viz., Prāṇa, Apāna, Samāna, Vyāna* and *Udāna*.

[11] *To the enjoyment etc.*—He makes people enjoy pleasure and pain according to their virtuous or vicious deeds.

[12] *First*—The word does not denote any priority of creation. It is called *first* because from the standpoint of *Vaiśvānara* or the waking state alone one can understand the other states, *i. e.*, as has been pointed out under the first Upaniṣad, we see *first* how from the waking state the dream state and the state of dreamless sleep are known.

[13] *No mistake*—The subjective is known as the *Adhyātma*. The *Adhidaiva* comprises the objective universe including the spheres of the sun, the moon, the stars, etc. *Adhyātma* is non-different from *Adhidaiva* because *both* these, as has already been pointed out, are but ideas imagined in *Ātman*. Hence there is no mistake in assuming *Ādhidaivika* members as forming the limbs of the *Adhyātma*.

[14] *From the standpoint etc.*—The gross physical aspects of both *Adhyātma* and *Adhidaiva*, known as *Virāṭ* (*i. e.*, the totality of all physical bodies), form the first quarter of the *Ātman* or Brahman. The subtle or *Sūkṣma* (namely, the *Apañcīkṛta*) aspects, known as the *Hiraṇyagarbha* (*i. e.*, the totality of the subtle), form the second quarter of the *Ātman* or Brahman. The *Kāraṇa* or causal aspect known as the *Avyākṛta* (unmanifested) or the *Iśvara* comprising both the *Adhyātma* and *Adhidaiva* is the third quarter. And the transcendental *(Turīya)* which is beyond all causal relations and which is the ultimate substratum of all appearances, *viz.*, *Virāṭ*, *Hiraṇyagarbha* and *Iśvara*, is the fourth quarter. In all these instances there is non-difference between the *Adhyātma* and *Adhidaiva*. Therefore there is no mistake in applying the limbs of *Adhidaiva* to *Adhyātma*.

[15] *In this way alone*—*i. e.*, by merging each of the three states step by step, in the *Turīya* or the transcendental.

[16] *Entire etc.*—*i. e.*, from Brahmā or the highest cosmic being to the mere blade of grass.

[17] *All beings*—*i. e.*, they are seen as mere imagination upon *Ātman*. Compare the following couplet from the *Manu Smṛti*:

सर्वभूतस्थमात्मानं सर्वभूतानि चात्मनि ।
संपश्यन्नात्मयाजी वै स्वराज्यमधिगच्छति ॥

[18] *Otherwise*—*i. e.*, by admitting the duality of *Adhyātma* and *Adhidaiva*.

[19] *Sāṁkhyas*—The *Sāṁkhya* doctrine admits the plurality of souls as based upon manifoldness of experience. The *Vedāntin* explains the plurality to be due to *Avidyā*.

[20] *Thy head etc.*—*i. e.*, if thou worshippest the effulgent region which is but a part of *Vaiśvānara* as the *Vaiśvānara* itself.

[21] *Identity*—*i. e.*, in the spiritual plane.

[22] *Taijasa*—The individual self while dreaming is called *Taijasa*.

[23] *The Unmanifested etc.*—The identity of *Iśvara* and *Prājña*. The individual self in the state of deep sleep *(Suṣupti)* is called *Prājña*.

[24] *Because etc.*—The *Prājña* or the causal self withdraws into itself at the time of deep sleep all distinctions of objects as well as the objects themselves experienced in waking and dream states. The *Iśvara* (the cosmic soul) too at the time of dissolution withdraws into itself all distinctions experienced in the planes of *Virāṭ* and *Hiraṇyagarbha* which correspond respectively to the waking and the dream states of the subjective.

## IV

स्वप्नस्थानोऽन्तःप्रज्ञः सप्ताङ्ग एकोनविंशतिमुखः
प्रविविक्तभुक्तैजसो द्वितीयः पादः ॥ ४ ॥

The second quarter *(Pāda)* is the *Taijasa* whose sphere (of activity) is the dream, who is conscious of internal objects, who has seven limbs and nineteen mouths and who experiences the subtle objects.

### Śaṅkara's Commentary

He is called the *Svapnasthāna* because the dream (state) is his (*Taijasa*) sphere. Waking consciousness, being associated as it is with many means,[1] and appearing[2] conscious of objects as if external, though (in reality) they are nothing but states[3] of mind, leaves in the mind corresponding[4] impressions. That the mind (in dream) without[5] any of the external means, but possessed of the impressions left on it by the waking consciousness, like[6] a piece of canvas[7] with the pictures painted on it, experiences the dream state also as if it were like the waking, is due to its being under the influence of ignorance, desire and their action.[8] Thus[9] it is said, '(And when he falls asleep) then after having taken away with him (portion of the) impression from the world during the waking state (destroying and building up again, he experiences dream by his own light)' (*Bṛhd. Up.*, 4. 3. 9). Similarly the *Atharvaṇa*, after introducing the subject with '(all the senses) become one in the highest[10] *Deva*, the mind', continues 'There the god (mind) enjoys in dream greatness'[11] (*Praśna Up.*). From[12] the standpoint of the sense-organs, the mind is internal. He (the *Taijasa*) is called the *Antaḥprajña* or conscious of the internal because his consciousness in dream becomes aware of the mental states, which are impressions left by the previous waking state. He is called the *Taijasa* because he appears as the subject though this (dream) consciousness is without any (gross) object and is of the nature of the essence of light. The *Viśva* (the subject of the waking state) experiences consciousness associated with gross external objects; whereas, here (in the dream state), the object of experience is consciousness consisting of *Vāsanās* (the impressions of past experience). Therefore this experience is called the experience[13] of the subtle. The rest is common (with the previous *Śruti*). This *Taijasa* is the second quarter (of *Ātman*).

[1] *Means*—Subject-object relationship, agency, instrumentality, etc.

[2] *Appearing*—According to *Vedānta*, external objects, perceived by the sense-organs, have no absolute reality. They appear as real on account of *Avidyā*. Their reality cannot be proved for the simple reason that they become non-existent when their essential character is enquired into.

[3] *States of mind*—External objects are nothing but mental existents produced by *Avidyā*. There are no such independent external entities as objects; they are but creations of the mind. In fact we are not conscious of any external objects independent of the mind. We take our mental creations to be such objects. Again those who seek for the cause of these mental creations or ideas, which we think we see as external objects, are led into a logical

*regressus*. This causal chain leads nowhere. It will be shown later on that the whole idea of cause and effect is unreal.

[4] *Corresponding etc.*—that is, like those experienced in the waking state These impressions are subsequently reproduced in the form of dream-objects.

[5] *Without any etc.*—It is because in dream no other separate entity than the mind of the dreamer, is present.

[6] *Like a piece etc.*—Dream experiences appear as real as the experiences of the waking state.

[7] *Like a piece of canvas etc.*—The picture painted on a piece of canvas appears to possess various dimensions though, in reality, the picture is on a plane surface. Similarly, dream-experiences, though really states of mind, appear to be characterized by the presence of externality and internality.

[8] *Action*—The word '*Karma*' is used in *Vedānta* in more senses than one. '*Karma*' primarily means 'action'. It also signifies the destiny forged by one in one's past incarnation or present: the store of tendencies, impulses, characteristics and habits, which determine one's future embodiment and environment. Another meaning of '*Karma*', often used in reference to one's caste or position in life, is ritual, the course of conduct, which one ought to follow in pursuance of the tendencies acquired in the past, with a view to work them out. The meaning of the word, here, is the tendencies generated in the mind by the activities of the waking state. *Avidyā* gives rise to *Kāma* or desire, and this in its turn, impels a man to action.

[9] *Thus etc.*—The *causal* relation between the waking and the dream states is sought to be established here on scriptural authority.

[10] *Highest etc.*—It is because in the dream state the *Jīva* is associated with the *Upādhi* of mind.

[11] *Greatness*—The *Jīva* in sleep, characterized by darkness, possesses the light by means of which the subject-object relationship is seen. The greatness of mind consists in the fact that in dream it can transform itself into knowledge, act of knowing and the object of knowledge.

[12] *From the standpoint of*—From the standpoint of the waking state alone when the sense-organs are active, one can review the dream experiences and thus come to know the internal activity of

the mind which acts in the dream state independently of the sense-organs of the waking state.

13 *Experience of the subtle*—The experiences of waking and dream states are of the same nature; for in both the states the perceiver is aware only of his mental states which are not related to any external objects, as they are non-existent. From the standpoint of dream, dream objects are as gross and material as those experienced in the waking state. From the view-point of the waking state alone, one may infer that the dream objects are subtle, that is, composed of mere impressions of the waking state, inasmuch as in the dream state no external (that is, gross) object exists at all..

## V

यत्र सुप्तो न कंचन कामं कामयते न कंचन स्वप्नं पश्यति तत्सुषुप्तम् । सुषुप्तस्थान एकीभूतः प्रज्ञानघन एवाऽऽनन्दमयो ह्यानन्दभुक् चेतोमुखः प्राज्ञस्तृतीयः पादः ॥ ५ ॥

That is the state of deep sleep wherein the sleeper does not desire any objects nor does he see any dream. The third quarter (*Pāda*) is the (*Prājña*) whose sphere is deep sleep, in whom all (experiences) become unified or undifferentiated, who is verily, a mass of consciousness entire, who is full of bliss and who experiences bliss, and who is the path leading to the knowledge (of the two other states).

### Śaṅkara's Commentary

The adjectival clause, *viz.*, 'Wherein the sleeper' etc., is put with a view to enabling one to grasp what the state of deep sleep (*Suṣupti*) signifies, inasmuch as sleep characterized by[1] the absence of the knowledge of Reality is the common feature of those mental modifications which are associated with (waking, that is) perception[2] (of gross objects) and (dream, that is the) non-perception[3] (of gross objects). Or[4] the object of the introduction of the adjectival clause may be to distinguish the state of deep sleep (of the sleeping person) from the two previous states as sleep characterized by the absence of knowledge of Reality is the common feature of the three states. 'Wherein', that is to say, in which state or time, the sleeping person does not see any dream, nor does he desire any desirable (object). For, in the state of deep sleep, there does not exist, as in the two other states, any desire or the dream experience whose characteristic is to take a thing for what it is not. He is called the '*Suṣuptasthāna*' because his sphere is this state of deep sleep. Similarly it is called *Ekībhūta*, *i.e.*, the state in which all experiences become unified—a state in which all objects of duality, which are nothing but forms[5] of thought, spread over the two states (*viz.*, the waking and the dream), reach the state[6] of indiscrimination or non-differentiation without losing their characteristics, as the day, revealing phenomenal objects, is enveloped by the darkness of night. Therefore conscious experiences, which are nothing but forms of thought, perceived during dream and waking states, become a thick mass (of consciousness) as[7] it were (in deep sleep); this state of deep sleep is called the '*Prajñānaghana*' (a mass of all consciousness unified) on account of the absence of all manifoldness (discrimination of variety). As at night, owing to the indiscrimination produced by darkness, all (precepts) become a mass (of darkness) as it were, so also in the state of deep sleep all (objects) of consciousness, verily, become a mass (of consciousness, verily, become a mass (of consciousness). The word '*eva*' ('verily') in the text denotes the absence[8] of any other thing except consciousness (in deep sleep). (At the time of deep sleep) the mind is free from the miseries[9] of the efforts made on account of the states of the mind being involved in the relationship of subject and object: therefore, it is called the *Ānandamaya*, that is, endowed with an abundance of bliss. But this is not Bliss Itself; because it[10] is not Bliss Infinite. As in common (experience) parlance, one, free from efforts, is called happy and enjoyer of bliss. As the *Prājña*[11] enjoys this state of deep sleep which is entirely free from all efforts, therefore it is called the '*Ānandabhuk*' (the experiencer of bliss). The *Śruti* also says, 'This is its highest bliss'. It is called the '*Cetomukha*' because it is the doorway[12] to the (cognition) of the two other states of consciousness known as dream and waking. Or because the *Ceta* (the perceiving entity) characterized[13] by (empirical) consciousness (*Bodha*) is its doorway leading to the experience of dreams etc., therefore it is called the '*Cetomukha*'. It is called *Prājña* as it is conscious of the past and the future as well as of all objects. It is called *Prājña*, the knower *par excellence*, even in deep sleep, because[14] of its having been so in the two previous states. Or it is called the *Prājña* because its peculiar feature is consciousness[15] undifferentiated. In the two other states consciousness exists, no doubt, but it is (there) aware of (the experiences of) variety. The *Prājña*, thus described, is the third quarter.

1 *By etc.*—The mere absence of desire or objects associated with waking or dream states is no characteristic of the Highest Knowledge; for, deep sleep, swoon, etc., are characterized by such absence. Therefore the knowledge of Reality is true *Jnānam*.

2 *Perception*—In the waking state one is aware of the mental modifications which are known as the perception of gross physical objects.

3 *Non-perception*—Dream experience is here designated as 'non-perception', as it is *distinct* from the perception of gross objects of the waking state. In the dream state the objects of perception, which are also modifications of the mind, are but the subtle impressions left by the objects of the waking state. That the

dream objects are such can only be known from the experience of the waking state.

[4] *Or*—The commentator gives two meanings of the first sentence of the text. The first meaning lays emphasis on '*yatra*' *i. e.*, wherein, because we are dealing here with the three states. The natural meaning of the text is that after describing the states of waking and dream the *Śruti* proceeds to describe the state of *Suṣupti* or deep sleep which is said to be distinguished from the two other states in not having desire etc., the common feature of the other two states. And such a distinction has to be made because all the three states have the common feature of the absence of knowledge of Reality. The second meaning emphasizes the word *supta* and explains it thus in this connection. *Jāgrat*, *Svapna* and *Suṣupti* are the three states which have for their perceiver one who experiences the three states. Though the perceiver of the three states has three different appellations yet the word *supta* is used as the common term for them by *Śruti* in a special sense, to denote the absence of knowledge of Reality. Therefore, in this sense, though the word *supta* means the same as the experiencer in the state of *Jāgrat*, and *Svapna* yet it is differentiated from the latter by the adjectival phrase. Wherein the sleeper does not see etc.

[5] *Forms of thought*—Mental or thought forms arise in *Ātman*, which constitute external and internal objects.

[6] *State of indiscrimination*—This is known in the empirical language as the causal state. One viewing *suṣupti* from the waking state takes it to be the causal state because he finds that the experiences of *jāgrat* and *svapna* merge in *suṣupti*. The mind moving within the sphere of causality further takes *suṣupti* to be the cause of the waking and the dream states, believing the former to be antecedent to the latter.

[7] *As it were*—As suggested in the previous note *suṣupti* is designated as the state of causal unity because the waking man looks upon it as the cause of waking and dream experiences. But even *suṣupti* is also a *vṛtti* or an idea of the waking man, which arises in his mind on account of his seeking for a cause of the waking and dream experiences. Therefore the *unity* experienced in *suṣupti* as understood by the wakeful man is not the *unity* of *Brahmajñāna*—otherwise the reappearance of multiplicity as real in the waking state would not be possible.

[8] *Absence etc.*—The state of *suṣupti* is characterized by the absence of the objects which one perceives in the waking or dreaming state.

[9] *Miseries of the efforts*—The perceiver in the *jāgrat* and *svapna* states who always experiences subject-object relationship, finds its absence in *suṣupti*.

[10] *It is not etc.*—The *suṣupti* is not the state of Bliss Infinite because the perceiver from the waking standpoint associates deep sleep with the *Upādhi* of the idea of the causal state.

[11] *Prājña*—The experiencer of *suṣupti*. That the *Prājña*, in deep sleep, enjoys bliss is viewed from waking state.

[12] *Doorway*—*Suṣupti* is the doorway because it leads to the experience of the waking and dream states. The state of unified existence of *suṣupti*, wherein all diversities disappear, is the invariable antecedent of the waking and dream experiences. Hence it is looked upon as the cause of the two other states.

[13] *Characterized etc.*—It is because the consciousness, present in *suṣupti*, is a necessary condition for becoming aware of the states of *jāgrat* and *svapna*. No experience is possible without consciousness.

[14] *Because etc.*—Though there are no specific states of consciousness in *suṣupti* still it is known as *Prājña* or the knower *par excellence* because all previous states of consciousness experienced in *jāgrat* and *svapna* are the same as that of *suṣupti*.

[15] *Consciousness etc.*—This consciousness, which exists as *Prājña* in deep sleep appears as particular (विशेष) states of consciousness in *jāgrat* and *svapna*.

## VI

एष सर्वेश्वर एष सर्वज्ञ एषोऽन्तर्याम्येष योनिः सर्वस्य
प्रभवाप्ययौ हि भूतानाम् ॥ ६ ॥

This is the Lord of all; this is the knower of all; this is the controller within; this is the source of all; and this is that from which all things originate and in which they finally disappear.

### Śaṅkara's Commentary

This in its natural[1] state, is the Lord (*Īśvara*) of all. All, that is to say, of the entire physical and super-physical universe. He (*Īśvara*) is not something separate from the universe as others[2] hold. The *Śruti* also says, 'O good one, *Prāṇa* (*Prājña* or *Īśvara*) is that in which the mind is bound'. He is omniscient because he is the knower[3] of all beings in their different conditions. He is the *Antaryāmin*, that is, he alone entering into all, directs everything from within. Therefore He is called the origin of all because from Him proceeds the universe characterized by diversity, as described before. It being so, He is verily that from which all things proceed and in which all disappear.

[1] *Natural state*—*Prājña* is the natural state because in deep sleep all diversities of waking and dream states merge. This state, being free from the conditions of the waking and dream states, manifests, in a marked degree Pure Consciousness.

[2] *Others*—The *Naiyāyikas* and others admit an extra-cosmic creator. Śaṅkara has refuted this theory in the commentary on the *Vedānta-Sūtras* (2-2-37). When seeking for the cause of the universe, *Vedānta* posits *Prājña* as the material as well as the efficient cause of the universe.

[3] *Knower*—The *Ātman* is the witness of the past, the present and the future as well as the three states. Knowledge of the three states implies the common knower of all.

Here commence Gauḍapāda's *Kārikās* in explanation of the *Māṇḍūkya Śruti*:

### Gauḍapāda-Kārikā

Regarding this there are these *Ślokas*.

### Śaṅkara's Commentary

In explanation of the foregoing (texts) there are these *Ślokas*.

*Gauḍapāda* takes up the preceding six texts of the Upaniṣad and comments upon them as follows:

बहिष्प्रज्ञो विभुर्विश्वो ह्यन्तःप्रज्ञस्तु तैजसः ।
घनप्रज्ञस्तथा प्राज्ञ एक एव त्रिधा स्मृतः ॥ १ ॥

1. Visva (*the first quarter*) *is he who is all-pervading and who experiences the external* (*gross*) *objects.* Taijasa (*the second quarter*) *is he who cognizes the internal* (*the subtle*) *objects.* Prājña *is he who is a mass of consciousness. It is one alone who is thus known in the three states.*

## Śaṅkara's Commentary

The implication of the passage is this: That *Ātman* is (as witness) distinct from the three states (witnessed) and that he is pure[1] and unrelated,[2] is established by his moving in three states, in[3] succession, and also on account of the knowledge, 'I am that', resulting from the experience which unites[4] through memory. The *Śruti* also corroborates it by the illustration[5] of the 'great fish' etc.

[1] *Pure*—The ideas of purity and impurity, weal and woe, pleasure and pain, etc., are the characteristics of the states and do not, in any way, pertain to *Ātman* who is only the witness of the three states. The *Jīva* or the reflected consciousness, which is identical with *Ātman*, falsely identifies himself with the states and considers himself to be impure, miserable, etc. *Ātman* is ever-pure.

[2] *Unrelated*—No relation of any kind, even that of causality, exists between the three states and *Ātman* as the latter alone exists. That *Ātman* is unrelated is further known from the fact that the experiences of the waking state do not, in reality, affect *Ātman* in the dream state, nor those of the dream state affect *Ātman* in the state of deep sleep.

[3] *In succession*—Though it appears that *Ātman* identifies itself with each of the three states for the time being, yet the fact that he moves from one state to another without being affected shows that he is only the witness of the three states.

[4] *Unites etc.*—From the standpoint of common experience we find a relationship between past, present and future. This is due to the unifying power of memory. Even this relationship between experiences is possible only if an *Ātman* is posited as the witness of them.

[5] *Illustration etc.*—This is taken from the *Bṛhd. Up.* As a powerful fish swims from one bank to another unimpeded by the currents of the river, so also *Ātman* moves in the three states totally unaffected by

them. As no characteristics of the banks, good or bad, affect the fish, so also no experiences of the three states affect the pure nature of *Ātman*. Another illustration is that of the bird, which flies unobstructed in the sky and unattached to the surrounding lands.

### KĀRIKĀ

दक्षिणाक्षिमुखे विश्वो मनस्यन्तस्तु तैजसः ।
आकाशे च हृदि प्राज्ञस्त्रिधा देहे व्यवस्थितः ॥ २ ॥

2. Viśva *is he who cognizes in the right eye*, Taijasa *is he who cognizes in the mind within and* Prājña *is he who constitutes the* Ākāśa *in the heart. Thus the one* Ātman *is (conceived as) threefold in the (one) body.*

### ŚAṄKARA'S COMMENTARY

This verse is intended to show that the threefold experience of *Viśva* etc. (*Taijasa* and *Prājña*) is realised in the waking[1] state alone. *Dakṣiṇākṣi*: the means of perception (of gross objects) is the right eye. The presence of *Viśva*, the cognizer of gross objects, is chiefly felt here. The *Śruti* also says, 'The person that is in the right eye is known as *Indha*—the Luminous One' (*Bṛhd. Up.*). *Indha*, which means the effulgent one, who is the *Vaiśvānara* and also known as the *Virāṭ Ātman* (the totality of gross bodies), the perceiver in the sun, is the same[2] as the perceiver in the eye.

(Objection)—The *Hiraṇyagarbha* is distinct from the knower of the body (*Kṣetra*) who is the cognizer, the controller of the right eye, who is also the general experiencer and who is the Lord of the body.

(Reply)—No, for, in reality, such a distinction is[3] not admitted. The *Śruti* says, 'One effulgent being alone is hidden in all beings'. The *Smṛti* also says, 'Me do thou also know, O Arjuna, to be the *Kṣetrajña* (the knower of the body) in all *Kṣetras* (bodies)' (*Gītā*, 13. 2), 'Indivisible, yet it exists as if divided in beings' (*Gītā*, 13. 16).

Though the presence of *Viśva* is equally felt in all sense-organs without distinction yet the right eye is particularly singled[4] out (as the chief instrument for its perception), because he (*Viśva*) makes a greater use of the right eye in perceiving objects. (The right eye is made here to represent all the sense-organs.) The one, who has his abode in the right eye, having perceived (external) forms, closes the eye; and then recollecting them within the mind sees[5] the very same (external objects) as in a dream, as the manifestation of the (subtle) impressions (of memory). As[6] is the case here (waking), so also is the case with dream. Therefore, *Taijasa*, the perceiver in the mind within, is verily the same as *Viśva*. With the cessation of the activity known as memory,[7] the perceiver (in the waking and dream states) is unified[8] with *Prājña* in the *Ākāśa* of the heart and becomes[9] verily a mass[10] of consciousness, because there is, then, a cessation of mental activities. Both perception and memory are forms of thought, in the absence of which the seer remains indistinguishably[11] in the form of *Prāṇa* in the heart alone. For, the *Śruti*[12] also says, '*Prāṇa* alone withdraws all these within'. *Taijasa* is identical[13] with *Hiraṇyagarbha* on account of its existence being realised in mind. Mind is the characteristic indication[14] (of both). This is supported by such scriptural passages as, 'This *Puruṣa* (*Hiraṇyagarbha*) is all mind' etc.

(Objection)—The *Prāṇa* (vital breath) of a deep sleeper is manifested.[15] The sense-organs (at the time of deep sleep) are merged in it. How, then, can it (*Prāṇa*) be said to be unmanifested?

(Reply)—This is no mistake, for the unmanifested[16] (*Avyākṛta*) is characterised by the absence (of the knowledge) of time and space. Though *Prāṇa*, in the case of a person who identifies himself with (particular) *Prāṇa*, appears to be manifested (during the time of waking and dream), yet even in the case of those who (thus) identify themselves with individualized *Prāṇa*, the *Prāṇa*, during deep sleep, loses (such) particular identification, which is due to its limitation by the body, and is verily the same as the unmanifested. As in the case of those who identify themselves with individualized *Prāṇas*, the *Prāṇa*, at[17] the time of death, ceases to be the manifested, so also in the case of those who think of themselves as identified with the individualized *Prāṇas*, the *Prāṇa* attains to the condition like the unmanifested, in the state of deep sleep. This *Prāṇa* (of deep sleep) further contains the seed (cause) of (future) creation[18] (as is the case with the *Avyākṛta*). The cognizer of the two states—deep sleep and *Avyākṛta*—is also one[19] (*viz.*, the Pure Consciousness). It (one in deep sleep) is identical[20] with the (apparently) different cognizers identifying themselves with the conditioned (in the states of waking and dream), and therefore such attributes as 'unified', 'mass of all consciousness' etc., as described above, are reasonably applicable to it (one in deep sleep). Other[21] reason, already stated, supports it. How does, indeed, the word *Prāṇa*[22] apply to the *Avyākṛta* (unmanifested)? It is supported by the *Śruti* passage, 'Oh, good one, the mind is tied to the *Prāṇa*'.

(Objection)—In that *Śruti* passage, the word *Prāṇa* indicates *Sat* (Existance,) *i.e.*, the *Brahman*, (not the *Avyākṛta*) which is the subject-matter under discussion, as the text commences with the passage, 'All this was *Sat* in the beginning'.

(Reply)—This is no mistake, for (in that passage) the *Sat* is admitted to be that which contains within it the seed[23] or cause (of creation). Though *Sat*, *i.e.*, *Brahman*, is indicated in that passage by the word '*Prāṇa*', yet the *Brahman* that is indicated by the words *Sat* and *Prāṇa* (in that connection) is not the one who is free from its attribute of being the seed or cause that creates all[24] beings. For if in that *Śruti* passage, *Brahman*, devoid of the causal relation (*i.e.*, the Absolute) were sought to be described, then the *Śruti* would have used such expressions as, 'Not this, Not this', 'Where from speech turns back', 'That is something other than both the known and the unknown', etc. The *Smṛti* also declares, 'It is neither *Sat* (existence) nor *Asat* (non-existence)' (*Gitā*). If by the text were meant the (Absolute) devoid of causal relation then the coming back, to the relative plane of consciousness, of those who were in deep sleep and unified with *Sat* at the time of *Praḷaya* (cosmic dissolution), could[25] not happen. Further, (in that case) the liberated souls would again come back to the relative plane of consciousness; for the absence of seed or cause (capable of giving birth to the world of names and forms) would be the common[26] feature of both.

Further, in the absence of the seed[27] (cause, *i.e.*, at the time of *Suṣupti* and *Praḷaya*) which can be destroyed by Knowledge (alone), Knowledge itself becomes futile. Therefore the word *Sat* (the text of the *Chāndogya Upaniṣad*, the passage under discussion) in that aspect in which causality is attributed to it, is indicated by *Prāṇa*, and accordingly has been described in all the *Śrutis* as the cause.[28] It is for this reason also that the Absolute *Brahman*, dissociated from its causal attribute, has been indicated in such *Śruti* passages as, 'It is beyond the unmanifested which is higher than the manifested', 'He is causeless and is the substratum of the external (effect) and the internal (cause)', 'Wherefrom words comeback....', 'Not this, not this', etc. That which is designated as *Prājña* (when it is viewed as the cause of the phenomenal world) will be described as *Turīya* separately when it is not viewed as the cause, and when it is free from all phenomenal relationship (such as that of the body, etc.) *i.e.*, in its absolutely Real aspect. The causal condition is also verily experienced in this body from such[29] cognition of the man who is awakened from the deep sleep, as, 'I did not know anything (at the time of deep sleep)'. Therefore it is said that (one) *Ātman* is perceived as threefold[30] in the (one) body.

[1] *Waking state alone*—From the ordinary empirical standpoint, *Viśva*, *Taijasa* and *Prājña* are generally related to three states, *viz.*, waking, dream and deep sleep. But the three states are comprehended from the standpoint of the waking state alone. That dream and deep sleep are two states, having different characteristics, is known in the waking state alone. Therefore these two become known to the waking consciousness. Besides *jāgrat* (waking), in so far as it denotes the absence of the knowledge of Reality, covers the dream and sleep states as well. The three apparent cognisers known as *Viśva*, *Taijasa* and *Prājña* are really one, because a plurality of perceivers in the same state, namely, the waking, and in the same body is an absurdity, as that would preclude the possibility of the continuity of perception as revealed through memory. Therefore the apparently three different perceivers are identical and their apparent distinction is due to their identification with the three states.

[2] *Same*—It is because, as already shown, the *Adhidaiva* is identical with *Adhyātma*.

[3] *Is it not admitted*—The difference is only imaginary and empirical and due to the identification with different bodies. Really speaking, one *Ātman* alone manifests itself in different forms, microcosmic or macrocosmic.

[4] *Singled out*—The assertion is based upon scriptural authority. In actual experience also one finds that the right eye is more efficient in the perception of objects than the left one.

[5] *Sees etc.*—*Viśva*, the perceiver of gross objects, becomes *Taijasa* when he closes the eyes and thinks within his mind about the gross objects. Cognisers of dream and ideas (in the waking state) are identical. Both, *viz.*, ideas and dream objects, possess, for the time being, the same characteristics.

[6] *As etc.*—There is no difference whatever between the dream state and the state of imagination in the waking, In both the states, the

perceiver cognizes the impressions of gross physical objects experienced in the preceding states. The only difference between the states of dream and imagination (in the waking state) is that dream represents a whole state whereas the reflection represents the part of a state.

[7] *Memory*—Memory is also a form of mental activity implying subject-object relationship. The impressions of gross external objects perceived in the waking state manifest themselves in the forms of memory and dream.

[8] *Unified*—That is, this state is characterised by the absence of subject-object relationship.

[9] *Becomes verily etc.*—Whenever in the waking state the mind ceases to be active, *i.e.,* whenever ideas disappear from it, the state is said to be *Suṣupti.* Even memory does not function then. This state is identical with deep sleep, when subject-object relationship is absent. This state is posited from the actual experience of the change from a state which was without the dual relationship of subject and object. The experience of the three states and the transition from the one to the other proves that there is only one perceiver who is the witness of the three states and their succession.

[10] *Mass of etc.*—That is, there is no particular cognition in that state.

[11] *Indistinguishably*—*i.e.,* in unmanifested form.

[12] *Śruti*—See *Bṛhd. Up.*

[13] *Identical*—That *Viśva* and *Virāṭ* as well as *Prājña* (deep sleep) and *Iśvara* (unmanifested) are identical, has been already shown. Now it is pointed out that *Hiraṇyagarbha* is identical with *Taijasa. Hiraṇyagarbha* and *Taijasa* are only what are termed as the cosmic mind and the individual mind respectively. Really speaking, macrocosm and microcosm, both being mere forms of thought, are identical. Therefore the perceivers, *Hiraṇyagarbha* and *Taijasa,* are identical because they are also forms of thought. Their different appellations are due to their identification with different *Upādhis* (adjuncts) namely, the thoughts of macrocosm and microcosm.

[14] *Indication*—Both are formed of the same stuff or the mind.

[15] *Manifested*—The manifestation of the activities of the *Prāṇa* of a deep sleeper is witnessed by on-lookers.

[16] *Unmanifested*—The characteristics of manifestedness and unmanifestedness of *Prāṇa* are predicated of it from the standpoint of waking and sleep states respectively.

[17] *At the time of death*—This illustration is given on the basis of the scriptural authority. Comp. *Bṛhd. Up.*, 4. 4. 2.

[18] *Creation*—Both the states of *Avyākṛta* and deep sleep (here called *Prāṇa*) are followed by a state in which names and forms are manifest. On account of the identity of effects, the causes are also said to be identical.

[19] *One*—The identity of deep sleep and *Avyākṛta* is further demonstrated from the identity of their common cogniser, *viz.*, Pure Consciousness.

[20] *Identical*—The meaning is that the perceiver of the three states is one and the same.

[21] *Other etc.*—*viz.*; the identity of *Adhyātma* and *Adhidaiva*.

[22] *Prāṇa*—The contention of the objector is that the ordinary meaning of *Prāṇa* is vital breath having five aspects, *viz.*,*Prāṇa*, *Apāna*, *Samāna*, *Vyāna* and *Udāna*.

[23] *Seed*—That is, the *Saguṇa Brahman*.

[24] *All etc.*—Both animate and inanimate.

[25] *Could not etc.*—For, after the realisation of the Absolute *Brahman* return to the plane of ignorance is not possible. But the person who goes into the *Suṣupti* or the *Avyākṛta* state without attaining *Jñānam* again returns to the plane of ignorance. It is the *Knowledge of Brahman* alone which is the condition of liberation but not mere absence of duality *without knowledge*, which can be experienced in deep sleep, swoon or trance.

[26] *Common feature*—If Existence free from causal relation, *i.e.*, the *Absolute Brahman*, be the meaning of *Sat* in the scriptural passage under discussion, then the reverting of the deep sleeper, who has not yet attained to *Jñānam*, to the dual plane of consciousness would not be possible. And if a person, after realising the *Absolute Brahman*, is to come back to the state of duality, then *Jñānam* or liberation would be impermanent. The meaning is this: At the time of *Pralaya* when the created beings become unified with *Sat* or Existence they do not become really the *Absolute Brahman*. They remain only in a seed or potential condition and therefore they re-appear at the time of creation. Similarly, an ignorant person who goes into deep sleep retains in a latent form, all his previous impressions of duality and gets them back after coming down from the state of *Suṣupti*. But a *Jñānī*, once realising his identity with *Absolute Brahman*, is never misled by the sense (of the reality) of dual existence.

[27] *Seed*—The causal standpoint comprises false apprehension and non-apprehension as well as their effects. The *Naiyāyikas* affirm this causal standpoint, popularly known as the cosmic ignorance, to be a *Padārtha* or independent category which arises in the absence of the contact of the sense-organ with its object. Therefore *Ajñānam*, according to them, is a negation or *abhāva*. But according to *Vedānta*, *Ajñānam* is not purely a negation (characterising the *Āvaraṇa* aspect), but a negation combined with an affirmation or creation (*Vikṣepa* aspect). It is not an independent category but dependent upon present consciousness and comprehended by it. This ignorance is destroyed by the knowledge of truth.

[28] *Cause*—It is because a causal explanation is necessary.

[29] *Such cognition*—The experience of the absence of knowledge in *Suṣupti* is possible only for a man who is awakened from deep sleep. From the perception in the waking state of a change involving names and forms, he thinks of the previous state of deep sleep as devoid of them. Therefore the knowledge of deep sleep is possible only in the waking state. This shows that *Suṣupti* is knowable only in *Jāgrat* consciousness.

[30] *As threefold*—The meaning is this: That the Ātman is the witness of the three states is known from the perception of the change of one state into another. The *Ātman* is the witness not only of the three states but also of their cognizers, *viz.*, *Viśva*, *Taijasa* and *Prājña*. In this body and in the *Jāgrat* state alone, the three states as well as their cognizers are perceived.

विश्वो हि स्थूलभुङ्नित्यं तैजसः प्रविविक्तभुक् ।
आनन्दभुक्तथा प्राज्ञस्त्रिधा भोगं निबोधत ॥ ३ ॥

3. Viśva *always experiences the gross (object)*, Taijasa *the subtle and* Prājña *the blissful. Know these to be the threefold experiences.*

स्थूलं तर्पयते विश्वं प्रविविक्तं तु तैजसम् ।
आनन्दश्च तथा प्राज्ञं त्रिधा तृप्तिं निबोधत ॥ ४ ॥

4. *The gross (object) satisfies* Viśva, *the subtle the* Taijasa *and the blissful the* Prājña. *Know these to be threefold satisfaction.*

ŚAṄKARA'S COMMENTARY

Verses 3 and 4 have already been explained.

त्रिषु धामसु यद्भोज्यं भोक्ता यश्च प्रकीर्तितः ।
वेदैतदुभयं यस्तु स भुञ्जानो न लिप्यते ॥ ५ ॥

5. *He who knows both the experiencer and the objects of experience that have been described (associated) with the three states, is not affected through experiencing the objects.*

ŚAṄKARA'S COMMENTARY

In the three states, namely, waking etc., the one[1] and the same object of experience appears in threefold forms as the gross, the subtle and the blissful. Further, the experiencer (of the three states) known (differently) as *Viśva*, *Taijasa* and *Prājña* has been described as one on account of the unity[2] of consciousness implied in such[3] cognition as, 'I am that' (common to all conditions), as well as from the absence[4] of any distinction in respect of the perceiver. He who knows the two (experiencer and the objects of experience), appearing as many in the form of subject and objects of experience, though enjoying them, is[5] not affected thereby; because[6] all objects (of experience) are experienced by one subject alone. As (the heat of the) fire[7] does not increase or decrease by consuming wood etc., so also nothing[8] is added to or taken away (from the knowingness or awareness of the *Ātman*) by its experience of that which is its object.

[1] *One and the same etc.*—It is because the experiences of the three states are only the different forms of thought or ideas.

[2] *Unity of etc.*—That the experiencer of the three states is one and identical is also known to the waking consciousness.

[3] *Such cognition etc.*—This cognition takes the following form: I, who now have been perceiving objects in the waking state, had seen forms (ideas) in dream and experienced nothing in deep sleep.

[4] *Absence etc.*—There is nothing to suggest that the experiencers of the three states are different.

[5] *Is not etc.*—He who knows that the three states are one and that their perceivers are also one, is not affected by the experiences of the states, nor does he identify himself with the (apparently separate) perceivers thereof. He is not affected because he clearly perceives that objects which appeared as real in the waking and dream states disappear again in the deep sleep. Therefore he is convinced of the unreality of dream and waking experiences. As a witness, he views unaffected the cropping up of these ideas of experience (in dream and waking) and also their disappearance in *Suṣupti*).

[6] *Because—i. e.*, it is because one *Ātman* in three forms alternately perceives the emergence and disappearance of the experiencer and all objects of experience. Hence he knows them to be unreal.

[7] *Does not etc.*—The *principle* or *character* of heat remains the same irrespective of the quantity of wood it consumes.

[8] *Nothing etc.*—The self or *Ātman*, when it knows that it is the witness of the three states, is not subject to any modification by the experiencer of the objects thereof. Because he knows these objects (including their perceivers) as mere मन: स्पन्दनं or his own thoughts, and hence unreal. An imaginary tiger or the one seen in the dream cannot harm its perceiver.

प्रभवः सर्वभावानां सतामिति विनिश्चयः ।
सर्वं जनयति प्राणश्चेतोंशून्पुरुषः पृथक् ॥ ६ ॥

6. *It is thoroughly established that the coming into effect can be predicated only of all positive entities that exist. The* Prāṇa *manifests all; the* Puruṣa *creates the conscious beings* (*the* Jīvas) *in their manifold form separately.*

## Śaṅkara's Commentary

The manifestation can be predicated of positive[1] entities comprehended as the different forms of *Viśva*, *Taijasa* and *Prājña*—whose existence, of the nature of illusory names and forms caused by an innate *Avidyā* (ignorance), cannot be denied. This is thus explained later on: 'Neither in reality nor in illusion can the son of a barren woman be said to be born.' For, if things could come out of non-entity, Brahman whose existence is inferred from experience[2] will itself be rendered a non-entity because of the absence of means of comprehension. That the snake (in the rope) appearing as such on account of an illusory cause (*Māyā*) which itself is the effect of ignorance (*Avidyā*), pre-exists in the form of the rope is a matter of common experience. For by no one is the illusion of the rope-snake or the mirage, etc., ever perceived without a substratum. As before the illusory[3] appearance of the snake, its existence was certainly there in the rope, so also all[4] positive entities before their manifestation certainly exist in the form of a cause, *i.e.*, *Prāṇa*. The *Śruti* also declares this in such passages as: 'All this (the phenomenal universe) was verily Brahman at the beginning' and 'All this existed, at the beginning as *Ātman*'. *Prāṇa* manifests all. As the rays proceed from the sun, so also all different centres of consciousness (*i.e.*, the *Jīvas*) which are like the (many) reflections of the same sun in the water and which are manifested differently as *Viṣva, Taijasa* and *Prājña*, comprising various physical forms of gods, animals, etc., proceed from the *Puruṣa*.[5] The *Puruṣa* manifests all these entities called as living beings, which are different from inanimate objects, but of the same nature as itself (*Puruṣa*), like fire and its sparks and like the sun with its reflections in water. *Prāṇa*, the causal self, manifests all other entities like the spider producing the web. There are such scriptural passages in its support as, 'The sparks from the fire', etc.

[1] *Positive etc.*—*Kārikās* from 6 to 9 give different views of the manifestation. The *Kārikā* under discussion points out that the manifested universe is not non-existent like the son of a barren woman. It has an empirical existence. The object of this is only

to show that no causal relation can be predicated of Brahman as *Prājña* unless we admit the positive existence of the world. The detailed discussion about causality will be found in the body of the *Kārikās*.

[2] *Will itself*—Those who depend upon causality to prove the existence of Brahman cannot but believe in the existence of the manifested objects through which alone they infer Brahman to be the cause of all.

[3] *Illusory*—*Vedānta* makes a distinction between *Avidyā* and *Māyā*, from the causal standpoint. *Māyā* is associated with *Īśvara* and it presents the variety in the universe. Comp. *Vedānta-Sūtras*, 1. 4. 3. and 2. 1. 14.

[4] *All*—It means here only the inanimate objects, as the manifestation of the animate is ascribed to the *Puruṣa*.

[5] *Puruṣa*—It is indicated by the text as well as the commentary that there are two manifestors, namely, the *Puruṣa* and the *Prāṇa*. The *Puruṣa* manifests the *Jīvas* and *Prāṇa* the inanimate objects. From the empirical standpoint we see two kinds of manifestations, *viz.*, the sentient and the insentient. Therefore we naturally ascribe these to two manifestors, *viz.*, *Puruṣa* and *Prāṇa*. (The general principal of causality is that the like produces the like.) But, in reality, *Prāṇa* is identical with *Puruṣa*. Brahman is looked upon as the manifestor of the universe; when he manifests the insentient objects he is said to be *Prāṇa*, and when he manifests the sentient beings he is called *Puruṣa*.

विभूतिं प्रसवं त्वन्ये मन्यन्ते सृष्टिचिन्तकाः ।
स्वप्नमायासरूपेति सृष्टिरन्यैर्विकल्पिता ॥ ७ ॥

7. *Those who think of (the process of) creation believe it to be the manifestation of the superhuman power of God; while others look upon it as of the same nature as dream and illusion.*

## Śaṅkara's Commentary

Creation is the manifestation of the superhuman power of God[1]; thus think those who reflect on (the process of) creation. But[2] those who intently think[3] of the Ultimate Reality find no interest in (the theory of) creation. It (that no interest should be attached to the act of creation) is also supported by such *Śruti* passages as, '*Indra* (the great god) assumed diverse forms through *Māyā*'. The juggler throws the thread up in the sky, climbs by it with his arms, disappears from the sight (of the spectators), engages himself in a fight (in the sky) in which his limbs, having been severed, fall to the ground and he rises up again. The on-looker, though witnessing the performance, does not evince any interest in the thought in regard to the reality of the jugglery performed by the juggler. Similarly there is a real juggler who is other than the rope and the one that climbs up the rope. The manifestation of deep sleep, dream and waking is analogous to the throwing up of the rope by the juggler (in the above illustration) and the (empirical selves known as) *Prājña*, *Viśva* and *Taijasa*, related to the three states, are similar to the juggler, who appears to have climbed up the rope. As he, the juggler, remains on the ground unseen (by the on-lookers) having veiled himself, as it were, by his illusion, so also is the truth about the Highest Reality known as *Turīya*.[4] Therefore those noble souls seeking *Mokṣa* evince interest in the contemplation of this (the *Turīya*) but not in the creation which is futile.[5] The word, '*Svapna-māyāsarūpā*'—meaning, alike dream and illusion—is intended to show that all[6] these (false) notions (regarding manifestation) belong only to those who imagine the process of creation or manifestation.

[1] *God*—He is naturally the Personal God. This is the theistic theory of creation.

[2] *But*—The seekers after God as creator may be either those who hold that creation is real or those who hold that creation is illusory. In the latter case *Śaṅkara* compares the seekers after truth to those who are interested in the magician and not in the magical feats.

[3] *Intently think*—*i. e.*, still pursuing the law of causation. Those who uphold the *Māyā* theory of the world see the illusion and infer *Turīya* as the Transcendental Cause.

[4] *Turīya*—The text contemplates two alternative theories of creation (सृष्टि) namely, (i) creation is real in so far as it is mere manifestation of God's real power. (ii) creation is manifested as an illusion by God (स्वप्नमाया). Both the alternative theories lay emphasis on the act of creation and this is pointed out by *Śaṅkara* in his commentary. *Śaṅkara* indicates in his commentary that those who seek the Highest Reality (परमार्थ) are not interested in any theory of creation.

[5] *Futile*—The truth about the Highest Reality can be realised only by the highest Knowledge and not by any thought bestowed upon creation.

[6] *All these etc.*—Because *Māyā* is also admitted to be a fact by the *Māyāvādins*, their theory does not also convey the highest truth.

इच्छामात्रं प्रभोः सृष्टिरिति सृष्टौ विनिश्चिताः ।
कालात्प्रसूतिं भूतानां मन्यन्ते कालचिन्तकाः ॥ ८ ॥

8. *Those who affirm (the existence of the created objects) attribute this manifestation to the mere will of God, while those who look upon time as real declare time to be the manifestor of all beings.*

ŚAṄKARA'S COMMENTARY

The manifestation (creation) proceeds from the mere will of God because His will in reality cannot[1] but achieve its purpose. Such objects as pot etc., are but[2] the (manifestation of the) will (of the potter). They can never be anything external or unrelated to such will. Some say manifestation proceeds from time.

[1] *Cannot etc.*—It is because they look upon the world as real, therefore they affirm that God whose will manifests the world cannot but be real.

[2] *But*—The potter, first of all, conceives in his mind the name and form of the object and then creates it.

भोगार्थं सृष्टिरित्यन्ये क्रीडार्थमिति चापरे ।
देवस्यैष स्वभावोऽयमाप्तकामस्य का स्पृहा ॥ ९ ॥

9. *Others think that the manifestation is for the purpose of enjoyment (of God) while still others attribute it to mere diversion (on the part of God). But it is the very nature of the Effulgent Being* (Ātman) *(for), what other desire is possible for Him whose desire is always in the state of fulfilment?*

## Śaṅkara's Commentary

Others think that the purpose of manifestation is only the enjoyment (by God of the objects so created), that creation is merely a diversion of God. These two theories are refuted (by the author) by the single assertion that it is the very[1] nature of the Effulgent (Brahman). Thus taking this standpoint (the nature of the Effulgent Being) all[2] the theories (of creation) herein (stated) are refuted[3] for the reason indicated by: 'What could be the desire for manifestation on the part of Brahman whose desires are ever in a state of fulfilment?' For the rope etc., to appear as snake, no[4] other reason can be assigned than *Avidyā*.

[1] *Very nature*—According to Gauḍapāda, what others see as the created universe, is nothing but the very nature or essence of Brahman. Brahman alone exists. What others designate as the universe of names and forms—subject to birth, change, death, etc.—is nothing but the non-dual Brahman. That one sees the world of duality instead of the non-dual Brahman and seeks its cause is due to *Avidyā* or ignorance.

[2] *All the etc.*—The following theories of creation have been stated in the preceding *Ślokas* of the *Kārikā*

(i) Creation is manifestation of the divine power of God (*K.* 6).
(ii) Creation is manifestation of the nature of dream or illusion (*K.* 6).
(iii) Creation is manifestation of the Divine Will which cannot but be fulfilled (*K.* 8).
(iv) Creation is manifestation which proceeds from Time. *Iśvara* is indifferent about it (*K.* 8).

The above four theories of creation may be classed as cosmological. The following two theories which may be designated as teleological are given in *Kārikā* 9:

(v) Creation is for the purpose of the enjoyment of God.

(vi) Creation is an act of God's sport.

Now all these theories are refuted by the simple statement that Brahman, whose desires are always in a state of fulfilment, cannot create the world for any purpose whatsoever. No causal theory can explain the relation of the appearance of the world to Brahman. The assumption of will, desire, enjoyment, diversion, etc., as the causes of creation is due to *Avidyā* or ignorance of the human mind regarding the real nature (आत्मकामत्व, आप्तकामत्व, अकामत्व) of Brahman. It only reveals the ignorance of the human mind in regard to the origin of the world which is one of the objects displaying God's superhuman powers. Those who look upon *the act of creation as real* and then explain it as of the same nature as dream and illusion, forget that dream and illusion are, after all, unreal and hence they cannot explain the supposed reality of the act of creation. Therefore, manifestation is not an act of creation. No *will* can be the *cause* of creation because a will implies an effort at gratifying some unsatiated desire. Brahman is Bliss (परमानन्द) which means the absence of all wants. Therefore the Divine Will cannot be the cause of the universe. The human mind, subject to *Māyā*, ascribes will, diversion, etc., as the cause of creation. This ascription is itself *Māyā*. Therefore it stands to reason that if anybody sees creation, it is only due to *Māyā*. Therefore all theories regarding creation are in fact मायामयी, that is, due to the ignorance of the mind that sees it. Viewed from the relative standpoint this *Māyā* inheres either in Brahman or in the perceiver. Assigning a substratum for *Māyā* depends upon one's standpoint. Viewed from the *Avidyā* standpoint *Māyā* has its locus in Brahman.

[3] *Refuted etc.*—The two theories implied by the first line of the *Kārikā* are refuted simply because 'enjoyment' and 'diversion' cannot be proved to be the object of creation. Creation or manifestation implies some adventitious or external factor, which idea is refuted by the statement of the Scripture that 'it is the very nature of the Effulgent Brahman'.

[4] *No other reason*—Comp. the Scriptural passage: आत्मनः आकाशः संभूतः—which means that it is the *Ātman* that appears as *Ākāśa*. The appearance is due to *Māyā* and no external cause.

### Śaṅkara's Introduction to Upaniṣad

The fourth[1] quarter which now comes in order (for explanation) has to be described. This is done in the words of the text: 'Not conscious of the internal object'. It (*Turīya*) does not admit of description or indication by means of words, for all uses (affirmative or negative) of language fail to express it. Therefore *Turīya* is sought[2] to be indicated by the negation of all attributes (characteristics).

(Objection)—Then it becomes mere void or *Śūnya*.

(Reply)—No,[3] because it is impossible for imagination to exist without[4] a substratum. The illusion of silver, a snake, a man or mirage etc., cannot be conceived as existing without the (corresponding) substratum of the mother-of-pearl, rope, stump or desert, etc.

(Objection)—If that be the case, *Turīya* ought to be indicatable by words and not by the negation of all attributes. For, it is the substratum of all imaginations such as *Prāṇa* etc., in the same way as jars etc., which being the substratum of water etc., are indicated as such by words.

(Reply)—The idea of *Prāṇa* etc., (supposed to exist in *Turīya*) is unreal like the false idea of silver etc., in the mother-of-pearl etc. A relation[5] between the real and the unreal cannot be expressed by words because such relation is, itself, non-existent. *Turīya* cannot be the object of any other instrument of knowledge (such as direct perception) like the cow etc., because of its unique nature, owing to the absence of *Upādhis*. *Ātman* cannot have anything like a generic property, like the cow etc., because it is devoid of all *Upādhis* or attributes; it has neither generic nor specific characteristics because it is one, without a second. It cannot be known by any activity (proceeding from it) as in the case of a cook; because it is devoid of all actions. It cannot be described by attributes such as blue etc., because it is without any attribute. Therefore it follows that *Turīya* cannot be indicated by any name.

(Objection)—Then it (*Turīya*) would be like the 'horns of a hare' and hence one's pursuit of it must be futile.[6]

(Reply)—No, the knowledge of *Turīya* as identical with Self (*Ātman*) destroys the hankering after objects[7] which are non-self just as the knowledge of mother-of-pearl (mistaken for silver) removes the desire for (illusory) silver. For, once the identity of *Turīya* and Self is realised there is no possibility of one's being deluded[8] by ignorance, desire and the like misapprehensions (which are the effects of ignorance) and there is no reason for *Turīya* not being known as identical with the Self. For all the Upaniṣads point to this end only as is evident from the following: 'That thou art', 'This *Ātman* is Brahman', 'That is real and that is *Ātman*', 'The Brahman which is directly and immediately cognized', 'He is both without and within, as well as causeless', 'All this is verily *Ātman*', etc. This very *Ātman* has been described as constituting the Highest Reality and its opposite[9] (the unreal) and as having four quarters. Its unreal (illusory) aspect has been described as due to ignorance, like the illusion of snake in the rope, having for its characteristics the three quarters and being of the same nature as the seed[10] and the sprout. Now is described (in the following *Śruti*) *Turīya* which is not of the nature of cause but which is of the nature of the Highest Reality corresponding to the rope—by negating[11] the three states, enumerated above, which correspond to the snake[12] etc.

1 *Fourth quarter*—The 'fourth' is not the *fourth state* or *condition* in which *Ātman* is to be viewed. *Turīya* which is indicated here as the 'fourth' comes in only for consideration after the three states have been considered. *Ātman* itself does not admit of any condition or state. Waking, dream and deep sleep are its three states or quarters and *Turīya*, as will be seen later on, is present in all these three. *Turīya* is designated here as the *fourth* because in the preceding texts,

three quarters of *Ātman* have been explained. It has occupied the 'fourth' place in respect of explanations.

[2] *Sought to be etc.*—It is because it cannot be directly pointed out like other objects of perception.

[3] *No etc.*—The contention of the opponent is this: You say that *Turīya* is not void (शून्य) as the illusion (विकल्प) of *Prāṇa* etc., cannot subsist without a substratum which is *Turīya*. In that case *Turīya* is not non-indicatable as it can be indicated as the substratum of *Prāṇa* etc. Therefore it must be such as can be indicated. But you say that it is arrived at by mere negation and therefore non-indicatable by words. If *Turīya* is indicatable as a substratum, then it becomes indicatable by that which is superimposed upon it as is the case with a pot which is indicatable by the water in it. In that case you contradict yourself as you have already said that Brahman is unindicatable by any word.

To this our reply is:

We would like to ask you if (i) your idea of indicatability of Brahman as the substratum is that of illusory superimposition, or (ii) is that of real superimposition.

It cannot be thereby illusory superimposition because the superimposition, in that case, would not appear as existing as it does. From the standpoint of the empirical reality of the appearance which is experienced by the ignorant persons, we say that *Turīya* is indicatable by the illusory ideas that are superimposed upon it. And if you admit the ideas (विकल्प) of *Prāṇa* etc., as unreal, then there is no disagreement between us.

Again this indicatability of *Turīya* as a substratum cannot be (due to) real superimposition or the superimposition of reality. For, as the idea of silver that is superimposed upon the mother-of-pearl is unreal, so also the idea of *Prāṇa* etc., that is superimposed upon *Turīya* is equally unreal. There cannot be any relationship between a real substratum and the unreal form superimposed on it.

Therefore the conclusion is that if one takes his stand upon the causal or relative plane, then *Turīya* may be indicated as a substratum of the illusory ideas of *Prāṇa* etc. But from the standpoint of Truth, *Turīya* cannot be indicated by any word which implies relationship. And *Śruti* also denies all relationship in Brahman.

[4] *Without etc.*—No illusion can be dissociated from the idea of

existence. The first impression that one gets of an illusion is that it exists and later on its existence is traced to a positive substratum.

5 *Relation*—Indicatability by words is possible in the following instances only: (i) Possessive case, (ii) conventional meaning of a word, (iii) generic or specific property, (iv) activity, (v) attribute and substance. But none of these applies to *Turīya* because it is one without a second and also it is without any attribute. Hence *Turīya* cannot be indicated by any word.

6 *Futile*—It is because no benefit can accrue from the knowledge of something which is as unreal as the 'mare's nest'.

7 *Objects*—Such as the illusory worldly objects to which the ignorant are attached.

8 *Deluded*—Delusion is the cause of all human misery.

9 *Its opposite*—*i.e.,* the illusory objects. As a matter of fact, only Brahman exists and He is the One and All. Nothing called unreal ever exists. What appears to the ignorant as unreal or illusory is also Brahman from the highest Advaitic standpoint. Therefore Brahman comprises everything.

10 *Seed and sprout*—The three states are characterised by the relation of cause and effect as the seed and the sprout are.

11 *Negating etc.*—The student, at first, by the process of negation separates Brahman from the superimposition and then realises that what has been negated as superimposition is, in fact, the very nature of Brahman. This is the highest Advaitic realisation.

12 *Snake etc.*—The rope is often mistaken for s snake or a garland or a stick or a streak of water or a fissure in the ground.

## VII

नान्तःप्रज्ञं न बहिष्प्रज्ञं नोभयतःप्रज्ञं न प्रज्ञानघनं न
प्रज्ञं नाप्रज्ञम् । अदृष्टमव्यवहार्यमग्राह्यमलक्षणमचिन्त्यम-
व्यपदेश्यमेकात्मप्रत्ययसारं प्रपञ्चोपशमं शान्तं शिवमद्वैतं
चतुर्थं मन्यन्ते स आत्मा स विज्ञेयः ॥ ७ ॥

*Turīya* is not that which is conscious of the internal (subjective) world, nor that which is conscious of the external (objective) world, nor that which is conscious of both, nor that which is a mass all sentiency, nor that which is simple consciousness, nor that which is insentient. (It is) unseen (by any sense organ), not related to anything, incomprehensible (by the mind), uninferable, unthinkable, indescribable, essentially of the nature of Consciousness constituting the Self alone, negation of all phenomena, the Peaceful, all Bliss and the Non-dual. This is what is known as the fourth (*Turīya*). This is the *Ātman* and it has to be realised.

( 'Consciousness ' as the nearest English word is used.)

## Śaṅkara's Commentary

(Objection)—The object was to describe *Ātman* as having four quarters. By the very descriptions of the three quarters, the fourth is established as being other than the three characterised by the ' conscious of the subjective ' etc. Therefore the negation (of attributes relating to the three quarters) for the purpose of indicating *Turīya* implied in the statement, ' *Turīya* is that which is not conscious of the subjective ' etc., is futile.

(Reply)—No. As the nature of the rope is[1] realised by the negation of the (illusory) appearances of the snake etc., so also it is intended to establish the very Self, which subsists in the three states, as *Turīya*. This[2] is done in the same way as (the great Vedic statement) ' Thou art that '. If *Turīya* were, in fact, anything different[3] from *Ātman* subsisting in the three states, then, the teachings of the Scriptures would have no meaning on[4] account of the absence of any instrument of knowledge (regarding *Turīya*). Or the other (inevitable) alternative would be to declare absolute nihilism (शून्य) to be the ultimate Truth. Like the (same) rope mistaken as snake, garland, etc., when the same *Ātman* is mistaken as *Antaḥprajña* (conscious of the subjective) etc., in the three states associated with different characteristics, the knowledge, resulting from the negation of such attributes as the conscious of the subjective etc., is the means of establishing the absolute absence of the unreal phenomena of the world (imagined) in *Ātman*. As a matter of fact, the two[5] results, namely, the negation of (superimposed) attributes and the disappearance of the unreal phenomena happen at the same time. Therefore no additional[6] instrument of knowledge or no other[7] effort is to be made or sought after for the realisation of *Turīya*. With the cessation of the idea of the snake etc., in the rope, the real nature of the rope becomes revealed and this happens simultaneously with the knowledge of the distinction between the rope and the snake. But those who say that the knowledge, in addition to the removal of the darkness (that envelopes the jar), enables[8] one to know the jar, may as well affirm[9] that the act of cutting (a tree), in addition to its undoing the relation of the members of the body intended to be cut, also functions (in other ways) in other parts of the body. As the act of cutting intended to divide the tree into two is said to be complete with the severance of the parts (of the tree) so also the knowledge employed to perceive the jar covered by the darkness (that envelopes it) attains its purpose when it results in removing the darkness, though that is not the object intended to be produced. In such case the knowledge of the jar, which is invariably[10] connected with the removal of the darkness, is not the result accomplished by the instrument of knowledge. Likewise, the knowledge, which is (here) the same as that which results from the negation of predicates, directed towards the discrimination of such attributes as 'the conscious of the subjective' etc., superimposed upon *Ātman*, cannot[11] function with regard to *Turīya* in addition to its act of negating of such attributes as 'the conscious of the subjective' which is not the object intended to be produced. For, with the negation of the attributes such as, 'conscious of the subjective' etc., is[12] accomplished simultaneously the cessation of the distinction between the knower, the known and the knowledge. Thus it will be said later on, 'Duality cannot exist when Gnosis, the highest Truth (non-duality), is realised'. The knowledge of duality cannot exist even for a moment immediately after the moment of the cessation of duality. If it should remain, there would[13] follow what is known as *regressus ad infinitum;* and consequently duality will never cease. Therefore it is established that the cessation of such unreal attributes as 'conscious of the subjective' etc., superimposed upon *Ātman* is[14] simultaneous with the manifestation of the Knowledge which, in itself, is the means (*pramāṇa*) for the negation of duality.

By the statement that it (*Turīya*) is 'not conscious of the subjective' is indicated that it is not '*Taijasa*'. Similarly by the statement that it is 'not conscious of the objective', it is denied that it (*Turīya*) is *Viśva.* By saying that it is 'not conscious of either', it is denied that *Turīya* is any intermediate state between[15] the waking and the dream states. By the statement that *Turīya* is 'not a mass all sentiency', it is denied that it is the condition of deep sleep—which is held to be a causal[16] condition on account of one's inability to distinguish the truth from error (in deep sleep). By saying that it is 'not simple consciousness', it is implied that *Turīya* cannot[17] simultaneously cognize the entire world of consciousness (by a single act of consciousness). And lastly by the statement that it is 'not unconsciousness' it is implied that *Turīya* is not insentient or of the nature of matter.

(Objection)—How,[18] again, do such attributes as 'conscious of the subjective' etc., which are (directly) perceived to subsist in *Ātman* become non-existent only by an act of negation as the snake etc. (perceived) in the rope etc., become non-existent (by means of an act of negation)?

(Reply)—Though[19] the states (waking and dream) are really of the essence of consciousness itself, and as such are non-different from each other (from the point of view of the substratum), yet one state is seen to change[20] into another as do the appearances of the snake, water-line, etc., having for their substratum the rope etc. But the consciousness itself is real because it never changes.

(Objection)—Consciousness is seen to change (disappear) in deep sleep.

(Reply)—No, the state of deep sleep is a matter of experience.[21] For the *Śruti* says, 'Knowledge of the Knower is never absent'.

Hence it (*Turīya*) is 'unseen';[22] and because it is unseen therefore it is 'incomprehensible'.[23] *Turīya* cannot be apprehended by the organs of action. *Alakṣaṇam* means 'uninferable',[24] because there is no *Liṅga* (common characteristic) for its inference. Therefore *Turīya* is 'unthinkable'[25] and hence 'indescribable'[26] (by words). It is 'essentially[27] of the nature of consciousness consisting of Self'. *Turīya* should be known by spotting that consciousness that never changes in the three states, *viz.*, waking etc., and whose nature is that of a Unitary Self. Or,[28] the phrase may signify that the knowledge of the one *Ātman* alone is the means for realising *Turīya*, and therefore *Turīya* is the essence of this consciousness or Self or *Ātman*. The *Śruti* also says, 'It should be meditated upon as *Ātman*'. Several attributes, such as the 'conscious of the subjective' etc., associated with the manifestation (such as, *Viśva* etc.) in each of the states have already been negated. Now by describing *Turīya* as 'the cessation of illusion', the attributes which characterise the three states, *viz.*, waking etc., are negated. Hence it is 'ever[29] Peaceful', *i.e.*, without any manifestation of change—and 'all[30] bliss'. As it is non-dual, *i.e.*, devoid of illusory ideas of distinction, therefore it is called '*Turīya*', the 'Fourth',[31] because it is totally distinct (in character) from the three quarters which are mere appearances. 'This, indeed, is the *Ātman* and it should be known', is intended to show that the meaning of the Vedic statement, 'That thou art', points to the relationless *Ātman* (*Turīya*) which is like the rope (in the illustration) different from the snake, line on the ground, stick, etc., which are mere appearances. That *Ātman* which has been described in such *Śruti* passages as, 'unseen, but the seer', 'the consciousness of the seer is never absent', etc., should be known. (The incomprehensible) *Turīya* 'should be known', and this[32] is said so only from the standpoint of the previously unknown condition, for *duality* cannot exist when the Highest Truth is known.

[1] *Is realised*—The rope did not cease to be the rope when it appeared as the snake. The rope, again, is seen in its true nature when the snake idea is removed. Similarly, *Ātman* appears as *Viśva, Taijasa* and *Prājña* in the three states. And the same *Ātman* is realised as *Turīya* when the *upādhis*, namely the states, are negated. *Turīya* is not a separate entity *nor is it a fourth state* succeeding the three other states. The real nature of *Turīya* cannot be realised without the negation of the *upādhis* of the three states.

[2] *This is etc.*—The real significance of 'That thou art', is *Turīya* and it is realised when the contrary qualities, known as the *upādhis*, indicated by the words 'That' and 'thou' are eliminated. Similarly, the Scripture of the negative process, removes the *upādhis* of the *Ātman* when associated with the three states and this reveals its eternal identity with *Turīya*.

[3] *Different*—From the relative or causal standpoint, the *Ātman* associated with any of the three states, is, no doubt, different from *Turīya*. But from the standpoint of *Turīya* there is no difference whatsoever between it and the *Ātman* associated with the three states. As a matter of fact, it is *Turīya* as the witness (साक्षि) that is revealed out by the three states.

[4] *On account of*—Ignorant person, for whom Scripture is prescribed for the attainment of Knowledge, moves in the relative plane of the

three states. To him the Scripture suggests the examination of the three states in order to arrive at the Knowledge of *Turīya*. If *Turīya* were something totally separate from and essentially unconnected with the three states and if the three states were not the means of realising *Turīya*, then no other instrument of Knowledge would be left for the realisation of *Turīya*. It cannot be contended that one can get the Knowledge of *Turīya* from the Scripture. Because the Scripture also teaches about *Turīya* by the method of repudiation (अपवाद) of the superimposed attributes (अध्यारोप) *i.e.*, by negating the *upādhis* which were superimposed upon *Turīya*. If *Turīya* were something totally different from the three states, then no scriptural teaching would be effective in establishing it. If *Turīya* cannot be established through the examination of the *Ātman* qualified by the three states, by following the scriptural method of negation, then one is faced with the only alternative that the Ultimate Reality is total non-existence (शून्य), because no other reality remains after the negation of the *upādhis* of the three states if the existence of *Turīya* be denied.

5 *Two results*—The instrument of Knowledge (प्रमाण) by means of which we become aware of the result of the negation of the *upādhis*, namely, the three states, reveals the relationless *Turīya*. It is like the seeing of the real rope (which is never absent) with the cessation of the illusory idea of the snake. It must be carefully noted that the realisation of *Turīya* is not the result of the *Pramāṇa* by means of which we become aware of the negation of the attributes of *Ātman*, *viz.*, the three states. The two results are simultaneous—and not successive in time as the language seems to imply. It is because no new entity known as *Turīya* is discovered (or comes into existence) after the negation of *upādhis*. *Turīya* is always present. Therefore there is no possibility of taking *Turīya* as the result of the negation of the *upādhis viz.*, the three states. *Turīya* being characterised by non-duality there is no subject-object relationship in *Turīya* in which case alone an instrument of Knowledge would have a meaning.

6 *Additional instrument etc.*—No instrument of Knowledge can establish *Turīya* on account of its non-relation and non-dual nature. Even the function of the *Śruti* which indicates *Turīya* is only to negate what is unreal, relative and non-Brahman.

7 *Other effort*—Even contemplation etc., which are the essential features of *Yoga* cannot establish *Turīya*, because it cannot be *proved* that *Yogic* contemplation can yield such Knowledge. Therefore the

realisation of *Turīya* cannot be characterised as the result of any particular instrument of Knowledge or of any *Yogic* practice.

[8] *Enables etc.*—This means that the instrument of Knowledge, besides removing the darkness enveloping the Jar, also yields another positive result that is the manifestation of the Jar.

[9] *Affirm*—This means that the act of cutting besides severing the parts to which it is directed also functions in other ways. But this is absurd because we have no knowledge of any other effect on the tree produced by the act of cutting.

[10] *Invariably etc.*—It is because the Jar always exists even when it is enveloped in darkness.

[11] *Cannot function.*—It is because *Turīya* is Knowledge itself. Hence no instrument of Knowledge can act upon it. *Turīya* does not stand in need of any demonstration or proof because it is ever-existent. The instrument of Knowledge only removed the super-impositions falsely attributed to *Ātman*. The instrument of Knowledge (perception) continues to act upon an object till the object is revealed (as Brahman).

[12] *Is accomplished*—The instrument of Knowledge, invariably connected with its employer and an object, can act only in the plane of duality. With the negation of duality, the instrument of Knowledge itself becomes ineffective, for it cannot function the next moment. The idea of time is also annihilated with the destruction of duality. When the non-dual *Turīya* is realised, all ideas of the instrument of Knowledge, the employer and the object with their distinction are destroyed. Only Brahman is.

[13] *Would follow etc.*—It is because a second instrument of Knowledge would be required to negate the residual Knowledge or instrument and a third would be necessary to negate the second and so on *ad infinitum*. An argument ending in a *regressus* is not allowed in logical discussion.

[14] *Is simultaneous*—Here *Pramāṇa* is the *Jñānam* that results from the negation of attributes. And through this instrument of Knowledge alone we know that all relative ideas have been negated. Simultaneously with this assurance, *Turīya* is realised.

[15] *Intermediate etc.*—It is the state when one experiences something like a ' day dream ' that is, he half sees the one and half sees the other.

[16] *Causal condition*—By seeing the manifestation in the waking

state one naturally infers that the preceding state, that is *Suṣupti*, is the cause of both the waking and dream experiences. In *Suṣupti*, specific states of consciousness, which manifest themselves as different objects in dream and waking states, remain in a state of indistinguishability. In deep sleep, no distinctions are perceived.

[17] *Cannot etc.*—By this are denied such attributes as omniscience etc., associated with *Iśvara*.

[18] *How etc.*—The contention of the objector is this: That the idea of the snake etc., in the rope is an illusion is a matter of common experience. When the error is pointed out, the idea of the snake disappears. Therefore the idea of such a snake can be said to be non-existent. But this is not the case with the attributes of *Ātman* which are sought to be negated. Such attributes are directly perceived by everyone and do not vanish even though they are negated. Therefore the phenomena of the three states cannot be said to be non-existent on the analogy of the rope and the snake.

[19] *Though etc.*—The reply is that the attributes, *viz*, the three states, can be demonstrated to be non-existent (unreal) by the act of negation. The illustration of the snake and the rope is quite apposite. The ideas of the snake, the water-line, etc., for which the rope is mistaken are first pointed out to be illusion because they are subject to change. Therefore, such objects as are indicated by the ideas are non-existent. Similarly it is a matter of common experience that the states of *Jāgrat*, *Svapna* and *Suṣupti* are subject to change. Therefore they are negatable. In any one state the two other states are negated. Besides, in the state of waking one can realise the three states as following one another. Therefore the three states partake of the nature of unreality as distinguished from Reality which is never subject to any change. Now, what is Reality? From the examination of the three states it becomes clear that though the states are changing and negatable the consciousness which is present therein is constant and invariable. Change of one state to another cannot affect the unchanging nature of Consciousness itself. Therefore *pure* Consciousness is real. Hence it follows that by constantly examining the changeable and negatable character of the attributes, *viz.*, the three states, one can realise their non-existent or unreal nature. The fallacy of the contention of the objector is due to the partial examination of Reality in only one state in which case the changeable nature of the attributes cannot be realized. But the examination of the three states

at once demonstrates their changeable and negatable nature and points out that consciousness itself which is the substratum of the changing attributes is the only Reality.

[20] *Change*—That is, no one is aware of consciousness in deep sleep.

[21] *Experience*—Consciousness cannot be dissociated from the state of deep sleep. *Suṣupti* is experienced from the *Jāgrat* state, that is to say, *Turīya* in *Jāgrat* state knows that it experienced deep sleep. Otherwise *Suṣupti* would have never been known to exist at all.

[22] *Unseen*—It cannot be recognised by any organ of perception. It is because *Turīya* is the negation of all the attributes. It cannot be made the object of any sense-organ.

[23] *Incomprehensible*—It cannot come within the cognizance of the senses; therefore *Turīya* cannot serve any purpose (अर्थक्रिया).

[24] *Uninferable*—'Existence, Knowledge and Infinity', by which Brahman is described in the *Taittirīya Upaniṣad* are not to be considered to be real and positive attributes for the purpose of drawing an inference about Brahman. They only serve a negative purpose indicating that Brahman is other than non-truth, non-consciousness and non-infinity. Besides, inference requires a common feature which always presupposes more objects than one. But Brahman is one and without a second. Therefore no inference is possible regarding Brahman.

[25] *Unthinkable*—It is because the predicates by which we can think about an entity have been totally eliminated from *Turīya*.

[26] *Indescribable*—*Turīya* cannot be described by words because it is unthinkable. That which one thinks in mind, is expressed by words.

[27] *Essentially etc.*—The elimination of all the attributes may make *Turīya* appear as a void to the unwary student. Therefore it is described as a positive existence which can be realised by spotting it as the changeless and the constant factor in the three states. The states, no doubt, do change but there is a unity of the subject implied in the conscious experience of 'I am that perceiver' common to all the three states.

[28] *Or*—The alternative meaning is that through consciousness of Self alone, which forms the basis of the three states, we can demonstrate *Turīya* which transcends all the states, or in other words, because there is Pure Consciousness, changeless and constant, known as *Turīya*, therefore we are aware of self-consciousness in the three states.

[29] *Ever-peaceful*—Free from attachment of love and hate, *i.e.*, changeless and immutable.

[30] *All-Bliss*—Pure and embodiment of the highest Bliss.

[31] *Fourth*—This does not signify any numerical relationship with the three other states narrated previously. *Turīya* is called the '*fourth*' because it occupies the 'fourth' place in order of explanation of Brahman of which the three states have previously been dealt with.

[32] *This is etc.*—The statement that 'It should be known', cannot be properly made with regard to the non-dual *Ātman* which is incomprehensible, etc. This objection is, no doubt, valid from the standpoint of *Turīya* where there cannot be a separate knower of *Ātman*. But *Turīya* is certainly unknown from the standpoint of any of the three states, and from that dual standpoint it is perfectly legitimate to speak of Brahman as something 'to be known'.

Here appear the following *ślokās:*

निवृत्तेः सर्वदुःखानामीशानः प्रभुरव्ययः ।
अद्वैतः सर्वभावानां देवस्तुर्यो विभुः स्मृतः ॥ १० ॥

10. *In it, indicated as the changeless and the Supreme Lord, there is a cessation of all miseries. It is the one without a second among all entities. It is known as the* Turīya (*Fourth*), *effulgent and all-pervading.*

### Śaṅkara's Commentary

In (the Knowledge of) *Īśāna*, meaning the *Turīya Ātman* there is a cessation[1] of all miseries characterised by the three states, *viz.*, *Prājña*,[2] *Taijasa* and *Viśva*. The word '*Īśāna*' is explained as '*Prabhu*', *i.e.*, the one who brings about the cessation of miseries. It is because misery is destroyed by one's own Knowledge[3] of it (*Turīya*). '*Avyaya*' means that which is not subject to any change, *i.e.*, which does not deviate from its own nature. How? It is so because *Turīya* is non-dual, all[4] other entities being illusory (unreal) like the idea of the snake etc., imagined in the rope. It is he who is recognised[5] as the *Deva* (on account of his effulgent nature), the *Turīya*, the fourth, the *Vibhu*,[6] that is the all-pervading one.

[1] *Cessation*—The three states are said to be in the *Ātman* because we, as *Turīya*, cognize them. Therefore all misery as well as its cause associated with the three states, are imagined by us to subsist in *Turīya*. It is because we do not realise this that we identify ourselves with the states and that we suffer from various kinds of miseries. But a complete cessation of miseries ensues if we realise *Ātman* as *Turīya* and thus witness the appearance and disappearance of the ideas, *viz*., the states without identifying ourselves with them.

[2] *Prājña*—The state of *Suṣupti*, devoid of the Knowledge of *Turīya* on the part of the sleeper, is characterised as unhappiness.

[3] *Knowledge*—Though *Turīya* is constant in all the states, yet we suffer from misery because we are not aware of the existence of the *Turīya*. It is only the Knowledge of *Turīya* that can destroy misery.

[4] *All other etc.*—Though *Viśva* etc., are perceived, they are really illusory like the ideas of the snake etc., in the rope. *Turīya* alone is real. Every part of *Viśva, Taijasa* and *Prājña* is nothing but *Turīya* as every part of the illusory snake is the rope. Therefore from the highest standpoint only *Turīya* is.

[5] *Recognised*—That is *Turīya*, as such, is known from the realisation of the wise.

[6] *Vibhu*—*Turīya* is called *Vibhu* because it pervades all the three states.

**कार्यकारणबद्धौ ताविष्येते विश्वतैजसौ ।**
**प्राज्ञः कारणबद्धस्तु द्वौ तौ तुर्ये न सिध्यतः ॥ ११ ॥**

11. Viśva *and* Taijasa *are conditioned by cause and effect. But* Prājña *is conditioned by cause alone. These two (cause and effect) do not exist in* Turīya.

### Śaṅkara's Commentary

The generic[1] and specific[2] characters of *Viśva* etc., are described with a view to determining the real nature of *Turīya*. '*Kārya*' or effect is that which is done, *i.e.*, which has the characteristic of result. '*Kāraṇa*' or the cause is that which acts, *i.e.*, it is the state in which the effect remains latent. Both *Viśva* and *Taijasa*, described above, are known as being conditioned by cause and effect,[3] characterised by both non-apprehension and mis-apprehension of Reality. But *Prājña* is conditioned by cause alone. Cause, characterised by the non-apprehension of Reality, is the condition of *Prājña*. Therefore these two, cause and effect, *i.e.*, non-apprehension and mis-apprehension of Reality, do not exist, *i.e.*, are not possible in *Turīya*.

[1] *Generic*—The Generic or the common characteristic of *Viśva* and *Taijasa* is that they are, both, characterised by the conditions of cause and effect.

[2] *Specific*—The special characteristic of *Prājña* is that it is characterised by the causal conditions alone.

[3] *Cause and effect*—Causal state (बीज) is that in which we do not know (अग्रहणं) the Truth. From it follows the result (फलं) which is the mis-apprehension of Truth (अन्यथाग्रहणं). It is because one does not know the rope (बीज) one mistakes it for the snake (फलं). *Prājña* or the state of non-apprehension as such is said to be the cause of the *Viśva* and *Taijasa* or the states of mis-apprehension. In dream and waking states there are both non-apprehension and mis-apprehension of Reality. But in deep sleep, there is only non-apprehension. As a matter of fact these two conditions mis-apprehension and non-apprehension, cannot be experienced separately. They have been differently classified only to facilitate understanding.

नाऽऽत्मानं न परांश्चैव न सत्यं नापि चानृतं ।
प्राज्ञः किंचन संवेत्ति तुर्यं तत्सर्वदृक्सदा ॥ १२ ॥

12. Prājña *does not know anything of the self or the non-self, nor truth nor untruth. But* Turīya *is ever existent and ever all-seeing.*

### ŚAṄKARA'S COMMENTARY

How is it that *Prājña* is conditioned by cause? And how is it, again, that the two conditions of non-apprehension and mis-apprehension of Reality do not exist in *Turīya?* It is because *Prājña* does not, like *Viśva* and *Taijasa*, perceive anything of the duality,[1] external to and other[2] than itself and born[3] of the cause known as *Avidyā*. Therefore it is conditioned by darkness characterised by non-apprehension of Reality which is the cause of mis-apprehension. As *Turīya* exists always, ever all-seeing,[4] on account of the absence of anything other than *Turīya*, it is never associated with the causal condition characterised by non-apprehension of Reality. Consequently mis-apprehension of Reality which is the result of non-apprehension is not found in *Turīya*. For, it is not possible to find in the sun, whose nature is to be ever-luminous, anything contrary to light, *viz.*, darkness, or any other light different from itself. The *Śruti* also says: 'The Knowledge of the seer is never absent.' Or the phrase may be explained thus: *Turīya* may be designated as ever all-seeing because it subsists in all, in dream and waking states and all the seers that cognize them (in those states) are *Turīyā* alone. This is also borne out by the following *Śruti* passage, 'There is no seer other than this'.

[1] *Duality*—This dual world is true from empirical standpoint. *Prājña* does not perceive it.

[2] *Other than etc.*—*Prājña* does not see the external world or the non-self. Therefore it does not see itself. Ego can be cognized only in relation to the non-ego.

[3] *Born etc.*—That is untruth. It is because *Prājña* does not see the unreal external world produced by *Avidyā*, therefore it is not aware of mis-apprehension.

[4] *Ever all-seeing*—It is because it exists in the seers and the things seen in both the states, it is ever all-seeing.

द्वैतस्याग्रहणं तुल्यमुभयोः प्राज्ञतुर्ययोः ।
बीजनिद्रायुतः प्राज्ञः सा च तुर्ये न विद्यते ॥ १३ ॥

13. *The non-cognition of duality is common to both* Prājña *and* Turīya. (*But*) Prājña *is associated with sleep in the form of cause and this* (*sleep*) *does not exist in* Turīya.

## Śaṅkara's Commentary

This *śloka* is meant to remove a doubt that has arisen incidentally. The doubt is this: How is it that it is *Prājña* alone and not *Turīya* that is bound by the condition of cause, since the non-cognition of duality is the common feature of both? This doubt is thus removed:[1] The meaning of the phrase *Bījanidrāyuta* is: *Nidrā* or sleep is characterised by the absence of the Knowledge of Reality. This is the cause which gives rise to the cognition of varieties. *Prājña* is associated with this sleep which is the cause. It is because *Turīya* is ever all-seeing, therefore the sleep characterised by the absence of the Knowledge of Reality does not exist in *Turīya*. Therefore the bondage in the form of causal condition does not exist in *Turīya*.

[1] *Removed*—The contention that *Turīya* and *Prājña* are both characterised by the condition of cause on account of the common feature of the non-perception of duality in both the cases, is due to a wrong inference based upon insufficient data. The *Prājña* is thought to be the causal state because it is the immediately preceding condition of the manifestations of the waking state etc. But this does not apply to *Turīya* because it is not the immediately preceding condition of any state. *Turīya* is not a state which is antecedent or subsequent to any other state. It is the substratum of all the states. *Turīya* is non-dual, changeless and pure consciousness itself. Hence it cannot be said to produce anything. Therefore causal condition cannot obtain in the case of *Turīya*.

स्वप्ननिद्रायुतावाद्यौ प्राज्ञस्त्वस्वप्ननिद्रया ।
न निद्रां नैव च स्वप्नं तुर्ये पश्यन्ति निश्चिताः ॥ १४ ॥

14. *The first two* (Viśva *and* Taijasa) *are associated with the conditions of dream and sleep;* Prājña *is the condition of sleep without dream. Those who have known the truth see neither sleep nor dream in* Turīya.

### Śaṅkara's Commentary

*Svapna* or dream is the misapprehension[1] of Reality like that of the snake in the rope. *Nidrā* or sleep has already been defined as darkness characterised by the absence of the Knowledge of Reality. *Viśva* and *Taijasa* are associated with these *viz.*, the conditions of dream and sleep. Therefore they have been described as conditioned by the characteristics of cause and effect. But *Prājña* is associated with sleep alone without dream; therefore it is described as conditioned by cause only. The knower of Brahman does not see them (dream and sleep) in *Turīya*,[2] as it would be inconsistent like seeing darkness in the Sun. Therefore[3] *Turīya* has been described as not associated with the conditions of cause and effect.

[1] *Misapprehension—i.e.*, when one, then, thinks of *Ātman* as endowed with body etc.

[2] *Turīya—Ajñāna* and its effects cannot exist in *Turīya* which is pure Knowledge.

[3] *Therefore*—It is because there is no *Nidrā* or sleep in *Turīya*.

अन्यथा गृह्णतः स्वप्नो निद्रा तत्वमजानतः ।
विपर्यासे तयोः क्षीणे तुरीयं पदमश्नुते ॥ १५ ॥

15. Svapna *or dream is the wrong cognition of Reality.* Nidrā *or sleep is the state in which one does not know what Reality is. When the erroneous knowledge in these two disappears,* Turīya *is realized.*

### Śaṅkara's Commentary

When is one established in *Turīya?* It is thus replied: During the states of dream and waking when one wrongly cognizes Reality like the perception of the snake in the place of the rope, he is said to be experiencing dream.[1] *Nidrā* or sleep,[2] characterised by the ignorance of Reality, is the common feature of the three states. *Viśva* and *Taijasa*, on account of their having the common feature of *Svapna* (dream) and *Nidrā* (sleep), form a single class. That *Nidrā* (sleep) which is characterised by the predominance of wrong apprehension (of Reality) constitutes the state of inversion which is *Svapna* (dream). But in the third state, *Nidrā* (sleep), alone, characterised by the non-apprehension of Reality is the only inversion. (This forms the second or the other class implied in the text which speaks only of dream and sleep as covering the three states.) Therefore when these two classes of the nature of effect and cause, characterised by the misapprehension and non-apprehension respectively (of Reality), disappear by the destruction of the inversion characterised by effect and cause, by the knowledge of the nature of the Highest Reality, then one realises *Turīya* which is the goal. Then one does not find in *Turīya* this condition, the characteristics of which are these two (effect and cause), and one thus becomes firm in the Highest Reality which is *Turīya*.

[1] *Dream—Svapna* includes dream and waking states, ordinarily so called, as in both the states there is a wrong apprehension of Reality. The inversion (absence of the Knowledge of Reality) which is the characteristic of sleep is found in dream and waking also. In other words, this is the common characteristic of all the three states.

[2] *Nidrā—Nidrā* includes the three states of waking, dream and sleep, ordinarily so-called, as all the three states are characterised by the absence of the Knowledge of Reality. The inversion, characteristic of *Nidrā*, is the non-apprehension of Reality and this is the only feature of *Prājña*. But *Svapna* (dream) including the waking state also is characterised by both non-apprehension and misapprehension of Reality.

अनादिमायया सुप्तो यदा जीवः प्रबुध्यते ।
अजमनिद्रमस्वप्नमद्वैतं बुध्यते तदा ॥ १६ ॥

16. *When the* Jīva *or the individual soul sleeping* (i.e., *not knowing the Reality*) *under the influence of the beginningless* Māyā, *is awakened, it, then, realises (in itself) the non-duality, beginningless and dreamless.*

## Śaṅkara's Commentary

One who is called the *Jīva*,[1] the individual soul, (whose characteristic is to be) subject[2] to the law of transmigration, sleeping[3] under the influence of *Māyā* which is active from time without[4] beginning and which has the double characteristics of non-apprehending (on account of its being of the nature of the cause) and misapprehending Reality, experiences such dreams as, 'This is my father, this is my son, this is my grandson, this is my property and these are my animals, I am their master, I am happy, I am miserable, I have suffered loss on account of this, I have gained on this account'. When the *Jīva* remains asleep experiencing these dreams in the two states[5] he is then thus awakened[6] by the gracious teacher who has himself realised the Reality indicated by *Vedānta:* 'Thou art not this, of the nature of cause and effect, but That thou art.' When the *Jīva* is thus awakened from sleep, he, then, realises his real nature. What is his nature? It (Self) is birthless, because it is beyond cause and effect and because it has none of the characteristics[7] such as birth etc., which are (inevitably) associated with all (relative) existence. It is birthless, *i.e.*, it is devoid of all changes associated with the object of relative existence including the conditions of cause and effect. It is *Anidram* (sleepless) because there does not exist in it *Nidrā* (sleep), the cause, of the nature of the darkness of *Avidyā*, which produces the changes called birth etc. *Turīyā*, is free from *Svapna* (dream) because it is free from *Nidrā* (sleep) which is the cause of misapprehension of Reality (dream). It is because the Self is free from sleep and dream therefore the *Jīva*, then[8] realises himself as the *Turīya Ātman*, birthless and non-dual.

[1] *Jīva*—It is the *Paramātman* or the Supreme Self who is thought to appear as world-bound on account of his assuming the characteristic of the *Jīva i. e.*, binding himself with the chain of cause and effect.

[2] *Subject etc.*—*i. e.*, world-bound.

[3] *Sleeping*—Sleep or ignorance is the common characteristic of the three states. See *Kārikā* 15.

[4] *Time without etc.*—*Māyā* is said to be *Ānādi* or beginningless from the standpoint of the relative, because it is something for which we cannot think of a cause. From the Absolute standpoint, *Māyā* does not exist.

[5] *Two states*—This covers the three states of waking, dream and deep sleep. See commentary on the previous *Kārikā*.

[6] *Awakened*—Awakening or realisation of Knowledge is possible only for one who is asleep, *i. e.*, who is ignorant.

[7] *Characteristics*—All entities of relative existence possess six characteristics, such as birth, duration, growth, change, decay and death. Brahman is free from them.

[8] *Then*—That is to say, when he is taught by the *Guru* what his real nature is. For the realisation of the Supreme Reality a competent teacher is absolutely necessary who alone is capable of dispelling the doubts that crop up in the mind of the student during the period of his inquiry into Truth.

प्रपञ्चो यदि विद्येत निवर्तेत न संशयः ।
मायामात्रमिदं द्वैतमद्वैतं परमार्थतः ॥ १७ ॥

17. *If the perceived manifold were real then certainly it would disappear. This duality (that is cognized) is mere illusion* (Māyā). *Non-duality is (alone) the Supreme Reality.*

## Śaṅkara's Commentary

If[1] the knowledge of non-duality (*Turīya*) be possible after the disappearance of the perceived manifold, how could non-duality be said to exist (always) while the perceptual manifold remains? This is explained thus: This would have been true if the manifold *really* existed.[2] This manifold being only a false imagination, like the snake in the rope, does not *really* exist. There is no doubt that it would (certainly) disappear if it *really* existed.[3] The snake imagined in the rope, through false conception, does not *really* exist and therefore does not disappear[4] through correct understanding. Nor, similarly, does the illusion of the vision conjured up by the magician exist and then disappear as though a veil thrown over the eyes of the spectators (by the magician) were removed. Similar is this duality of the cognized universe called the Phenomenal or manifold, (मायामात्रं द्वैतं) a mere illusion. Non-duality *Turīya* like the rope and the magician (in the illustrations) is alone the Supreme Reality.[5] Therefore the fact is that there is no such thing as the manifold about which appearance or disappearance can be predicated.

[1] *If*—This is the contention of the opponent: Your assertion that there is anything like the non-dual *Turīya* cannot be a fact: for, a second entity known as the manifold universe does exist, and is perceived. But if you say that the realisation of the non-dual *Turīya* is not inconsistent with that of the dual manifold, because *Turīya* can be realised as such only by the destruction of the manifested manifold, then, so long as the manifold is there as reality and does not disappear, *Turīya* cannot be established as the eternally existent non-duality.

[2] *Existed*—The manifold does not exist in the sense of a separate Reality. If it had any such existence then alone could it obstruct the eternally non-dual nature of the *Turīya* by the appearance (of the manifold). If anyone says that the manifold disappears that is only because he believes in its reality. But this is not the Truth, because the appearance of the manifold is only an illusion and not a reality.

[3] *Really existed*—People say that duality disappears only because they believe in its reality. But really duality does not exist, therefore it does not disappear. If any one believes in the reality of such illusory appearance then can one believe in the reality of the disappearance.

[4] *Does not disappear*—The rope is mistaken for an illusory snake. There is no real snake. When one is pointed out the real rope, no such thing as a snake *actually* disappears, for no such thing as a *real* snake existed. It is the illusion due to ignorance that makes one see the snake that disappears but no *real* snake. The illusion disappears because it is not a reality. That which is liable to be negated cannot be said really to exist at all.

[5] *Supreme Reality*—That is, it is never absent. If one contends that *Turīya* does not exist when the manifold is seen, we reply that the manifold is nothing but Brahman; only the illusion which manifests the manifold as separate from Brahman comes and goes but the manifold, having for its substratum Brahman, always exists.

This *Kārikā* deals with the crux of the *Vedānta* Philosophy. *Vedānta* says that non-duality (*Turīya*) alone is real and ever-existent. But the opponent points out to him the fact of the existence of the universe which incontestably proves duality. If this universe be real, then non-duality (*Turīya*) cannot be a fact. If non-duality is realised only after the disappearance of the objective universe, then non-duality cannot certainly exist so long as the universe exists.

*Vedānta* shows its boldest genius in answering this question. It at once states that non-dual Brahman alone exists. Whatever is, is nothing but Brahman. The manifold is Brahman. As Brahman, it always exists and never undergoes any change. If a man realises the universe as Brahman, then he is never subject to any illusion regarding its reality. The difference between a *Jñānī* and an *Ajñānī* is that a wise man sees the universe as Brahman and therefore never sees in it any appearance or disappearance. But the ignorant person believes in the reality of the universe as apart from Brahman and therefore talks about its disappearance. What really disappears is the illusion that the manifold exists as something other than Brahman. The universe as Brahman does not appear and disappear. It always is. The meaning of the disappearance of the universe really is the disappearance of one's *notion* of the illusion (*i. e.*, the existence of the universe as something other than Brahman). It is like the illusion conjured up by the magician. When the real nature of the rope is pointed out, what disappears is only the illusion which presented the rope as other than it is. The on-looker, after his error is pointed out, realises that what he considered as snake is really the rope. It is illusion which made the rope appear as other than what it is. Knowledge removes this illusion. This illusion is unsubstantial and unreal, hence its appearance and disappearance cannot affect the nature of Reality.

विकल्पो विनिवर्तेत कल्पितो यदि केनचित् ।
उपदेशादयं वादो ज्ञाते द्वैतं न विद्यते ॥ १८ ॥

18. *If anyone has ever imagined the manifold ideas (such for instance as the teacher, the taught, and the scripture), they might disappear. This explanation is for the purpose of teaching. Duality (implied in explanation) ceases to exist when the Highest Truth is known.*

### Śaṅkara's Commentary

(Objection)—How[1] could (duality implied in) ideas such as the teacher, the taught and the scripture disappear?

(Reply)—This is thus explained. If[2] such ideas had ever been imagined by someone then they might be supposed to disappear. As the manifold is like the illusion (conjured up by the magician or) of the snake in the rope, so[3] also are the ideas of the teacher etc. These ideas, namely, the ideas of teacher, taught, and scripture are for[4] the purpose of teaching which are (therefore appear) true till one realises the Highest Truth. But duality does not exist when one, as a result of the teaching, attains knowledge, *i.e.*, realises the Highest Reality.

[1] *How could etc.*—If even the idea of teacher etc., existed, non-duality could not be established. If such ideas be meant for the purpose of *inferring Turīya,* as the smoke is thought of for inferring fire, then duality cannot be refuted. For, the experience of smoke and fire, as existing together, does not demonstrate non-duality.

[2] *If etc.*—Such ideas as teacher, student and scripture have their applicability till one realises the Highest Truth of non-duality (*Turīya*). Such ideas, possible only from the standpoint of ignorance, cannot contradict *Turīya* because they are unreal and negatable by knowledge. The analogy of the smoke and fire is not appropriate. Brahman cannot be logically inferred from the world like the fire from the smoke. For, fire and smoke are objective realities of the same order and seen to exist together by a perceiver. That is not so with Brahman and the world. But the seeing of an object implies the seer. So Brahman may only be indicated.

[3] *So also etc.*—The entire manifold is an illusion, it is not reality. It appears as real till one attains to the Highest Knowledge. The idea of the teacher etc., is a part of this manifold. Hence such ideas have no absolute reality. The appearance is also due to the non-apprehension of Reality.

[4] *For the purpose of*—If one sees duality and seeks an explanation, one of the explanations, offered is that ideas are imagined for the purpose of attaining the Truth.

It has been seen in the previous *Kārikā* that the manifold is Brahman. As the wave is non-different from water, so also the world is non-different from Brahman. The idea that what we see is not Brahman and has got such attributes as birth, changeability, destruction, etc., is illusion which being negated enables one to realise the Highest Truth. Similarly the various ideas one has with regard to the manifold, are non-different from Brahman. Even the so-called illusion of the manifold universe has no existence other than that of Brahman. As the wind that arises from the air, disappears in the air and is identical with the air, so also the manifold is non-different from Brahman. As in dream, the objects that are experienced as the elephant etc., with their names and forms are nothing but the mind-stuff, so also in the state of ignorance what are experienced as the objects with their distinctive names and forms are nothing but Brahman. As in the same dream the idea that I have seen an elephant is non-different from the mindstuff which creates the elephant, so also the idea that there is a distinction between the teacher etc., is not separate from *Brahman*. The cognition of ideas as teacher etc., as separate from *Brahman* is due to one's still persisting in the relative plane, and this is explained as being useful for the realisation of Truth. But after enlightenment these ideas are realised as non-different from *Brahman*. The Highest Truth is that the manifold as well as various thoughts associated with it are identical with *Brahman*. The non-duality (*Turīya*) alone is.

## VIII

**सोऽयमात्माऽध्यक्षरमोङ्कारोऽधिमात्रं पादा मात्रा मात्राश्च पादा अकार उकारो मकार इति ॥ ८ ॥**

The same *Ātman* (which has been described above as having four quarters) is, again, *Aum*, from the point of view of the syllables (अक्षरम्). The *Aum* with parts is viewed from the standpoint of sounds (letters, मात्राः). The quarters are the letters (parts) and the letters are the quarters. The letters here are *A*, *U* and *M*.

### Śaṅkara's Commentary

In the word *Aum* prominence is given to that which is indicated by several names. The word *Aum* which has been explained before as *Ātman* having four quarters is again the same *Ātman* described here from the standpoint of syllable where prominence is given to the name. What, again, is that syllable? It is thus replied: *Aum*. It is that word *Aum* which being divided into parts, is viewed from the standpoint of letters. How? Those which constitute the quarters of the *Ātman* are[1] the letters of *Aum*. What are they? The letters are *A*, *U* and *M*.

In the first Upaniṣad it is said, '*Aum*, the word, is all this'. The word *Aum* is the name (अभिधान) which indicates everything (अभिधेय) past, present, future and all that which is beyond even the conception of time. Thus *Aum* is the name for Brahman. The second Upaniṣad declares that Brahman is the *Ātman*. The *Ātman* with its four quarters has been explained in the following Upaniṣads. Therefore all these explanations are of *Aum* from the standpoint of *Ātman* where prominence is given to that which is indicated by names. Now the same *Aum* is explained from the standpoint of the word itself, that is the name which indicates *Ātman* or the Supreme Reality.

The Highest Truth as explained above by the process of the refutation of the erroneous superimposition can be grasped only by the students of sharp or middling intelligence. But those ordinary students who cannot enter upon philosophical reflection regarding the Supreme Reality as given in the previous texts, are advised to concentrate on *Aum* as the symbol of the Ultimate Reality.

[1] *Are etc.*—It is because the quarters and the letters are identical.

## IX

जागरितस्थानो वैश्वानरोऽकारः प्रथमा मात्राऽऽप्तेरादिमत्त्वा-
द्वाऽऽप्नोति ह वै सर्वान्कामानादिश्च भवति य एवं वेद ॥ ९ ॥

He who is Vaiśvānara, having for its sphere of activity the waking state, is *A*, the first letter (of *Aum*) on account of its all-pervasiveness or on account of being the first (these being the common features of both). One who knows this attains to the fulfilment of all desires and becomes the first (of all).

### Śaṅkara's Commentary

Points of specific resemblance between them are thus pointed out. That which is *Vaiśvānara*, whose sphere of activity is the waking state, is the first letter of *Aum*. What is the common feature between them? It is thus explained: the first point of resemblance is pervasiveness.[1] All sounds are pervaded[2] by *A*. This is corroborated by the *Śruti* passage, 'The sound *A* is the whole of speech'. Similarly the entire universe is pervaded by the *Vaiśvānara* as is evident from such *Śruti* passages as, 'The effulgent Heaven is the head of this, the *Vaiśvānara Ātman*' etc. The identity of the name and the object, indicated by the name, has already been described.

The word '*Ādimat*' means that this has a beginning. As[3] the letter *A* is with a beginning, so also is *Vaiśvānara*. *Vaiśvānara* is identical with *A* on account of this common feature. The knower of this identity gets the following result:[4] One who knows this, *i.e.*, the identity described above, has all his desires fulfilled and becomes the first of the great.

[1] *Pervasiveness*—*A* (अ) pervades all sounds. It is present in all sounds. No articulate sound can be produced without opening the mouth and the sound that is thus produced is *A* (अ).

[2] *Pervaded etc.*—It has been already stated that the knowledge of all other states are possible only from the waking state. The three states constitute our entire experience of the universe. Therefore the waking state pervades the whole of the universe.

[3] *As etc.*—This is the second point of resemblance. *A* is the first of all sounds or letters. Therefore *A* has a beginning because no other sound or letter precedes *A*. Similarly from our common experience it is known that the states of dream and deep sleep are preceded by the waking state which is therefore the first of the three states.

[4] *Result*—The enumeration of the merits is for the purpose of inducing students to understand the meaning of *Aum*.

## X

स्वप्नस्थानस्तैजस उकारो द्वितीया मात्रोत्कर्षादुभयत्वाद्वोत्कर्षति ह वै ज्ञानसंततिं समानश्च भवति नास्याब्रह्मवित्कुले भवति य एवं वेद ॥ १० ॥

*Taijasa*, whose sphere of activity is the dream state, is *U* (उ), the second letter (of *Aum*) on account of superiority or on account of being in between the two. He who knows this attains to a superior knowledge, is treated equally by all alike and finds no one in his line who is not a knower of Brahman.

### Śaṅkara's Commentary

He who is *Taijasa* having for its sphere of activity the dream state is *U* (उ) the second letter of *Aum*. What is the point of resemblance? It is thus replied: The one common feature is superiority. The letter *U* is, as it were, 'superior'[1] to *A*; similarly *Taijasa*[2] is superior to *Viśva*. Another common feature is: the letter *U* (उ) is in between the letters *A* (अ) and *M* (म). Similarly *Taijasa* is in between *Viśva* and *Prājña*. Therefore this condition of being in the middle is the common feature. Now is described the result of this knowledge. The knowledge (of the knower of this identity) is always on the increase, *i.e.*, his power of knowing increases considerably. He is regarded in the same way by all, *i.e.*, his enemies, like his friends, do not envy him. Further, in his family not one is born who is not a knower of Brahman.

[1] *Superior*—As a matter of fact, *A* being the first of all sounds is superior to all letters. But *U* coming after *A* may be said to be superior to *A* in an indirect way.

[2] *Taijasa*—*Taijasa* is superior to *Viśva* as it is associated with ideas (in dream state) whereas *Viśva* is associated with gross objects (in the waking state). In dream alone one realises the world as states of mind (मनःस्पन्दन) which knowledge brings the student nearer to truth.

## XI

सुषुप्तस्थानः प्राज्ञो मकारस्तृतीया मात्रा मितेरपीतेर्वा मिनोति
ह वा इदं सर्वमपीतिश्च भवति य एवं वेद ॥ ११ ॥

*Prājña* whose sphere is deep sleep is *M* (म) the third dart (letter) of *Aum*, because it is both the measure and that wherein all become one. One who knows this (identity of *Prājña* and *M*) is able to measure all (realise the real nature of the world) and also comprehends all within himself.

ŚAṄKARA'S COMMENTARY

One who is *Prājña* associated with deep sleep is *M* (म) the third sound (letter) of *Aum*. What is the common feature? It is thus explained. Here this is the common feature: The *Miti* in the text means 'measure'. As barley is measured by *Prastha* (a kind of measure), so also *Viśva* and *Taijasa* are, as it were, measured[1] by *Prājña* during their evolution (उत्पत्ति) and involution (प्रळय) by their appearance from and disappearance into *Prājña* (deep sleep). Similarly[2] after once finishing the utterance of *Aum* when it is re-uttered, the sounds (letters) *A* and *U*, as it were, merge into and emerge from *M*. Another common feature is described by the word '*Apītiḥ*' which means 'becoming one'. When the word *Aum* is uttered the sounds (letters) *A* and *U* become[3] one, as it were, in the last sound (letter) *M*. Similarly, *Viśva* and *Taijasa* become one (merge themselves) in *Prājña* in deep sleep. Therefore *Prājña* and the sound *M* are identical on account of this common basis that underlies them both. Now is described the merit of this knowledge. (One who knows this identity) comprehends all this, *i.e.*, the real[4] nature of the universe. Further he realises himself as the *Ātman*, the cause of the universe, *i.e.*, *Iśvara*. The enumeration of these secondary[5] merits is for the purpose of extolling the principal means (of knowledge).

[1] *Measured*—Both the waking and dream states appear (during their evolution) from and disappear (at the time of their involution) into deep sleep. Therefore *Prājña* is, as it were, the container in which *Viśva* and *Taijasa* are contained. The nature of *Viśva* and *Taijasa* (non-apprehension of Reality) is known from the nature of *Prājña*—because it is the cause of the two other states. Therefore *Prājña* is here described as the measure of the two other states.

[2] *Similarly*—When the word '*AUM*' is uttered quickly several times, the sound actually heard is *Maum* and not *Aum*, in which case it may be said that the sounds *A* and *U* emerge out of and merge into *M*.

[3] *Become one*—*i.e.*, merge themselves.

[4] *Real Nature*—That is, the universe experienced in the dream and waking states is of the same stuff as the *Prājña*.

[5] *Secondary merits*—The enumeration of these secondary merits is for the satisfaction of those that still move in the causal plane.

Here appear the following *ślokas*:

विश्वस्यात्वविवक्षायामादिसामान्यमुत्कटम् ।
मात्रासंप्रतिपत्तौ स्यादाप्तिसामान्यमेव च ॥ १९ ॥

19. *When the identity of* Viśva *and the sound (letter)* A *is intended to be described, the conspicuous ground is the circumstance of each being the first (in their respective position); another reason for this identity is also the fact of the all-pervasiveness of each.*

ŚAṄKARA'S COMMENTARY

When the *Śruti* intends to describe *Viśva* as of the same nature as *A* (अ), then the most prominent ground is seen to be the fact of each being the first, as described in the Upaniṣad discussed above. '*Mātrā Sampratipat*' in the text means the identity of *Viśva* and *A*. Another prominent reason for such identity is their all-pervasiveness.

तैजसस्योत्वविज्ञान उत्कर्षो दृश्यते स्फुटम् ।
मात्रासंप्रतिपत्तौ स्यादुभयत्वं तथाविधम् ॥ २० ॥

20. *The clear ground of realising* Taijasa *as of the same nature as* U *is the common feature of 'Superiority'. Similarly another plain reason of such identity is being in 'the middle'.*

ŚAṄKARA'S COMMENTARY

When *Taijasa* is intended to be described as '*U*', the reason of their being 'Superior' (in respective cases) is seen to be quite clear. Their being in 'the middle' is also another plain ground. All these explanations are as before.

मकारभावे प्राज्ञस्य मानसामान्यमुत्कटम् ।
मात्रासंप्रतिपत्तौ तु लयसामान्यमेव च ॥ २१ ॥

21. *Of the identity of* Prājña *and* M (म) *the clear reason is the common feature,* i.e., *they both are the 'measure'. The other reason for such identity is another common feature, namely, all become one in both* Prājña *and* M.

ŚAṄKARA'S COMMENTARY

Regarding the identity of *Prājña* and *M* the plain common features are that both of them are the 'measure' as well as that wherein all merge.

त्रिषु धामसु यत्तुल्यं सामान्यं वेत्ति निश्चितः ।
स पूज्यः सर्वभूतानां वन्द्यश्चैव महामुनिः ॥ २२ ॥

22. *He who knows without doubt, what the 'common features' are in the three states, is worshipped and adored by all beings and he is also the greatest sage.*

ŚAṄKARA'S COMMENTARY

One who knows positively, *i.e.,* without a shadow of doubt, the common[1] features that are found in the three states, is worshipped and adored in the world. He is a knower[2] of Brahman.

[1] *Common features*—That is, the three quarters of *Ātman, viz., Viśva, Taijasa* and *Prājña* associated with waking, dream and deep sleep states are identical with the three sounds (letters) of *Aum, viz. A, U,* and *M* respectively for reasons stated above.

[2] *Knower etc.*—The knower of this identity is highly extolled for this reason: From the standpoint of *Ātman, Viśva* merges in *Taijasa* and *Taijasa* in *Prājña;* similarly from the standpoint of *Aum* the sound *A* merges in *U* and *U* merges in *M*. The quarters of *Ātman* are identical with the sound of *M*. He who knows this

identity also knows that the entire universe of the dream and waking experiences emerges from and merges into *Prājña*. This *Prājña* is Brahman though it appears as the causal self (बीज) to those whose mind still moves in the plane of causality. It is only the knower of Brahman that knows *Prājña* also as *Turīya*.

अकारो नयते विश्वमुकारश्चापि तैजसम् ।
मकारश्च पुनः प्राज्ञं नामात्रे विद्यते गतिः ॥ २३ ॥

23. *The sound (letter)* A *helps its* worshipper *to attain to* Viśva, U *to* Taijasa, *and* M *to* Prājña. *In the 'Soundless' there is no attainment.*

### Śaṅkara's Commentary

Having identified the quarters of *Ātman* with the sounds (letters) of *Aum*, on account of the common features stated above, he who realises the nature of the sound *Aum*, described above, and meditates upon it, attains to *Viśva* through the help of *A*. The meaning is that he who meditates on *Aum* having[1] for his support *A* becomes *Vaiśvānara*.[2] Similarly the meditator of *U* becomes *Taijasa*.[3] Again the sound *M* leads its meditator to *Prājña*.[4] But when *M* too disappears, causality[5] itself is negated. Therefore about such *Aum*, which thus becomes soundless,[6] no[7] attainment can be predicated.

[1] *Having etc.*—*i.e.*, one who meditates on *Aum* laying emphasis upon *A* or the waking experiences, realises the entire universe experienced in the waking state as comprehended in the sound *A*.

[2] *Vaiśvānara*—*Vaiśvānara* is the macrocosmic aspect of *Viśva* and and the same as *Virāṭ*.

[3] *Taijasa*—*i.e.*, the *Hiraṇyagarbha*. One who meditates upon *Aumkāra* laying emphasis upon *U*, realises the world as forms of thought like the world experienced in dream. Such worshipper attains to *Hiraṇyagarbha* who is the cosmic mind.

[4] *Prājña*—That is, *Īśvara*, *Prājña* is the cause of the experiences of the waking and dream states as well as it is that wherein all these

finally disappear. *Īśvara* is also he who is the cause of the Universe as well as that of its final disappearance. The meditator on *M* merges *A* in *U* and *U* in *M*. That is, he merges the gross universe of the waking state in the world of ideas experienced in dream and finally realises the dream as one with the state of deep sleep.

[5] *Causality*—It is the idea of causality that makes a man think that he realises the same world after *Suṣupti* which he had seen before going to sleep.

[6] *Soundless*—*i.e.*, it cannot be identified with any of the sounds or their corresponding states.

[7] *No etc.*—Because soundless *Aum* is the same as *Turīya Brahman*.

## XII

अमात्रश्चतुर्थोऽव्यवहार्यः प्रपञ्चोपशमः शिवोऽद्वैत एवमोंकार
आत्मैव संविशत्यात्मनाऽऽत्मानं य एवं वेद ॥ १२ ॥

That which has no parts (soundless), incomprehensible (with the aid of the senses), the cessation of all phenomena, all bliss and non-dual *Aum*, is the fourth and verily the same as the *Ātman*. He who knows this merges his self in the Self.

### Śaṅkara's Commentary

The अमात्रः (soundless[1]) is that which has no parts (sounds etc., or letters). This partless *Aum* which is the fourth, is nothing but Pure *Ātman*. It is incomprehensible, because both speech and mind which correspond to the name[2] and the object disappear or cease; the name and the object (that is indicated by the name) which are only forms of speech and mind cease or disappear (in the partless *Aum*). It is the cessation[3] of the (illusion of) phenomena and all[4] bliss and is identical with non-duality.[5] *Aum*, as[6] thus understood, has three sounds which are the same as the three quarters and therefore *Aum* is identical[7] with *Ātman*. He who knows this merges[8] his self in the Self which is the Highest Reality.

Those who know Brahman, *i.e.*, those who realise the Highest Reality merge into Self, because in their case the notion of the cause which corresponds to the third quarter (of *Ātman*) is destroyed (burnt). They[9] are not born again, because *Turīya* is not a cause. For, the illusory snake which has merged in the rope on the discrimination of the snake from the rope, does not reappear as before, to those who know the distinction between them, by any effort[10] of the mind (due to the previous impressions). To the men of dull or mediocre intellect who still consider themselves as students of philosophy, who having renounced the world, tread on the path of virtue and who know the common features between the sounds (मात्राः) and the quarters (or parts) as described above—to them *Aum*, if meditated upon in a proper way, becomes a great[11] help to the realisation of Brahman. The same is indicated in the *Kārikā* later on thus: 'The three inferior stages of life....' etc. (*Māṇḍ. Kārikā*, *Advaita* Chapter, 16.)

[1] *Soundless*—It is because *Amātra Aum* cannot be expressed by any sound. It is relationless and therefore it cannot be described as the substratum of three other sounds. Sound points out, by contrast, the soundless *Aum*. All sounds must, at some time or other, merge in soundlessness. This *Amātra Aum* is identical with *Turīya Ātman* as described in a previous text (Upaniṣad 7).

[2] *Name etc.*—Name is but a form of speech or sound. All objects are again forms of mind. Both the name and the object are therefore mere ideas (मनःस्पन्दनम्). They disappear with the disappearance of the mind at the dawn of knowledge. Therefore soundless *Aum* like *Turīya* cannot be expressed by a name or pointed out as an object. Therefore it is incomprehensible.

[3] *Cessation*—As the rope is realised when the illusion of snake disappears so partless (soundless) *Aum* is realised when the illusion of duality vanishes.

[4] *All bliss*—This is a state of infinite and eternal bliss because no illusion which is the cause of misery exists there.

*Fourth*—*Amātra* is called fourth because it occupies the fourth place in order of explanation of *Aum*, of which three other states have previously been dealt with. Fourth does not signify any numerical relationship with the three aspects of *Aum* described previously.

[5] *Non-duality*—From the standpoint of the relative world, the soundless state is the substratum of all illusory appearances. One can speak of duality only in the relative world.

[6] *As thus etc.*—*i.e.*, with reference to the identity of the sounds and quarters as explained above.

[7] *Identical with*—Three quarters, *Viśva, Taijasa*, and *Prājña* are imagined to subsist in *Ātman*. *Viśva* merges in *Taijasa, Taijasa* in *Prājña* and finally *Prājña* which is looked upon as the cause of the two preceding states merges in *Turīya Ātman*. Similarly the three sounds *A, U* and *M* ultimately merge in the soundless *Aum*. In soundless *Aum*, the three sounds become identical with it as the three states are identical with *Turīya* from the absolute standpoint. Therefore *Turīya Ātman* is the same as soundless *Aum*.

[8] *Merges*—That is, the knower realises himself as *Turīya*.

[9] *They are etc.*—It may be contended that like a man coming back to the realm of duality having experienced deep sleep, the knower of Self who has identified himself with *Turīya* may also come back to the illusory universe, for *Prājña* and *Turīya* are identical having a common feature of the perception of non-duality. This contention is without ground, because *Turīya* is not a cause. Hence it cannot give rise to the world of illusory experience. Unlike *Prājña* it is beyond all relations of cause and effect. Therefore one who has identified himself with *Turīya* can never see the *illusion* of the manifold.

[10] *Effort of mind*—All efforts of mind are nothing but ideas. Our so-called illusory experiences and their opposite in the relative plane are nothing but ideas (मनःस्पन्दनम्). To a man who has realised ideas as non-different from Brahman, no illusion which is of the nature of existence separate from Brahman, is possible.

[11] *Great help*—Those students who cannot at once think of the soundless *Aum* or *Turīya Ātman* proceed step by step and ultimately realise the Highest Truth.

(Here ends the *Māṇḍūkya Upaniṣad*
with the Commentary of Śaṅkara.)

The following verses explain the foregoing Upaniṣadic texts:

ओंकारं पादशो विद्यात् पादा मात्रा न संशयः ।
ओंकारं पादशो ज्ञात्वा न किंचिदपि चिन्तयेत् ॥ २४ ॥

24. *(The meaning of) Aumkāra should be known quarter by quarter. There is no doubt that quarters are the same sounds (letters). Having grasped the (meaning of) Aumkāra nothing else should be thought of.*

### Śaṅkara's Commentary

Here are, as before, the following verses:

*Aumkāra* should be known along with the quarters; for the quarters[1] are identical with sounds (letters) because of their common features described before. Having[2] thus understood *Aumkāra*, no other object, seen or unseen, should be thought of; for, the knower of *Aumkāra* has all his desires fulfilled.

[1] *Quarters*—It is because the quarters of *Ātman* are identified with the sounds (letters) of *Aum*. Therefore *Aum* should be meditated upon as *Ātman*.

[2] *Having etc.*—That is, by realising *Aum* as Brahman.

युञ्जीत प्रणवे चेतः प्रणवो ब्रह्म निर्भयम् ।
प्रणवे नित्ययुक्तस्य न भयं विद्यते क्वचित् ॥ २५ ॥

25. *The mind should be unified with (the sacred syllable)* Aum. *(For)* Aum *is Brahman, the ever-fearless. He who is always unified with* Aum *knows no fear whatever.*

### Śaṅkara's Commentary

The word *Yuñjīta* means to unify, *i.e.*, to absorb. The mind should be absorbed in *Aum*, which is of the nature of the Supreme Reality, as explained before. The *Aum* is Brahman, the ever-fearless. He who is always unified with *Aum* knows no fear whatever; for the *Śruti* says, 'The knower of Brahman is not afraid of anything'.

He who is proficient or perfect in the knowledge of *Aum*, acquired by an enquiry into its parts, *i.e.*, he who has unified himself with the soundless (partless) *Aum* by merging the three sounds in it, has annihilated the entire dualistic illusion and thereby attained to the supreme goal. But those who cannot do so and those who always depend upon the teachings of others for acquiring knowledge, should meditate upon *Aum* in the manner described in the *Śruti*.

प्रणवो ह्यपरं ब्रह्म प्रणवश्च परः स्मृतः ।
अपूर्वोऽनन्तरोऽबाह्योऽनपरः प्रणवोऽव्ययः ॥ २६ ॥

26. (*The sacred syllable*) Aum *is verily the Lower Brahman, and it is also admitted to be the Supreme Brahman.* Aum *is without beginning* (*cause*), *unique, without anything outside itself, unrelated to any effect and changeless.*

### Śaṅkara's Commentary

*Aum* is both the Lower[1] Brahman and the Supreme *Turīya*. When from the highest standpoint, the sounds and quarters disappear (in the soundless *Aum*) it is verily the same as the Supreme Brahman. It is without cause because no cause can be predicated of it. It is unique because nothing else, belonging to any other species separate from it, exists. Similarly nothing else exists outside it. It is further not related to any effect (because it is not the cause of anything). It is without cause and exists everywhere, both inside and outside, like salt in the water of the ocean.

[1] *Lower Brahman*—That is, the Brahman which is looked upon as the cause of the universe. The dull and mediocre intellect should meditate upon *Aum* as described in the first line of *Kārikā*. The second line describes the soundless aspect of *Aum* or the *Turīya Ātman* which can be understood only by one possessing the keenest intellect.

सर्वस्य प्रणवो ह्यादिर्मध्यमन्तस्तथैव च ।
एवं हि प्रणवं ज्ञात्वा व्यश्नुते तदनन्तरम् ॥ २७ ॥

27. Aum *is verily the beginning, middle and end of all. Knowing* Aum *as such, one, without doubt, attains immediately to that (the Supreme Reality).*

## ŚAṄKARA'S COMMENTARY

*Aum*[1] is the beginning, middle and end of all; that is, everything originates from *Aum*, is sustained by it and ultimately merges in it. As[2] the magician, etc. (without undergoing any change in themselves) stand in relation to the illusory elephant, (the illusion of) snake-rope, the mirage and the dream, etc., so also is the sacred syllable *Aum* to the manifested manifold such as *Ākāśa* (either) etc. The meaning is that he who knows thus, the *Aum*, *Ātman*, which, like the magician etc., does not undergo any change, at[3] once becomes unified with it.

[1] *Aum*—When a cause, etc. of the universe is sought, *Aum* is pointed out as such. This is in accordance with the *Pariṇāmavāda*.

[2] *As the magician etc.*–This is from the standpoint of the *Vivartavāda*. The magician, the rope, the desert, etc., appear as the elephant, the snake, the mirage, etc., without undergoing any change in themselves. Similarly *Aum* also, from the relative standpoint, appears to have become the entire manifested manifold without undergoing any change in itself. But from the standpoint of soundless *Aum*, there is no manifested manifold. It is not the cause of anything nor does it appear in any way other than itself. *Aum* is inferred as a juggler (मायावी) by those who see the fact of creation and explain it as *Māyā*. Therefore, idea of the juggler is also an illusion and it lasts as long as we look upon the manifold as *Māyā*. It vanishes as soon as the *Māyā* or illusion disappears.

[3] *At once*—*Jnāña* or knowledge is alone the cause of *Mukti* which does not depend upon anything else. The moment we know the real nature of *Aum*, we become unified with it.

प्रणवं ह्रीश्वरं विद्यात् सर्वस्य हृदि संस्थितम् ।
सर्वव्यापिनमोंकारं मत्वा धीरो न शोचति ॥ २८ ॥

28. *Know* Aum *to be Īśvara, ever present in the mind of all; the man of discrimination realising* Aum *as all-pervading does not grieve.*

### Śaṅkara's Commentary

Know *Aum* as the Īśvara present in the mind, which is the seat[1] of memory and perception, of all things. The man of discrimination realising *Aumkāra* as all-pervading[2] like the sky, *i.e.*, knowing it as the *Ātman*, not bound by the law of transmigration, does not grieve; for, there is no cause[3] of misery for him. The Scriptures also abound in such passages as, 'The knower of *Ātman* goes beyond grief'.

[1] *Seat etc.*—The knowledge of past and present consists of ideas in the mind of the perceiver. From the recollection of the past one forms the idea of the future.

[2] *All-pervading*—From the highest standpoint *Aum* is not confined to any particular space. It is beyond the limitation of time, space, etc. Therefore the knower of the all-pervading *Aum* transcends grief which is the outcome of limitation. *Aum* is called all-pervading because whatever we perceive or cognize is in consciousness.

[3] *Cause of misery*—One can go beyond grief only by realising the Highest Truth by *Viveka* or discrimination of real and unreal.

अमात्रोऽनन्तमात्रश्च द्वैतस्योपशमः शिवः ।
ओंकारो विदितो येन स मुनिर्नेतरो जनः ॥ २९ ॥

29. *One who has known* Aum *which is soundless and of infinite sounds and which is ever-peaceful on account of negation of duality is the (real) sage and none other.*

### Śaṅkara's Commentary

*Amātra*[1] or soundless *Aum* signifies *Turīya*. *Mātrā* means 'measure'; that which has infinite measure or magnitude is called *Anantamātra*. That is to say, it is not possible to determine its extension or measure by pointing to this or that.

It is ever-peaceful on account of its being the negation of all duality. He who knows *Aum,* as explained above, is the (real) sage because he has realised the nature of the Supreme Reality. No[2] one else, though he may be an expert in the knowledge of the Scriptures, is a sage.

[1] *Amātra*—It is because there is no sound or part beyond the *AUM*, *i.e.*, the soundless and partless quarter (*Amātra*) is not indicated by any letter.

[2] *No etc.*—Book-learning without the direct realisation of Truth is of no value.

Here ends the first chapter of Gauḍapāda's *Kārikā* with the Commentary of Śaṅkara.

**Aum Salutation to Brahman**

CHAPTER II

# ILLUSION

**वैतथ्यं सर्वभावानां स्वप्न आहुर्मनीषिणः ।**
**अन्तःस्थानात्तु भावानां संवृतत्वेन हेतुना ॥ १ ॥**

1. *The wise declare the unreality of all the objects seen in the dream, they all being located within (the body) and on account of their being in a confined space.*

## Śaṅkara's Commentary

*Aum.* It has been already said, 'Duality does not exist when (true) knowledge arises,' and this is borne out by such *Śruti* passages as, 'It (*Ātman*) is verily one and without a second' etc. This is all based merely on the authority[1] of the *Śruti*. It[2] is also equally possible to determine the unreality (illusoriness) of duality through pure reasoning; and for this purpose is begun the second chapter which commences with the words *Vaitathyam* (unreality) etc. The word, *Vaitathyam* signifies the fact of its being unreal or false. Of what is this (unreality) predicated? Of all objects, both internal[3] and external,[4] perceived in the dream. It is thus declared by the wise, *i.e.*, those who are experts in the use of the means (*pramāṇas*) of arriving at true knowledge. The reason of this unreality is stated thus: For, the objects perceived are found to be located within the body. All these entities such as a mountain, an elephant etc., perceived in the dream are cognized there[5] (*i.e.*, within) and not outside the body. Therefore they must be regarded as unreal.

(Objection)—This ('being within') is no valid reason. A jar and other things on account of their being perceived within a cover, such as a cloth etc. (cannot be called unreal).

(Reply)—On account of their being confined in a limited space, that is, within the body (where dream objects are cognized). It is not possible for the mountain, the elephant, etc., to exist in the limited space (within the nerves[6] of the body) which are within the body. A mountain does not or cannot exist inside[7] a body.

[1] *Authority of the Śruti*—The subject-matter, namely, the illusoriness of duality, has been proved in the first chapter solely on Scriptural authority.

[2] *It is etc.*—Śaṅkara contends that the illusoriness of the duality can be proved by reasoning also ***independently of*** the *Sruti*. The Scripture, no doubt, convinces those who believe in its authority. But the philosophy of ***Vedānta*** can hold its ground against those who do not believe in the authority of the *Vedas*, *e. g.*, the ***Buddhists***, the *Jains*, the ***Cārvākas*** and others. All fair discussions are based on reason which is the common platform for all. It betrays ignorance of higher *Vedānta* to say that the reasoning employed in the ***Vedānta*** philosophy to arrive at the Ultimate Truth is always subservient to Scriptural authority. The second chapter of the ***Kārikā*** establishes the unreality of duality through reasoning independent of Scriptural authority.

[3] *Internal*—*i. e.*, such ideas as those of happiness, misery, etc.

[4] *External*—*e. g.*, a pot, a mountain, etc. This distinction between internal ideas and external objects is made here from the dream standpoint. But from the waking standpoint all dream experiences are internal.

[5] *There*—*i. e.*, within the body. The dream is an activity of the mind and according to the common-sense view, mind is within the body. Therefore objects seen in dream are said to exist within the body.

[6] *Nerves*—It is said in the Scriptures that the mind moves about during the time of sleep along some nerves and this produces the dream experiences.

[7] *Inside etc.*—If a mountain cannot exist within a body, it is still more impossible for it to exist within a nerve, which is an old-world view.

अदीर्घत्वाच्च कालस्य गत्वा देशान्नपश्यति ।
प्रतिबुद्धश्च वै सर्वस्तस्मिन्देशे न विद्यते ॥ २ ॥

2. *On account of the shortness of time it is not possible for the dreamer to go out of the body and see (the dream objects). Nor does the dreamer, when he wakes up, find himself in the place (seen in his dream).*

### Śaṅkara's Commentary

That all that is perceived to exist in dreams is located in a limited space, is not a fact. For a man sleeping in the east, often finds himself, as it were,[1] experiencing dreams in the north. Anticipating this objection (of the opponent) it is said: The dreamer does not go to another region outside his body where he experiences dream. For, it is found that as soon as a man falls asleep he experiences dream objects, as it were, at a place which is hundreds of *Yojanas*[2] away from his body and which can be reached only in the course of a month. The long period of time which is necessary to go to that region (where dream objects are perceived) and again to come back (to the place where the sleeper lies) is not found to be an actual fact. Hence on account of the shortness of time the experiencer of the dream does not go to another region. Moreover, the dreamer when he wakes up, does not find himself in the place where he experiences the dream. Had the man (really) gone to another place while dreaming and cognized (or perceived) the dream-objects there, then he would have certainly woken up there alone. But this does not happen. Though a man goes to sleep at night he feels as though he were seeing objects in the day-time and meeting many persons.

(If that meeting were real) he ought to have been met by those persons (whom he himself met during the dream). But this does not happen; for if it did, they would have said, 'We met you there to-day'. But this does not happen. Therefore one does not (really) go to another region in dream.

[1] *As it were*—The dream experiences, though they appear to be real to the dreamer, are not really so.

The experiences of dream are unreal on account of the absence of the appropriate time and place with which such experiences are associated. And this unreality can be known from the waking condition alone. The unreality of dream-experiences is proved here from the standpoint of time and space. For, those who believe in the reality of time and space cannot but admit the illusoriness of dream-experiences.

[2] *Yojana*—It is a measure of distance of eight or nine miles.

अभावश्च रथादीनां श्रूयते न्यायपूर्वकम् ।
वैतथ्यं तेन वै प्राप्तं स्वप्न आहुः प्रकाशितम् ॥ ३ ॥

3. *Following reason,* (*as indicated above*) Śruti *declares the non-existence of the chariots etc.* (*perceived in dream*). *Therefore it is said* (*by the wise*) *that* Śruti *itself declares the illusoriness* (*of the dream-experiences*), *established* (*by reason*).

## Śaṅkara's Commentary

For this reason also the objects perceived to exist in dream are illusory. For, the absence of the chariots etc. (perceived in dream) is stated by *Śruti*, in such passage as, 'There[1] exists neither chariot etc., its assertion being based on reason.[2] In the opinion of the wise, *i.e.*, the knowers of Brahman, the illusoriness (of the dream objects) has been established on the ground of their being perceived within the contracted space in the body. The *Śruti* only reiterates it in order to establish the self-luminosity[3] (of *Ātman*) in dream.

[1] *There etc.*—Comp. *Bṛhd. Up.*, 4. 3. 10.

[2] *Reason*—The reason, as adduced in the previous *Kārikā* is the absence of the appropriate time and space for the real existence of such dream objects.

[3] *Self-luminosity*—Comp. *Bṛhd. Up.*, 4. 3. 14. Mere examination of the waking experiences cannot prove that *Ātman* is self-luminous. For, it may be contended that various activities, associated with the waking state, are due to the functioning of the sense organs under the influence, as the *Śruti* says, of the various luminous deities as the sun, the fire, etc. But in sleep various activities are experienced by the dreamer and these activities, in the absence of the functionings of the sense-organs, are due to the self-luminosity of *Ātman*

अन्तःस्थानात्तु भेदानां तस्माज्जागरिते स्मृतम् ।
यथा तत्र तथा स्वप्ने संवृतत्वेन भिद्यते ॥ ४ ॥

4. *Different objects cognized in dream* (*are illusory*) *on account of their* being perceived to exist. *For the same reason, the objects seen in the waking state are illusory. The nature of objects is the same in the waking state and dream. The only difference is the limitation of space* (*associated with dream objects*).

## ŚAṄKARA'S COMMENTARY

The proposition to be established (*Pratijñā*) is the illusoriness of objects that *are perceived* in the waking state. 'Being perceived' is the 'ground' (*Hetu*) for the inference. They are like the objects that *are perceived* in dream is the illustration (दृष्टान्तः). As the objects perceived to exist in dream are illusory so also are the objects perceived in the waking state. The common feature of 'being perceived' is the relation (*Upanaya*) between the illustration given and the proposition taken for consideration. Therefore the illusoriness is admitted of objects that are perceived to exist in the waking state. This is what is known as the reiteration (*Nigamanam*) of the proposition or the conclusion. The objects perceived to exist in the dream are different[1] from those perceived in the waking state in respect of their being perceived in a limited space within the body. The fact of *being seen* and the (consequent) illusoriness are common to both.

[1] *Different*—This difference is noted only from the waking condition. No inappropriateness of space is noticed during the dream.

*Śaṅkara's* commentary on the *Kārikā* is in the form of a syllogism.

स्वप्नजागरितस्थाने ह्येकमाहुर्मनीषिणः ।
भेदानां हि समत्वेन प्रसिद्धेनैव हेतुना ॥ ५ ॥

5. *The thoughtful persons speak of the sameness of the waking and dream states on account of similarity of objects (perceived in both the states) on grounds already described.*

## ŚAṄKARA'S COMMENTARY

The identity[1] (of the experiences) of the dream and waking states is declared by the wise on account of the reason, already stated, *i.e.,* the experience of objects (in both the states) is associated with subject-object[2] relationship. This *Kārikā* enunciates the conclusion that has already been arrived at in the previous inference by the wise.

[1] *Identity*—Sometimes experience is said to be of three kinds. *Pāramārthika, Prātibhāsika,* and *Vyāvahārika,* making the last two different from each other. Gauḍapāda does not make any distinction between the dream (प्रातिभासिक) and waking (व्यावहारिक) experiences. Compare *Kārikā* 14 (1st chapter).

[2] *Subject-object*—The two factors, namely, the seer and the seen, are equally present in both the waking and the dream states.

The dream and the waking experiences are identical because both are characterised by the same condition, *viz.,* the characteristic of 'being perceived'. Therefore they, both are unreal. The reason of 'being seen', as already described, is a matter of common experience.

आदावन्ते च यन्नास्ति वर्तमानेऽपि तत्तथा ।
वितथैः सदृशाः सन्तोऽवितथा इव लक्षिताः ॥ ६ ॥

6. *That which is non-existent at the beginning and in the end, is necessarily so (non-existent) in the middle. The objects are like the illusions we see, still they are regarded as if real.*

## Śaṅkara's Commentary

The objects perceived to exist in the waking state are unreal for this reason also,[1] that they do not really exist either at the beginning or at the end. Such objects (of experience) as mirage etc., do not really exist either at the beginning or at the end. Therefore they do not (really) exist in the middle either. This is the decided[2] opinion of the world. The several objects perceived to exist really in the waking state are also of the same[3] nature. Though they (the objects of experience) are of the same nature as illusory objects, such as mirage, etc., on account of their non-existence at the beginning and at the end, still they are regarded as real by the ignorant, that is, the persons that do not know *Ātman*.

[1] *Also*—This is an additional reason for the illusoriness of the waking objects.

[2] *Decided etc.*—The reason for the illusoriness of the objects perceived to be real is that such (illusory) existence is not perceived at the beginning or at the end. If it be contended that a perceived object exists at the beginning as the cause, it will be shown later on that this causal conception is itself illusory.

[3] *Same etc.*—*i. e.*, illusory. According to Gauḍapāda, illusory objects are those that have no existence at the beginning and at the end. This is exactly the characteristic of objects perceived to exist outside of us. Changeability is the characteristic of all perceived objects. Change implies non-existence at the beginning and at the end. As all perceived objects are of this nature, they are called illusory.

In this *Kārikā* emphasis is laid on the non-existence of the perceived objects at the beginning and at the end. The ego is the perceiver (*Dṛk*) of all objects seen. The ego does not change as it is the witness of all changes. The perceived objects are known to be illusory or unreal in comparison with the perceiver

सप्रयोजनता तेषां स्वप्ने विप्रतिपद्यते ।
तस्मादाद्यन्तवत्वेन मिथ्यैव खलु ते स्मृताः ॥ ७ ॥

7. *The serving a purpose (as means to an end), of them (the objects of waking experience) is contradicted (opposed) in dream. Therefore they are undoubtedly admitted to be illusory on account of their (both waking and dream) being with a beginning and an end.*

### Śaṅkara's Commentary

(Objection)—The assertion that the objects perceived to exist in the waking state are illusory like those of the dream state is illogical. It is so because the objects of the waking experience, such as food, drink or vehicles, etc., are seen to serve some purpose, that is, they appease hunger and thirst as well as do the work of carrying a man to and fro. But this is not the case with the objects perceived in dream. Therefore the conclusion that the objects perceived in the waking state are unreal like those seen in dream is mere fancy.

(Reply)—It is not so.

(Objection)—Why?

(Reply)—It is because the serving as means to some end or purpose which is found in respect of food, drink, etc. (in the waking state) is contradicted in dream. A man, in the waking state, eats and drinks and feels appeased and free from thirst. But as soon as he goes into sleep, he finds himself (in dream) afflicted with hunger and thirst as if he were without food and drink for days and nights. And the contrary also happens to be equally true. A man satiated with food and drink in dream finds himself, when awakened, quite hungry and thirsty. Therefore the objects perceived in the waking state are contradicted in dream. Hence, we think that the illusoriness of the objects perceived in the waking state like those of dream need not be doubted. Therefore[1] both these objects are undoubtedly admitted to be illusory on account of their common feature of having a beginning and an end.

[1] *Therefore*—Therefore the original assertion that the objects seen in the waking and dream states are illusory on account of their being characterised by a beginning and an end need not be doubted.

The test of reality is thought by some to be 'what works' (as the *Arthakriyākāryavādins* hold). As the dream objects do not work in the waking state therefore they are unreal. The *Vedāntin* says that dream objects are means to dream ends as the waking ones are to waking ends. A sense of causal relation is present in the dream mind as in the waking mind. But what is considered logical sequence in the waking state is not thought to be such in the dream. Each has its own notion of propriety and each is stultified by the other in spite of its appearing to be real.

अपूर्वं स्थानिधर्मो हि यथा स्वर्गनिवासिनाम् ।
तानयं प्रेक्षते गत्वा यथैवेह सुशिक्षितः ॥ ८ ॥

8. *The objects* (*perceived by the dreamer*), *not usually met with* (*in the waking state*) *undoubtedly, owe their existence to the* (*peculiar*) *condition in which the cognizer, that is, his mind, works for the time being, as in the case of those residing in heaven. The dreamer associating himself* (*with the dream conditions*) *experiences those* (*objects*), *even as the one, well-instructed here* (*goes from one place to another and sees objects belonging to those places*).

### Śaṅkara's Commentary

(Objection)—The assertion about the illusoriness of objects perceived in the waking state on account of their similarity to those perceived in the dream state is not correct.

(Reply)—Why?

(Objection)—The illustration does not agree with the thing to be illustrated.

(Reply)—How?

(Objection)—Those objects that are cognized in the waking state are not seen in dream.

(Reply)—What then are they (dream experiences)?

(Objection)—A man perceives in dream objects which are never usually seen in the waking state. He finds himself (in dream) to be with eight hands and seated on an elephant with four tusks. Similarly various other unusual (abnormal) objects are seen in the dream. These (dream objects) are not like other illusory objects. They are, without doubt, real (in themselves). Therefore the illustration does not agree. Hence, the statement that the waking experiences are unreal like those of dream is not correct.

(Reply)—No, your conclusion is not correct. You think that the objects perceived in dream are extraordinary (not like those usually seen in the waking state), but these are not absolutely real in themselves. What, then, is their nature? They[1] are only peculiar to the circumstances of the perceiver associated with those (dream) conditions, *i.e.*, of the dreamer associated with the dream-conditions. As[2] the denizens of heaven, such as Indra etc., have the characteristics of being endowed with a thousand eyes etc. (on account of the very condition of their existence in heaven), so also there are the (peculiar) unusual (abnormal) features of the dreamer (on account of the peculiar condition of the dream state). These[3] (dream experiences) are not absolutely real like the absolute reality of the perceiver. The dreamer associated with the (dream) conditions, while in the dream state, sees all these abnormal or peculiar objects which are but the imaginations of his own mind. It is like the case of a man, in the waking experience, who is well instructed regarding the route to be taken to reach another country, and who while going to that country sees on the way objects belonging to that locality.

Hence as[4] perception of snake in the rope and the mirage in the desert which are due to the (mental) conditions of the perceiver are unreal, so also the objects transcending the limits of the waking experience, perceived in dream, are unreal on account of their being due to the (peculiar) condition of the dream state itself. Therefore the illustration of dream is not incorrect.

[1] *They are etc.*—The dream experiences have no causal relation with the waking experience. A causal relation between two objects of even waking experiences, as will be seen later on, cannot be proved to be true. The objects of our experiences, whether in dream or in waking state, are but the creations of the mind (चित्तस्पन्दनम्) and it is due to ignorance that we relate them causally. In dream, the mind is associated with those experiences which are realised as creations of dream.

[2] *As etc.*—It is only some particular forms of thought which create heaven etc., with their peculiar denizens. They are not absolutely real but are only our imaginations. The moment we imagine heaven, we imagine it also to be peopled with Indra etc., inasmuch as our mind Indra etc., are ever associated with heaven.

[3] *These etc.*—The experiences of dream are not real because of their changing nature. But the perceiver of dream is real because it is unchangeable and witnessing the changes. Even the so-called *sentient* beings we perceive in dream are insentient because they are also objects of perception (दृश्य) and they appear and disappear.

[4] *As etc.*—The illusory perception of mirage etc., is due to the peculiar mental condition of the cognizer. These illusions last as long as the mental conditions that create them last. The objects perceived to be real in the waking state, the illusions experienced in that state and the objects perceived in the dream state have the same nature, *i.e.*, they are all seen (दृश्य) and as such they are all forms of thought (मनःस्पन्दनम्). Hence they are all illusory. No reality can be attached to any of them.

It has been said before that both of dream and waking experiences are alike in nature. But a line of demarcation is sought to be drawn between them, contending that the dream percepts being most of them queer, fantastic and even unnatural, the like of them do not find a place in the world of the wakeful man. But such percepts, however grotesque or abnormal, appear perfectly normal, to the dreamer. The dreamer evidently has his own notion of space, distance and form. But his standards have no applicability to the wakeful man. And the notions of the latter in regard to space etc., have no place in the dreamer's world, though for each everything is normal and real.

स्वप्नवृत्तावपि त्वन्तश्चेतसा कल्पितं त्वसत् ।
बहिश्चेतोगृहीतं सद्दृष्टं वैतथ्यमेतयोः ॥ ९ ॥
जाग्रद्वृत्तावपि त्वन्तश्चेतसा कल्पितं त्वसत् ।
बहिश्चेतो गृहीतं सद्युक्तं वैतथ्यमेतयोः ॥ १० ॥

9-10. *In dream, also, what is imagined within by the mind is illusory and what is cognized outside (by the mind) appears to be real. But (in truth) both these are known to be unreal. Similarly, in the waking state, also, what is imagined within by the mind is illusory; and what is experienced outside (by the mind) appears to be real. But in fact, both should be rationally held to be unreal.*

## Śaṅkara's Commentary

Having refuted the contention of the opponent that there exists no similarity between objects of the waking state and the abnormal (unusual) objects seen in dream, (the text proceeds to point out) the truth of the objects of waking state being (unreal) like those of dream. In the dream state also those which are mere modifications of the mind, cognized within, are illusory. For, such internal objects vanish the moment after they are cognized. In that very dream such objects as pot etc., cognized by the mind and perceived by the sense-organs, eyes, etc., as existing outside, are[1] held to be real. Thus, though all the dream experiences are, without doubt, known[2] to be unreal, yet they arrange themselves as[3] real and unreal. Both kinds of objects (in dream), imagined by the mind internally and externally, are found to be unreal.

Similarly in the waking experience objects known as real and imaginary (mental) should be rationally held to be unreal. Objects, internal and external, are creations of the mind (whether they be in the dream or in the waking state). Other matters have already been explained.

1 *Are held to be real*—That is, by the subject in the dream.

2 *Known etc.*—We know the illusoriness of the dream experiences from the waking state.

3 *As etc.*—*i.e.*, at the time of dreaming.

This is another ground for proving the similarity of the dream and the waking states and the consequent unreality of the latter. It may be contended that in the waking state we make a distinction between 'real' and 'unreal' and that the latter corresponds to all dream objects. To this the reply of the *Vedāntist* is: In dreams also we make a distinction between 'real' and 'unreal'. We see unreal objects in dream and feel surprised when the picture wears off, which impression we consider unreal in dream itself. Therefore there exists a sense of distinction between the 'real' and the 'unreal' in the one state as in the other. For, while the dream lasts, to the dreamer not only are dream objects real but also is the dream state a waking one. The whole of dream experiences is known to be illusory only from the waking standpoint. Similarly the whole of waking experiences, including its so-called subjective imaginations and objective realities, is equally unreal from the standpoint of true knowledge.

उभयोरपि वैतथ्यं भेदानां स्थानयोर्यदि ।
क एतान्बुध्यते भेदान्को वै तेषां विकल्पकः ॥ ११ ॥

11. *If the objects cognized in both the conditions (of dream and of waking) be illusory, who cognizes all these (illusory objects) and who again imagines them?*

## Śaṅkara's Commentary

The opponent asks, 'If the objects, cognized in the waking and dream states, be devoid of reality, who[1] is the cognizer of these—objects imagined by the mind, both inside (subjective), and outside (objective)? Who is, again, their imaginer?' In short, what is the support (substratum) of memory and knowledge? If[2] you say none, then we shall be led to the conclusion that there is nothing like *Ātman* or Self.

[1] *Who etc.*—It is the subject or the ego who, remembering his past experiences, has similar experiences in the present. We can infer a subject only from the facts of memory and experience. If experience and memory be unreal, the subject also would be unreal or non-existent.

[2] *If etc.*—If the Self (*Ātman*) and the objective world be unreal, then all categories of experience, *viz.*, knower, known and knowledge become mere illusion. That is the same as believing in absolute nihilism in which the existence of even *Ātman* or Self is denied. But this contention is invalid. One cannot deny the existence of *Ātman*. For, one who refutes *Ātman* (the knower) takes the position of *Ātman*. Therefore the theory of the non-existence of *Ātman* cannot be admitted.

कल्पयत्यात्मनाऽऽत्मानमात्मा देवः स्वमायया ।
स एव बुध्यते भेदानिति वेदान्तनिश्चयः ॥ १२ ॥

12. Ātman, *the self-luminous, through the power of his own* Māyā, *imagines in himself by himself* (*all the objects that the subject experiences within or without*). *He alone is the cognizer of the objects* (*so created*). *That is the decision of the Vedānta.*

## Śaṅkara's Commentary

The self-luminous[1] *Ātman* himself,[2] by[3] his own *Māyā*, imagines[4] in [5]himself the different[6] objects, to be described hereafter. It is like the imagining of the snake etc., in the rope etc. He[7] himself cognizes them, as[8] he has imagined them. There[9] is no other substratum of knowledge and memory. The aim of Vedānta is to declare that knowledge and memory are not without support as the Buddhistic nihilists maintain.

[1] *Self-luminous*—The self-luminosity of *Ātman* is predicated from the relative standpoint. Objects otherwise insentient, appear sentient on account of the conscious *Ātman* pervading everywhere.

[2] *Himself*—There is no extra-cosmic creator of the universe who, like the potter, is separate from his creation.

[3] *By his own Māyā*—When one looks upon the creation as a fact and seeks its cause, *Māyā* or ignorance is pointed out as such cause. The *Māyā* inheres in Brahman as viewed from the same causal standpoint. It is like the ignorance which, inhering in the perceiver, makes him see his own mind appearing as various dream objects. The causal ignorance of the knowledge of the mind's act of imagining which makes *Ātman* appear as the manifested manifold, is here called *Māyā*.

[4] *Imagines*—There is no actual creation. It is an imagination due to the perceiver's ignorance.

[5] *In himself*—From the causal standpoint *Ātman* is both the material and the efficient cause of the universe. There is no inert matter or anything else, separate from *Ātman*, which he has fashioned into the universe.

[6] *Different objects*—All perceived objects consisting of the ego and the non-ego.

[7] *He himself*—*Ātman* creates this world with his own *Māyā* and then he himself being reflected in *Buddhi* (mind), appears as *Jīva* who perceives the objects.

[8] *As he etc.*—Agency etc. associated with *Ātman*, are not absolutely real. It is because *Ātman* imagines himself, owing to *Māyā*, as an agent, that he is looked upon as the subject.

[9] *There is etc.*—Knowledge and memory, categories of relative perception. inhere in *Ātman* (Self from the subjective standpoint) and in the creator (Brahman from the objective standpoint). Brahman and *Ātman* are identical.

This illusory *Jīva*, *Īśvara* and the world last as long as ignorance (*Māyā*) lasts. Solipsism cannot be a charge against Vedānta. For, according to Vedānta, the ego is not the creator of the non-ego. They come into existence together. One cannot exist without the other. From the relative standpoint both ego and non-ego are the products of the mentation of *Īśvara* or the cosmic mind.

**विकरोत्यपरान्भावानन्तश्चित्ते व्यवस्थितान् ।**
**नियतांश्च बहिश्चित्त एवं कल्पयते प्रभुः ॥ १३ ॥**

13. *The Lord* (Ātman), *with his mind turned outward, variously imagines the diverse objects (such as sound etc.), which are already in his mind (in the form of* Vāsanas *or* Saṅkalpas *or desires). The* Ātman *again (with his mind turned within), imagines in his mind various (objects of) ideas.*

## Śaṅkara's Commentary

How does he imagine the ideas? It is described thus: The word '*Vikaroti*' means creates or imagines, *i.e.*, manifests in multiple forms. Lord, *i.e.*, *Ātman*, with[1] his mind turned outward, imagines in diverse forms various objects, perceived in the (outside) world, such as sound etc., as well as other objects,[2] and also various objects permanent (such as earth etc.), and impermanent,[3] *i.e.*, which exist only for the moment, *i.e.*, as long as that imagination lasts—all being of the nature of subtle ideas (*Vāsanas*) in his mind and not yet fully manifested. Similarly, turning his mind within, the Lord imagines various ideas which are subjective. '*Prabhu*' in the text means the Lord (*Īśvara*) *i.e.*, the *Ātman*.

[1] *With his etc.*—The distinction of objects as internal and external is due to the association of the two organs of perception, namely, mind and sense-organs. When mind alone is concerned we cognize internal objects, when sense-organs are associated with mind we perceive external objects; or in other words, the *Ātman* with the association of sense-organs externalises the internal ideas, *i.e.*, makes them appear as gross physical objects, This division of externality and internality is not true.

[2] *Other etc.*—Such as heavenly worlds etc., mentioned in the Scriptures.

[3] *Impermanent*—Such as lightning etc.

As a potter or a weaver, in order to produce a pot or a cloth, first of all, imagines these in his mind and subsequently manifests them outside, associating them with appropriate names and forms, so also the great Lord, first of all, conceives in his mind, as an idea, the external world to be and then projects it outside associating it with suitable means and forms.

The world that is seen extended in time and space, with its permanent and impermanent objects as well as the various ideas which are distinguished from matter, are all nothing but the ideas in the mind of the Creator *i.e.*, *Ātman* as *Īśvara*. This *Ātman* or the causal Self creates by his imagination the ego and the non-ego as well as their mutual relationship.

The word 'Imagination' is used as the equivalent of '*Kalpana*'. The English term is generally used to denote the mental construction of the individual soul or self. The Sanskrit term applies to both *Īśvara* (the *Ātman*) and the individual soul.

चित्तकाला हि येऽन्तस्तु द्वयकालाश्च ये बहिः ।
कल्पिता एव ते सर्वे विशेषो नान्यहेतुकः ॥ १४ ॥

14. *Those that are cognized within only as long as the thought of them lasts, as well as those that are perceived by the senses and that conform to two points of time, are all mere imaginations. There is no other ground for differentiating the one from the other.*

### ŚAṄKARA'S COMMENTARY

A[1] doubt is raised as to the statement that everything is mere imagination of mind like the dream. For, the imagination of mind, such as desire etc., determined[2] by mind, is different from objects[3] perceived to exist outside, on account of the latter being determined by two points in time. This objection is not valid. Objects perceived to exist within, only as long as the thought about them lasts, signify those (subjective) ideas which[4] are only determined by mind; *i.e.*, such objects have no other time to determine them except that wherein the idea in the mind exists (when imagining such ideas). The meaning is that such (subjective) ideas are experienced at the time when they are imagined. Objects related to two points of time signify those external objects which are cognizable by others at some other point of time and which cognize the latter in their turn. Therefore such objects are said to be mutually limited by one another. As for example, when it is said that he remains[5] till the cow is milked, the statement means, 'The cow is milked as long as he remains and he remains as long as the cow is milked'. A[6] similar instance is the following: 'It is like that, that is like this'. In this way, the objects perceived to exist outside mutually determine one another. Therefore they are known as '*Dvayakālāh*', that is, related to two points in time. Ideas perceived within and existing as long as the mind that cognizes them lasts, as well as the external objects related to two points in time, are all mere imaginations.[7] The[8] peculiar characteristic of being related to two points in time of the objects that are perceived to exist outside is not due to any other cause except their being imagined by the mind. Therefore the illustration of dream well applies here.

[1] *A doubt—i.e.*, the imaginary objects exist as long as the mind that imagines them lasts. They have no existence beyond that time. But the external objects that are perceived in the waking state exist at other times also even when the mind does not imagine them. Therefore external objects cannot be proved to be illusory by the mere illustration of dream experiences.

[2] *Determined etc.*—The mental imagination has no corresponding reality existing outside. Such an idea, as the objective illusion of the snake in the rope, created within by the mind, is of the nature of mind and is perceived to exist within the mind alone. Such ideas exist only as along as the perceiving mind exists. They cannot be proved to exist by any other instrument of knowledge.

[3] *Objects etc.*—But the different external objects are mutually cognized by one another from different points in time. The consciousness that such objects exist does not depend upon the perceiving mind alone. Therefore such objects cannot be of the same nature as dream or imaginary objects.

[4] *Which are etc.—i.e.,* external objects are perceived by other minds existing previous to or subsequent to the present perceiving mind.

[5] *He remains etc.*—The two external objects of cognition, *e.g.,* the milking of a cow and the remaining of a man are mutually related to each other in respect of two points in time. The cow may be milked independently of a man's existence and a man may exist independently of the milking of the cow. Those objects that are in this manner mutually cognized are said to answer to two points in time.

[6] *A similar instance*—As long as a pot serves a purpose, so long it is said to exist. Here also the time is the limiting factor. Thus all objects that are perceived to exist outside are determined by the present or any other time. They are independent of the mind of the perceiver. They are, rather, dependent upon the time in which they exist.

[7] *Imaginations*—That a thing exists independently of the perceiving mind is also an idea. That the world existed before I was born or will continue to exist after I die or that many things exist at present of which I am not conscious—these are all mere ideas in the mind at the present time. Past, present and future are nothing but ideas present in the mind at the moment.

[8] *The peculiar etc.*—This can be better understood from the analogy of the dream. A man may dream for five minutes in which time he may see objects existing during as many years. Different objects perceived in dream, answering to different points in time, are but the imagination of the dreamer who only dreams for a few moments. Similarly in the waking state a man, by mere force of imagination, sees objects conforming to different points in time extending over hundreds of years. Though from the waking standpoint dream objects are known to be illusory, yet they are perceived to be actually existing at the time of dream. Similarly it is quite reasonable to believe in the illusory nature of the waking experience from the standpoint of Truth. There is no difference between the objects perceived in dream and waking states on account of their possessing a common feature, namely, 'capability of being seen'.

अव्यक्ता एव येऽन्तस्तु स्फुटा एव च ये बहिः ।
कल्पिता एव ते सर्वे विशेषस्त्विन्द्रियान्तरे ॥ १५ ॥

15. *Those that exist within the mind (as mere subjective imaginations) and are known as the unmanifested as well as those that exist without in a manifested form (as perceived objects)—all are mere imaginations, the difference lying only in the sense-organs (by means of which the latter are cognized).*

## Śaṅkara's Commentary

Though[1] the objects perceived within, as mere mental impressions, are unmanifested, and though[2] the objects perceived outside through the sense-organs such as eyes etc., are known as manifested (gross entities), yet the distinction[3] is not due to anything substantial in the nature of the (two kinds of) objects. For, such distinction is seen in dreams as well. What is, then, the cause of this distinction? It[4] is only due to the difference in the use of sense-organs (by means of which these objects are perceived). Hence, it is established that the objects perceived in the waking state are as much imagination of the mind as those seen in the dream.

1 *Though etc.*—Objects perceived within the mind are mere products of imagination. The characteristic of such objects is their unmanifestedness. Therefore they are known as 'ideas' in contradistinction to 'gross' objects perceived outside.

2 *Though etc.*—Those perceived to exist outside and cognized by different sense-organs are known as gross manifested objects and as such they are distinguished from ideas in the mind.

3 *The distinction etc.*—This distinction between the gross objects and the subtle ideas is not due to anything substantial or real in the very nature of the objects. They belong to one and the same class, *i.e.*, both these are mere forms of thought or the imagined ideas of the perceiver. Though there is this distinction of manifestedness and unmanifestedness, yet one cannot be less illusory than the other. For, we see the same distinction in dream experiences as well, yet the whole of dream is illusory or imagination of the mind.

4 *It is etc.*—This distinction is due to the following reason. Ideas are cognized within the mind. External objects are perceived by sense-

organs such as the eyes etc. The distinction regarding the nature of perceived objects is due to the nature of the organs by means of which they are perceived. In spite of this difference, ideas and physical objects do not admit of any distinction as regards their real nature. In dreams also there are sense-organs of the dream. There is therefore no real difference.

जीवं कल्पयते पूर्वं ततो भावान्पृथग्विधान् ।
बाह्यानाध्यात्मिकांश्चैव यथाविद्यस्तथास्मृतिः ॥ १६ ॥

16. *First of all, is imagined the* Jīva *(the embodied being) and then are imagined the various entities, objective and subjective, that are perceived. As is (one's) knowledge so is (one's) memory of it.*

### Śaṅkara's Commentary

What is the source of the imagination of various objects, subjective[1] and objective[2] that are perceived and appear to be related to one another as cause and effect? It is thus explained: The *Jīva* is of the nature of cause and effect and is further characterised by such ideas as, 'I do this, I am happy and miserable'. Such *Jīva* is, at first, imagined[3] in the *Ātman*[4] which is pure and devoid of any such characteristics, like[5] the imagination of a snake in a rope. Then for the knowledge of the *Jīva* are imagined[6] various existent entities, both subjective and objective, such as *Prāṇa* etc., constituting different ideas such as the agent, action and the result (of action). What is the cause of this imagination? It is thus explained: It, the *Jīva*, who is the product of imagination and competent to effect further imagination, has its memory determined by its own inherent knowledge. That is to say, its knowledge is always followed by a memory, similar to that knowledge. Hence,[7] from the knowledge of the idea of cause results the knowledge of the idea of the effect. Then follows the memory of both cause and effect. This memory is followed by its knowledge which results in the various states of knowledge characterised by action, actor and the effect. These are followed by their memory, which, in its turn, is followed by the states of knowledge. In this way are imagined various objects, subjective and objective, which are perceived and seen to be related to one another as cause and effect.

[1] *Subjective*—Such as, pain and pleasure, knowledge, attachment, etc.

[2] *Objective*—Such as, various objects perceived outside of us. These objects appear to cause various subjective feelings in us, which, in their turn, seen to create external objects. Therefore, subjective and objective entities appear to be mutually related as cause and effect.

[3] *Imagined*—The *Ātman* itself imagines the idea of a *Jīva* through the power of *Māyā*.

[4] *Ātman*—*Ātman*, pure and unrelated, appears as the substratum of all ideas.

[5] *Like etc.*—No illusory superimposition is possible without a real substratum. This is the reply to the Buddhistic nihilism.

[6] *Imagined*—That is to say, by the *Jīva* itself through the power of *Māyā* which is postulated from the causal standpoint.

[7] *Hence etc.*—It is seen from common experience that the idea of food and drink is followed by the idea of satisfaction. One is not possible in the absence of the other. Following this method of agreement and difference we imagine thus. From the idea of knowledge of food etc., which is the cause, follows the idea of the knowledge of satisfaction which is the effect. Next day, we get the memory of this cause and effect experienced on the previous day. Then we have the idea of a duty which may be described as a result of the previous experience Accordingly we begin the act of cooking etc., with the help of rice, fuel, etc. After eating the food thus prepared, we derive certain definite states of knowledge characterised by the idea of satisfaction etc. This satisfaction inheres in us as the memory which stimulates us, next day, to similar action. We perform the action which is followed by an identical result. Thus ideas succeed one another and appear to be related as cause and effect. That these ideas need not have any counter-part in the gross physical world of the waking state can be understood

by the analysis of the dream experiences. As a matter of fact, it cannot be rationally proved that even, in the waking state, an idea can produce a corresponding effect in the world perceived to exist outside of us.

अनिश्चिता यथा रज्जुरन्धकारे विकल्पिता ।
सर्पधारादिभिर्भावैस्तद्वदात्मा विकल्पितः ॥ १७ ॥

17. *As the rope, whose nature is not really known, is imagined in the dark to be a snake, a water-line etc., so also is the* Ātman *imagined (in various ways).*

### Śaṅkara's Commentary

It has been said that the imagination of *Jīva* (the *Jīva*-idea) is the source of all (other) imaginations (ideas). What is the cause of this *Jīva*-idea? It is thus explained by an illustration: It is found in common experience that a rope, not known as such, is imagined, in hazy darkness, as snake, water-line, stick or any one of the many similar things. All this is due to the previous absence of knowledge regarding the real nature of the rope. If previously the rope had been known in its real nature, then the imagination of snake etc., would not have been possible, as in the case of one's own fingers.

Similarly, *Ātman* has been variously imagined as *Jīva*, *Prāṇa* and so forth[1] because It is not known in its own nature, *i.e.*, pure[2] essence of knowledge itself, the non-dual *Ātman*, quite distinct from such phenomenal characteristics indicated by the relation of cause and effect etc., which are productive of misery. This is the unmistakable verdict of all the Upaniṣads.

[1] *So forth etc.*—*e.g.*, the ideas of agent, enjoyer, etc.
[2] *Pure etc.*—*i.e.*, without birth, death, form, etc.

निश्चितायां यथा रज्ज्वां विकल्पो विनिवर्तते ।
रज्जुरेवेति चाद्वैतं तद्वदात्मविनिश्चयः ॥ १८ ॥

18. *When the real nature of the rope is ascertained all illusions about it disapppear and there arises the conviction that it is the one (unchanged) rope and nothing else; even so is the nature of the conviction regarding* Ātman.

### Śaṅkara's Commentary

When it is determined that it is nothing but the rope alone, then all illusions regarding the rope disappear and the (non-dual) knowledge that there exists nothing else but the rope, becomes firmly established. Similar is the knowledge—like the light of the sun—produced by the negative Scriptural statements which deny all phenomenal attributes (in *Ātman*)—statements like 'Not this', 'Not this', etc., leading to the knowledge of the real nature of *Ātman*, as, 'All this is verily *Ātman*', '(It is) without cause and effect, without internality and externality', '(It is) ever without and within and beginningless', '(It is) without decay and death, immortal, fearless, one and without a second'.

प्राणादिभिरनन्तैश्च भावैरेतैर्विकल्पितः ।
मायैषा तस्य देवस्य यया संमोहितः स्वयम् ॥ १९ ॥

19. *The* Ātman *is imagined as* Prāṇa *and other endless objects. This is due to* Māyā (*ignorance*) *of the luminous* (Ātman *itself*) *by which It is (as it were) deluded.*

### Śaṅkara's Commentary

If it be definitely ascertained that *Ātman* is verily one, how could it be imagined as the endless objects like *Prāṇa* etc., having the characteristics of the phenomenal experience? It is thus explained: This is due to the *Māyā* (ignorance) inhering in the luminous *Ātman*. As the illusion conjured up by the juggler makes[1] the very clear sky appear covered with trees blooming with flowers and leaves, so[2] does this luminous *Ātman* become deluded, as it were, by his own *Māyā*. 'My *Māyā* cannot be easily got over' declares the *Gītā*.

[1] *Makes etc.*—Even when under the influence of the juggler's illusion, the sky appears to be filled with trees etc., it does not, in reality, lose its natural clearness.

[2] *So etc.*—*Māyā* as the explanation of the manifold is from the causal standpoint. Even when the *Ātman* appears to be transformed into the universe, it does not, in reality, lose its non-dual character.

प्राण इति प्राणविदो भूतानीति च तद्विदः ।
गुणा इति गुणविदस्तत्वानीति च तद्विदः ॥ २० ॥

20. *Those*[1] *that know only* Prāṇa,[2] *call It* (Ātman) Prāṇa, *those*[3] *that know* Bhūtas *call It* Bhūtas,[4] *those*[5] *knowing* Guṇas *call It* Guṇas,[6] *those*[7] *knowing* Tattvas, *call It* Tattvas.[8]

[1] *Those—e.g.,* the *Vaiśeṣikas* and the worshippers of *Hiraṇyagarbha* etc.

[2] *Prāṇa*—They hold *Prāṇa, i.e., Hiraṇyagarbha* or extra-cosmic God, to be the cause of the universe. This is mere imagination of the mind. There is no rational proof of the reality of an extra-cosmic God or Person as the cause of the world.

[3] *Those etc.—e.g.,* the *Cārvākas* or the atheists.

[4] *Bhūtas*—They designate the four elements, such as, earth, water, fire and air, which are directly perceived by them, as the cause of the universe. The insentient elements cannot be the cause of the sentient beings. Therefore, this theory also is an imagination.

[5] *Those etc.,—e.g.,* the *Sāṁkhyas*.

[6] *Guṇas*—According to the *Sāṁkhyas,* the state of equilibrium of the three *Guṇas, viz., Sattva, Rajas* and *Tamas,* produces *Mahat* etc., and through them the universe. This is also mere idea.

[7] *Those etc.—i.e.,* the *Śaivas*.

[8] *Tattvas*—The *Śaivas* enumerate three *Tattvas* or categories, *viz., Ātman, Avidyā* and *Śiva* as the cause of the universe. This is also an imagination and hence untenable. For, *Śiva* being an entity separated from *Ātman,* becomes an object like a pot etc.

पादा इति पादविदो विषया इति तद्विदः ।
लोका इति लोकविदो देवा इति च तद्विदः ॥ २१ ॥

21. *Those acquainted with the quarters*[1] (Pādas) *call It quarters; those*[2] *with objects, the objects*[3]; *those*[4] *with* Lokas, *the* Lokas[5]; *those*[6] *with* Devas, *the* Devas[7].

These different conceptions of *Ātman* are nothing but imaginations of the mind.

[1] *Quarters—e.g., Viśva, Taijasa* and *Prājña*. *Ātman,* being without parts and also unrelated, cannot be really divided into quarters or parts.

[2] *Those etc.—i.e.,* thinkers like *Vātsyāyana* etc.

[3] *Objects*—Such as, sound, colour, etc., *i.e.,* the objects perceived by the different sense-organs. The objects, on account of their changeable and negatable nature, cannot be the Ultimate Reality.

[4] *Those etc.—i.e.,* the *Paurāṇikas* or the believers in Mythology.

[5] *Lokas*—Such as *Bhūḥ, Bhuvaḥ* and *Svaḥ*. These being three in number are limited.

[6] *Those etc.—i.e.,* the *Karma-Mīmāṁsakas* or the believers in the *Karma* portions of the *Vedas*.

[7] *Devas*—Such as, *Agni* (Fire), *Indra,* etc. According to this theory, *Agni, Indra,* etc., the various conscious deities, though not occupying the actual position of God (*Īśvara*), apportion the results of our various works. The conception of a separate God is not necessary. They cannot be Ultimate Reality.

वेदा इति वेदविदो यज्ञा इति च तद्विदः ।
भोक्तेति च भोक्तृविदो भोज्यमिति च तद्विदः ॥ २२ ॥

22. *Those knowing the Vedas call It the Vedas;*[1] *those*[2] *acquainted with the sacrifices, call It the sacrifices*[3] (*Yajña*); *those*[4] *conversant with the enjoyer, designate It as the enjoyer*[5] *and those*[6] *with the object of enjoyment, call It such.*

[1] *Vedas—e.g.,* the four *Vedas, Ṛg, Yajus, Sāma* and *Atharva*. These *Vedas* cannot be the Ultimate Reality inasmuch as they are sounds.

[2] *Those etc.—i.e.,* sages such as Bodhāyana and others who are adept in the performance of sacrifices.

[3] *Sacrifices*—The upholders of sacrifices and rituals like the *Yajñas* think that sacrifices, such as *Jyotiṣṭoma* etc., constitute the Highest Reality. But this is also an illusion. For, according to them, the sacrifice signifies the object (offered), the deity and the act of offering. Any one of these, *singly*, does not constitute sacrifice. Again three of them, combined together, do not constitute any real entity.

[4] *Those etc.*—*viz.*, the *Sāṁkhyas*.

[5] *Enjoyer*—According to the *Sāṁkhyas* the Ultimate Reality is the *Puruṣa* who is not the agent or doer but a mere enjoyer. This theory is not rational; for enjoyment means some change in the enjoyer which thus contradicts the idea of his being eternal and changeless. If enjoyment be predicated as the inherent nature of *Puruṣa*, then the conception of extraneous objects, conducive to its enjoyments, is inconsistent.

[6] *Those etc.*—That is, the cook, to whom the only reality appears to be delicious dishes.

सूक्ष्म इति सूक्ष्मविदः स्थूल इति च तद्विदः ।
मूर्त इति मूर्तविदोऽमूर्त इति च तद्विदः ॥ २३ ॥

23. *The Knowers*[1] *of the subtle designate It as the subtle,*[2] *the Knowers*[3] *of the gross call It the gross.*[4] *Those*[5] *that are familiar with a Personality (having form) call It a person,*[6] *and those*[7] *that do not believe in anything having a form call It a void.*[8]

[1] *Knowers*—*i.e.*, those who *believe* (or take) the *Ātman* to be subtle like an atom.

[2] *Subtle*—This theory is irrational: for, we feel consciousness simultaneously all over the body.

[3] *Knowers*—A sect of materialists who believe the gross body to be real.

[4] *Gross*—The gross body cannot be the Ultimate Reality as a dead or sleeping man, in spite of the body being in existence, is unconscious. Any single limb of the body is insentient. Therefore even their aggregate cannot constitute the conscious Reality.

[5] *Those etc.*—*i.e.*, the *Āgamikas* who believe a person, *e.g.*, *Śiva* with a trident or *Viṣṇu* with a disc, to be the Ultimate Reality. These are also imaginary.

[6] *Person*—This is also an illusion.

[7] *Those etc.—i.e.*, The Buddhistic ritualists.

[8] *Void*—The idea that the Ultimate Reality is an absolute void is also an illusion, as a void also should have a knower, and so cannot be the substratum of the positive fact of the empirical universe.

काल इति कालविदो दिश इति च तद्विदः ।
वादा इति वादविदो भुवनानीति तद्विदः ॥ २४ ॥

24. *The Knowers*[1] *of time call It time*[2]*; the Knowers of space (ether) call It space (ether). Those versed in disputation call It the problem in dispute and the Knowers of the worlds call It the worlds.*[3]

[1] *Knowers etc.*—Such as the astrologers (astronomers).

[2] *Time*—This theory is also fallacious as time is divided into various parts as moment, minute, hour, etc. Time is also an object (thought) of the perceiving mind.

[3] *Worlds*—This is also an illusory conception.

मन इति मनोविदो बुद्धिरिति च तद्विदः ।
चित्तमिति चित्तविदो धर्माधर्मौ च तद्विदः ॥ २५ ॥

25. *The Cognizers*[1] *of the mind call It the mind*[2]*; of*[3] *the* Buddhi *(intellect) the* Buddhi[4]*; of the* Citta *(mind-stuff), the* Citta[5]*; and the Knowers*[6] *of* Dharma *(righteousness) and* Adharma *(unrighteousness) call It the one*[7] *or the other.*

[1] *Cognizers etc.—i.e.*, a sect of the materialists.

[2] *Mind*—This theory is also not tenable as mind is also an object, an instrument of the perceiving ego.

[3] *Of etc.*—They are a class of Buddhists.

[4] *Buddhi*—This is also a wrong view of the Reality, as the functionings of *Buddhi* disappear at the time of deep sleep. Further *Buddhi* is also an object cognized by the perceiver.

[5] *Citta*—*Citta* is an aspect of mind which has no particular external form. It cannot be *Ātman* for the reasons given regarding mind.

[6] *Knowers etc.—i..e*, the *Mīmāṁsakas*.

[7] *The one etc.*—None of these can be the Ultimate Reality because one cannot be conceived without the other and they have no absolute standard. They vary with different conditions of time and country.

पञ्चविंशक इत्येके षड्विंश इति चापरे ।
एकत्रिंशक इत्याहुरनन्त इति चापरे ॥ २६ ॥

26. *Some*[1] *say that the Reality consists of twenty-five categories, others*[2] *twenty-six, while there are others*[3] *who conceive It as consisting of thirty-one categories and lastly people are not wanting who think such categories to be infinite.*

[1] *Some—i.e.*, the *Sāṁkhyas* according to whom the Reality consists of twenty-five categories, *viz.*, *Prakṛti*, *Mahat*, *Ahaṁkāra*, five *Tanmātras* (subtle elements), five organs of perception, five organs of action, five objects, mind and the *Puruṣa*.

[2] *Others—i.e.*, the followers of Patañjali who add *Īśvara* to the categories of the *Sāṁkhyas*.

[3] *Others—i.e.*, the *Pāśupatas* who add to the categories of *Sāṁkhyas* six more, *viz.*, *Rāga*, *Avidyā*, *Kāla*, *Kalā*, *Māyā* and *Niyati*.

The mutual contradiction among these different schools prove the fallacious character of their theories. The difference of opinion is due to the ignorance of the nature of Reality.

लोकाँल्लोकविदः प्राहुराश्रमा इति तद्विदः ।
स्त्रीपुंनपुंसकं लैङ्गाः परापरमथापरे ॥ २७ ॥

27. *Those*[1] *who know only to please others call It* (*Reality*) *such*[2] *pleasure; those*[3] *who are cognizant of the* Āśramas *call It the* Āśramas; *the grammarians call It the male, female or the neuter, and others know It as the* Para[4] *and* Apara.

[1] *Those etc.—i.e.*, a sect of the atheists.

[2] *Such etc.*—This is also a delusion as it is impossible to please everybody on account of the different tastes of the people.

[3] *Those etc.—i.e.*, men like Dakṣa etc.

[4] *Para etc.—i.e.*, the Brahman who is regarded as high and low. An entity, subject to division of any sort, can never be the Supreme Reality.

सृष्टिरिति सृष्टिविदो लय इति च तद्विदः ।
स्थितिरिति स्थितिविदः सर्वे चेह तु सर्वदा ॥ २८ ॥

28. *The Knowers*[1] *of creation call It creation; the Knowers of dissolution describe It as dissolution and the believers in subsistence believe It to be subsistence. Really speaking, all*[2] *these ideas are always imagined*[3] *in* Ātman.

[1] *Knowers etc.*—*i.e.*, the *Paurāṇikas* (the believers in Mythology) who believe in the reality of creation, preservation and destruction.

[2] *All these*—*i.e.*, those enumerated above and which may be enumerated by others in future.

[3] *Imagined*—So long as men are given to imagining, they have recourse to all such imaginations regarding *Ātman*. But *Ātman*, from its own standpoint, does not imagine anything. It is because all these ideas, described above, are mere imaginations, that they cannot be the underlying Reality.

## Śaṅkara's Commentary

20–28. *Prāṇa* means *Prājña* (the *Jīva* associated with deep sleep) and *Bījātmā* (the causal self). All the entities from *Prāṇa* to the *Sthiti* (subsistence) are only various effects of *Prāṇa*. These and other popular ideas of their kind, imagined by all beings, are like the imaginations of the snake etc., in the rope etc. These are through ignorance imagined in *Ātman* which is free[1] from all these distinctions. These fancies are due to the lack of determination of the real nature of the Self. This is the purport of these *ślokas*. No attempt is made to explain the meaning of each word in the texts beginning with *Prāṇa* etc., on account of the futility of such effort and also on account of the clearness of the meaning of the terms.

[1] *Free from etc.*—*Ātman* is free from all these imaginations. It is because of the ignorance of the real nature of the *Ātman* that it is thought to be the substratum (another entity) of all imaginations.

No useful purpose can be served by the discussion of imaginations which are unreal and illusory.

यं भावं दर्शयेद्यस्य तं भावं स तु पश्यति ।
तं चावति स भूत्वाऽसौ तद्ग्रहः समुपैति तम् ॥ २९ ॥

29. *He* (*the inquirer*) *cognizes only that idea that is presented to him. It* (Ātman) *assumes the form* (*of what is cognized*) *and thus protects* (*the inquirer*). *Possessed by that* (*idea*) *he realises it* (*as the sole essence*).

### Śaṅkara's Commentary

What more is to be gained (by this kind of endless discussion)? Whatever idea or interpretation of such things as *Prāṇa*[1] etc., narrated above or omitted, is shown to the inquirer by the teacher or other trustworthy person. He realises[2] that as the sole essence (*Ātman*), *i.e.*, he understands that as, 'I am that or that is mine'. Such conception about *Ātman* as is revealed to the inquirer, appears to him as the sole essence and protects him, *i.e.*, keeps him away from all other ideas (because it appears to him as the highest ideal). On[3] account of his devotion (attachment) to that ideal, he realises it as the sole essence in due course, *i.e.*, attains his identity with it.

[1] *Prāṇa*—All interpretations of *Ātman* must be included in the *Prāṇa*, as *Prāṇa* or the causal Self is the highest manifestation of *Ātman* in the relative plane.

[2] *Realises etc.*—It is because such inquirer, for want of proper discrimination, accepts the words of the teacher as the highest truth. The teacher also, realising the limited intellectual capacity of the student, teaches him, at first, only a partial view of truth.

[3] *On account etc.*—Such student only gets a partial view of Reality though he takes it as the sole essence, He shuts his eyes to other views. On account of his single-minded devotion to that ideal he becomes intolerant of other view-points. But he who takes a particular idea to be the Reality and condemns other ideas as untrue, has not realised the Highest Truth. For, to a knower of Reality, all imaginations are identical with *Brahman* and hence have the same value. This is the mistake generally committed by the mystics who, for want of the faculty of the rational discrimination, do not see any truth in the views of others.

एतैरेषोऽपृथग्भावैः पृथगेवेति लक्षितः ।
एवं यो वेद तत्त्वेन कल्पयेत्सोऽविशङ्कितः ॥ ३० ॥

30. *This* Ātman, *though non-separate from all these, appears, as it were, separate. One who knows this truly imagines (interprets) (the meaning of the Vedas) without hesitation.*

## Śaṅkara's Commentary

Though this *Ātman* is verily non-separate[1] from these, the *Prāṇa* etc.—like the rope from such imaginary ideas as the snake etc.—it appears as separate to the ignorant persons. But to the Knower (of truth), the *Prāṇa* etc., do not exist apart from *Ātman*, just as the snake etc., falsely imagined in the rope, do not exist apart from the rope. For, the *Śruti* also says, 'All that exists is verily *Ātman*'. One who thus knows truly, that is, from Scriptures as well as by reasoning[2] that *Prāṇa* etc., imagined in *Ātman*, do not exist separately from *Ātman* (as in the illustration) of the (illusory) snake and the rope, and further knows that *Ātman* is ever pure[3] and free from all imaginations—construes,[4] without hesitation, the text of the Vedas according to its division.[5] That is to say, he knows that the meaning of this passage is this and of that passage is that. None but the Knower of *Ātman* is able to know truely the (meaning of the) Vedas. 'None but the Knower of *Ātman* is able to derive any benefit from his actions', says Manu.

[1] *Non-separate*—It is because that which is superimposed cannot exist apart from the substratum. Therefore the *Prāṇa* etc., which are superimposed upon *Ātman*, are non-separate from *Ātman* from the standpoint of Reality.

[2] *Reasoning*—That is, the reasoning stated in the fourth verse of this chapter. That which is accepted on the authority of the *Śruti* can also be demonstrated by reasoning.

[3] *Ever-pure etc.*—Even while *Ātman* is imagined by the ignorant as *Prāṇa* etc., it is known to the *Jnānī* (Knower of Truth) as pure and simple and free from all imaginations. For, to the *Jnānī* such imaginations as *Prāṇa* etc., are identical with *Ātman*. For his *Ātman* never undergoes any modifications. He knows 'All that exists is verily *Ātman*'.

[4] *Construes*—A Knower of Reality does not follow any fixed rule for the interpretation of the Vedas. 'A Knower of Reality is never a slave to the Vedas. But whatever interpretation he gives of the Vedas is their real meaning' (Ānandagiri).

[5] *Division*—That is to say, the Knowledge-portion of the Vedas, *viz.*, the Upaniṣad directly leads to the non-dual *Brahman*, whereas the Works-portion (*i.e.*, the *Karma-kāṇḍa*) explains Reality from the causal or relative standpoint and thus indirectly indicates it.

स्वप्नमाये यथा दृष्टे गन्धर्वनगरं यथा ।
तथा विश्वमिदं दृष्टं वेदान्तेषु विचक्षणैः ॥ ३१ ॥

31. *As are dreams and illusions or a castle in the air seen in the sky, so is the universe viewed by the wise in the Vedānta.*

## Śaṅkara's Commentary

The unreality of duality has been demonstrated by reason.[1] The same also can be deduced from the evidence[2] of Vedānta Scriptures. Therefore it is stated: Dream objects and illusion, though unreal when their true nature is considered, are thought, in spite of their unreality, as real by the ignorant. As an imaginary city in the sky, filled with shops full of vendable articles, houses, palaces and villages frequented by men and women, though appearing real to us, is seen to vanish suddenly as dream and illusion, which are known to be unreal (though they appear to be real)—so also is perceived this entire duality of the universe to be unreal. Where is this taught? This is thus taught in the Vedānta Scriptures: 'There is no multiplicity here', '*Indra* (assumed diverse forms) through the powers of *Māyā*', 'In the beginning all this existed as Brahman', 'Fear rises verily from duality', 'That duality does never exist', 'When all this has become *Ātman* then who can see whom and by what?' In these and other passages, the wise men, *i.e.,* those who see the real nature of things, declare (the unreal nature of the universe). The *Smṛti* of Vyāsa also supports this view in these words: 'This duality of the universe, perceived by the wise like a hole seen in darkness in the ground, is unstable like the bubbles that appear in rain-water, always undergoing destruction, ever devoid of bliss, and ceasing to exist, after dissolution.'

[1] *Reason*—It has been demonstrated at the beginning of this chapter that the illusion of duality can be established by reason independent of Scriptures.

[2] *Evidence etc.*—If a conclusion arrived at by reasoning and corroborated by actual experience is further supported by the words of the teacher and the Scriptures, then alone it can be accepted as true.

न निरोधो न चोत्पत्तिर्न बद्धो न च साधकः ।
न मुमुक्षुर्न वै मुक्त इत्येषा परमार्थता ॥ ३२ ॥

32. *There is no dissolution, no birth, none in bondage, none aspiring for wisdom, no seeker of liberation and none liberated. This is the absolute truth.*

### Śaṅkara's Commentary

This verse sums up the meaning of the chapter. When duality is perceived to be illusory and *Ātman* alone is known as the sole Reality, then it is clearly established that all our experiences, ordinary or religious (Vedic), verily pertain to the domain of ignorance. Then one perceives that there is no dissolution *i.e.,* destruction (from the standpoint of Reality): no birth or creation *i.e.,* coming into existence; no one in bondage *i.e.,* no worldly being; no pupilage *i.e.,* no one adopting means for the attainment of liberation; no seeker after liberation, and no one free from bondage (as bondage does not exist). The Ultimate Truth is that the stage of bondage etc., cannot exist in the absence of creation and destruction. How can it be said that there is neither creation nor destruction? It is thus replied: There is no duality (at any time). The absence of duality is indicated by such Scriptural passages as, 'When duality *appears* to exist......', 'One who *appears* to see multiplicity......', 'All this is verily *Ātman*', '*Ātman* is one and without a second', 'All that exists is verily the *Ātman*', etc. Birth[1] or death can be predicated only of that which exists and never of what does not exist, such as the horns of a hare etc. That[2] which is non-dual *(Advaita)* can never be said to be born or destroyed. That it should be non-dual and and at the same time subject to birth and death, is a contradiction in terms. It[3] has already been said that our dual experience characterised by (the activities of) *Prāṇa* etc., is a mere illusion having *Ātman* for its substratum, like the snake imagined in the rope which is its substratum. The imagination characterised by the appearance of the snake in the rope cannot be produced from nor dissolved in the rope[4] (*i.e.*, in any external object), nor is produced from the imaginary snake or dissolved in the mind,[5] nor even in both[6] (*i.e.*, the rope and the mind). Thus[7] duality being non-different from mental (subjective) imagination (cannot have a beginning or an end). For,[8] duality is not perceived when one's mental activities are controlled (as in *Samādhi*) or in deep sleep. Therefore[9] it is established that duality is a mere illusion of the mind. Hence it is well said that the Ultimate Reality is the absence of destruction etc., on account of the non-existence of duality (which exists only in the imagination of the mind).

(Objection)—If this be the case, the object of the teachings should be directed to prove the negation of duality and not to establish as a positive fact non-duality, inasmuch as there is a contradiction (in employing the same means for the refutation of one and the establishment of another). If this were admitted, then the conclusion will tend to become Nihilistic[10] in the absence of evidence for the existence of non-duality as Reality; for, duality has already been said to be non-existent.

(Reply)—This contention is not consistent with reason. Why[11] do you revive a point already established *viz.*, that it is unreasonable to conceive of such illusions as the snake in the rope etc., without a substratum?

(Objection)—This analogy is not relevant as even the rope, which is the substratum of the imaginary snake, is also an imaginary entity.

(Reply)—It is not so. For,[12] upon the disappearance of the imagination, the unimagined substratum can be reasonably said to exist on account of its unimagined character.

(Objection)—It may be contended that like the imagination of the snake in the rope, it (the unimaginary substratum) is also unreal.

(Reply)—It cannot be so. For, it (Brahman) is ever unimagined, because it is like the rope that is never the object of our imagination and is real even before the knowledge of the unreality of the snake. Further,[13] the existence of the subject (knower or witness) of imagination must be admitted to be antecedent to the imagination. Therefore it is unreasonable to say that such subject is non-existent.

(Objection)—How[14] can the Scripture, if it cannot make us understand the true nature of the Self (which is non-duality), free our mind from the idea of duality?

(Reply)—There[15] is no difficulty. Duality is superimposed upon *Ātman* through ignorance, like the snake etc., upon the rope. How is it so? I am happy, I am miserable, ignorant, born, dead, worn out, endowed with body, I see, I am manifested and unmanifested, the agent, the enjoyer, related and unrelated, decayed and old, this is mine—these and such other ideas are superimposed upon *Ātman*. The notion[16] of *Ātman* (Self) persists in all these, because no such idea can ever be conceived of without the notion of *Ātman*. It is like the notion of the rope which persists in (all superimposed ideas, such as) the snake, the water-line, etc. Such being the case, the Scripture has no function with[17] regard to the *Ātman* which, being of the nature of the substantive, is ever self-evident. The function of the Scripture is to accomplish that which is not accomplished yet. It does not serve the purpose of evidence if it is to establish what has been already established. The *Ātman* does not realise its own natural condition on acconnt of such obstacles as the notion of happiness etc., superimposed by ignorance; and the true nature is realised only when one knows it as such. It[18] is therefore the Scripture, whose purpose is to remove the idea of happiness etc., (associated with *Ātman*) that produces the consciousness of the not-happy (*i.e.*, attributeless) nature of *Ātman* by such statements as, 'Not this', 'Not this', '(It is) not gross', etc. Like the persistence of *Ātman* (in all states of consciousness) the not-happy (attributeless) characteristic of *Ātman* does not inhere in all ideas such as of being happy and the like. If it were so, then one would not have such specific experience as that of being happy etc., superimposed upon *Ātman*, in the same manner as coldness cannot be associated with fire whose specific characteristic is that of heat. It is, therefore, that such specific characteristics as that of being happy etc., are imagined in *Ātman* which is, undoubtedly, without any attributes. The Scriptural teachings which speak of *Ātman* as being not-happy etc., are meant for the purpose of removing the notion that *Ātman* is associated with such specific attributes as happiness etc. There is the following aphoristic statement by the knowers of the *Āgama*: 'The validity of Scripture is established by its negating all positive characteristics of *Ātman* (which otherwise cannot be indicated by Scriptures).'

[1] *Birth etc.*—Birth or death can be imagined only in the realm of duality. But from the standpoint of the Ultimate Reality duality is as non-existent as the horns of a hare. Therefore, from the standpoint of Reality birth or death is inconceivable, as neither birth nor death can be imagined of the horns of a hare or the son of a barren woman.

[2] *That etc.*—Birth or death implying an antecedent or subsequent non-existence cannot be conceived of non-dual *Ātman* which is ever-existent. Further, birth or death implying a change cannot be brought about except by another factor which brings about the change. This position is also untenable from the non-dual standpoint. Non-duality being the only Reality, there is neither birth nor death from the standpoint of Truth.

[3] *It etc.*—The dealings in the plane of duality, which is illusory, are also illusory from the standpoint of Truth. Therefore all dealings in the dual realm are mere imaginations like our dealings with the false snake perceived in the rope.

[4] *Rope etc.*—This is the refutation of the realistic contention. The illusion of the mind which perceived the snake in the rope does not exist in the rope. For, such illusion, in that case, would have been experienced by all. When an explanation is sought, from the empirical standpoint, of the illusion of the snake in the rope, it is, no doubt, said that the rope produces the illusion. This explanation may be justified when such illusion is admitted to be a fact. But from the standpoint of the Ultimate Reality, illusion does not exist; hence no birth and disappearance can be predicated of anything non-existent or illusory.

[5] *Mind*—This is the refutation of the contention of the idealists. The illusion of the snake in the rope cannot be produced by the mind. That is because our subjective idea does not correspond to the objects perceived outside. Therefore the illusion cannot be produced by the mind alone. Further, from the standpoint of Truth, mind, associated with its dual functionings (*saṅkalpa* and *vikalpa*) does not exist—as a reality. Being non-existent in itself it cannot produce anything new.

[6] *Both*—This may be taken as the refutation of the Kantian view that our perceptions in the dual world are caused both by mind and

external objects (things-in-themselves). The contention of Kant cannot also be correct, the thing-in-itself being unknown and unknowable and also being beyond the law of causation cannot produce anything. Again, from the non-dual standpoint both mind and the external object (the thing-in-itself) are known to be non-existent. Hence they cannot produce anything new.

[7] *Thus etc.*—Dual perception is totally non-different from subjective imagination which produces the illusion of the snake in the rope. All illusory objects being non-existent from the standpoint of Truth, the duality is also non-existent from the standpoint of the Ultimate Reality.

[8] *For etc.*—It is because in the state of trance or deep sleep, the mind, with its double aspects (of imagination and volition), does not exist. Therefore no duality can be perceived in the absence of the mind.

[9] *Therefore*—It is because duality is perceived when mind functions and it is not perceived when mind does not function. Therefore the existence of duality depends entirely upon the imagination of the perceiving subject.

[10] *Nihilistic*—This is the contention of the Buddhistic Nihilists who, after the negation of duality, find void as the only Reality.

[11] *Why etc.*—An illusion cannot exist without a substratum. The imagination or idea of the snake cannot be perceived without the substratum of the rope. Therefore the illusion of duality must have the non-dual *Ātman* the knower, as its substratum.

[12] *For etc.*—Unless one is aware of the unimagined factor (*Ātman*), one cannot know that this or any object is unreal. We know of a thing as unreal only as distinguished from something which is real. The illustration of the snake and the rope is given only for the purpose of an analogy. No exact analogy can be given with regard to non-duality as it is one without a second. Analogy always belongs to the realm of duality.

[13] *Further*—Without a perceiver, there cannot be any imagination. Even if our analysis of the dualistic world leads to the experience of the void or total negation, as the Buddhists contend, there must be an *experiencer* of this negation. If the mind always seeks the cause of the substratum, the discussion ends in a *regressus*. But even then there is a perceiver of that *regressus* without which the argument of '*regressus ad infinitum* is not possible. Therefore no one can escape the 'Perceiver" (*Dṛk*) which is the *Ātman*.

[14] *How etc.*—Scriptures can be applied only to the sphere of duality. In the absence of duality, Scriptures cannot function. In your opinion duality consisting of birth, death, etc., does not exist. Therefore the Scripture is also an illusion. Hence the Scripture cannot remove duality and lead to the realisation of non-duality or *Ātman*.

[15] *There etc.*—From the standpoint of ignorance, duality certainly exists as we see it. Therefore the Scripture is a means to remove this illusion of duality.

[16] *Notion*—The *Ātman* persists through all our experiences; for at no time is it possible to conceive that *Ātman*, in the form of the perceiver, *(Dṛk)* is absent or non-existent.

[17] *With regard etc.*—The Scripture cannot directly describe the real nature of *Ātman*. It serves no purpose for the knower of the Ultimate Reality.

[18] *It is etc.*—The Scripture serves a negative purpose, *i.e.*, it helps us to remove all attributes, which are the ideations (*vṛttis*) of our mind, generally associated with *Ātman*. By associating *Ātman* with any attribute such as the condition of being happy etc., we make it an object (*viṣaya*). But *Ātman* is the eternal subject—or witness of all ideas.

**भावैरसद्भिरेवायमद्वयेन च कल्पितः ।**
**भावा अप्यद्वयेनैव तस्माद्द्वयता शिवा ॥ ३३ ॥**

33. *This (the* Ātman) *is imagined both as unreal objects that are perceived as the non-duality. The objects* (Bhāvas) *are imagined in the non-duality itself. Therefore, non-duality (alone) is the (highest) bliss.*

## Śaṅkara's Commentary

The reason for the interpretation of the previous verse is thus stated: Just as in a rope, an unreal snake, streak of water or the like is imagined, which are non-separate (non-dual) from the existing rope—the same (rope) being spoken of as this snake, this streak of water, this stick, or the like—even so this *Ātman* is imagined to be the innumerable objects such as *Prāṇa* etc., which are unreal[1] and perceived only through ignorance, but not from the standpoint of the Ultimate Reality. For,[2] unless the mind is active, nobody is ever able to perceive any object. But no action is possible for *Ātman*. Therefore the objects that are perceived to exist by the active mind can never be imagined to have existence from the standpoint of the Ultimate Reality. It is therefore this (non-dual) *Ātman* which alone is imagined as such illusory objects as *Prāna* etc., which are perceived, as well as the[3] non-dual and ultimately real *Ātman* (which is the substratum of illusory ideas, such as *Prāṇa* etc.) in the same manner as the rope is imagined as the substratum of the illusion of the snake. Though[4] always one and unique (*i.e.*, of the nature of the *Ātman*), the *Prāṇa* etc., the entities that are perceived, are imagined (from the standpoint of ignorance) as having the non-dual and ultimately real *Ātman* as their substratum. For, no illusion is ever perceived without a substratum. As 'non-duality' is the substratum of all illusions (from the standpoint of ignorance) and also as it is, in its *real* nature, ever unchangeable, non-duality alone is (the highest) bliss even[5] in the state of imagination, *i.e.*, the empirical experiences. Imaginations alone (which make *Prāṇa* etc., appear as separate from *Ātman*) are the cause of misery.[6] These imaginations cause fear etc., like the imaginations of the snake etc., in the rope. Non-duality[7] is free from fear and therefore it is the (highest) bliss.

[1] *Unreal*—It is because the one characteristic of these perceived forms of objects is their changeability.

[2] *For etc.*—From the standpoint of Ultimate Reality, there is no *Kalpanā*, or ideation which makes the *Bhāvas* or the perceived objects appear as separate from *Brahman*. From that standpoint *Brahman* is always everything and everywhere. This ideation is due to ignorance—an explanation which is given from the empirical standpoint.

[3] *The non-dual etc.*—This non-dual characteristic of the *Ātman* is a correlative of the duality. Hence this conception of non-duality is not free from ignorance. In contrast to the changeable *Bhāvas*, the *Ātman* is imagined as the non-dual entity. Hence they stand and fall together. *Ātman* is beyond all *Kalpanā* or metnal activity. Therefore *Ātman*, from the highest standpoint, cannot be called one, if the term is used as a contrast to the many or duality. Non-duality is a negation of all thoughts of duality,

[4] *Though etc.*—Such entities as *prāṇa* etc., which are perceived to exist, are from the highest standpoint identical with *Ātman*. They are like the dream objects which are found, on waking up, to be identical with the mind. Only from the waking standpoint we know them as illusion; and seeking a cause for such illusion we point out *Ātman* as its substratum.

[5] *Even etc.*—Even when the mind moves in the empirical plane it attains peace when it discovers the unity underlying the variety. Non-duality alone dispels our doubts and makes us happy.

[6] *Misery etc.*—*Kalpanā* or imagination that makes the *Bhāvas*, or the objects that are perceived appear as separated from Brahman, is the cause of fear, as in that state of duality people are assailed with all kinds of fear arising from hatred, jealousy, animosity, etc. When the snake, imagined in the rope, is perceived to be other than the rope, it gives rise to all kinds of fear etc.

[7] *Non-duality etc.*—When the student attains to the state of non-duality, he enjoys real bliss, as in that state there exists nothing of which he can be afraid.

This verse explains the previous one as well as the two other verses in the *Āgama Prakaraṇa* (17 and 18). The highest teaching of Vedānta is that Brahman alone is real. What are known as *Bhāvas* or multiple phenomena are nothing but Brahman. As the snake is identical with the rope from the standpoint of knowledge, or as the dream objects are nothing but the mind, so are the various objects perceived by us nothing but Brahman. When one perceives the snake as other than the rope, he is afraid. This fear is based upon ignorance. Similarly, when one finds the objects as separate from *Ātman* he feels attached to or disgusted with them and suffers accordingly. But the highest bliss is realised when one finds everything as Brahman. From the standpoint of Truth, *Prapañca* or the phenomenal world or even the idea of perceiving them does not exist as separate from Brahman. Therefore no birth or death can be predicated of what exists ultimately. Therefore to a man of the highest wisdom there is nothing to be added to or subtracted from. All is non-dual *Ātman*. Even what appears as unreal *Bhāvas* to the ignorant is non-dual *Ātman* to the *Jñānī*.

नाऽऽत्मभावेन नानेदं न स्वेनापि कथंचन ।
न पृथङ्नापृथक्किंचित् इति तत्त्वविदो विदुः ॥ ३४ ॥

34. *This manifold does not exist as identical with* Ātman *nor does it ever stand independent by itself. It is neither separate from Brahman nor is it non-separate. This is the statement of the wise.*

### Śaṅkara's Commentary

Why is non-duality called the highest bliss? One suffers from misery when one finds differences in the form of multiplicity, *i.e.*, when one finds an object separate from another. For[1] when this manifold of the universe with the entire relative phenomena consisting of *Prāṇa* etc., imagined in the non-dual *Ātman*, the Ultimate Reality is realised to be identical with the *Ātman*, the Supreme Reality, then alone multiplicity ceases to exist, *i.e.*, *Prāṇa* etc., do not appear to be separate from *Ātman*. It[2] is just like the snake that is imagined (to be separate from the rope) but that does no longer remain as such when its true nature is known with the help of a light to be nothing but the rope. This manifold (*Idam*) does never really exist as it appears to be, that is to say, in the forms of *Prāṇa* etc., because[3] it is imaginary just like the snake seen in the place of the rope. Therefore different objects, such as *Prāṇa* etc., do not exist as separate from one other as a buffalo appears to be separate from a horse. The idea of separation being unreal, there is nothing which exists as separate from an object of the same nature or from other objects (of different nature). The Brāhmaṇas, *i.e.*, the Knowers of Self, know this[4] to be the essence of the Ultimate Reality. Therefore the implication on the verse is that non-duality alone, on account of the absence of any cause that may bring about misery, is verily the (highest) bliss.

[1] *For etc.*—Does this insentient manifold exist as one with *Ātman?* This position is untenable as the sentient *Ātman* and insentient universe can never be identical. For, if it be admitted that the manifold is identical with *Ātman* which is one and without a second, then multiplicity cannot exist.

[2] *It is etc.*—The snake, which in the darkness appeared to be separate from the rope, is known with the help of a light, to be the same as the rope. The light does not show that the rope is identical with the snake, as such identity is an impossibility, but it reveals that the only thing that exists is the rope and even that which appeared as the snake in the dark was nothing but the rope. Similarly, *Ātman* alone exists and the phenomenon, which appears through ignorance to be separate from *Ātman,* is also *Ātman* from the standpoint of Truth.

[3] *Because*—It is because the idea of separation is unreal. A pot is known only in relation to a cloth or another object. One cannot totally exclude another. Therefore the objects, that are perceived to exist, are not mutually independent from the standpoint of Truth. It is the non-dual *Ātman* alone which appears as multiple objects, having relations, through ignorance.

[4] *This*—*i.e.,* duality or multiplicity does never exist, as it cannot be demonstrated.

वीतरागभयक्रोधैर्मुनिभिर्वेदपारगैः ।
निर्विकल्पो ह्ययं दृष्टः प्रपञ्चोपशमोऽद्वयः ॥ ३५ ॥

35. *By the wise, who are free from attachment, fear and anger and who are well versed in the meaning of the Vedas, this (Ātman) has been verily realised as totally devoid of all imaginations (such as those of* Prāṇa *etc.), free from the illusion of the manifold, and non-dual.*

## Śaṅkara's Commentary

The perfect knowledge as described above, is thus extolled.[1] The sages who are always[2] free from all blemishes such as attachment, fear, spite, anger, etc., who are given to contemplation, who can discriminate between the real and the unreal and who can grasp the essence of the meaning of the Vedas, *i.e.*, who are well versed in the Vedānta (*i.e.*, the Upaniṣads) do[3] realise the real nature of this *Ātman* which is free from all imaginations and also free from this the illusion of the manifold. This *Ātman* is the total negation of the phenomena of duality and therefore it is non-dual. The intention of the *Śruti* passage is this: The Supreme Self can be realised only by the Saṁnyāsins (men of renunciation) who are free from all blemishes who are enlightened regarding the essence of the Upaniṣads and never other, *i.e.*, those vain logicians whose mind is clouded by passion etc., and who find truth only[4] in their own creeds and opinions.

[1] *Extolled*—The purpose of this praise is to attract the attention of the pupils towards the realisation of Truth.

[2] *Always*—The student fails to realise Truth if his mind is, at any moment, clouded by passion etc. It is therefore laid in the Vedānta that a student, before aspiring to realise Truth, must be well established in the fourfold pre-requisites, such as, discrimination between the real and the unreal, renunciation of the unreal, total self-control and a strong hankering after realisation.

[3] *Do realise*—This is to refer to the contention of the agnostics that Reality is ever unknown and unknowable. Reality can certainly be known and realised if the student has got the necessary equipments for such realisation.

[4] *Only etc.*—It is only the ignorant person who says that his vision of Reality is alone true. But to a wise man everything is Brahman. To him anything that may be called non-Brahman is ever non-existent.

तस्मादेवं विदित्वैनं अद्वैते योजयेत्स्मृतिम् ।
अद्वैतं समनुप्राप्य जडवल्लोकमाचरेत् ॥ ३६ ॥

36. *Therefore knowing the* Ātman *to be such, fix your attention on non-duality. Having realised non-duality behave in the world like on insensible object.*

## Śaṅkara's Commentary

As non-duality, on account of its being the negation of all evils, is bliss and fearlessness, therefore knowing it to be such, direct your mind to the realisation of the non-dual *Ātman*. In other words, concentrate your memory on the realisation of non-duality alone. Having known this non-dual Brahman which is free from hunger etc., unborn and directly perceptible as the Self and which transcends all codes[1] of human conduct, *i.e.*, by attaining to the consciousness that 'I am the Supreme Brahman', behave with others as one not knowing the Truth; that is to say, let[2] not others know what you are and what you have become.

[1] *Codes etc.*—It is because the non-dual Brahman is beyond the duality of the manifested manifold.

[2] *Let not etc.*—A wise man does not broadcast his realisation before the world. The sentence may mean that a wise man, on account of his being established in the non-dual *Ātman,* does not see others as separate from him; and therefore he does not assume *consciously* the role of a Knower *(Jñānī).*

निस्तुतिर्निर्नमस्कारो निःस्वधाकार एव च ।
चलाचलनिकेतश्च यतिर्यादृच्छिको भवेत् ॥ ३७ ॥

37. *The man of self-restraint should be above all praise, salutation and all rites prescribed by the Smṛti in connection with the departed ancestors. He should have this body and the* Ātman *as his support and depend upon chances,* i.e., *he should be satisfied with those things for his physical wants, that chance brings to him.*

ŚAṄKARA'S COMMENTARY

What should be his code of conduct in the world? It is thus stated: He[1] should give up all such formalities as praise, salutation, etc., and be free[2] from all desires for external objects. In other words, he should take up the life of a *Paramahaṁsa Saṁnyāsin*.[3] The *Śruti* also supports this view in such passages as, 'Knowing this *Ātman*....' etc. This is further approved in such *Smṛti* passages as, 'With their consciousness in That (Brahman), their self being That, intent on That, with That for their Supreme Goal....' (*Gītā*) etc. The word '*calam*' in the text signifying 'changing' indicates the 'body' because it changes every moment. The word '*Acalam*' signifying 'unchanging' indicates the 'Knowledge of Self'. He[4] has the (changing) body for his support when he, for the purpose of such activities as eating etc., forgets the Knowledge of the Self, the (real) support of *Ātman*, unchanging like the *Ākāśa*, (ether) and relates himself to egoism. Such[5] a wise man never takes shelter under external objects. He entirely depends upon circumstances, that is to say, he maintains his body with whatever food or strips of cloth, etc., are brought to him by[6] mere chance.

[1] *He etc.*—No wise man recites any hymn to the deities or bows down before them, as he has no desires which can be fulfilled by their favour or grace. The word *Svadhā* in the text refers to the ceremonies known as *Śrāddha*, a rite performed for the propitiation of the departed ancestors. Every offering in that ceremony is accompanied by the utterance of that word. The sense is that the wise man renounces even those actions connected with the dead which are obligatory for all people of the three higher castes. This is because the man of Knowledge, on account of the realisation of the non-dual *Ātman*, does not find anything separate or different from his own self.

[2] *Free etc.*—It is because such objects do not exist for a knower of Truth.

[3] *Paramahaṁsa Saṁnyāsin*—Such a man belongs to the highest

order of monks and moves in the world like other men ; only he does not declare that he is a Knower of the Highest Reality.

[4] *He etc.*—A wise man, in this text, is said to have both body and self for his abode. The meaning is this : When he mediates on the *Ātman*, detaching his mind from all external desires, then he is said to have the *Ātman* for his support and abode. But when his mind comes down to the consciousness of the body on account of his feeling the necessity for food etc., he is said to have his body for his support and abode.

[5] *Such etc.*—The wise man, described in this verse, never takes the 'external objects as real' like the ignorant persons. But the word '*yati*' (man of self-control) does not signify the man of the highest realisation, as it is not all possible for the latter to *forget* at any time the Knowledge of Brahman. This verse refers to the student aspiring after the Highest Knowledge. The next verse indicates the condition of a *Jñānī*.

[6] *By mere etc.*—That is to say, such a man does not make any conscious effort to procure his food or clothing.

तत्त्वमाध्यात्मिकं दृष्ट्वा तत्त्वं दृष्ट्वा तु बाह्यतः ।
तत्त्वीभूतस्तदारामः तत्त्वादप्रच्युतो भवेत् ॥ ३८ ॥

38. *Having known the truth regarding what exists internally* (i.e., *within the body*) *as well as the truth regarding what exists externally* (i.e., *the earth etc.*) *he becomes one with Reality, derives his pleasure from It and never deviates from the Real.*

### Śaṅkara's Commentary

The truth[1] regarding external objects such as the earth etc., and the truth regarding internal objects characterised by body etc., is that these are as unreal as a snake seen in the rope, or objects seen in dream or magic. For, there are such *Śruti* passages as, 'Modification being only a name, arising from speech', etc. The *Śruti* further declares, '*Ātman* is both within and without, birthless, causeless, having no within or without, entire, all-pervading like the *Ākāśa* (ether), subtle, unchanging, without attributes and parts, and without action. That is Truth, That is *Ātman* and That thou art'. Knowing it to be such from the point of view of Truth, he becomes one with Truth and derives his enjoyment[2] from Truth and not from any external[3] object. But a person[4] ignorant of Truth, takes the mind to be the Self and believes the *Ātman* to be active like the mind, and becomes active. He thus thinks his self to be identified with the body etc., and deviated from *Ātman* saying, 'Oh, I am now fallen from the Knowledge of Self'. When his mind is concentrated he sometimes thinks that he is happy and one with the Self. He declares, 'Oh, I am now one with the essence of Truth'. But,[5] the knower of Self never makes any such statement, as *Ātman* is ever one changeless and as it is impossible for *Ātman* to deviate from its own nature. The[6] consciousness that 'I am Brahman' never leaves him. In other words, he never loses the conciousness regarding the essence of the Self. The *Smṛti* supports this view in such passages as, 'The wise man views equally a dog or an outcaste', 'He sees who sees the Supreme Lord remaining the same, in all beings' (*Gītā*).

[1] *Truth etc.*—Body, mind, etc., and the earth, the sun, etc., when looked upon as separate from the self, are as illusory as the snake seen in the rope etc. But every unreal superimposition, from the standpoint of Truth, is identical with the substratum as dream objects are one with the mind and the snake is one with the rope.

[2] *Enjoyment*—There being no existing entity other than *Ātman*, this thought makes a man happy.

[3] *External objects*—It is because no objects external or separate from him exist.

[4] *Some person etc.*—This is the case with those *yogis* or mystics who think that the *Ātman* can be realised only by withdrawing the mind from external objects and concentrating it on something within.

[5] *But etc.*—It is because even when the mind is active and creating ideas, the man of realisation knows it to be the *Ātman*. If one sees multiplicity, this multiplicity is nothing really existent which can make

the non-dual *Ātman* become dual. The *act* of becoming, creation or manifestation is an illusion. The rope never becomes the snake.

[6] *The consciousness*—Even when a *Jñānī* eats or drinks or does any other act he only sees the non-dual Brahman. He never deviates from the real. His condition has thus been described in the *Gītā*: 'Brahman is the offering, Brahman the oblation, by Brahman is the oblation poured into the fire of Brahman; Brahman verily shall be reached by him who always sees Brahman in action.' The state of a student has been described in the previous verse. A student, when urged by hunger and thirst, thinks himself as something different from Reality. A mystic or a *yogi* thinks that he can realise Truth only by withdrawing his mind from the external objects. But a man of the highest realisation, who knows that he is the Supreme Reality, never loses that consciousness and even in the midst of the world keeps intact the Knowledge of his identity with the non-dual Brahman.

Here ends the Gauḍapāda *Kārikā* on Illusion and Śaṅkara's Commentary on the Chapter.

**Aum Salutation to Brahman**

CHAPTER III

# ON ADVAITA

ॐ

उपासनाश्रितो धर्मो जाते ब्रह्मणि वर्तते ।
प्रागुत्पत्तेरजं सर्वं तेनासौ कृपणः स्मृतः ॥ १ ॥

1. *The* Jīva *betaking itself to devotion* (upāsanā) *thinks itself to be related to the Brahman that is supposed to have manifested Himself. He is said to be of narrow intellect because he thinks that before creation all was of the nature of the unborn (Reality).*

Śaṅkara's Commentary

While determining the meaning of *Aum*, it has been stated in the form of a proposition that '*Ātman* is the negation of phenomena, blissful and non-dual'. It has been further stated that 'Duality does not exist when the reality is known'. Further, in the chapter on Illusion, that duality does not exist really has been established by the illustrations of dream, magic, castle-in-the-air, etc., and also by reasoning on the grounds of '*the capability of being seen*' and '*the being finite*', etc. Now it is asked whether non-duality can be established only by scriptural evidence or whether it can be proved by reasoning as well. It is said in reply that it is possible to establish non-duality by reasoning[1] as well. How is it possible? This is shown in this chapter on *Advaita*. It has been demonstrated in the last chapter that the entire realm of dualism including the object and the act of devotion is illusory,[2] and the attributeless, non-dual *Ātman* alone is the Reality. The word '*upāsanāśritaḥ*' in the text, meaning the one[3] betaking himself to devotion, signifies him who has recourse to devotional exercises as means to the attainment of liberation and who further thinks that he is the devotee and Brahman is his object of worship. This *Jīva* or the embodied being further thinks that through devotional practices he, at present related to the evolved[4] Brahman (Personal God), would attain to the ultimate Brahman after the dissolution of the body. Prior[5] to the manifestation, according to this *Jīva*, everything including itself, was unborn. In other words he thinks, 'I shall, through devotional practices, regain that which was my real nature before manifestation, though at present I subsist in the Brahman that appears in the form of the manifold'. Such a *Jīva*, that is the aspirant, betaking itself to devotion, inasmuch as it knows only a partial aspect of Brahman, is called of narrow[6] or poor intellect by those who regard Brahman as eternal[7] and unchanging. The *Upaniṣad* of the *Talavakāra* (Kena) supports this view in such statements as, 'That which is not expressed (indicated) by speech and by which speech is expressed, That alone know as Brahman and not that which people here adore' etc.

[1] *Reasoning*—The truth arrived at by reasoning may be corroborated by one's own experience and further supported by the *Śruti*.

[2] *Illusory*—It is because these belong to the realm of duality.

[3] *One etc.*—One who does not know the eternal and unchanging nature of the Self, thinks of himself as separate or different from his real nature and has recourse to various spiritual practices in order to regain his Brāhmic nature, which he thinks he does, after death. Compare the Christian view of the 'Fall of man'. These views are given in the Hindu scriptures also but refuted at the end from the standpoint of Truth. which is that even when a man thinks himself to

be ignorant and tries to attain Knowledge by means of spiritual practices, he *is* Brahman. The nature of the non-dual Brahman never undergoes any change or transformation. There is no act of creation.

[4] *Evolved Brahman*—The *Jīva* in his state of imaginary 'fall' worships a Personal God or a Cosmic Soul. He cannot think of the non-dual Self; but he imagines the *Saguṇa Brahman* to be Reality.

[5] *Prior*—This ignorant *Jīva* thinks that only after death he will realise his eternal Brāhmic nature, which was his real nature before he came into dual existence.

[6] *Narrow*—It is because an ignorant person has no idea of the changeless non-dual Self. For, according to his view the *non-dual* Self is also limited by time and change which characterise the dual universe.

[7] *Eternal etc.*—According to the Knower of Truth, Brahman never undergoes any manifestation. The phenomena of birth and death are mere illusion.

अतो वक्ष्याम्यकार्पण्यमजाति समतां गतम् ।
यथा न जायते किंचित् जायमानं समन्ततः ॥ २ ॥

2. *Therefore I shall now describe that (Brahman) which is free from limitations, unborn and which is the same throughout; and from this, one understands that it is not (in reality) born though it appears to be manifested everywhere.*

## Śaṅkara's Commentary

One unable to realise *Ātman*, which is both within and without and birthless, and therefore believing oneself to be helpless through *Avidyā*, thinks, 'I am born, I subsist in the Brahman with attributes (*saguṇa*) and through devotion to It I shall become Brahman', and thus becomes *Kripaṇa* (narrow-minded). Therefore, I shall describe Brahman which has never been subject to any limitation and which is birthless (changeless). The narrowness of mind has been described in such *Śruti* passages as, 'When one sees another, hears another, knows another, then there is limitedness (littleness), mortality and unreality', 'Modification is only a name arising from speech, but the truth is that all is clay', etc. But contrary to it is Brahman known as *Bhūmā* (great) which is both within and without and which is free from all limitations. I shall now describe that Brahman, free from all limitations, by realising which one gets rid of all narrowness superimposed by ignorance. It (Brahman) is called *Ajāti*, birthless, inasmuch as none knows its birth or cause. It is the same always and everywhere. How is it so? It is so because there does not exist in it (Brahman) any inequality caused by the presence of parts or limbs. For, only that which is with parts may be said to be born (or to have taken new form) by a change of its parts. But as *Ātman* is without parts, it is always the same and even, that is to say, it does not manifest itself in any new form through a change of the parts. Therefore it is without birth and free from limitation. Now listen as to how[1] Brahman is not born, how it does not undergo change by so much as a jot, but ever remains unborn, though it appears, through ignorance, to be born and to give birth to others, like the rope[2] and the snake.

[1] *How etc.*—Brahman (*Ātman*) is always non-dual even during the perception of duality by the ignorant. Non-duality is the Reality and duality is illusion.

[2] *Rope*—The truth is that the rope does not become or produce the snake. It is only through ignorance that one sees the snake in the rope. Similarly Brahman which is birthless, causeless, changeless and attributeless is imagined by the ignorant as producing or becoming the universe.

आत्मा ह्याकाशवज्जीवैर्घटाकाशैरिवोदितः ।
घटादिवच्च संघातैर्जातावेतन्निदर्शनम् ॥ ३ ॥

3. Ātman *may be said to be similar to* Ākāśa (*ether*) *manifested in the forms of the* Jīvas (*embodied selves*) *which may be compared to the ether enclosed in pots. Again, as pots etc.,*

*are said to be produced from the* Ākāśa (*ether*), *similarly* (*gross*) *bodies are said to be evolved from the* Ātman. *This is the illustration of the manifestation* (*from Brahman, if any*).

## Śaṅkara's Commentary

It has been said in the previous text, 'I shall now describe Brahman, birthless and free from all narrowness'. Now I shall give an illustration and a reason to substantiate the proposition. As the Supreme *Ātman* is like the *Ākāśa*, subtle, without parts and all-pervasive, it is compared to the *Ākaśa*. The Supreme Self again, who is likened to the *Ākaśa*, is said to be manifested as the embodied beings (*Jīvas*) or *Kṣetrajñas* (Knowers of bodies), and are likened to the *Ghaṭākāśas* or the *Ākāśa* enclosed in jars. This is the Supreme Self which is like the *Ākāśa*. Or the sentence may be explained thus: As the totality of the *Ākāśa* enclosed within the pots is said to constitute what is known as the *Mahākāśa* or the great expanse of ether, similarly the totality of the embodied beings (*Jīvas*) constitutes the Supreme Being. The creation or manifestation of the *Jīvas* (embodied beings) from the Supreme Self, as stated in the Vedānta, is like the creation or manifestation of the *Ghaṭākāśa* (*i.e.*, the ether enclosed in a jar) from the *Mahākāśa* (or the great and undifferentiated ether). That is to say, creation or manifestation is not[1] real. As[2] from that *Ākāśa* are produced such physical objects as the pot etc., similarly from the Supreme Self which is like the *Ākāśa*, are produced the entire aggregate of material entities, such as the earth etc., as well as the individual bodies, all[3] characterised by causality, the entire[4] production being nothing but mere imagination like that of the snake in the rope. Therefore it is said, 'The aggregates (of the gross bodies) are produced like the pot' etc. When[5] the *Śruti*, with a view to the enlightenment of the ignorant, speaks of the creation or manifestation (of the *Jīvas*) from the *Ātman*, then such manifestation, being admitted as a fact, is explained with the help of the illustration of the creation of the pot etc., from the *Ākāśa*.

[1] *Not real*—As the *Ākāśa* does not really create the *Ākāśa* enclosed within the pot etc., but appears as enclosed on account of the association of the *upādhis* of the pot etc., similarly the Supreme Self does not manifest or create any *Jīva* but appears as *Jīva* on account of its association with the *upādhis* of ignorance *(Avidyā)*. This is an explanation of creation from the empirical standpoint when such creation is admitted as a fact. But from the standpoint of Reality there is no creation.

[2] *As etc.*—The pot etc., cannot be produced without space. They exist in space. Similarly no physical body can exist without the substratum of *Ātman*. Therefore, *Ātman* is said to have created the physical bodies.

[3] *All etc.*—All phenomenal objects are characterised by the law of cause and effect.

[4] *Entire etc.*—*Vedānta* accepts both the theories of *Vivarta* and *Pariṇāma* as explanation of the phenomenal universe. Brahman is imagined to manifest himself as the universe through *Māyā*, and then the universe follows the law of causation.

[5] *When etc.*—Creation through *Māyā* is only an explanation of the universe when one takes it to be real. It is not truth. *Māyā* is only a statement of fact, an explanation of the world we perceive in a state of ignorance. From the standpoint of Reality neither the universe nor *Māyā* exists. Brahman alone exists.

घटादिषु प्रलीनेषु घटाकाशादयो यथा ।
आकाशे संप्रलीयन्ते तद्वज्जीवा इहाऽऽत्मनि ॥ ४ ॥

4. *As on the destruction of the pot etc., the ether enclosed in the pot etc., merges in the* Ākāśa *(the great expanse of ether), similarly the* Jīvas *merge in the* Ātman.

ŚAṄKARA'S COMMENTARY

As the creation of ether enclosed within the pot etc., follows the creation of the pot etc., and as the merging of the same ether (in the *Mahākāśa*) is consequent on the destruction of the pot etc.; in the same manner the creation or manifestation of the *Jīva* follows that of the aggregate of the body etc., and the merging of the *Jīva* in the Supreme Self follows in the wake of the destruction of the aggregate of the body etc. The meaning is that neither the creation nor destruction is in itself real (from the standpoint of the Absolute).

Both the creation and destruction of the universe, and consequently its existence, are due to ignorance. In truth, there is neither creation, nor existence nor destruction. Destruction is impossible in the absence of creation. Therefore, the *Śruti* passages describing the process of creation and destruction do not antagonise the reality of the non-dual *Ātman*, as such fact is admitted by the *Advaitin* to be possible in the realm of ignorance.

यथैकस्मिन्घटाकाशे रजोधूमादिभिर्युते ।
न सर्वे संप्रयुज्यन्ते तद्वज्जीवाः सुखादिभिः ॥ ५ ॥

5. *As any portion of* Ākāśa *enclosed in a pot being soiled by dust, smoke, etc., all such other portions of* Ākāśa *enclosed in other pots are not soiled, so is the happiness etc., of the* Jīvas, *i.e., the happiness, misery, etc., of one* Jīva *do not affect other* Jīvas.

ŚAṄKARA'S COMMENTARY

The dualists contend that if one *Ātman* exists in all bodies then the birth, death, happiness, etc., of one *Ātman* (as *Jīva*) must affect all and, further, there[1] must follow a confusion regarding the results of the action (done by individuals). This contention is thus refuted: As[2] the *Ākāśa* enclosed within one jar being soiled by dust, smoke, etc., does not make the *Ākāśa* enclosed in other jars soiled with the dust and the smoke, so all created beings are not affected by the happiness etc. (of one *Jīva*)

(Objection)[3]—Is it not your contention that there is only one *Ātman*?

(Reply)—Yes, we admit it. Have you not heard that there is only one *Ātman* like the all-pervading space, in all bodies?

(Objection)—If[4] there be only one *Ātman* then it must always and everywhere feel misery and happiness.

(Reply) — This objection cannot be raised by the *Sāṁkhyas*. For,[5] the *Sāṁkhyas* do not admit that misery, happiness, etc., ever cling to the *Ātman*; for they assert that happiness, misery, etc., belong inseparably to *Buddhi*.[6] Further, there is no evidence for imagining multiplicity of *Ātman* which is of the very nature of knowledge.

(Objection)—In the absence of the multiplicity of *Ātman* the theory that the *Pradhāna* or *Prakṛti* acts for the sake of others[7] does not hold good.

(Reply)—No, this argument is not valid; for whatever the *Pradhāna* or *Prakṛti* may be supposed to accomplish by itself for another cannot inseparably inhere in *Ātman*. If bondage[8] and liberation accomplished by the *Pradhāna inseparably* inhered in the multiple *Puruṣas*, then the theory that the *Pradhāna* (*Prakṛti*) always acts for the sake of others would not be consistent with the unity of *Ātman* existing everywhere. And the theory of the *Sāṁkhyas* regarding the multiplicity of *Ātman* would be reasonable. But the *Sāṁkhyas* do not admit that the purpose of bondage or liberation can ever be inseparably associated with the *Puruṣa*. For, they admit that the *Puruṣas* are attributeless and are centres of Pure Consciousness. Therefore,[9] the very existence of the *Puruṣa* is their support for the theory that the action of *Pradhāna is* directed to serve the purpose of others (the *Puruṣas*). But the supposition of the multiplicity of *Puruṣas* need not be made for this purpose. Therefore the theory of the *Pradhāna* seeking to serve the purpose of others cannot be an argument for the supposition of the multiplicity of *Ātman*. The *Sāṁkhyas* have no other argument in support of their supposition regarding the multiplicity of *Ātman*. The *Pradhāna* takes upon itself bondage and liberation only through the instrumentality[10] of the *existence* of the other (the *Puruṣa*). The *Puruṣa* which is of the very nature of knowledge, is the cause of the activity of the *Pradhāna* by the fact of its very *existence* and not on account of its any specific[11] qualities. So it is through ignorance alone that people imagine the *Puruṣa* (*Ātman*) to be many and also thereby give up the real[12] import of the Vedas.

The *Vaiśeṣikas*[13] and others assert that attributes such as desire etc., are inseparably related to *Ātman*. This[14] view is also not correct. For, the *Saṁskāras* (the impressions) which are the cause of memory cannot have any inseparable relation with *Ātman* which has no[15] parts. Further, if[16] it be contended that the origin of memory lies in the contact of *Ātman* with the mind, we say that this contention is not valid ; for, in that case there will no principle regarding memory. Memory of all things will come simultaneously. Besides[17] mind can never be related to the *Ātman* which is devoid of all sensations such as touch etc., and which belongs to a class other than that of the mind. Further the *Vaiśeṣikas* do not admit that the attributes (*Guṇa*) such as forms (*Rūpas*) etc., action (*Karma*), generality (*Sāmānya*), particularity (*Viśeṣa*) and inherence (*Samavāya*), can exist independently of the substance (*Dravya*). If these are totally independent of one another, the contact between the *Ātman* and desire etc., and also between the attributes (*Guṇa*) and the substance (*Dravya*) will be an absurdity.

(Objection)—The contact characterised by an inseparable inherence is possible in the case of entities where such relation is proved to be *innate*.

(Reply)—This[18] objection is not valid; for such *innate* relationship cannot be reasonable, as the *Ātman*, the ever permanent, is antecedent to the desires etc., which are transitory. And if desires etc., be admitted to have inseparable innate relationship with *Ātman*, then[19] the former would be as permanent as such innate attributes of *Ātman* as greatness etc. That is not desirable, for then there would be no room for liberation of the *Ātman*. Further, if inseparable relationship (*Samavāya*) were something separate from the substance, then another factor must be stated which can bring about the relationship between *Samavāya* and the substance—as in the case of the substance and the attributes. Nor can it be stated that *Samavāya* is a constant inseparable relationship with *Ātman*; for, in that case, the *Ātman* and *Samavāya* on account of their constant and inseparable relationship can never be different from one another. If, on the other hand, the relationship of *Samavāya* be totally different from the *Ātman* , and the attributes also be different from the substance, then the possessive case cannot be used to indicate their mutual relation which is possible only when the two terms connected by the possessive are not totally different. If *Ātman* be inseparably connected with such categories as desires etc., which have both 'beginning' and 'end', then it would itself be impermanent. If *Ātman* be considered to have parts and undergo changes, like the body etc., then, these two defects always associated with the body etc., would be inevitable in the case of the *Ātman*. (Therefore the conclusion is that) as the *Ākāśa* (ether), on account of the superimposition of ignorance (*Avidyā*), is regarded as soiled by dust and smoke, in like manner, the *Ātman* also, on account of the limiting condition of the mind caused by the erroneous attribution of *Avidyā*, appears to be associated with the contamination of misery, happiness, etc. And such being the case, the idea of bondage and liberation, being empirical in nature, does not contradict (the permanent nature of *Ātman* from the standpoint of Truth). For, all the disputants admit the relative experience to be caused by *Avidyā* and deny its existence from the standpoint of the Supreme Reality. Hence it follows that the supposition of the multiplicity of *Ātman* made by the logicians is without basis and superfluous.

[1] *There*—In the case of the unity of *Ātman*, the action of one individual must affect others who are not responsible for the action. Then there cannot be any possible relation between action and the results of actions. The law of causality becomes futile.

[2] *As*—The reply is that birth, death, misery, happiness, etc., are admitted to be facts experienced in the practical world. There the multiplicity of *Ātman* is also admitted. But this multiplicity of *Ātman* is due to the limitation of the (*upādhi*) of the mind caused by *Avidyā* (ignorance), which does not exist in the Supreme Reality.

[3] *Objection*—This objection is supposed to be raised by the adherents of the *Sāṁkhya* philosophy.

[4] *If etc.*—The contention of the *Sāṁkhya* philosopher is that in case the unity of *Ātman* is upheld, one must always feel miserable or happy as the result of the good and the bad actions of others must affect him.

[5] *For etc.*—According to the *Sāṁkhya* theory, the *Ātman* or the *Puruṣa* is without parts and attributes and is of the very nature of consciousness. *Prakṛti* or *Pradhāna* is insentient, dull, and endowed with the qualities of misery, happiness, etc. All the activities of *Prakṛti* are directed to serve the purpose of the conscious *Puruṣa*. *Prakṛti*, being insentient, cannot enjoy the result of her own work. According to the *Sāṁkhya* theory, *Prakṛti* is one, but the *Puruṣas* are as numerous as there are bodies. Each *Puruṣa* by coming in contact with *Prakṛti* catches the reflection of misery or happiness, which are the characteristics of the latter (*Prakṛti*) and thinks itself as happy or miserable.

[6] *Buddhi*—According to the *Sāṁkhya* philosophy there are twenty-five categories. *Buddhi* is first evolved as the result of the contact of

*Prakṛti* with *Puruṣa*. The three qualities of *Sattva*, *Rajas* and *Tamas* which give rise to misery, happiness, etc., lie in an undifferentiated state in *Prakṛti*. But when *Prakṛti* evolves into *Buddhi*, these qualities become differentiated. Hence, misery, happiness, etc., have been stated as inseparably related to *Buddhi*.

7 *Others*—*i.e.*, the *Puruṣas*. See note *Ante 5*.

8 *Bondage etc.*—According to the *Sāṁkhya* philosophy the contact of *Prakṛti* with *Puruṣa* causes the latter to fall into bondage. But as soon as *Puruṣa* realises his independence, he is liberated. Therefore according to the *Sāṁkhyas*, *Prakṛti* is the cause of bondage and liberation and the *Puruṣa*, in itself, is of the very nature of knowledge. All the activities of *Prakṛti*, which are otherwise meaningless, are directed to make the *Puruṣa* realise his real nature.

9 *Therefore etc.*—According to *Vedānta*, the ideas of both bondage and liberation belong to the world of relativity. It is due to ignorance. From the standpoint of Truth, there is neither bondage nor liberation; for the *Ātman* is always free.

10 *Instrumentality etc.*—*Vedānta* does not disagree with this position. According to it, the fact of the multiplicity of relative phenomena is explained by the presence of the non-dual *Ātman*. Every illusion has its substratum.

11 *Specific qualities*—This is the view of *Patañjali*. According to his system, known as the philosophy of *Yoga*, there is an *Īśvara* or Personal God, possessed of attributes, who is the cause of the created universe.

12 *Real import etc.*—*i.e.*, the non-dual *Ātman* is the only Reality.

13 *Vaiśeṣikas*—The followers of the *Vaiśeṣika* philosophy hold that there are six categories, *viz.*, *Dravya* (substance), *Guṇa* (quality), *Karma* (activity), *Sāmānya* (generality), *Viśeṣa* (particularity), and *Samavāya* (inherence). All these categories exist independently of one another. The *Dravya* of substance (*Ātman*) has nine special attributes, *viz.*, *Buddhi* (intellect), *Sukha* (happiness), *Duḥkha* (misery), *Icchā* (desire), *Dveṣa* (aversion), *Prayatna* (effort), *Dharma* (merit), *Adharma* (demerit) and *Saṁskāra* (impression).

14 *This etc.*—If desire etc., are inseparably connected with *Ātman*, then desire, misery, happiness, etc., of one being would imply those of another.

[15] *No parts*—If it be contended that desire etc., inhere in one part of the *Ātman* then the reply is that *Ātman* unlike the pot etc., has no parts.

[16] *If etc.*—The opponent contends that the origin of memory is to be found in the contact of the mind with *Ātman*. But this argument is not valid. For, *Ātman* is ever present. In that case the mere effort of the mind to remember anything should bring its memory. But this does not happen. In spite of all our efforts we often fail to bring back the memory of many past events. Further, *Ātman* is indivisible and without parts. Therefore any impression that arises in the *Ātman* cannot be confined to any particular part of the *Ātman*. If such be the case, then all beings should remember a thing at the same time. Still another difficulty of this theory is that, *Ātman* being without parts, one should remember all things at one and the same time. Hence no rule exists regarding memory.

[17] *Besides etc.*—Contact is possible between two things of the same species.

[18] *This objection etc.*—Śaṅkara criticises this view of the relation between substance and quality. If the two are inseparably related, the inseparability must refer to space, time or nature. The two are not inseparable in space, since we see the redness of a red lotus disappearing. If inseparability in time is the essence of the *Samavāya* relation, then the right and the left horns of a cow would be related in that way. If it be inseparability in nature or character, then it would be impossible to make any further distinction between substance and quality, since the two are one.

[19] *Then etc.*—But we know that desires etc., are impermanent.

रूपकार्यसमाख्याश्च भिद्यन्ते तत्र तत्र वै ।
आकाशस्य न भेदोऽस्ति तद्वज्जीवेषु निर्णयः ॥ ६ ॥

6. *Though form, function and name are different here and there yet this does not imply any difference in the* Ākāśa (*which is one*). *The same is the conclusion* (*truth*) *with regard to the* Jīvas.

ŚAṄKARA'S COMMENTARY

(Objection)—If[1] *Ātman* be one then how is it possible to justify the variety of experiences pointing to the multiplicity of *Ātman* (which is explained as being) due to *Avidyā* (ignorance)?

(Reply)—This is thus explained: In our common experience with regard to this *Ākāśa* (which is really one), we find variety of forms, such as large, small, etc., in respect of the *Ākāśa* enclosed in a pot, a water-bowl and a cover. Similarly there are various functions (of the same *Ākāśa*) such as fetching water, preserving water and sleeping. Lastly there are various names as the ether enclosed in a jar (*ghata*), the ether enclosed in a water-bowl (*karaka*), etc., caused by different *upādhis*. All these different forms, functions and names are matters of common experience. This variety of experience caused by different forms etc., is not true from the standpoint of the ultimate Reality. For, in reality *Ākāśa* never admits of any variety. Our empirical activities based upon the difference in *Ākāśa* are not possible without the instrumentality of an adventitious *upādhi*.[2] As in this illustration, the *Jīvas* (embodied beings) which may be compared to the *Ākāśa* enclosed in a jar, are regarded as different, this difference[3] being caused by the *upādhis*. This is the conclusion of the wise.

This text gives one of the explanations of the empirical world as stated by the wise.

[1] *If etc.*—The contention of the opponent is this: The variety of names, forms and functions is an indubitable experience of the relative world. This can be explained only if we admit the multiplicity of *Ātman*. Therefore there are infinite number of *Ātmans*, each having a different name and form and each performing a different function. The unity of *Ātman* cannot explain this variety.

[2] *Upādhi*—*i.e.*, The form of a pot, water-bowl, etc.

[3] *Difference*—The apparent difference in our empirical experience is caused by *upādhis* which are unreal. These *upādhis* are unreal on account of their changeable and negatable nature. Therefore from the standpoint of Reality, *Ātman*, like the *Ākāśa*, is only one and without a second.

This explanation that this apparent difference of the empirical experience is caused by *Avidyā* is given from the relative standpoint when such difference is admitted as a fact. But from the standpoint of the ultimate Reality, the difference does not exist.

नाऽऽकाशस्य घटाकाशो विकारावयवौ यथा ।
नैवाऽऽत्मनः सदा जीवो विकारावयवौ तथा ॥ ७ ॥

7. *As the* Ghaṭākāśa (*i.e., the ether portioned off by the pot*) *is neither the* (*evolved*) *effect nor part of the* Ākāśa (*ether*), *so is the* Jīva (*the embodied being*) *neither the effect nor part of the* Ātman.

### Śaṅkara's Commentary

(Objection)—Our experience of the variety of forms, functions, etc., associated with the ether enclosed in the pot etc., is true from the standpoint of the ultimate Reality (and not illusory, as you say).

(Reply)—No, this[1] cannot be so. For, the ether enclosed in the pot cannot be the evolved effect of the real ether in the same way as the ornament[2] etc., are the effect of gold or the foam, bubble, moisture, etc., are the effect of water. Nor, again is the *Ghaṭākāśa* (the *Ākāśa* in the pot) similar to the branches and other parts of a tree. As *Ghaṭākāśa* is neither a part (limb) nor an evolved effect of the *Ākāśa*, so also the *Jīva* (the embodied being), compared to the *Ākāśa* enclosed in the pot, is neither, as in the illustrations given above, an effect nor part (limb) of the *Ātman*, the ultimate Reality, which may be compared to the *Mahākāśa* (*i.e.*, the undifferentiated expanse of ether). Therefore the relative experience based upon the multiplicity of *Ātman* is an illusion (from the standpoint of the ultimate Reality).

[1] *This etc.*—For, it is admitted by all that the ether is without parts and cannot undergo any modification.

[2] *Ornament etc.*—We explain a necklace or foam, etc., as the modification of gold or water respectively. We also explain the branches or the leaves as the parts of the tree. But *Jīva* is neither modification, nor manifestation, nor part of the *Ātman*. *Jīva* is *Ātman* itself which never undergoes a change.

यथा भवति बालानां गगनं मलिनं मलैः ।
तथा भवत्यबुद्धानामात्माऽपि मलिनो मलैः ॥ ८ ॥

8. *As the ether appears to the ignorant children to be soiled by dirt, similarly, the* Ātman *also is regarded by the ignorant as soiled.*

### Śaṅkara's Commentary

As[1] the diversity of experiences such as forms, functions, etc., is caused by the admitted differences of the *Ghaṭākāśa* etc., so also is the experience of birth, death, etc., consequent on the perception of the different *Jīvas*, due to the limitations caused by *Avidyā* (ignorance). Therefore the contamination of misery, action and result (of action) caused by *Avidyā* does not really inhere in the *Ātman*. In order to establish this meaning by an illustration, the text says: As in our ordinary experience it is found that the ignorant regard the *Ākāśa* (ether)—which, to those who know, the real nature of a thing by discrimination, is never soiled by any contamination—as soiled with cloud, dust and smoke, so also the Supreme *Ātman*, the Knower, the innermost Self directly perceived within, is regarded by those who do not know the real nature of the innermost Self, as affected by the evils of misery, action and result. But this is not the case with those who can discriminate. As in the desert are never found foam,[2] waves, etc., though thirsty creatures falsely attribute these things to it, similarly the *Ātman* also is never affected by the turbidity of misery[3] etc., falsely attributed to it by the ignorant.

The opponent may contend thus: The statement that the *Jīvas* are neither an evolved effect nor a part of Brahman but identical with it is not correct. For, Brahman is ever pure and non-dual whereas the *Jīvas* are many and ever affected by the contamination of passion, attachment, etc. The text refutes this contention.

[1] *As etc.*—In our relative experience we make a distinction between the different forms of *Ākāśa* enclosed by a jar, an eye of a needle, or an extensive field. This knowledge of distinction, caused by various *upādhis*, unreal from the standpoint of Truth, makes us associate the undifferentiated *Ākāśa* with different forms, functions and names. In like manner, ignorant persons make a distinction of the *Jīvas* by associating the *Ātman* with the attributes of different bodies etc., and consequently think of the *Ātman* as suffering from the effects of birth, death, misery, etc. This distinction in the non-dual *Ātman* which gives rise to the notion of birth, death, etc., is due to *Avidyā* which is subjective or which proceeds from the perceiver. This distinction does not, in reality, exist; hence *Ātman* is ever uncontaminated by the evils of birth, death, etc.

[2] *Foam etc.*—The ignorant, subject to the illusion of the mirage, associate the desert with foam, waves, etc. All the waters of the mirage, taken as real by the ignorant, do not soak one grain of sand in the desert as this water is unreal. Similarly all the evils attributed falsely to the *Ātman* by undiscriminating persons do not make it lose its innate purity by so much as an iota.

[3] *Misery*—Misery or *Kleśa* has been defined by *Patañjali* as that which causes misery to the *Jīvas*. This *Kleśa* is of five kinds, *viz.*, *Avidyā* (*i.e.*, thinking the body which is non-self as the Self), *Asmitā* (*i.e.*, regarding the *Ātman* as one with *Buddhi* or mind), *Rāga* (*i.e.*, attachment), *Dveṣa* (*i.e.*, the anger which a man feels when his desire to attain a particular object is frustrated), *Abhiniveśa* (*i.e.*, the fear of death etc.).

मरणे संभवे चैव गत्यागमनयोरपि ।
स्थितौ सर्वशरीरेषु आकाशेनाविलक्षणः ॥ ९ ॥

9. Ātman, *in regard to its birth, death, going and coming* (*i.e.*, *transmigration*) *and its existing in different bodies, is not dissimilar* to the Ākāśā (*i.e.*, the Ghaṭākāśa *or the ether portioned off by a jar*).

ŚAṄKARA'S COMMENTARY

The point which has been just stated is again thus developed: Birth, death, etc., of the *Ātman* as seen in all bodies is like the creation, destruction, coming, going and existence of the *Ghaṭākāśa* (or ether enclosed within a jar).

It may be contended that the *Jīva* after death, as a result of the meritorious deeds done in his life, goes to heaven, If a sinner, he is thrown into hell. After his enjoyment of happiness or misery in heaven or hell, he again takes birth. In due course he departs from this world. This theory of transmigration is inconsistent with that of the non-dual *Ātman*. The text refutes this contention. All these diverse experiences regarding *Ātman* are due to *Avidyā* and therefore not real. Like the ether, *Ātman* which is pure, undifferentiated and one, can never be subject to transmigration etc., which are falsely superimposed upon it through *Avidyā*.

संघाताः स्वप्नवत्सर्वे आत्ममायाविसर्जिताः ।
आधिक्ये सर्वसाम्ये वा नोपपत्तिर्हि विद्यते ॥ १० ॥

10. *All aggregates (such as body, etc.) are produced by the illusion of the* Ātman *(i.e., the perceiver) as in a dream. No rational arguments can be adduced to establish their reality, whether they be equal or superior (to one another).*

ŚAṄKARA'S COMMENTARY

The aggregates of body etc., answering to the pots etc., in the illustration, are produced—like the body etc., seen in dream or conjured up by the magician—by the illusion[1] of the *Ātman, i.e.*, the *Avidyā* (ignorance) which is in the perceiver. That[2] is to say, they do not exist from the standpoint of the ultimate Reality. If[3] it be argued, in order to establish their reality, that there is a superiority (among the created beings)—as in the case of the aggregates of cause and effect constituting gods who are superior to lower beings, such as birds and beasts—or that there is an equality (of all created beings), yet no cause[4] can be set forth regarding their creation or reality. As there is no cause therefore all these are due to *Avidyā* or ignorance; they have no real existence.

[1] *Illusion etc.*—If one, subject to *Avidyā* sees multiplicity, then this *Avidyā* is in the perceiver. *Avidyā* is not objective, *i. e.*, it does not exist outside the perceiver.

[2] *That is etc.*—As in the case of the dream objects etc., which have no real existence.

[3] *If etc.*—The opponents may argue that the bodies of gods etc., on account of their superiority and adorability cannot be unreal. This is an argument of the ignorant, as all bodies, whether belonging to gods or lower animals, are constituted of five elements. Hence there is no intrinsic difference between gods and other beings. It is like the various objects seen in the dream, such as gods, birds, men, beasts, etc. They are made of the same thing, *viz.*, the mindstuff. Therefore, they are of the same nature and known to be unreal when the dream vanishes. Similarly a wise man knows all bodies from *Brahmā* to the blade of grass to be unreal.

[4] *Cause*—The idea of creation or coming into existence is due to *Avidyā*. With the removal of *Avidyā*, the idea of creation also vanishes. This topic will be discussed at full length later on.

रसादयो हि ये कोशा व्याख्यातास्तैत्तिरीयके ।
तेषामात्मा परो जीवः खं यथा संप्रकाशितः ॥ ११ ॥

11. The *Supreme* Jīva (*i.e., the non-dual Brahman*) *is the self of the* (*five*) *sheaths, such as the physical etc., which have been explained in the* Taittirīyaka Upaniṣad. *That the Supreme* Jīva *is like the* Ākāśa *has already been described by us* (*in the third verse of this chapter*).

## Śaṅkara's Commentary

Now statements are made in order to show that the existence of the essence of *Ātman* which is non-dual and without birth etc., can[1] as well be proved on the evidence of the *Śruti*. *Rasa* etc., are the five[2] sheaths such as the physical sheath (*Annarasamaya*), the vital sheath (*Prāṇamaya*) etc. These are called 'sheaths' (*Kośa*) because they[3] are like the sheath of the sword, the previous[4] sheaths being outer than the following ones. These have been clearly explained in the *Taittirīyaka*, *i.e.*, in a chapter of the *Taittirīyaka-śākhā Upaniṣad*. It is the Self (*Ātman*) of these sheaths. By It, the innermost Self, the five sheaths are regarded as alive. It is again called *Jīva* as it is the cause of the life of all. What is It? It is the Supreme Self which has been described before as 'Brahman which is Existence, Knowledge and Infinity'. It has been further stated that from this *Ātman* the aggregates of the body known as *Rasa* etc., having the characteristics of the sheath, have[5] been created by its (*Ātman's*) power called ignorance, this creation being like illusory creation of objects seen in a dream or in a performance of jugglery. We have described this *Ātman* as the ether (*Ākāśa*) in the text, 'The *Ātman* is verily like the *Ākāśa*' (*Gauḍ. Kārikā*, 3. 3). This *Ātman* cannot be established by the reasoning[6] of a man who follows the logician's method of arguments as the *Ātman* referred to by us is different from the *Ātman* of the logicians.

[1] *Can etc.*—That *Jīva* is identical with non-dual Brahman has already been established through reason. Now the same is again proved by the evidence of the Vedas.

[2] *Five etc.*—The five sheaths are the *Annamayakośa* (the physical sheath), the *Prāṇamayakośa* (the vital sheath), the *Manomayakośa* (the mental sheath), the *Vijñānamayakośa* (the sheath of intellect) and the *Ānandamayakośa* (the sheath of Bliss).

[3] *They etc.*—The *kośas* are compared to sheaths. As the sheath is external to the sword, so also the *kośas* are external to the *Ātman* which is the innermost Self of all.

[4] *Previous etc.*—The *Annamayakośa* is the sheath wherein is encased the *Prāṇamayakośa*, the *Prāṇamayakośa* is the sheath wherein is encased the *Manomayakośa* and so on. The *Ānandamayakośa* is encased in the *Vijñānamayakośa*.

[5] *Have been etc.*—This is no real creation. The phenomena of creation, which is illusory, are regarded as such from the empirical standpoint.

[6] *Reasoning*—The rational method of arriving at the Truth sought in the *Vedānta* philosophy is mainly described in the *Kārikā* of Gauḍapāda. This consists of the analysis of the three states, known as the waking, the dream and the deep sleep and the co-ordination of the experiences of these states.

द्वयोर्द्वयोर्मधुज्ञाने परं ब्रह्म प्रकाशितम् ।
पृथिव्यामुदरे चैव यथाऽऽकाशः प्रकाशितः ॥ १२ ॥

12. *The description by pairs, as that of the* Ākāśa, *which is in the earth as also in the stomach (though referred to separately), applies equally to the Supreme Brahman described in the* Madhu-Brāhmaṇa *(a chapter in the* Bṛhadāraṇyaka Upaniṣad), as *being both in the corporeal* (Adhyātma) *and in the celestial* (Adhidaiva) *regions.*

Śaṅkara's Commentary

Moreover, in the words[1] 'All this is the Supreme *Ātman*, the Brahman, the bright, the immortal Person who is both the celestial (superphysical—*Adhidaiva*) and the corporeal (*Adhyātma*), who is in this earth as well as the Knower incorporated in the body '—Brahman alone is described in order to indicate the limit at which duality vanishes. Where does this occur? It is thus replied: It occurs in the *Madhu-Brāhmaṇa* chapter which is known as the chapter dealing with the Knowledge of Brahman. It is because therein is described the nectar (*i.e.*, immortality) which is known as *Madhu*, *i.e.*, honey, as it gives us the highest bliss. This Brahman is like the *Ākāśa* which is said to be the same or identical though separately indicated as existing in the earth and in the stomach.

[1] *Words etc.*—The text of the *Bṛhadāraṇyaka Upaniṣad* (2.5.1) referred to here begins thus: 'This earth is the honey (*Madhu*, the effect)

of all beings and all beings are honey (*Madhu*, the effect) of this earth. Likewise this bright, immortal person in this earth and that bright immortal person incorporated in the body (both are *Madhu*). He is indeed the same as that Self, that Immortal, that Brahman, that All.' The purport of this *Śruti* passage is this: The Supreme Brahman alone has been described as existing in all the pairs of the corporeal (*Adhyātma*) and the superphysical (*Adhidaiva*).

जीवात्मनोरनन्यत्वमभेदेन प्रशस्यते ।
नानात्वं निन्द्यते यच्च तदेवं हि समञ्जसम् ॥ १३ ॥

13. *As the identity of* Jīva *and* Ātman, *through their non-dual character, is praised and multiplicity is condemned (in the scriptures), therefore, that (non-duality) alone is rational and correct.*

### Śaṅkara's Commentary

The *Śāstras*[1] as well as the sages like Vyāsa etc., extol the identity of *Jīva* and the Supreme Self through the negation of all differences—the conclusion arrived at by reasoning and supported by the scriptures. Further, the experiences of multiplicity which are natural (to the ignorant) and common to all beings—the view propounded by those who do not understand the real import of the *Śāstras* and who indulge in futile reasoning—have been condemned[2] thus: 'But there is certainly nothing corresponding to the dual existence', 'Fear arises from the consciousness of duality', 'If he sees the slightest difference (in *Ātman*) then he is overcome with fear', 'All this is verily *Ātman*', 'He goes from death to death who sees here (in this *Ātman*) multiplicity'. Other Knowers of Brahman as well as the scriptures (quoted above) extol identity (of *Jīva* and Brahman) and condemn multiplicity. Thus alone this praise and condemnation can be comprehended; in other words, it accords with reason. But the false views (vainly) advanced by the logicians,[3] not easy of comprehension, cannot be accepted as facts (Truth).

[1] *Śāstras*—Comp. 'One who knows Brahman verily becomes Brahman'.

[2] *Condemned*—That which is condemned cannot be Reality.

[3] *Logicians*—This refers to the followers of the *Vaiśeṣika* and other systems of thought.

There is no scriptural quotation which praises duality and condemns non-duality (*Advaita*).

जीवात्मनोः पृथक्त्वं यत् प्रागुत्पत्तेः प्रकीर्तितम् ।
भविष्यद्वृत्त्या गौणं तन्मुख्यत्वं हि न युज्यते ॥ १४ ॥

14. *The separateness of* Jīva *and* Ātman *which has been declared in (the ritual portion of the) Upaniṣad, dealing with the origin (of the universe), is only figurative, because this portion (of the Vedas) describes only what is to be. This statement regarding separateness can never have any meaning as truth.*

## Śaṅkara's Commentary

(Objection)—Even the *Śruti* has already declared the separateness of the *Jīva* and the Supreme Self in that part of the Upaniṣad which describes the creation (of the universe), *i.e.*, in the ritual portion (*Karmakāṇḍa*) of the Vedas. The texts of the *Karmakāṇḍa*, referred to here, describe the Supreme *Puruṣa* who had multiple desire, in such words as, 'desirous of this', 'desirous of that', 'He,[1] the Highest, supported the heaven and the earth' etc. This being the case, how is it possible, when there is a conflict between the knowledge portion and the ritual portion of the Vedas, to conclude that the unity underlying the meaning of the knowledge portion (of the Vedas) is alone reasonable and accurate?

(Reply)—Our reply is as follows:—The seperateness (of *Jīva* and *Paramātman*) described in the *Karmakāṇḍa* (ritual portion of the Vedas)—anterior to such Upaniṣadic statements dealing with the creation of the universe as, 'That from which all these beings emanate', 'As small sparks (come out) from fire', 'The *Ākāśa* has evolved from that which is this *Ātman*', 'It created heat'—is not real from the absolute standpoint.

(Objection)—What is it then?

(Reply)—It has only a secondary meaning. The separateness (between *Jīva* and *Paramātman* implied in these passages) is like that between the undifferentiated[2] ether (*Mahākāśa*) and the ether enclosed in the jar (*Ghaṭākāśa*). This statement is made with reference to a future[3] happening as in the case of another statement we often make, 'He is cooking rice'. For, the words describing separateness (of *Jīva* and *Paramātman*) can never reasonably uphold such separateness as absolutely real, as the statements regarding the separateness of *Ātman* only reiterate the multiple experiences of those beings who are still under the spell of their inborn[4] *Avidyā* or ignorance. Here[5] in the Upaniṣads, the texts regarding the creation, destruction, etc., of the universe are meant only to establish the identity of *Jīva* and the Supreme Self, as is known from the texts, 'That thou art', 'He does not know who knows I am another and he is another'. In other words, in the Upaniṣads the purpose of the *Śruti* is to establish the identity (of *Jīva* and Brahman). Keeping in view this identity which is going to be established later on, the (dualistic) texts only reiterate the common[6] experience of multiplicity (due to ignorance). Therefore these (dualistic) texts are only metaphorical. Or, the *Kārikā* may be explained thus: The scriptural text, 'He is one and without a second' declares the (complete) identity of *Jīva* and Brahman even before creation, denoted by such passages as, 'He saw', 'He created fire', etc. The culmination is, again, that identity as is known from such *Śruti* passages as, 'That is the Reality; He is the *Ātman*. That thou art'. Now, if keeping in view this future identity, the separateness of *Jīva* and *Ātman* has been declared in some texts, it must have been used in a metaphorical way as is the case with the statement 'He is cooking rice'.

[1] *He—i. e., Hiraṇyagarbha* or the cosmic soul.

[2] *Undifferentiated etc.*—The difference between the *Ghaṭākāśa* and the *Mahākāśa* is only due to the *upādhi* or the limiting adjunct of the *ghaṭa* or the jar. In reality it is the identical *Ākāśa* that is perceived in the great expanse of the ether, as well as in the jar. Similarly, the *Jīva* is thought of as different from the *Ātman* when the former is limited by the *upādhis* of *Antaḥkaraṇa* and body.

[3] *Future etc.*—The Vedas make the statement regarding the separateness of *Jīva* and Brahman keeping in view the experience of multiplicity by the ignorant people. The idea of past, present and future is formed only in the realm of ignorance. When the grain (*i. e.*, the uncooked rice) is boiled, people say that the rice (cooked rice) is boiled. This sort of statement is common parlance. Here the present tense is used keeping in view a future happening. Similarly the scriptures speak of duality before creation with a view to indicating the future state of Knowledge when multiplicity is known to be unreal.

[4] *Inborn*—It is because no cause can be traced of *Avidyā*.

[5] *Here etc.*—The aim of the dualistic statements of the *Śruti* is to establish ultimately the identity of *Jīva* and Brahman. The Upanisads accept the empirical view of the world as it appears and explain it by saying that Brahman who is both the material and efficient cause of the universe, created the world with all its beings and then entered into all as the living Self. This explanation establishes the unity of Brahman and *Jīva*, the apparent difference being ascribed to ignorance. The import of the *Śruti* is this: The non-dual Brahman alone exists. He is birthless, causeless and changeless. If one sees multiplicity that is also Brahman. The experience of multiplicity in the non-dual Brahman is due to *Avidyā*.

[6] *Common etc.*—This is due to ignorance.

मृल्लोहविस्फुलिङ्गाद्यैः सृष्टिर्या चोदिताऽन्यथा ।
उपायः सोऽवताराय नास्ति भेदः कथंचन ॥ १५ ॥

15. *(The scriptural statements regarding) creation as illustrated by examples of earth, iron, sparks, etc., or otherwise, (only) serve the purpose of (ultimately) explaining the unity (of* Jīva *and Brahman). (Really speaking) multiplicity does not exist in any manner.*

### Śaṅkara's Commentary

(Objection)—Before[1] creation all this might have been unborn, one and non-dual; but after creation, all this evolved world and the embodied beings (*Jīvas*) denote multiplicity.

(Reply)—No, it cannot be so. For, the scriptural passages dealing with creation have another meaning. This difficulty raised here has already been solved by the statements that[2] the aggregates (entities) of body etc., like dream-objects, are produced through illusion of the subject (*Ātman*) and that creation and the differences of the *Jīvas* are like the creation and the differences of the *Ghaṭākāśas*, *i.e.*, the bits of *Ākāśa* enclosed in different jars. The scriptural[3] statements dealing with creation and differences (of the created beings), have again been referred to here in order to show that such statements regarding creation have the purpose of determining the unity of *Jīva* and Brahman. The[4] (theory of) creation has been described in the scripture through the illustrations of earth, iron, sparks, etc. or otherwise; but all these modes of creation are meant for enlightening our intellect so that it may comprehend the identity of *Jīva* and Brahman. It is just like the story[5] of the organs of speech (*vāk*) etc., being smitten with evil by the *Asuras* (demons) as described in the chapter on *Prāṇa* (vital breath), where the real purpose of the *Śruti* is to demonstrate the special importance of *Prāṇa*.

(Objection)—We[6] do not accept this meaning as indicated.

(Reply)—Your contention is not correct. For[7] this story about *Prāṇa* etc., has been differently narrated in different recensions of the Vedas. If the story of *Prāṇa* were literally true, there should have been one version only in all recensions. Different versions of contradictory nature would not have been narrated. But we do come across such different versions in the Vedas. Therefore the scriptural passages recording stories of *Prāṇa* are not meant to serve any purpose of their own, *i.e.*, they should not be taken literally. The scriptural[8] statements regarding creation should also be understood in a similar manner.

(Objection)—There have been different creations in different cycles. Therefore, the scriptural statements regarding creations (of the universe) and stories (of *Prāṇa*) are different as they refer to the creations in different cycles.

(Reply)—This contention is not valid. For, they (the illustrations of earth, iron, etc., as well as the stories of *Prāṇa*) serve no other useful purpose than clearing our intellect as stated above. No one can imagine any other utility of the scriptural statements regarding creation and *Prāṇa*.

(Objection)—We[9] contend that these are for the purpose of meditation so that one may ultimately attain to that end.

(Reply)—This is not correct either; for no one desires to attain his identity with the *dispute* (in the case of the *Prāṇa* narrative), or with the creation or destruction (in the case of the scriptural statements regarding creation etc.). Therefore we have reasonably to conclude that the scriptural statements regarding creation etc., are for the purpose of helping the mind to realise the oneness of *Ātman*, and for no other purpose whatsoever. Therefore, no multiplicity is brought about by creation etc.

[1] *Before etc.*—There are definite scriptural statements regarding creation. These statements are *literally* true. Therefore multiplicity caused by creation is also true.

[2] *That etc.*—In *Kārikās* 3 and 10 (Chapter III), it has been established that the perception of ego and non-ego as separate from Brahman is due to ignorance.

[3] *Scriptural etc.*—It has been explained in the previous text that the scriptural statements regarding creation etc., are for the purpose of explaining the illusory nature of the universe to those who take it as real. But the purpose of this *Kārikā* is to enable us to understand the identity of *Jīva* and Brahman.

[4] *The creation etc.*—The meaning is that we should not take these scriptural statements in the literal sense but must get at their underlying significance.

[5] *Story etc.*—The reference is to the second part of the first chapter of the *Chāndogya Upaniṣad.* This story cannot be accepted in a literal sense as the organs of speech etc., being themselves unconscious, cannot quarrel with one another. The significance of the story is to demonstrate the superiority of *Prāṇa* over other *Indriyas* (organs). The story referred to here is as follows: The *Devas* and *Asuras*, both of the race of Prajāpati, fought with one another. The *Devas* (Gods) and the *Asuras* (Demons) are explained as good and evil inclinations of man. The *Devas* took the *Udgītha*, thinking that they would be able to vanquish the *Asuras* with it. The *Udgītha* stands for the sacrificial act to be performed by the *Udgātṛ*, the *Sāmaveda* priest, with the *Udgītha* hymns. They meditated on the *Udgītha* as the breath in the nostril, but the *Asuras* smote the breath with evil. Then they meditated on *Udgītha* as the speech, the eye, the ear, the mind ; but all these sense organs were smitten with evil by the *Asuras*. Then they meditated on *Udgītha* as *Prāṇa* (vital breath) and the *Asuras* failed to smite it with evil. Therefore *Prāṇa* is superior to all sense-organs.

[6] *We etc.*—We do not accept your explanation, for, the organs of speech etc., have been designated as gods. Therefore they cannot be insentient matter.

[7] *For etc.*—This story about *Prāṇa* has been differently stated in different Upaniṣads. This cannot happen if the story is to be accepted as literally true.

[8] *Scriptural etc.*—The story regarding creation, as in the case of *Prāṇa*, has been differently stated in different parts of the Upaniṣads. In some places we read that the *Ākāśa* was first evolved ; again we find that the fire was first evolved and still in another place it is mentioned that *Prāṇa* was first evolved. Therefore, on account of the contradictory

natures of these stories they should not be taken as true. They serve some other purpose, *viz.*, the establishment of the absence of variety, or the oneness of *Ātman* (Brahman).

[9] *We contend etc.*—It is said in the *Śruti* that the worshipper ultimately realises the oneness of *Ātman*.

आश्रमास्त्रिविधा हीनमध्यमोत्कृष्टदृष्टयः ।
उपासनोपदिष्टेयं तदर्थमनुकम्पया ॥ १६ ॥

16. *There are three stages of life corresponding to three—the lower, the middle and the high—powers of comprehension. The Scripture, out of compassion, has taught this devotion (or discipline) for the benefit of those (who are not yet enlightened).*

### Śaṅkara's Commentary

(Objection) - If according to such *Śruti* passages as, '*Ātman* is one and without a second' etc., the *Ātman* alone, the one, the eternally pure, illumined and free, is the highest and the ultimate Reality and all else is unreal, what then is the purpose of the devotion and spiritual practices implied in such *Śruti*[1] passages as, 'Oh dear, *Ātman* alone is to be seen', 'The *Ātman* who is free from....', 'He desired', 'It should be worshipped as *Ātman*', etc.? Further, what is the utility of *Karma* (Vedic works) like *Agnihotra* etc.?

(Reply)—Yes, listen to the reasons. *Āśrama* signifies those who are competent to follow the disciplines of life as prescribed for the different stages.[2] The word (in the text) also includes those who belong to the (different) castes[3] and therefore who observe the rites (prescribed for those castes). The application of the word '*Āśrama*' implies that these castes are also three in number. How? It is because they are endowed with three kinds of intellect, *viz.*, low,[4] middle[5] and high.[6] This discipline as well as the (various) *Karmas* (works) are prescribed for the *Āśramis* of low and average intellect, by the *Śruti*, out of compassion, so that they also, following the correct disciplines, may attain to the superior knowledge. That[7] this discipline is not for those who possess the right understanding, *i.e.*, who are already endowed with the Knowledge of *Ātman* which is one and without a second, is supported by such *Śruti* passages as, 'That which cannot be known by the mind, but by which, they say, the mind is able to think, that alone know to be Brahman, and not that which people here adore', 'That thou art', 'All this is verily *Ātman*', etc.

In the previous *Kārikās* it has been proved that the Scriptural statements regarding creation etc., do not conflict with the non-dual *Ātman*. This *Kārikā* states that the prescription of various disciplines associated with different *Varṇas* and *Āśramas* also does not contradict the view of the non-dual *Ātman*. The statements regarding creation etc., as well as the various spiritual disciplines are only meant for the unenlightened in order to assist them to understand the oneness of *Ātman*.

[1] *Śruti passages*—It is because all these *Śruti* passages require, on the part of the students, either meditation, or spiritual disciplines or devotion. This has no meaning if the non-dual *Ātman* alone is the Reality.

[2] *Stages*—These are the orders of *Brahmacarya*, *Gārhasthya*, *Vānaprastha* and *Saṁnyāsa*.

[3] *Castes*—The word *Varṇa*, here, implies the three castes, *viz.*, the *Brāhmaṇa*, *Kṣatriya* and *Vaiśya*.

[4] *Low*—Those who look upon the phenomenal universe (the *Kārya Brahman*) as real, are said to possess low intellect.

[5] *Middle*—Those who worship the *Kāraṇa Brahman*, that is the Brahman as the cause of the universe, are said to possess mediocre intellect, because they still live on the causal plane.

[6] *High*—Those who have realised the non-dual (*Advaita*) *Ātman* are said to possess superior power of understanding.

[7] *That etc.*—As the possessor of the Knowledge of non-dual *Ātman* is free from all distinction of *Āśrama* and *Varṇa*, it is therefore not necessary for him to perform any *Vedic* work or practise any spiritual discipline.

The meaning of the *Kārikā* is this: The *Āśramas* and the *Varṇas* described in the *Śruti*, and the different functions ascribed to them have only a disciplinary value; the main purpose is to train the student to understand the unity of *Jīva* and Brahman.

स्वसिद्धान्तव्यवस्थासु द्वैतिनो निश्चिता दृढम् ।
परस्परं विरुध्यन्ते तैरयं न विरुध्यते ॥ १७ ॥

17. *The dualists obstinately cling to the conclusions arrived at by their own enquiries (as being the truth). So they contradict one another; whereas the* Advaitin *finds no conflict with them.*

### Śaṅkara's Commentary

The knowledge of the non-dual Self is established by both Scriptures and reasoning. Therefore, it is alone the perfect knowledge. Other views, on account of their being devoid of the bases of Scriptures and reasoning, lead to false systems. The views of the dualists are false on account of this additional reason, that they are the fruitful sources of the vices of attachment and hatred etc. How is this? The dualists following the views of Kapila, Kaṇāda, Buddha and Jina etc., hold firmly to the conclusions as outlined and formulated by their respective schools. They[1] think that the view they hold is alone the ultimate Reality, whereas other views are not so. Therefore they become attached to their own views and hate others whom they consider to be opposed to them. Thus being overcome with attachment and hatred, they contradict one another, the reason being the adherence to their own convictions as the only truth. But our view, *viz.*, the unity of *Ātman*, based upon the identity of all, supported by the Vedas, does not conflict with others who find contradictions among themselves—as[2] one's limbs such as hands, feet, etc., do not conflict with one another. Hence the purport of the *Śruti* is that the knowledge of the oneness of *Ātman*, as it is free from the blemish of attachment and aversion, is the true knowledge.

This *Kārikā* proves the superiority of the *Advaita* knowledge over other views as it does not contradict the scriptural statements regarding creation and exercises (*Upāsana*), and also because it does not clash with other theories. *Advaita* alone harmonises all other doctrines and theories. It alone gives the rationale of other relative views regarding Truth.

[1] *They etc.*—It is because the dualists take the relative truth to be the ultimate view of Reality.

[2] *As etc.*—If in the course of physical movements, the hands or feet strike any part of the body, the body does not feel irritated as the body knows the limbs to be its own integral parts. Similarly the non-dualist, on account of his knowledge of identity with all created beings and thoughts, does not feel angered at the hostility of his opponents, as he knows his so-called opponents to be his own self. The Knower of Brahman realises the entire world as the projection of his thought (*Kalpana*). The thoughts are also identical with Brahman as the various dream-objects are identical with the mind. Therefore the theories of others are not in conflict with non-duality because they are also identical with Brahman. *Comp.* the Scriptural passage, 'All this is verily Brahman'.

अद्वैतं परमार्थो हि द्वैतं तद्भेद उच्यते ।
तेषामुभयथा द्वैतं तेनायं न विरुध्यते ॥ १८ ॥

18. *As non-duality is the ultimate Reality, therefore duality is said to be its effect* (Kārya *or* Bheda). *The dualists perceive duality either way (*i.e., *both in the Absolute and in the phenomena). Therefore the non-dual position does not conflict with the dualist's position.*

## Śaṅkara's Commentary

How is it that the non-dualist does not conflict with the dualist? The reason is thus stated: As[1] non-duality is the ultimate Reality, therefore duality or multiplicity is only its effect. The Scriptural passages such as, 'He is one and without a second', 'He created fire', etc., support this view. It[2] is further borne out by reason as duality is not perceived in the states of swoon, deep sleep or trance (*samādhi*), in the absence of the activity of the mind. Therefore duality is said to be the effect of non-duality. But the dualists perceive duality alone either[3] way, that is, from both the absolute and the relative standpoints. As duality is perceived only by the deluded and non-duality by us who are enlightened,[4] therefore our view does not clash with their views. For, the Scripture also says, 'Indra (the Supreme Lord) created all these diverse forms through *Māya*', 'There exists nothing like duality'. It[5] is like the case of a man on a spirited elephant, who knows that none can oppose him, but who yet does not drive his beast upon a lunatic who though standing on the ground, shouts at the former, 'I am also on an elephant, drive your beast on me'. Therefore from the standpoint of Reality, the Knower of Brahman is the very self of (even) the dualists. Hence, our, *viz.*, the non-dualistic view does not clash with other views.

It may be asked in view of the differences between the dualistic and the non-dualistic views, how it can be said that the latter does not find any contradiction with the former. The text of the *Kārikā* gives the reply. It says that the so-called duality does not exist at all. Whatever exists is non-dual Brahman alone. Therefore the non-dualist cannot quarrel with a thing which is ultimately non-existent.

[1] *As etc.*—We learn from Scriptural evidence that duality is the effect of the non-dual unity. The effect, relatively speaking, is other than the cause, otherwise, one cannot make a distinction between the cause and the effect. Again the *Śruti* says that all effects consisting of names are mere figures of speech, like the effects of clay, and therefore unreal. The cause, like the clay, alone is real. Therefore effects, being unreal, cannot contradict the cause. Hence non-duality does not clash with duality. Here the word '*Bheda*', implying *effect* is not used in the *Sāṁkhya* sense of modification.

[2] *It is etc.*—One perceives duality on account of the activity of the mind. When the mind is at rest, duality is not perceived as in the case of deep sleep, swoon, or *Samādhi*. Therefore duality is the effect. The non-dualist admits the fact of duality during the state of ignorance.

But he denies its reality. Therefore from the standpoint of Reality, non-duality does not contradict duality, as the latter is really non-existent.

[3] *Either way.*—That is to say, the dualist holds duality both as the highest Reality and as the relative Reality.

[4] *Enlightened*—It is because our view is supported both by Scripture and reason.

[5] *It is etc.*—The dualist is self-deluded like the madman who, though standing on the earth, thinks that he is really on an elephant. The person who is driving the elephant does not listen to the foolish cry of the lunatic. Similarly the dualist possessed of a partial view of the truth, thinks of himself as having realised the ultimate Truth, and throws his challenge to the non-dualist, calling upon him to refute his position. But the non-dualist, secure in his position, laughs at this challenge and he bears no ill-will against the dualist as he is the very self of the dualist, his so-called opponent.

मायया भिद्यते ह्येतन्नान्यथाऽजं कथंचन ।
तत्त्वतो भिद्यमाने हि मर्त्यताममृतं व्रजेत् ॥ १९ ॥

19. *This unborn (changeless, non dual Brahman) appears to undergo modification only on account of* Māyā *(illusion) and not otherwise. For, if this modification were real, the Immortal (Brahman) would become mortal.*

## Śaṅkara's Commentary

If duality[1] were the effect of non-duality, then it could be contended that duality also, like the *Advaita,* is the Supreme Reality. In order to remove this doubt which may crop up in the minds of some, it is said that non-duality which is the Supreme Reality appears manifold through *Māyā,*[2] like the one moon appearing as many to one with defective eye-sight and the rope appearing (to the deluded) as the snake, the water-line, etc. This manifold is not real, for *Ātman* is without any part. An object endowed with parts may be said to undergo modification by a change of its parts, as clay undergoes differentiation into pots etc. Therefore the purport is that the changeless (unborn) *Ātman* which is without parts cannot, in any manner, admit of distinction excepting through *Māyā* or the illusion of the perceiver. If[3] the appearance of manifoldness were real, then the *Ātman*, the ever-unborn and non-dual, which is, by its very nature, immortal would become mortal as though fire would become cold (which is an absurdity). The[4] reversal of one's own nature is not desired by any—as it is opposed to all means of proofs. Therefore the Reality—which is *Ātman*—changeless and unborn, appears to undergo a modification only through *Māyā*. Hence it follows that duality is not the ultimate Reality.

[1] *Duality etc.*—For, the effect always partakes of the nature of the cause.

[2] *Māyā–Māyā* explains the appearance of the manifold consistently; not the *Pariṇāmavāda* (or the theory of actual transformation) adumbrated by the *Sāṁkhyas.*

[3] *If etc.*—For, by changing into the universe, the non-dual *Ātman* which is admitted to be immortal, would undergo destruction and become mortal. A thing cannot retain its own nature while undergoing a change.

[4] *The reversal etc.*—One of the tests of Reality is that it never admits of any change of its innate nature The non-dual *Ātman* being the Reality, can never really change into the dual universe. Therefore the *act* of creation or modification is an illusion. Hegel's theory of *logical necessity* or Bradley's Absolute *somehow* becoming the phenomena cannot be borne out by reason.

अजातस्यैव भावस्य जातिमिच्छन्ति वादिनः ।
अजातो ह्यमृतो भावो मर्त्यतां कथमेष्यति ॥ २० ॥

20. *The disputants (*i.e., *the dualists) contend that the ever-unborn (changeless) entity* (Ātman) *undergoes a change. How could an entity which is changeless and immortal partake of the nature of the mortal?*

ŚAṄKARA'S COMMENTARY

Some interpreters of the Upaniṣads, who[1] are garrulous and who put on the airs of the Knowers of Brahman, admit that the Reality—the *Ātman*—which is by nature ever-unborn (changeless) and immortal, really passes[2] into birth (*i.e.*, becomes the universe). If,[3] according to them, the *Ātman* really passes into birth it must undergo destruction. But,[4] how is it possible for the *Ātman* which is, by its very nature, ever-unborn (changeless) and immortal to become mortal, *i.e.*, to be subject to destruction? It can never become mortal which is contrary to its very nature.

[1] *Who etc.*—*i.e.*, who, in reality, do not know anything about Brahman.

[2] *Passes etc.*—That is, it creates itself into the manifold universe.

[3] *If etc.*—For, destruction is the inevitable consequence of all objects that are born.

[4] *But etc.*—Birth means change of nature. An entity cannot be changeless while giving birth to other objects. Hence the theory that *Ātman* somehow changes into the universe is fallacious.

न भवत्यमृतं मर्त्यं न मर्त्यममृतं तथा ।
प्रकृतेरन्यथाभावो न कथंचिद्भविष्यति ॥ २१ ॥

21. *The immortal cannot become mortal, nor can the mortal ever become immortal. For, it is never possible for a thing to change its nature.*

ŚAṄKARA'S COMMENTARY

As in common experience the immortal never becomes mortal, nor the mortal ever becomes immortal; therefore it is, in no way, possible for a thing to reverse its nature, *i.e.*, to become otherwise than what it is. Fire can never change its character of being hot.

स्वभावेनामृतो यस्य भावो गच्छति मर्त्यताम् ।
कृतकेनामृतस्तस्य कथं स्थास्यति निश्चलः ॥ २२ ॥

22. *How can he, who believes that the naturally immortal entity becomes mortal, maintain that the Immortal, after passing through change, retains its changeless nature?*

### Śaṅkara's Commentary

The disputant who maintains that the naturally immortal entity becomes mortal, *i.e.*, really passes into birth, makes[1] the futile proposition that that entity before creation is by its very nature, immortal. How can he assert that the entity is of immortal nature if it be admitted that it passes[2] into birth? That is to say, how can the immortal retain its immortal nature of changelessness if it should undergo a change? It cannot, by any means, be so. Those[3] who hold that the *Ātman* passes into birth (*i.e.*, undergoes a change), cannot speak of the *Ātman* as ever birthless. Everything, according to them, must be mortal. Hence[4] there cannot be a state called liberation.

It may be contended that Brahman, as the cause, is immortal before creation. But as effect, subsequent to the creation, it becomes mortal. Therefore there is no contradiction in associating with Brahman both immortal and mortal aspects which apply to its two states. This *Kārikā* refutes this contention.

[1] *Makes etc.*—For, according to these disputants, the cause (*i. e.*, Brahman), even before creation must contain within it the possibility of change; otherwise it cannot undergo a change. If this were admitted then the cause can no longer be called immortal.

[2] *Passes etc.*—If an entity undergoes a change, that shows its impermanent characteristic inasmuch as it admits of the destruction of its inherent nature.

[3] *Those etc.*—The so-called Absolute of the dualists is also a mortal entity. For, nothing that passes through birth, can be immortal.

[4] *Hence etc.*—That is to say, *Mukti* or liberation in the sense of an immutable and permanent condition becomes an absurdity.

भूततोऽभूततो वाऽपि सृज्यमाने समा श्रुतिः ।
निश्चितं युक्तियुक्तं च यत्तद्भवति नेतरम् ॥ २३ ॥

23. *The passing into birth may be real or illusory. Both these views are equally mentioned in the* Śruti. *That which is supported by* Śruti *and corroborated by reason, is alone true and not the other.*

ŚAṄKARA'S COMMENTARY

(Objection)—Those[1] who do not admit the change or the passing into birth of Brahman, cannot justify the Scriptural passages which support creation.

(Reply)—Yes, we also admit the existence of Scriptural texts supporting creation as actual, but such texts serve other purposes. Though the question has already been disposed of, the contention is here again made and refuted in order to allay all doubts regarding the applicability or otherwise of the Scriptural texts to the subject-matter[2] that is going to be dealt with. The Scriptural text regarding creation is the same, whether the creation of things is taken in the real sense or as a mere illusion produced by the juggler.

(Objection)—If words admit of metaphorical and direct meanings, it is reasonable to understand the world according to their direct meaning.

Reply—We do not admit it. For,[3] creation, in any sense other than illusion, is unknown to us, and further, no purpose is served by admitting (the act of) creation. All[4] creation, whether metaphorical or actual, refers to the apparent creation caused by *Avidyā* but not to any creation from the standpoint of Reality. For the Scripture says, 'Though existing both within and without, he (the *Ātman*) (is really) changeless'. Therefore we have stated in the foregoing part of this work only what is supported by reason and determined by the *Śruti* such words as, 'He is one and without a second and is free from birth and death'. That alone is the true import of the Scripture and not anything else.

[1] *Those etc.*—There are some Scriptural passages which state that the *Ātman* brings about the creation by following the law of causality.

[2] *Subject-matter*—The purport of the *Śruti* is not to establish any act of creation, whether actual or illusory, but to prove the *Ajāti* or eternal changelessness of Brahman.

[3] *For etc.*—According to the *Advaita* philosophy, all creation, whether actual or metaphorical (secondary) whether in dream or in the waking state, is equally illusory from the standpoint of Reality. Further, if creation be admitted as real, no purpose whatsoever is served by creation. It does not help anyone to attain to liberation.

[4] *All etc.*—The creation of objects in dream is called metaphorical or secondary in comparison with the creation of objects such as pot etc., in the waking state. As the dream objects become unreal in the waking state, similarly the objects perceived in the waking state are known to be unreal when one attains to the knowledge of *Ātman*. Therefore from the standpoint of *Ātman*, all objects, perceived in dream or the waking state, are equally unreal.

नेह नानेति चाऽऽम्नायादिन्द्रो मायाभिरित्यपि ।
अजायमानो बहुधा मायया जायते तु सः ॥ २४ ॥

24. *From such Scriptural passages as, 'There is no multiplicity in* Ātman', '*Indra through* Māyā', *we know that the* Ātman, *though ever unborn, verily appears to have become many (only) through* Māyā.

## Śaṅkara's Commentary

It may be asked how the changelessness *(Ajāti)* of *Ātman* is the final conclusion of the *Śruti*. In reply it is said that if creation were real, then the existence of the variety of objects would be absolutely real. Consequently there ought not to be Scriptural texts implying their unreality. But there are such Scriptural texts as, 'In this *(Ātman)* there is no multiplicity' etc., which negate the existence of duality. Therefore creation (imaginary) has been imagined in order to help the understanding of the non-duality of *Ātman*. It[1] is like the story of *Prāṇa*. And this is further borne out by the use of the word, '*Māyā*', denoting unreality (in connection with creation) in such Scriptural texts as, 'Indra[2] through *Māyā* assumed diverse forms'.

(Objection)—The word denotes knowledge (*Prajñā*).

(Reply)—It is true, but sense-*knowledge* is illusory. The word[3] '*Māyā*' is used to denote that (sense-) *knowledge*. Hence there is no blemish (in such use of the word). The word '*Māyābhiḥ*' (through *Māyā*) in the Scriptural text means through sense-knowledge, which is illusory. For, the Scripture again says, 'Though unborn he appears to be born in many ways'. Therefore *Ātman* passes into birth through *Māyā* alone. The word '*Tu*' ('verily') in the text (of the *Kārikā*) denotes certainty, that is to say, it[4] indicates that creation is possible only through *Māyā* or illusion and not in any real sense. For, birthlessness and birth in various forms cannot be predicated of the same object, as fire cannot be both hot and cold. Further, from such *Śruti* passages as, 'How can there be any delusion and any grief for him who sees unity' etc., we know that the knowledge of the unity of *Ātman* is alone the conclusion of *Śruti* on acconnt of the (good) result it brings to the knower. Again, the perception of differentiation implied by creation has been condemned in such *Śruti* passages as, 'He goes from death to death (who sees here many)'.

[1] *It is etc.*—As the *Śruti* described the disputes of *Prāṇa* and the sense-organs in order to prove the superiority of the vital breath (*Mukhya-Prāṇa*), so also creation has been described in order to help the understanding of the student to grasp the unity of *Atman*. (See *Kārikā* 3-15)

[2] *Indra*—The word is used here in the sense of the Supreme Lord.

[3] *The word etc.*—The word '*Māyā*' is sometimes used to denote empirical knowledge or the knowledge derived by the contact of the sense-organs with their objects. This knowledge does not indicate the Highest Consciousness or the knowledge of Reality. Hence creation through *Māyā* is necessarily illusory.

[4] *It etc.*—If one believes in creation then the only plausible explanation is that of the *Vivartavāda* and not any other theory such as *Pariṇāmavāda*.

संभूतेरपवादाच्च संभवः प्रतिषिध्यते ।
को न्वेनं जनयेदिति कारणं प्रतिषिध्यते ॥ २५ ॥

25. *Again, by the negation of creation* (Sambhūti) *the passing into birth is refuted. Causality (in respect of* Ātman) *is denied by such a statement as, 'Who can cause it to pass into birth?'*

ŚAṄKARA'S COMMENTARY

By the condemnation of *Sambhūti*[1] (*i.e., Hiraṇyagarbha*) as something fit to be meditated upon, in such *Śruti*[2] passage as, 'They enter into blind darkness who worship *Sambhūti*', the whole[3] creation (evolution) is negatived. For, if *Sambhūti* were absolutely real, then its condemnation, in such manner, would not be reasonable.

(Objection)—The[4] condemnation of *Sambhūti* is meant here for co-ordinating *Sambhūti* with *Vināśa*[5] as is the case with the *Śruti* passage,[6] 'They enter into blind darkness who worship *Avidyā*'.

(Reply)—Yes, it is indeed true that the condemnation of the exclusive worship of *Sambhūti* is made for the purpose of co-ordinating the meditation regarding *Sambhūti* with the *Karma* (ritual) known as *Vināśa*. Still it should not be forgotten that as the purpose of the *Karma* known as *Vināśa* is to transcend death—whose nature is the desire consequent upon the inborn ignorance of man—so also the aim[7] of the co-ordination of the meditation on *Devatā* (*i.e.*, *Sambhūti* or *Hiraṇyagarbha*) with the *Karma* (called *Vināśa*) undertaken for the purpose of the purification of the mind of man, is to transcend death—which[8] is of the nature of the attachment to ritual and its results characterised by the dual hankering after the end and the means. For, thus alone man becomes free from death which is of the nature of impurity and is characterised by the dual impulse of end and means. Therefore the co-ordination of the meditation of *Devatā* and of *Karma*—which is *Avidyā*—leads to freedom from death. Thus[9] the realisation of *Vidyā* (the highest knowledge), characterised by the identity of the Supreme Self and *Jīva*, is inevitable[10] for one who has transcended death—of the form of *Avidyā* and characterised by the dual impulses (of the means and the end)—and who is established in renunciation and also devoted to the meaning of the import of the Upaniṣad. It is therefore said thus[11]: *Brahmavidyā* *i.e.*, the knowledge of Brahman—which is the means for the attainment of Immortality and which is (from the relative standpoint) *subsequent* to the state of the antecedent *Avidyā* (ignorance) being related to the same person (who is still in the state of ignorance), is said to be co-ordinated with *Avidyā*. Hence the negation of *Sambhūti* is for the purpose of condemnation as it serves a purpose other[12] than the knowledge of Brahman which (alone) is the means to the attainment of Immortality. Though it serves the purpose of removing impurity yet the devotion to *Sambhūti* does not enable one to realise (directly) immortality. (Therefore the condemnation of *Sambhbūti* is reasonable.) Hence, *Sambhūti* being thus negatived, it can be said to have only a relative existence. Having regard to the unity of *Ātman*, the ultimate Reality, creation (symbolised by *Hiraṇyagarbha*) which is known as immortal[13] (only from the relative standpoint) is negated. Such[14] being the case, who can bring into being the *Jīva* who is seen as created only through illusion (*Māyā*) and who exists only while ignorance (*Avidyā*) lasts? This *Jīva* reverts to its original nature (of Brahman) with the disappearance of *Avidyā*. For, no one can verily bring into being the snake (falsely) superimposed upon the rope through *Avidyā* and which disappears when one knows (the true nature of the rope). Therefore no one can produce or create the *Jīva*. The words '*Ko nu*' ('who can?') in the text, being in the form of interrogation refute the idea of causality. The purport of the *Kārikā* is that there can be no cause for a thing which is seen to be born only through ignorance and which disappears with the destruction of the said ignorance. The *Śruti* also says, 'This[15] *Ātman* is not born from any cause nor is anything born from it'.

[1] *Sambhūti*—The word '*Bhūti*' means 'Aiśvarya' (ऐश्वर्य) *i.e.*, power, and the word *Sambhūti* indicates one who possesses all powers. It is a deity known as *Hiraṇyagarbha* (The Golden Germ) who is the first of all the evolved effects and from whom, as the matrix, the whole evolution proceeds. It is described in the *Vedāntic* texts as the summation of all subtle bodies.

[2] *Śruti passage*—This is a quotation from the *Īśa Upaniṣad* (12). This *Kārikā* is based on this text of the Upaniṣad.

[3] *Whole etc.*—By the condemnation of *Hiraṇyagarbha* from whom the entire creation is said to proceed, the whole of the subsequent effects is negatived. Therefore the entire effect which is seen in the form of the manifold, is unreal.

[4] *The etc.*—The reference is to the text of the *Īṣa Upaniṣad* (14) which runs thus: 'Those who worship the unmanifested *Prakṛti* and *Hiraṇyagarbha* (Destruction, *Vināśa*) together, get over death through the worship of *Hiraṇyagarbha* and attain immortality through the worship of *Prakṛti*.' The contention of the opponent is this: The condemnation of *Sambhūti* is not for the purpose of proving its unreality. Its purpose is to combine the worship of *Prakṛti* and *Hiraṇyagarbha*. The exclusive worship of *Hiraṇyagarbha* is condemned. (See Śaṅkara's Commentary on verse 14 of the *Īśa Upaniṣad*.)

[5] *Vināśa*—The word '*Vināśa*' means that object whose character-

istic attribute is destruction, the abstract being here used for the concrete. *Vināśa* means the worship of *Hiraṇyagarbha*. The contention of the opponent is that the purpose of the condemnation of the exclusive worship of *Sambhūti* is to prescribe the co-ordination of its meditation with some ritualistic worship and not to imply the unreality of *Sambhūti* or the first cause.

[6] *Śruti etc.*—The reference is to the 9th verse of the *Īśa Upaniṣad* which condemns *Vidyā* (the exclusive meditation on the deities) and *Avidyā* (the exclusive ritualistic ceremonies without any meditation) and prescribes their co-ordination.

[7] *Aim etc.*—The purport of the 9th verse of the *Īśa Upaniṣad* is this: *Avidyā* is something other than *Vidyā* or knowledge; hence it is *Karma:* for *Karma* is opposed to knowledge. Those who are continuously performing *Agnihotra-sacrifice etc.*, alone, fall into darkness. Those who having given up *Karma*, are always bent upon acquiring the knowledge of the deities, fall into greater darkness. Who knows that both these should simultaneously be followed by the same person, he alone, so combining the two, *gradually* secures the one desirable end. That is to say, his mind is purified of all impurities. The pure mind, then, is able to grasp the meaning of the Upaniṣad which alone enables the student to know the ultimate Reality. The aim of such *Karma* as the *Agnihotra-sacrifice* etc., prescribed by the Scripture, is to turn the mind of the student away from the pursuit of worldly objects, not sanctioned by the Scriptures. By the co-ordination of *Karma* with meditation (on the deities) the student frees himself from all impulse of desires. Even then he has not realised the Highest Truth which is possible only through *Jñānam* or knowledge.

[8] *Which is etc.*—Death means the endless cycle of birth and death which is inevitable unless one has attained to the knowledge of Brahman. The endless chain is caused by the desire for relative objects.

[9] *Thus etc.*—The knowledge of Brahman can never be combined with co-ordination of *Karma* and *Upāsanā* as the latter belongs to the realm of ignorance. *Brahmavidyā* and ignorance are as unrelated as light and darkness.

[10] *Inevitable*—There is no other obstacle for the realisation of the Supreme Reality when all the impurities have been removed by the practice of *Karma* and *Upāsanā*.

[11] *Thus etc.*—No co-ordination is possible between the knowledge of Brahman and any other relative knowledge. Still it is found that the

student, at first, through a process of relative knowledge gets his mind purified and *then* becomes fit for *Brahma-Jñānam*. Thus from a relative standpoint it is seen that the knowledge of Brahman arises *subsequent to* the relative knowledge. Really speaking, the knowledge of Self is ever present and ignorance is non-existent. As from the relative standpoint it is seen that an ignorant person gradually attains to the highest knowledge, therefore from that standpoint *Vidyā* and *Avidyā* are said to be related to the same person.

[12] *Other than etc.*—That is to say, the purpose of the meditation on *Sambhūti* is the purification of the mind. As this is not the same as the knowledge of Brahman, therefore, *Sambhūti* is condemned.

[13] *Immortal*—In comparison with the phenomenal *Jīva*, *Sambhūti* or *Hiraṇyagarbha* is said to be immortal, as the cosmic soul exists even after the death of the *Jīva*. But from the standpoint of Brahman, *Hiraṇyagarbha* is also mortal and impermanent. Therefore it is condemned.

[14] *Such etc.*—There is no act of creation from the standpoint of Reality, because the very idea of creation is due to ignorance. Creation is but an idea of the mind and hence negated.

[15] *This etc.*—*i.e.*, the idea of causality cannot apply to Brahman. It is only an explanation of things in the phenomenal world due to the ignorance of the real nature of Brahman.

स एष नेति नेतीति व्याख्यातं निह्नुते यतः ।
सर्वमग्राह्यभावेन हेतुनाऽजं प्रकाशते ॥ २६ ॥

26. *As the* Śruti *passage, 'It is not this, not this', on account of the incomprehensibility of* Ātman, *negates all (dualistic) ideas described; (as the means for the attainment of* Ātman), *therefore the birthless* (Ātman *alone*) *exists* (*and not any duality*).

## Śaṅkara's Commentary

The *Śruti*[1] in such passage as, 'This is the final instruction. It is not this, not this,' has determined the nature of *Ātman* by the refutation of all specific characteristics. But knowing this *Ātman* to be incomprehensible[2] the *Sruti* has again sought to establish the very same *Ātman* through other means and finally refuted what have been described (as the means for the attainment of *Ātman*). That is to say, the *Śruti*, in such passage as, 'It is not this, not this', demonstrates the incomprehensibility of *Ātman* or in other words, refutes the idea that *Ātman*[3] can be realised or understood. Those[4] who do not understand that the means (suggested for the realisation of *Ātman*) have only one purpose, *viz.*, the realisation of the end (*i.e.*, the non-dual *Ātman*), make a mistake by thinking that what are suggested as the means have the same reality as the end. In order to remove this error, the *Śruti* negates the reality[5] of the means by[6] pointing out the incomprehensibility of *Ātman*, as its reason. Subsequently,[7] the student knows that the means serve their purpose by pointing only to the end and the end itself is always one and changeless. To such a student the knowledge of the unborn Self which is both within and without reveals itself.[8]

[1] *The Śruti*—The reference is to the *Bṛhadāraṇyaka Upaniṣad* (2. 3. 1) which begins with the statement: 'There are two forms of Brahman, the material and the immaterial, the mortal and the immortal, the solid and the fluid . . .' The chapter ends thus: 'Next follows the teaching (of Brahman) by "No, no"; for, there is nothing else higher than this (if one says): "It is not so" . . . .' Those who cannot meditate on Brahman, free from all attributes, are advised to concentrate on some characteristics (of Brahman) superimposed upon Brahman for the facility of meditation. Then the students are asked to negate those attributes also, because thus alone can they realise the undifferentiated Brahman which alone is the Supreme Reality.

[2] *Incomprehensible*—It is because the knowledge of the Self is extremely subtle.

[3] *Ātman etc.*—That is to say, the *Ātman* is never the effect of any thought or words. It is not an object of meditation or speech. For it is our very self. Thus the *Śruti* advises the students to dissociate from *Ātman* all words, or thoughts which were at first accepted as means for its realisation. That which is thought by the mind is merely an idea. It is changeable and negatable. Hence it is not Reality. Therefore any idea associated with *Ātman* is not the *Ātman* itself.

[4] *Those etc.*—The unwary students, unable to understand the real significance of *Vedānta,* make the mistake of thinking that the attributes which are superimposed upon Brahman are as real as Brahman itself. That is to say, they think that these attributes have an independent existence.

[5] *Reality—i. e.,* a reality independent of Brahman.

[6] *By pointing out*—This is the Advaitic method of reasoning. Brahman or *Ātman,* being beyond time, space and causality, is ever incomprehensible through any empirical means. It is the eternal subject having no object through which one can comprehend it. This incomprehensibility of *Ātman* is the very reason for refuting any attribute that may be otherwise associated with it. If *Ātman* can be known by any positive attribute, it no longer remains incomprehensible. It becomes an object of our thought like any other perceived object. Such *Ātman* can never be the changeless Absolute.

[7] *Subsequently etc.*—The discriminating student, through his superior power of reasoning, refutes all attributes superimposed upon *Ātman.* He realises that these attributes have no independent reality. Then he understands that all attributes are the same as the non-dual Brahman, as one who knows the true nature of the rope realises that what he formerly thought of as the snake is nothing but the rope. That which was superimposed upon the rope is identical with the substratum. Only the idea of the existence of the snake *apart from* the rope is illusion. Similarly all attributes of *Ātman,* such as materiality or immateriality etc., are, in reality, identical with *Ātman.* To concede any separate existence to the attributes independent of *Ātman* is illusion. *Ātman,* the non-dual, changeless, and causeless Reality, alone exists. All that exists is *Ātman.* Even that which is imagined as means for the realisation of *Ātman* is not separate from *Ātman.*

[8] *Itself—i. e.,* the final revelation of *Ātman* does not depend upon *Śruti* or anything else. A knower of *Ātman* realises that *Ātman* always exists and is self-luminous; and needs no external means to illumine it.

सतो हि मायया जन्म युज्यते न तु तत्त्वतः ।
तत्त्वतो जायते यस्य जातं तस्य हि जायते ॥ २७ ॥

27. *That which is ever-existent appears to pass into birth through illusion* (Māyā) *and not from the standpoint of Reality.*

*He who thinks that this passing into birth is real asserts, as a matter of fact, that what is born is born again (and so on without end).*

ŚAṄKARA'S COMMENTARY

Thus hundreds of Scriptural passages conclude that the essence which is the non-dual and birthless Self, existing both within and without, is the only Reality, and that nothing else, besides the Self, exists. Now, in order to determine this very Reality through reason, again it is stated:

(Objection)—It may also be true that if Reality be incomprehensible then the knowledge of Self would be unreal.

(Reply)—No, this cannot be, for[1] the effect is comprehended. As the effects, that is to say, creation (of new things), come from a really existent magician through *Māyā* (magic), so also the comprehension of the effects, in the form of the creation of the universe, leads us to infer the *existence of the Ātman*, the Supreme Reality, who, like the magician, is, as it were, the substratum of the illusion which is seen in the form of the creation of the universe. For, the creation of the universe is possible only with a Reality, *i.e.*, an existing cause, like the birth of the effects, such as the elephant etc., conjured up through illusion (by an existing magician); and this creation is never possible with a non-existing cause. It is not, however, possible for the unborn *Ātman* to really pass into birth. Or,[2] the first line of the text may be explained in another manner. As a really existing entity, such as the rope etc., passes into such effects as the snake etc., only *through Māyā* and not in reality, similarly, the real and the incomprehensible *Ātman* is seen to pass into birth, in the form of the universe, like the rope becoming the snake, only through illusion. The birthless *Ātman* cannot pass into birth from the standpoint of Reality. But the disputant who holds that the unborn *Ātman*, the Supreme Reality, is really born in the form of the universe, cannot assert that the *unborn* is born, as this implies a contradiction.[3] In that case he must admit that, in fact, what is (already) born, again passes into birth. If, thus, birth is predicated of that which is already born, then the disputant is faced with what is known in logic as *regressus ad infinitum*. Therefore it is established that the Essence which is *Ātman* is ever unborn and non-dual.

It has already been established on scriptural evidence that the *Ātman* which is the Supreme Reality is birthless and non-dual. All duality is mere imagination due to ignorance and hence unreal. This is now established independently by reason. Śaṅkara always maintains a dual aspect. For those who believe in Scripture, Śaṅkara quotes the Scripture to establish his point. Again for those who do not believe in the Vedas as the supreme authority but who depend upon reason alone, Śaṅkara gives rational proof of his conclusion.

[1] *For etc.*—The opponent believes in causality but denies *Ātman*. This is illogical. If one admits the creation of the universe then one must believe in its cause also. Every effect presupposes a cause. Even every illusion must have a substratum. A positive effect cannot be produced from a non-existing cause. The position of the *Advaitin* is this: If you believe in the universe as a created entity, you must admit its cause, namely, Brahman. The positive effect of the universe cannot come from a non-existing cause. Brahman or *Ātman,* however, does not really create the universe nor transform itself into the universe, as the rope does not really create the snake nor does it become the snake. The appearance of creation is due to ignorance. Therefore the theory of *Māyā* or *vivarta* which posits a real *Ātman* is the best explanation of the universe when such universe is recognised as a fact.

[2] *Or etc.*—The first interpretation of the first line points to *Ātman* as the instrumental cause (*Nimitta Kāraṇa*) of the universe, though the very perception of the creation is due to illusion. This interpretation stresses the *Reality* of *Ātman*. The second interpretation stresses on the fact that the idea of the unborn *Ātman* passing into birth is due to ignorance. The process of creation and creation itself are illusory.

[3] *Contradiction*—It is because the unborn cannot give birth to a new thing. If this causality be admitted then the so-called unborn

cause must itself come from another cause and so on *ad infinitum.* Thus we never come across *an unborn* cause. There will be thus an endless past in the case of causes and an equally endless future in the case of effects. If the cause produces an effect, that effect, in its turn, must produce new effect and so on *ad infinitum* (Hegel's position). Thus there can be no *mukti* or liberation which means freedom from the causal chain.

असतो मायया जन्म तत्त्वतो नैव युज्यते ।
वन्ध्यापुत्रो न तत्त्वेन मायया वाऽपि जायते ॥ २८ ॥

28. *The unreal cannot be born either really or through* Māyā. *For the son of a barren woman is neither in reality nor in illusion.*

## Śaṅkara's Commentary

There are those who hold that all entities are unreal, that the non-existent produces this world. But production, by the non-existent, of any thing either in reality or in illusion is not possible. For we know nothing like it in our experience. As the son of a barren woman is not seen to be born either really or through *Māyā*, the theory of the non-existence of things is in truth[1] untenable.

If the ultimate Reality be non-existent, then it cannot pass into birth. Again if what we perceive be unreal, its production is likewise impossible. In either case causality is unreal. We have seen from the previous *Kārikā* (27) that the Reality, which is the unborn *Ātman*, cannot be said to pass into birth, without our being forced into an infinite regress. This *Kārikā* shows that production is an impossibility if the ultimate Reality be non-existent, or if the thing we perceive be unreal. So, causality or production or passing into birth is an absurdity.

1 *In truth*—In case the *Ātman* is a Reality, the passing into birth may be explained by *Māyā;* but in this case even that explanation cannot hold, for there is no evidence in our actual experience to justify the presumption that either something comes out of nothing or nothing comes out of something.

यथा स्वप्ने द्वयाभासं स्पन्दते मायया मनः ।
तथा जाग्रद्द्वयाभासं स्पन्दते मायया मनः ॥ २९ ॥

29. *As in dream the mind acts through* Māyā *presenting the appearance of duality, so also in the waking state the mind acts, through* Māyā, *presenting the appearance of duality.*

## Śaṅkara's Commentary

How is it possible for the Reality to pass into birth through *Māyā*? It is thus replied: As the snake imagined in the rope, is real[1] when seen as the rope, so also the mind,[2] from the standpoint of the knowledge of the ultimate Reality, is seen to be identical with *Ātman*. This mind, in dream, appears to us as dual in the forms of the cogniser and the cognised through[3] *Māyā*, as the snake appears to be separate from the rope through ignorance. Similarly, indeed the mind acts (in a dual form) in the waking state through *Māyā*. That[4] is to say, the mind appears to act.

[1] *Real etc.*—The snake is unreal when we try to see it as separated from the rope. But when the real nature of the rope is known then it is realised that the snake, which appeared, is really identical with the rope. The substratum (*Adhiṣṭhāna*) is the same as that which is superimposed (*Āropita*) upon it.

[2] *Mind*—The mind as the substratum of the dream experiences, is identical with Reality or *Ātman*.

[3] *Through Māyā*—In dream we have the experience of the separate existence of the perceiver, the object of perception and the act of perceiving. But in the waking state we know these threefold experiences to be nothing but the mind so appearing. The idea that the dream experiences are different from the mind is due to the ignorance which exists in the dream state. The knower of the real nature of the rope finds it to be identical with the snake.

[4] *That etc.*—For, in reality Brahman does not act. The action of the mind is due to *Māyā*. The *Śruti* also says that mind in reality is Brahman.

अद्वयं च द्वयाभासं मनः स्वप्ने न संशयः ।
अद्वयं च द्वयाभासं तथा जाग्रन्न संशयः ॥ ३० ॥

30. *There is no doubt that the mind, which is, in fact, non-dual appears as dual in dream ; in like manner undoubtedly that which is non-dual, appears as dual in the waking state also.*

## ŚAṄKARA'S COMMENTARY

Really speaking, the snake is identical with the rope. In like manner, the mind which is non-dual[1] as *Ātman* appears undoubtedly in dual forms in dreams. Verily in dream, such objects of perception as elephants etc., or their perceivers such as eyes etc., have[2] no existence independently of consciousness (mind). Similar[3] is the case in the waking state as well. For (conciousness) mind, which is the highest Reality, is common to both.

The opponent may contend that the previous *Kārikā* admits duality. This *Kārikā* shows that the perception of duality is due to our ignorance. The only Reality, both in the dream and the waking states, is mind or consciousness which appears as dual, *i. e.*, the perceiver and the perceived, on account of ignorance.

[1] *Non-dual etc.*—This is known in *Suṣupti* or deep-sleep when the mind remains as pure and non-dual.

[2] *Have etc.*—That the perceiver and the perceived in the dream state have no existence independent of the mind is known in the waking state.

[3] *Similar etc.*—In the waking state also what is perceived is only the act of the mind. The same consciousness is common in both the states. The idea of a mind having the dual characteristics of determination and volition is superimposed upon the substratum, *i. e.*, consciousness ; and as a result, the phenomenal world is perceived. It should not be thought that there is any other cause for the appearance of duality excepting ignorance.

मनोदृश्यमिदं द्वैतं यत्किंचित्सचराचरम् ।
मनसो ह्यमनीभावे द्वैतं नैवोपलभ्यते ॥ ३१ ॥

31. *All these dual objects, comprising everything that is movable and immovable, perceived by the mind (are mind alone). For, duality is never experienced when the mind ceases to act.*

### Śaṅkara's Commentary

It has been said that it is the mind alone which appears as dual (objects) like the appearance of the snake in the rope. But what is its proof? Our answer is this: We make the statement on the strength of an inference following the method of agreement and difference. The proposition is that all this duality perceived as such by the imagination of the mind is, in reality, nothing but the mind. The reason for such inference is that duality is perceived when the mind acts and it vanishes when the mind ceases to act; that is to say, when the (activity, *i.e.*, the *Vṛttis* of the) mind is withdrawn[1] unto itself by the knowledge got through discrimination, repeated practice and renunciation—like the disappearance of the snake in the rope—or during deep sleep.[2] Hence on account of the disappearance of duality it is established that duality is unreal or illusory. That the perception of duality is due to the action of the mind is further proved in this *Kārika*.

[1] *Withdrawn etc.*—This may be called *Samādhi*. But Vedānta does not prescribe any mechanical method for the attainment of this state. The Vedāntic method for the control of the mind is the discrimination between the real and the unreal (repeated discrimination), all based upon reasoning.

[2] *Deep sleep*—Although there is a difference, *Suṣupti* has often been pointed out by the Vedāntic Seers as similar to the state of *Nirvikalpa-Samādhi*. *Suṣupti* is the state when the mind ceases to act. Consequently in it duality is not perceived.

आत्मसत्यानुबोधेन न संकल्पयते यदा ।
अमनस्तां तदा याति ग्राह्याभावे तदग्रहम् ।। ३२ ।।

32. *When the mind does not imagine on account of the knowledge of the Truth which is* Ātman, *then it ceases to be mind and becomes free from all idea of cognition, for want of objects to be cognised.*

### Śaṅkara's Commentary

How does the mind become naught? It is thus replied: The *Ātman* alone is the Reality like[1] the clay; as in the *Śruti* passage, 'All modifications are mere names arising from efforts of speech. The clay alone is real'. That knowledge of the reality of *Ātman* comes through the Scripture[2] and the teacher. The mind having attained to that knowledge does not imagine, as[3] there remains nothing to be imagined. The mind then is like fire when there is no fuel to burn. When the mind thus does no longer imagine, it *ceases to be mind*, that is, the mind, for want of any object to be cognised, becomes free from all cognition.

[1] *Like etc.*—The only reality in the pots, jars, plates, etc., (made of clay) is the clay. The names and forms, on account of their changeability and negatability, are unreal. Similarly the only reality in this universe is *Ātman*; all other objects which are mere acts of mind, being changeable and negatable, are unreal.

[2] *Scripture etc.*—The Scripture and the teacher only tell the student what is not *Ātman*. They follow the negative method for pointing out the Reality, which is the rational method pursued in philosophy proper.

[3] *As etc.*—The acts of mind which conjure up the world of duality belong to the empirical realm, *i. e.*, to the realm wherein the duality of the subject and the object is recognised. But such action becomes impossible in the absolute state where there is no consciousness of subject and object. In that state Brahman alone is realised and hence the mind, consisting of determination and volition, ceases to exist. Then mind becomes identical with Brahman which is free from all duality of cognition.

अकल्पकमजं ज्ञानं ज्ञेयाभिन्नं प्रचक्षते ।
ब्रह्मज्ञेयमजं नित्यमजेनाजं विबुध्यते ॥ ३३ ॥

33. *The knowledge* (Jñānam) *which is unborn and free from all imaginations is ever inseparable from the knowable. The immutable and birthless Brahman is the sole object of knowledge. The birthless is known by the birthless.*

## Śaṅkara's Commentary

If all this duality be illusory, how is the knowledge of the Self to be realised? It is thus replied: The Knowers of Brahman describe knowledge, *i.e.*, the mere essence of thought, which is unborn and free from all imaginations as[1] non-different from Brahman, the ultimate Reality, which is also the object of knowledge. This is supported by such Scriptural passages as, 'Like heat from fire, knowledge (*Jñānam*) is never absent from the knower (*Ātman*)', 'Brahman is Knowledge and Bliss', 'Brahman is Reality, Knowledge and Infinity', etc. The knowledge of which Brahman is the object, is non-different from (the knowable) Brahman, as is the heat from the fire. The Essence of the Self, which is the object of knowledge, verily knows itself by means of unborn knowledge, which is of the very nature of *Ātman*. Brahman which is of the nature of one homogeneous mass of eternal consciousness, does not depend upon another[2] instrument of knowledge (for its illumination), as is the case with the sun, which being of the nature of continuous light (does not require any instrument to illumine itself).

[1] *As non-different etc.*—The *Jñānam* or knowledge is the same as Brahman; otherwise no knowledge would be able to tell us what Brahman is. Darkness cannot illumine the sun. Only the light of the sun which is the sun itself, can illumine the sun.

[2] *Another instrument*—Such as scripture etc., which only tell us what is not self.

To the *Jñānī*, even when he acts in this empirical world, the knower, the knowledge and the object of knowledge are all Brahman. And yet all these, being of the nature of Brahman, are without birth (*Aja*).

निगृहीतस्य मनसो निर्विकल्पस्य धीमतः ।
प्रचारः स तु विज्ञेयः सुषुप्तेऽन्यो न तत्समः ॥ ३४ ॥

34. *The behaviour of the mind that is under control,* i.e., *which is free from all imaginations and that is endowed with discrimination, should be known. The condition of the mind in deep sleep is of another sort and not like that.*

### Śaṅkara's Commentary

It has been stated before that the mind, free from imagination on account of the knowledge[1] of Truth, which is *Ātman*, becomes tranquil for want of external objects, like the fire not fed by fuel. Such mind may be said to be under control. It has been further stated that duality disappears when the mind thus ceases to act. The *Yogīs* should particularly know the behaviour[2] of the mind which is thus brought under discipline, which is free from all imaginations and which is possessed of discrimination.

(Objection)—In[3] the absence of all specific consciousness the mind, in the state of deep sleep, behaves exactly in the same manner as does the mind under control. What is there to be known in the absence of all specific knowledge?

(Reply)—To this objection we reply thus: Your objection is not valid. For, the behaviour of the mind in deep sleep, overcome by the darkness of delusion caused by ignorance, and still full of many potential desires which are the seeds of numerous future undesirable activities, is quite different from the behaviour of the mind well under control and free from the ignorance which produces activities that give rise to numerous afflictions, and from which has been burnt away by the fire of self-knowledge the ignorance which contains the harmful seed of all potential tendencies to act. The behaviour of the latter kind of mind is quite different.[4] Therefore it is not like the mind in deep sleep. Hence the behaviour of such mind should be known. This[5] is the purport.

[1] *Knowledge etc.*—This implies the discrimination between real and unreal.

[2] *Behaviour*—The word '*Pracāra*' in the text implying behaviour of activity shows that by '*Nigraha*' or discipline is not meant the Yogic discipline leading to *Nirvikalpa-Samādhi*; for, in that state the mind loses all activity and movement. To a *Jñānī* the *Pracāra* or the ideation of the mind is also Brahman. Therefore these ideations should be examined or analysed.

[3] *In the etc.*—The opponent evidently mistakes the Vedāntic tranquillity of mind arrived at by discrimination etc., for the Yogic *Samādhi* which is cultivated by controlling the activities of the mind. Hence his objection to Yogic trance, like deep sleep, is associated with absence of mental ideation. *Śaṅkara* in his commentary on the *Brahmasūtras* (2. 1. 9) and in various other places puts *Yogic Samādhi* and deep sleep under the same category.

[4] *Different*—It is because the mind of the *Jnānī* is always established in Brahman.

[5] *This etc.*—The purport is that the mind of a man, who has not known the Truth of Self, becomes absorbed in *Avidyā* at the time of deep sleep or *Samādhi*. Such mind is free from all activities and remains in a motionless, *i. e.*, inactive condition, concealing within it all the seeds of future dual activities. But the mind of a *Jñānī* is well under discipline by the constant practice of discrimination. That mind is always saturated with the *thought* of Brahman. Hence the mind of a *Jñānī* does not lose its activities which are identical with the non-dual Brahman itself.

लीयते हि सुषुप्ते तन्निगृहीतं न लीयते ।
तदेव निर्भयं ब्रह्म ज्ञानालोकं समन्ततः ॥ ३५ ॥

35. *As the mind is withdrawn at the time of deep sleep and not so in the case of the (Vedāntic) discipline, (therefore there is a difference between the condition of the mind of a sleeper and that of a* Jñānī). *That (mind of a* Jñānī) *becomes identical with fearless Brahman whose all-round illumination is consciousness alone.*

ŚAṄKARA'S COMMENTARY

Now is stated the reason for the distinction between the behaviour (of the mind of a sleeper and that of a *Jñānī*). The mind in deep sleep, with the desires which are the cause of all experiences during the state of ignorance, goes[1] back to the seed-like condition of potentiality characterised by the undifferentiated[2] feature of darkness; but the[3] mind (of a *Jñānī*) which is disciplined by discrimination is not so withdrawn, that is to say, does not go back to the seed-like state of darkness. Therefore is made the distinction between the behaviour of the mind in deep sleep and that of a *Jñānī* whose mind is under control. When the mind becomes free from all ideas of the perceiver and the perceived—the dual evils caused by ignorance—it verily becomes one with the Supreme and the non-dual Brahman. Therefore the mind becomes free from all fear; for, in that state, the perception of duality, which is the cause of fear, is absent. Brahman is peace and fearlessness. Having realised Brahman, the *Jñānī* is not afraid of anything. This is thus further amplified: *Jñānam* means the essence of Knowledge, *i.e.*, the consciousness which is the very nature of *Ātman* or the Self. Brahman is that whose expression is the Knowledge thus described. In other words, Brahman is the one mass of sentiency. The word, 'all-round' in the text, implies that this knowledge of Brahman is without[4] break and all-pervading like the ether.

It is implied in the previous text of the *Kārikā* that there is a difference between the mind of a *Jñānī* and that of a deep sleeper. The reason for this difference is stated in this *Kārikā*.

[1] *Goes back etc.*—For, an ignorant man, when he wakes up from deep sleep, again experiences these desires. Therefore the desires are said to remain in a potential state in deep sleep.

[2] *Undifferentiated etc.*—It is because the experience of deep sleep is characterised by the absence of all that is known. The man describing the condition of deep sleep says, 'I know nothing during that state'.

[3] *The mind etc.*—But the case of a *Jñānī* is quite different. By the practice of discrimination, he can distinguish reality from unreality. All objects of cognition, being changeable and negatable, are known to the *Jñānī* as unreal. Therefore the knowledge of Brahman does not denote a state in which the desires remain in potential condition. For, the desires of a *Jñānī* are destroyed for ever by the knowledge of the non-dual Brahman. Hence, a man having attained to the knowledge of Brahman does not experience any desire, which implies cogniser and cognised. The *Jñānī* knows the activities of his mind as identical with the non-dual Brahman.

[4] *Without break etc.*—That is to say, the *Jñānī* may be engaged in any activity, but in everything he realises Brahman alone. The experiences of a *Jñānī* have thus been described in the *Gītā* (4. 24): 'Brahman is the offering, Brahman is the oblation poured into the fire of Brahman. Brahman verily shall be reached by him who always sees Brahman in action.'

अजमनिद्रमस्वप्नमनामकमरूपकम् ।
सकृद्विभातं सर्वज्ञं नोपचारः कथंचन ॥ ३६ ॥

36. *(This Brahman is) birthless, free from sleep and dream, without name and form, ever-effulgent and omniscient. Nothing has to be done in any way (with respect to Brahman).*

## Śaṅkara's Commentary

Brahman is both within and without as well as unborn, as there is no cause for its passing into birth. For, we have already stated that (the phenomenon of) birth is seen on account of the ignorance (of the real nature of a thing), as[1] is the case with the rope giving birth to the (illusion of the) snake. It is birthless because all ignorance is destroyed by the knowledge of Truth which is the *Ātman*. Hence it is free from sleep;[2] for *Ātman*, which is, by nature, non-dual, is always free from sleep the nature of which is that of beginningless delusion characterised by ignorance. Therefore it is free from dream.[3] Name and forms which are ascribed to it are due to the ignorance of its real nature. These names and forms are destroyed by Knowledge. It is like the (destruction of the illusion of the) snake seen in the rope. Hence Brahman cannot be described by any name, nor can it be in any manner described to be of any form. To support this, there are such *Śruti* passages as, 'From which words come back' etc. Moreover, it[4] is ever effulgent or it is of the very nature of effulgence. For,[5] it is free from (the ideas of) manifestation and non-manifestation characterised by wrong-apprehension and non-apprehension. Apprehension and non-apprehension are (as inseparable) as day and night. Darkness is the characteristic of ignorance.' These are the causes of the non-manifestation (of the real nature of *Ātman*). These[6] are absent in *Ātman*. Moreover *Ātman* is always of the nature of consciousness and effulgence. Therefore it is reasonable to speak of *Ātman* as ever-effulgent. It is all-knowing, that is to say, *Ātman* is all that exists and *Ātman* is consciousness (awareness) itself. As regards such Brahman (*i.e.*, the one that knows such Brahman) no action can be enjoined, as may be in the case of others, who (on account of their ignorance of the real nature of Brahman) are asked to practise concentration etc., on the nature of *Ātman*. The[7] purport is that besides the destruction of ignorance it is not possible to prescribe any disciplinary action (for the knowledge of Brahman), as Brahman is always of the nature of purity, knowledge and freedom.

The nature of Brahman, which is the subject-matter under discussion is thus described in other ways. The purport of the *Kārikā* is that apart from tho realisation of one's identity with the attributeless Brahman no effort is to be made by him. The categorical imperative of Kant has no meaning for a knower of *Ātman*. *Yogic Samādhi* is not the same as the goal of *Jñāna-Yoga* as described in the philosophy of Advaita Vedānta or the *Kārikā.*

[1] *As etc.*—The phenomenon of the rope producing the snake is due to ignorance of the real nature of the rope.

[2] *Sleep*—Sleep or *Nidrā* means the non-apprehension of objects, as is the characteristic of the mind in deep sleep. In the causal world this *Nidrā* or ignorance is known to be beginningless, as no beginning of it can be found.

[3] *Dream*—The dream or *Svapna* is characterised by wrong apprehension of objects. This is not possible in the case of *Ātman* which is of the nature of eternal purity, knowledge and illumination.

[4] *It is etc.*—The *Ātman* is that which gives us the idea of light. It is not itself what is described as light in the waking state.

[5] *For etc.*—The ideas of non-apprehension and wrong apprehension are correlatives. The one implies the other. Similarly the ideas of manifestation and non-manifestation are correlatives. When an empirical *Jīva* becomes oblivious of himself, as in deep sleep, he is said to be in a state of non-manifestation characterised by the non-perception of objects. Similarly, the empirical *Jīva* is said to be manifested, as in dream or waking state, when he apprehends objects in a wrong way, *i. e.*, not as they are in their true character which is the non-dual Brahman. But Brahman cannot be identified with the dualistic concepts of non-apprehension or wrong apprehension and non-manifestation or manifestation, as it is the witness of all these conditions.

[6] *There are etc.*—The ideas of manifestation and non-manifestation cannot inhere in *Ātman* from the standpoint of Reality. These are attributed to *Ātman*, as one says that *Ātman* is unmanifested to us previous to the realisation of knowledge and it is manifested to us

subsequent to that realisation. These statements are made from the empirical standpoint. But Brahman is always of the nature of illumination which never decreases or increases under any circumstances. In common parlance the advent of day and night is associated with the rising and the setting of the sun. But the sun neither rises nor sets. It is always bright and effulgent. If one takes his stand in the sun he sees neither the night nor its correlative the day. But if a man is away from the sun, he imagines the rising and setting of the sun and consequently experiences day and night which have no meaning from the standpoint of the sun.

[7] *The purport etc.*—All imaginations regarding *Samādhi* etc., may have their application in the state of ignorance when one does not realise the ever-illumined nature of his self.

सर्वाभिलापविगतः सर्वचिन्तासमुत्थितः ।
सुप्रशान्तः सकृज्ज्योतिः समाधिरचलोऽभयः ॥ ३७ ॥

37. *(This* Ātman *is) beyond all expression by words, beyond all acts of mind; (It is) all peace, eternal effulgence, free from activity and fear and attainable by concentrated understanding (of the* Jīva*).*

### Śaṅkara's Commentary

Now is explained the reason for indicating Brahman as without name etc., as stated above. The word *Abhilāpa*, meaning expression, denotes here the instrument of sound by which all sounds are expressed. Brahman is beyond speech. The instrument of sound is used in the sense of metonymy *i.e.*, it also implies other instruments of sense-knowledge. The purport is that the *Ātman* is beyond all external sense-organs. Similarly, it is beyond all activities of the mind. The word '*Cintā*' in the text stands for 'mind' (or the internal organ of thought). For, the *Śruti* says, 'It is verily without *Prāṇa* and without mind', 'It is higher than the imperishable Supreme', It is all peace as it is free from all distinctions. The *Ātman* is ever-effulgent, that is to say, being of the nature of self-consciousness which is its very essence, it is eternal light. The *Ātman* is denoted by the word *Samādhi*[1] as it can be realised only by the knowledge arising out of the deepest concentration (on its essence) or, the *Ātman* is denoted by *Samādhi* because the *Jīva* concentrates his mind on *Ātman*. It is immovable, *i.e.*, beyond change· Hence, it is fearless as it is free from change.

[1] *Samādhi*—This state of complete identity with non-dual Brahman, arrived at as a result of discrimination and negation of phenomena, is the Vedāntic conception of *Samādhi* (which is quite different from any mystical or mechanical state described as *Samādhi* in the *Yoga* system).

ग्रहो न तत्र नोत्सर्गश्चिन्ता यत्र न विद्यते ।
आत्मसंस्थं तदा ज्ञानमजाति समतां गतम् ॥ ३८ ॥

38. *In that Brahman which is free from all acts of mind there is neither any idea of acceptance nor any idea of giving up (of anything). Established in the* Ātman *(Self), knowledge attains to the state of birthlessness and sameness, that is to say, changelessness.*

### Śaṅkara's Commentary

As Brahman alone has been described in the previous text as *Samādhi* (*i.e.*, the sole object of concentration) and as free from activity and fear, therefore in that Brahman there[1] is nothing to accept nor is there anything to give up. For, acceptance or abandonment is possible only where there is change or the possibility of change. But both these are inconsistent with Brahman—as nothing else exists which can cause a change in Brahman, and further because Brahman is without parts. Therefore, the meaning is that in Brahman there is no possibility of either accepting or giving up anything. The purport of the *Kārikā* is this: How can there be any acceptance or abandonment (in Brahman) where, in the absence of the mind, no[2] mentation whatsoever is possible? When the knowledge of Reality which is the Self, ensues, then Knowledge, for want of any object to rest upon, becomes[3] established in *Ātman*, like the heat of fire (in the absence of fuel). *Ajāti*, *i.e.*, free from birth. It attains to the state of supreme non-duality. Thus is concluded, by means of reasoning and Scriptural authority what was stated before as a proposition in the following words: 'Now I shall describe the non-dual Brahman which is free from limitation and birth and which is the same everywhere.' Everything else, other than the knowledge of Reality which is the Self, birthless and homogeneous, implies limitation. The *Śruti* also says, 'O Gārgī, he who departs from this world without knowing that Imperishable One, is, indeed, narrow-minded'. The purport is that everyone, realising this knowledge, becomes established in Brahman and attains to the fulfilment of all desires.

This *Kārikā* tells us that the changeless non-dual Brahman is beyond all injunctions, mandatory or prohibitory, as enjoined by Scriptures or society. These injunctions apply only to the realm of ignorance,

[1] *There is etc.*—All ethics, prescribing moral codes to be followed of immoral acts to be shunned, apply to the dual world. They have no meaning in respect of Brahman or the Knower of Brahman, which are identical.

[2] *No mentation*—For, it is the activities of the mind alone which conjure up the phenomena of a dual world with all its injunctions, prohibitory or mandatory.

[3] *Becomes etc.*—Knowledge of Brahman is the same as Brahman.

अस्पर्शयोगो वै नाम दुर्दशः सर्वयोगिभिः ।
योगिनो बिभ्यति ह्यस्मादभये भयदर्शिनः ॥ ३९ ॥

39. *This* Yoga, *which is not in touch with anything, is hard to be attained by all* Yogis *(in general). The* Yogis *are afraid of it, for they see fear in it where there is really fearlessness.*

### Śaṅkara's Commentary

Though[1] such is the nature of the knowledge of the Supreme Reality, yet it is described in the Upaniṣads[2] as *Yoga* not in touch with anything; for, it is free from all touch implying relations (with objects). It is hard to be attained by the *Yogis*[3] who are devoid of the knowledge taught in the Vedānta philosophy. In other words, this truth can be realised only by the efforts culminating in the knowledge of *Ātman* as the Sole Reality. The *Yogis* shrink from it, which is free from all fear, for[4] they think that this *Yoga* brings about the annihilation of their self. In other words, the *Yogis*, being devoid of discrimination, who, through fear, apprehend the destruction of their self, are afraid of it which is, in reality, fearlessness.[5]

[1] *Though etc.*—The word '*Yoga*' signifying union, generally means contact between two. But derivatively *Jñāna-Yoga* is not in touch with any idea or object, as there exists nothing else but the non-dual Brahman. Therefore it is called the *Asparśa-Yoga*, *i. e.*, a spiritual discipline which does not admit of relation or touch with anything else.

[2] *Upaniṣads*—The Upaniṣad says that the knowledge of *Ātman* is ever uncontaminated by any touch of action sinful or virtuous.

[3] *Yogis*—That is to say, those who are called *Yogis* according to *Patañjali*. Their aim is to attain to the trance-condition by some mystical or mechanical means and thereby become oblivious of the miseries of the world. But Vedānta says that the world as it is, if seen in its true character, is Brahman.

[4] *For etc.*—The *Yogis* are afraid of losing their individual consciousness which is the pivot of enjoyments in the world. But Vedānta says that the true nature of an individual is his identity with the non-dual Brahman. The idea of individual existence is due to the ignorance of one's own nature.

[5] *Fearlessness*—Brahman is fearless because it is ever-free, ever-illumined and ever-pure. There is nothing else of which it can be afraid. Fear comes from the sense of duality.

मनसो निग्रहायत्तमभयं सर्वयोगिना(णा)म् ।
दुःखक्षयः प्रबोधश्चाप्यक्षया शान्तिरेव च ॥ ४० ॥

40. *The* Yogis (*who do not follow the method of* Jñāna-Yoga *as described in the* Kārikā) *depend on the control of their mind for fearlessness, destruction of misery, the knowledge of self and eternal peace.*

ŚAṄKARA'S COMMENTARY

Those[1] who regard mind and the sense-organs, when seen apart from their identity with the very nature of Brahman, as mere imagination—like that of the snake when seen apart from its identity with the rope—and who thus deny the sole reality of the mind and the sense-organs (independent of Brahman), *i.e.*, those who look upon themselves as of the very nature of Brahman, spontaneously enjoy, as quite natural to them, fearlessness and eternal peace known as Freedom, (perfect knowledge) for which they (the *Jñānīs*) do not depend upon any mechanical effort (such as the control of the mind etc.). We have already stated that no duty (effort), whatsoever, exists for the *Jñānī*. But those other *Yogis* who are also traversing the path (leading to Truth), but who possess inferior[2] or middling understanding and who[3] look upon the mind as separate from but related to *Ātman*, and who[4] are ignorant of the knowledge regarding the reality of *Ātman*—the *Yogis* belonging to this class can experience fearlessness as a result of the discipline of the mind. To them[5] the destruction of misery is also dependent upon mental control. The ignorant can never experience the cessation of misery, if the mind, (considered) related to *Ātman*, becomes active. Besides, their knowledge of self is dependent on their control of the mind. And similarly, eternal peace, known as *Mokṣa* (or liberation), in their case, depends upon the mental discipline.

This *Kārikā* applies to those who look upon the mind as separate from *Ātman* and think that peace, knowledge, etc., depend upon its control.

[1] *Those etc.*—The *Jñānī* knows the mind and sense-organs to be identical with the non-dual Brahman. It is like the identity of the snake with the rope. As the snake in the illusion of the snake in the rope has no existence apart from the rope, similarly, the mind has no existence separate from Brahman. To see the mind as separate from Brahman is a freak of imagination. They, the *Jñānīs* knowing this truth, do not care for the control of the mind. For, the mind, as such, does not exist for them. One who realises mind as Brahman, finds spontaneously, peace, fearlessness, etc. Fear, misery, etc., are the outcome of duality. Duality is seen on account of the activity of the mind. But the *Jñānī* sees the identity of the mind and Brahman. Therefore duality does not exist for him. Hence he does not experience any fear, misery, etc. Therefore, peace, fearlessness, etc., in his case are natural.

[2] *Inferior etc.*—That is to say, they do not possess the sharp intellect that can distinguish the real from the unreal. For them the *Yogic* practices are recommended.

[3] *Who etc.*—It is because they find the mind as separate from Brahman that they try to keep it under control. According to them, the mind is acted upon by *Ātman*.

[4] *Who are etc.*—For they see a duality of the *Ātman* and the mind.

[5] *To them etc.*—The *Yogis* think that misery is caused by the activities of the mind. Hence they direct all their energy to the suppression of the *Vṛttis* of the mind. But the *Vṛttis* reappear if the attempt is slightly relaxed. The *Yogīs*, on account of their ignorance of the real nature of the mind, fight with their own shadows. The *Jñānī*, on the other hand, realises the mind as well as all its activities as identical with the non-dual Brahman. Hence, the activities of mind do not stand in the way of his eternal happiness.

**उत्सेक उदधेर्यद्वत्कुशाग्रेणैकबिन्दुना ।**
**मनसो निग्रहस्तद्वद्भवेदपरिखेदतः ॥ ४१ ॥**

41. *The mind can be brought under control only by an unrelenting effort like that which is required to empty an ocean, drop by drop, with the help of a (blade of)* Kuśa-*grass.*

### Śaṅkara's Commentary

As one may try to empty the ocean, by draining off its water drop by drop, with the help of a (blade of) *Kuśa*-grass, even so may one control the mind by making the same effort with a heart which becomes neither[1] depressed nor tired.

This *Kārikā* gives us an idea of the effort that a *Yogī* should make to control his mind completely. But it appears that the complete suppression of the mental *Vṛttis* is impossible in this way. And as the happiness of a *Yogī* is dependent upon such suppression, he can never attain to eternal Truth by the *Yogic* method. *Jñāna-yoga* is the royal road for the attainment of eternal Truth and peace.

[1] *Neither depressed etc.*—The *Yogī* at every step meets with defeat. While closing the eyes, he sees no object; with the eyes open, he perceives the phenomenal world. In either case, he does not realise Brahman. But these must not depress his heart.

**उपायेन निगृह्णीयाद्विक्षिप्तं कामभोगयोः ।**
**सुप्रसन्नं लये चैव यथा कामो लयस्तथा ॥ ४२ ॥**

42. *The mind distracted by desires and enjoyments as also the mind enjoying pleasure in oblivion (trance-like condition) should be brought under discipline by the pursuit of proper means. For, the state of oblivion is as harmful as desires.*

### Śaṅkara's Commentary

Is untiring effort the only way for bringing the mind under discipline? We say, in reply, no. One should, with untiring effort, follow the means, to be stated presently, in order to bring the mind under discipline, that is to say, bring it back to *Ātman*,[1] when the mind turns towards objects of desires and enjoyments. The word '*Laya*'[2] in the text indicates *Suṣupti*, *i.e.*, deep sleep in which state one becomes oblivious of all things. The[3] (injunction implied in the) words 'should be brought under discipline', should also be applied in the case of the mind when it feels happy, that is to say, free from all worries in the state of *Laya* or oblivion. Why should it be further brought under discipline if it feels pleasure (in that state)? It is thus replied: Because the state of oblivion is as[4] harmful as desire, the mind should be withdrawn from the state of oblivion as it should be withdrawn from objects of enjoyment.

One practising *Yoga* meets with four kinds of obstacles which are in his way of realising the Highest Reality. They are known as *Laya* (a state of oblivion analogous to *Yogic Samādhi* or deep sleep), *Vikṣepa* (distraction), *Sukha* (happiness in temporary success) and *Rāga* (attachment to any particular phase of realisation). The mind should be trained to keep away from these obstacles. The means are described in the next *Kārikā*.

[1] *Ātman*—It is because the ultimate aim of all spiritual practices is the realisation of *Ātman* or the true nature of the Self.

[2] *Laya*—The state of *Laya* realised by the *Yogī* in *Samādhi* is non-different from the state of *Suṣupti* or deep sleep. Both are characterised by the absence of subject-object relationship. Again in both these states, the student is not aware of the real nature of his self. The difference between the two states is this: The *Yogī* can induce *Samādhi* at his mere will, but *Suṣupti*, for an ordinary man, is not under his control.

[3] *The words etc.*—The state of *Samādhi* induced by *Yoga* should not be considered as the goal. No doubt, one feels a sort of pleasure in such *Samādhi* on account of the absence of worries consequent on the withdrawal of the mind from external objects, but this does not indicate that the *Yogī* has realised the Supreme *Truth*. Seeking after pleasure or the avoidance of misery indicates the exhaustion of the inquiring mind. The real seeker after Truth cannot rest satisfied till he has attained to it.

[4] *As harmful etc.*—It is because both these states are characterised by the absence of the knowledge of *Ātman*. Thirst for external objects and attachment to the pleasure one feels in *Samādhi* are equally harmful for the realisation of Truth. A *Yogī* can realise Truth if he supplements his own method by the Vedāntic discipline of discrimination between the real and the unreal, and meditation on the nature of *Ātman*.

दुःखं सर्वमनुस्मृत्य कामभोगान्निवर्तयेत् ।
अजं सर्वमनुस्मृत्य जातं नैव तु पश्यति ॥ ४३ ॥

43. *The mind should be turned back from the enjoyment of pleasures, remembering that all this is attended with misery. If it be remembered that everything is the unborn (Brahman), the born (duality) will not be seen.*

## Śaṅkara's Commentary

What is the way of disciplining the mind? It is thus replied: Remember that all[1] duality is caused by *Avidyā* or illusion and therefore afflicted with misery. Thereby dissuade the mind from seeking enjoyments produced by desires. In other words, withdraw the mind from all dual objects by impressing upon it the idea of complete non-attachment.[2] Realise from the teachings of the Scriptures and the *Ācāryas* that all this is verily the changeless Brahman. Then you will not see anything to the contrary, *viz.*, duality; for it does not exist.

It has been said in the previous *Kārikā* that the mind should be disciplined by following the right method. This verse of the *Kārikā* points out complete detachment to be the right method.

[1] *All duality etc.*—All dual objects, on account of their changeable and negatable nature, are attended with misery.

[2] *Non-attachment*—It implies the spirit of dispassion for all dual objects, because they are always associated with misery.

लये संबोधयेच्चित्तं विक्षिप्तं शमयेत्पुनः ।
सकषायं विजानीयात्समप्राप्तं न चालयेत् ॥ ४४ ॥

44. *If the mind becomes inactive in a state of oblivion awaken it again. If it is distracted, bring it back to the state of tranquillity. (In the intermediary state) know the mind containing within it desires in potential form. If the mind has attained to the state of equilibrium, then do not disturb it again.*

## Śaṅkara's Commentary

When[1] the mind is immersed in oblivion, *i.e.*, in *Suṣupti*, then rouse it up by means of knowledge and by detachment. That is to say, turn the mind to the exercise of discrimination which leads to the knowledge of the Self. The word '*Citta*' in the text bears the same meaning as '*Manas*' or mind. Bring[2] the mind back to the state of tranquility if it is distracted by the various objects of desires. When the mind is thus, by constant practice, awakened from the state of inactivity and also turned back from all objects, but not yet established in equilibrium,[3] that is to say, when the mind still dwells in an intermediary state—then know[4] the mind to be possessed of attachment. Then the mind contains within it the seeds of desires for enjoyment and inactivity. From[5] that state also, bring the mind, with care, to the realisation of equilibrium. Once the mind has realised the state of equilibrium, that is, when it is on the way to realise that state, then do not disturb it again. In other words, do not turn it to (by attachment) external objects.

[1] *When the etc.*—This is the warning given against pursuing the *Yogic Samādhi* as the state of the highest spiritual realisation. The mind seeking Truth and frightened at the immensity of effort necessary for its realisation often seeks relief in *Samādhi*. The commentator exhorts us to practise discrimination even when the mind passes into the passivity of *Samādhi* and to extricate it from that state by cultivating the spirit of non-attachment to any pleasure experienced in the state of *Samādhi*. The object of life is not to enjoy any bliss arising out of inactivity as one experiences in *Samādhi* or deep sleep, but to know the real nature of the Self.

[2] *Bring etc.*—The *Yogic* method may be followed with certain advantages by the student of mediocre intellect who wants to turn his turbulent mind from the pursuit of external objects. The *Yogic* method gives him control over his mind. But even in such a case, *Yoga* serves only a temporary or subordinate purpose.

[3] *Equilibrium*—The non-dual Brahman which is characterised by sameness throughout.

[4] *Know etc.*—This is another state of the mind. In this state the mind is roused from the state of inactivity. It is also withdrawn from objects. But it has not yet realised its identity with the non-dual Brahman. In this intermediary state, the mind contains, in potential form, the desires for the enjoyment of external objects or the bliss in a state of inactivity.

[5] *From etc.*—This intermediary state also should not be taken as the state of Ultimate Realisation.

नाऽऽस्वादयेत्सुखं तत्र निःसङ्गः प्रज्ञया भवेत् ।
निश्चलं निश्चरच्चित्तमेकीकुर्यात्प्रयत्नतः ॥ ४५ ॥

45. *(The mind) should not be allowed to enjoy the bliss that arises out of the condition of* Samādhi. *It should be freed from attachment to such happiness through the exercise of discrimination. If the mind, once attaining to the state of steadiness seeks externality, then it should be unified with the* Ātman, *again, with effort.*

## Śaṅkara's Commentary

The seeker should not taste that happiness that is experienced by the *Yogis* seeking[1] after *Samādhi*. In other words, he is not to be attached to that happiness. What then should be done by the student? He should be unattached to such happiness, by gaining knowledge through discrimination, and think that whatever happiness is experienced is false[2] and conjured up by ignorance. The mind should be turned back from such happiness. When, however, having been once withdrawn from happiness and fixed on the state of steadiness, the mind again manifests its outgoing propensities, then control it by adopting the above-mentioned[3] means; and with great care, make it one[4] with *Ātman*; that is, make the mind attain to the condition of pure existence and thought.

The purpose of this *Kārikā* is to dissuade the mind from enjoying the happiness that the *Yogis* experience in the state of *Samādhi*.

[1] *Seeking etc.*—That is in the state of *Samādhi*, the *Yogi* fails to see that the non-dual Brahman alone exists. He seeks *Samādhi* because he believes in the existence of the mind as separate from *Ātman*, and therefore tries to control it. By some mechanical means he brings the mind to a state of inactivity and thus makes himself free from all worries. But this is not the Vedāntic goal of Truth.

[2] *False*—All objects which are experienced by us are changeable and negatable. Therefore they are unreal.

[3] *Above-mentioned*—*i.e.*, discrimination etc.

[4] *One etc.*—The truth is that the mind is identical with *Ātman*. Mind is *Ātman*. It is only through ignorance that we separate the mind from *Ātman*.

यदा न लीयते चित्तं न च विक्षिप्यते पुनः ।
अनिङ्गनमनाभासं निष्पन्नं ब्रह्म तत्तदा ॥ ४६ ॥

46. *When the mind does not merge in the inactivity of oblivion, or become distracted by desires, that is to say, when the mind becomes quiescent and does not give rise to appearances, it verily becomes Brahman.*

## Śaṅkara's Commentary

When the mind brought under discipline by the above-mentioned[1] methods, does not fall into the oblivion of deep sleep, nor is distracted by external objects, that is to say, when the mind becomes quiescent[2] like the flame of a light kept in a windless place; or when[3] the mind does not appear in the form of an object—when the mind is endowed with these characteristics, it verily becomes one[4] with Brahman.

[1] *Above-mentioned etc.*—*i.e.*, the practice of knowledge and discrimination.

[2] *Quiescent*—This steadiness is quite different from the condition of *Samādhi*. In this steady condition the mind realizes the non-dual Brahman alone everywhere.

[3] *When etc.*—The external objects are nothing but the activities of the mind itself. Comp. *Kārikā* 3. 31.

[4] *One etc.*—Then the mind realizes its real nature.

स्वस्थं शान्तं सनिर्वाणमकथ्यं सुखमुत्तमम् ।
अजमजेन ज्ञेयेन सर्वज्ञं परिचक्षत ॥ ४७ ॥

47. *This highest bliss is based upon the realisation of Self, it is peace, identical with liberation, indescribable and unborn. It is further described as the omniscient Brahman, because it is one with the unborn Self which is the object sought by Knowledge.*

### Śaṅkara's Commentary

The above-mentioned bliss which is the highest[1] Reality and which is characterised by the knowledge of the *Ātman* is[2] centred in the Self. It is all peace, characterised by the cessation of all evils. It is the same as liberation.[3] It is indescribable as[4] nobody is able to describe it; for, it is totally different from all objects. This ultimate bliss is directly realized by the *Yogis*.[5] It is unborn because it is not produced like anything resulting from empirical perceptions, It is identical with the Unborn which is the object sought by Knowledge. The Knowers of Brahman describe this bliss verily as the omniscient Brahman, as it is idéntical with that Reality which is omniscient.

Now is described the nature of the mind in the state of the highest realisation.

[1] *Highest*—It is distinguished from the happiness described in *Kārikā* 45, which is of the same class as relative bliss.

[2] *Is centred etc.*—This is to show that Self-realisation does not depend upon anything external to itself.

[3] *Liberation*—The state of liberation, on account of its identity with Truth, is characterised by the attainment of all-absorbing happiness and cessation of all miseries.

[4] *As etc.*—It is because this happiness transcends all subject-object relationship.

[5] *Yogis*—These *Yogis* are not like the ordinary ones. The nature of their *Yoga* has been described as the *Asparśa Yoga* in *Kārikā* 3. 39.

न कश्चिज्जायते जीवः संभवोऽस्य न विद्यते ।
एतत्तदुत्तमं सत्यं यत्र किंचिन्न जायते ॥ ४८ ॥

48. *No* Jīva *is ever born. There does not exist any cause which can produce it. This is the highest Truth that nothing is ever born.*

### ŚAṄKARA'S COMMENTARY

All these ideas regarding the discipline of the mind, evolution resembling the creation of forms from iron and clay, as well as the ideas regarding devotional exercises, are given as means[1] to the realisation of the nature of the Ultimate Reality. They have, in themselves, no meaning whatsoever. The[2] truth regarding the ultimate Reality is that no *Jīva* is ever born. The *Jīva* whom one knows as the agent and the enjoyer is not born in any way whatsoever. Therefore, no cause can ever exist which may produce the *Ātman* which is, by nature, unborn and non-dual. In other words, no *Jīva* can ever be born, as the cause which may produce it does not exist. Of all the (relative) truths described above as means (for the realisation of the Ultimate Reality), this alone is the Supreme Truth that nothing whatsoever is ever born in or of that Brahman which is of the nature of the Ultimate Reality

Various empirical means such as the practice of *Yoga* etc., have been suggested above. If these means which naturally are related to the dual realm be true, then the position of the non-dual Brahman cannot be maintained. If these means be untrue, then they cannot serve any purpose. To remove this difficulty this *Kārikā* suggests that these means help us to realise Brahman; but they do not reveal Brahman.

[1] *Means*—These means have their applicability only in the realm of duality where a man, through ignorance, does not know his real nature.

[2] *The truth etc.*—The Ultimate Truth is that there is only one entity which may be called either *Jīva* or Brahman. The *Jīva* as separate from Brahman, does never exist.

Here ends the third chapter, on Advaita, of the *Kārikā* of Gauḍapāda with the Commentary of Śrī Śaṅkara.

**Aum Salutation to Brahman**

CHAPTER IV

# QUENCHING OF FIRE-BRAND

ज्ञानेनाऽऽकाशकल्पेन धर्मान्यो गगनोपमान् ।
ज्ञेयाभिन्नेन संबुद्धस्तं वन्दे द्विपदां वरम् ॥ १ ॥

1. *I bow to that best among men who by means of knowledge, which is like* Ākāśa *and non-different from the object of knowledge* (i.e., *the* Dharma), *realised the nature of the* Dharmas (i.e., *the* Jīvas) *which are, again, like the* Ākāśa.

## Śaṅkara's Commentary

The proposition regarding *Advaita* (as the Supreme Truth) has been based upon scriptural evidence, by[1] determining the nature of *Aum*. That proposition has been established by proving[2] the unreality of the distinction implied by the external objects (of experience). Again the third chapter dealing with *Advaita* has directly established the proposition on the authority of scripture and reason with the concluding statement[3] that 'This alone is the Ultimate Truth'. At the end of the previous chapter it has been hinted that the opinions of the dualists and the nihilists, who are opposed to the philosophy of *Advaita* which gives the true import of the scriptures, bear the name of true philosophy. But that is not true because of their mutual contradictions and also because of their being vitiated by attachment to their own opinions and aversion to those of others. The philosophy of *Advaita* has been extolled as the true philosophy on[4] account of its being free from any vitiation (referred to above regarding the theories of the dualists and nihilists). Now is undertaken the chapter styled *Alātaśānti* (*i.e.*, on the quenching of the fire-brand) in order to conclude the final examination for the establishment of the philosophy of *Advaita*, by following the process known as the method[5] of disagreement, which is done by showing here in detail that other systems cannot be said to be true philosophy. For there are mutual contradictions implied in them. The first verse has for its purpose the salutation to the promulgator[6] of the philosophy of *Advaita,* conceiving him as identical with the *Advaita* Truth. The salutation to the teacher is made in commencing a scripture in order to bring the undertaking to a successful end. The word '*Ākāśakalpa*' in the text means *resembling Ākāśa*, that is to say, slightly[7] different from *Ākāśa*. What is the purpose of such knowledge which resembles *Ākāśa*? By such *Knowledge* is known the nature of the *Dharmas*[8] (*i.e.*, the attributes of *Ātman*). The attributes are the same as the substance. What is the nature of these *Dharmas*? They also can be known by the analogy[9] of *Ākāśa*, that is to say, these *Dharmas* also resemble *Ākāśa*. The word '*Jñeyābhinna*' in the text is another attribute of '*Jñānam*' or Knowledge and means that this knowledge is not[10] separate from the *Ātmans* (*Jīvas*) which are the objects of knowledge. This identity of the knowledge and the knowable is like the identity of fire[11] and heat and the sun and its light. I bow to the God, known as *Nārāyaṇa*,[12] who by knowledge, non-different from the nature of *Ātman* (the object of knowledge) and which resembles *Ākāśa*, knew the *Dharmas* which, again, may be compared to *Ākāśa*. The import of the words '*Dvipadām Varam*' (Supreme among the bipeds), is that *Nārāyaṇa* is the greatest of all men, characterised by two legs, that is to say, He is the

'*Puruṣottama*', the best of all men. By the adoration of the teacher it is implied that the purpose of this chapter is to establish, by the refutation of the opposite views, *Advaita* which gives the philosophy of the Ultimate Reality, characterised by the identity of the knower, knowledge and the object of knowledge.

[1] *By the etc.*—This has been done in the first chapter of the book, *viz.*, the *Āgama Prakaraṇa* which deals with the subject-matter from the scriptural standpoint.

[2] *Proving etc.*—This has been done in the second chapter.

[3] *Statement—Comp.* the 48th verse of the *Kārikā* of the third chapter.

[4] *On account etc.*—One of the tests of Truth is that it does not contradict anything. The Ultimate Truth is that by knowing which everything else becomes known. The fact of non-duality satisfies this condition and therefore it is called the Ultimate Truth or Reality.

[5] *Method of etc.*—This is one of the processes of inference; the other is known as the method of agreement. It has been shown in the second chapter that what is caused or what comes into being is unreal. Here it is shown that what is not untruth is not caused also. That is to say, the *Kārikā* will show in this chapter the absence of causality in *Ātman* and thus establish the Ultimate Reality of Self.

[6] *Promulgator etc.*—*Nārāyaṇa* or the Lord Himself is said to be the promulgator of this philosophy which was handed down to Gauḍapāda. The salutation is made to Nārāyaṇa at the commencement of the chapter.

[7] *Slightly etc.*—*Ākāśa* or ether contains within it elements of inert matter. Therefore it is slightly different from knowledge which is all sentiency. The analogy is made with reference to the all-pervading characteristic of *Ākāśa* which is similar to *Jñānam* or knowledge.

[8] *Dharmas*—The word '*Dharma*' literally means attribute. Attribute, according to Vedānta, is non-different from substance. Hence '*Dharma*' also is non-different from Brahman. The word *Dharma* is, in the texts, synonymous with knowledge or *Jñānam*. The word '*Dharma*' is used by Gauḍapāda to mean '*Jīva*' or embodied being. '*Jīva*' is identical with 'knowledge', 'Brahman'. The plural number is used on account of the plurality of '*Jīvas*' which is admitted from the empirical standpoint.

[9] *Analogy etc.*—The *Jīva* is, as Brahman is, in reality, as all-pervading as the *Ākāśa* (or *Jnānam*).

[10] *Not separate etc.*—If knowledge is intrinsically separate from its object. *i. e.*, the *Jīva* or the Brahman, then one can never know, by such knowledge, the nature of *Jīva* or Brahman. The knower, knowledge and the object of knowledge are really identical and denote the same Reality.

[11] *Fire etc.*—That is to say, from the standpoints of the fire and the sun, the heat and the light are identical with the fire and the sun.

[12] *Nārāyaṇa*—The story runs thus: In ancient times Gauḍapāda retired to *Badarikāśrama*, in the interior of the Himālayas, and there worshipped with great austerity the human figure of the Almighty Lord.

अस्पर्शयोगो वै नाम सर्वसत्वसुखो हितः ।
अविवादोऽविरुद्धश्च देशितस्तं नमाम्यहम् ॥ २ ॥

2. *I salute this* Yoga *known as the* Asparśa (i.e., *free from all touch which implies duality*), *taught through the scripture*—the Yoga *which promotes the happiness of all beings and conduces to the well-being of all and which is free from strife and contradictions.*

Śaṅkara's Commentary

Now salutation is made to the *Yoga* taught by the *Advaita* Philosophy, in order to extol it. The word *Asparśa-yoga*[1] in the text means the *Yoga* which is always and in all respects free from *sparśa* or relationship with anything and which is of the same[2] nature as Brahman. This *Yoga* is well known as the *Asparśayoga* to all Knowers of Brahman. This *Yoga* is conducive[3] to the happiness of all beings. There are certain forms of *Yoga* such as *Tapas* or austerity, which though conducive to the supreme happiness, are associated with misery. But this is not of that kind. Then what is its nature? It tends to the *happiness* of *all* beings. It may however be contended that the enjoyment of certain desires gives pleasure but certainly does not tend to one's well-being.

But this *Asparśayoga* condūces to both[4] happiness and well-being. For,[5] it never changes its nature. Moreover, this[6] *Yoga* is free from strife, that is to say, in it there is no room for any passage-at-words, which is inevitable in all disputes consisting of two opposite sides. Why so? For, it is non-contradictory[7] in nature. To this kind of *Yoga*, taught in the scripture, I bow.[8]

[1] *Asparśayoga*—As a matter of fact there is a contradiction involved in this word. For, the word '*Asparśa*', meaning freedom from relation, indicates only non-duality which by its very nature has no contact with any other thing, as such a thing is ever non-existent. The word *Yoga*, 'meaning contact' implies more than one. Gauḍapāda names the path of knowledge as *Asparśayoga*, as the word *Yoga* was used in his time also to denote the method for realising the Ultimate Truth.

[2] *Same nature etc.*—The *Jñānam* through which the aspirant realises Brahman is identical with Brahman itself.

[3] *Conducive etc.*—Because *Jñāna-Yoga* is the surest and most direct method for the realisation of the highest Truth.

[4] *Both etc.*—It is because the aim of this *Yoga* is the realisation of Self which is of the nature of Existence-Knowledge-Bliss-Absolute.

[5] *For etc.*—The idea of duality and change, implying loss, is at the root of all miseries. This *Yoga* enables us to realise the Self which is free from all ideas of change.

[6] *This yoga etc.*—The non-dualist knows that even those who come to quarrel with him are, in reality, his own self. Therefore he does not look upon any one as his opponent.

[7] *Non-contradictory*—One who knows everything as his own self does not contradict others. For, one cannot contradict his own self.

[8] *Bow*—The salutation is meant to direct the attention of the students to this most valuable and easy way of realising the Truth.

भूतस्य जातिमिच्छन्ति वादिनः केचिदेव हि ।
अभूतस्यापरे धीरा विवदन्तः परस्परम् ॥ ३ ॥

3. *Quarrelling among themselves, some disputants postulate that an existing entity undergoes evolution, whereas other disputants, proud of their understanding, maintain that evolution proceeds from a non-existing entity.*

ŚAṄKARA'S COMMENTARY

How do the dualists quarrel with one another? It is thus replied:[1] Some disputants, such as the followers of the *Sāṁkhya* system, admit production as the effect of an entity that is already existent. But this is not the view of all the dualists. For the intelligent followers of the *Nyāya* and the *Vaiśeṣika* systems, that is to say, those who believe that they possess wisdom, maintain that evolution proceeds from a non-existing cause. The meaning is that these disputants, quarrelling among themselves, claim victory over their respective opponents.

[1] The disputation among the dualists is mentioned here in order to make clear the non-contradictory nature of the non-dualists. All the dualists believe in the act of creation or evolution.

भूतं न जायते किंचिदभूतं नैव जायते ।
विवदन्तोऽद्वया ह्येवमजातिं ख्यापयन्ति ते ॥ ४ ॥

4. *The existent cannot (again) pass into (birth) existence. Nor can the non-existent be born or come into being as existent. Thus disputing among themselves, they, as a matter of fact tend to establish the* Advaita *view and support the* Ajāti *or the absolute non-evolution (of what exists).*

ŚAṄKARA'S COMMENTARY

What do they, by refuting each other's conclusions and quarreling among themselves, really establish? It is thus replied: No[1] entity which is already in existence can again pass into birth. The reason is that as entity, it already exists. It is just like the *Ātman,* which already being in existence, cannot be born again as a new entity. Thus argues the supporter of evolution from *non-ens* (*i.e.*, from a non-existing cause) and refutes the *Sāṁkhya* theory that an existing cause is born again as an effect. Similarly, the follower of the *Sāṁkhya* theory refutes the supporter of the *non-ens* view regarding creation by a non-existing cause. He declares that a non-existing[2] cause, on account of its very non-existence, cannot, like the horns of a hare, produce an effect. Thus[3] quarrelling among themselves, by supporting 'existent' and 'non-existent' causes, they refute their respective opponent's views and declare, in effect, the truth that there is no creation at all.

[1] *No etc.*—This is the view of the followers of the *Naiyāyika* and *Vaiśeṣika* systems. According to them, an existing entity cannot be born as an effect. If an entity already exists, it is not said to be produced again. This view can be stated thus: A cannot produce B, as A is always A and B is always B. It may be contended that A+C may produce B. Therefore C is something which does not exist in the cause A. Therefore the effect B does not come out of the cause A.

[2] *Non-existing etc.*—This is the view of the followers of the *Sāṁkhya* system. According to them, the existing entity cannot undergo any annihilation; nor can the non-existing entity pass into existence. The existing entity is existent in times, past, present and future. A non-existing entity, such as the child of a barren woman, is always non-existent. By 'birth', the *Sāṁkhyas* mean manifestation and by 'death', they understand the return of the effect into the cause. The sesame seed produces oil. It means that oil, already existent in the seed, manifests itself in the form of the effect when the seed (the cause) is pressed. But one cannot get oil by pressing sand, as oil is never present in the sand. The clay which contains in potential form the pot, manifests the pot. Again the destruction of the pot means its going back to the original cause, *viz*,, the clay. There is no absolute destruction of the pot.

[3] *Thus etc.*—Both the theories are based upon causality. But by refuting each other, they, in fact, refute causality itself. For, if an existing thing is produced from an existing cause (as the *Sāṁkhyas* profess) then there cannot be, in truth, any causal relation. Similarly, it is absurd to say that a positive thing can be produced by a non-existing cause. Thus the entire theory of causality is refuted. This

only establishes the *Advaita* position of *Ajāti* which means that there is no act of creation or manifestation.

ख्याप्यमानामजातिं तैरनुमोदामहे वयम् ।
विवदामो न तैः सार्धमविवादं निबोधत ॥ ५ ॥

5. *We approve the* Ajāti *or non-creation declared by them. We do not quarrel with them. Now, hear from us (the Ultimate Reality) which is free from all disputations.*

### Śaṅkara's Commentary

We simply accept the view of the *Ajāti* or the absolute non-causation declared by them[1] and say, 'Let it be so'. We do not quarrel with them by taking either side in the disputation. In other words, like them, we do not quarrel with each other. Hence Oh ye pupils, know from us the Ultimate Reality as taught by us, which is free from dispute.

[1] *Them*—The followers of the *Sāṁkhya* as well as the *Nyāya* and the *Vaiśeṣika* systems.

Both schools by finding fault with each other's views regarding 'causal' relation tend to establish the truth of *Ajāti* or the absolute non-manifestation of *Ātman*. With regard to causality, we accept that theory that is not refuted by any party, but which must be admitted by all, *viz.*, *Ajāti*.

अजातस्यैव धर्मस्य जातिमिच्छन्ति वादिनः ।
अजातो ह्यमृतो धर्मो मर्त्यतां कथमेष्यति ॥ ६ ॥

6. *The disputants* (i.e., *the dualists*) *contend that the ever-unborn* (*changeless*) *entity* (Ātman) *undergoes a change. How does an entity which is changeless and immortal partake of the nature of the mortal?*

### Śaṅkara's Commentary

The word 'disputant' in the text includes all the dualists, *viz.*, those who believe that evolution proceeds from an existing cause, as well as those who believe its opposite. This verse has already been commented upon.

For the commentary and the note of this *Kārikā* see *Kārikā* 20 of the previous chapter.

न भवत्यमृतं मर्त्यं न मर्त्यममृतं तथा ।
प्रकृतेरन्यथाभावो न कथंचिद्भविष्यति ॥ ७ ॥

7. *The immortal cannot become mortal, nor can the mortal ever become immortal. For, it is never possible for a thing to change its nature.*

स्वभावेनामृतो यस्य धर्मो गच्छति मर्त्यताम् ।
कृतकेनामृतस्तस्य कथं स्थास्यति निश्चलः ॥ ८ ॥

8. *How can he, who believes that the naturally immortal entity becomes mortal, maintain that the immortal, after passing through birth, retains its changeless nature?*

### Śaṅkara's Commentary

These verses have already been explained. They are repeated here in order to justify our view that the disputants mentioned above only contradict each other.

See *Kārikās* 21 and 22 of the previous chapter.

सांसिद्धिकी स्वाभाविकी सहजा अकृता च या ।
प्रकृतिः सेति विज्ञेया स्वभावं न जहाति या ॥ ९ ॥

9. *By* Prakṛti *or the inherent nature of a thing is understood that which, when acquired, becomes completely part and parcel of the thing, that which is its very characteristic quality, that which is part of it from its very birth, that which does not depend upon anything extraneous for its origin and that which never ceases to be itself.*

### Śaṅkara's Commentary

Even[1] the nature of a thing in ordinary experience does not undergo any reversal. What is meant by the nature of a thing? This is thus replied: The word '*saṁsiddhi*' means 'complete attainment'. The nature of a thing is formed by such complete attainment as in the case of the perfected *Yogis* who attain to such superhuman powers as *Aṇimā*[2] etc. These powers thus acquired by the *Yogis* never undergo any transformation in the past and future. Therefore these constitute the very nature of the *Yogis*. Similarly, the characteristic quality of a thing, such as heat or light of fire and the like, never undergoes any change either in time or space. So also the nature of a thing which is part of it from its very birth, as the flying power of the bird etc., through the sky, is called its *Prakṛti*. Anything else which is not produced by any other cause (except the thing itself), such as the running downwards of water is also called *Prakṛti*. And lastly, anything which[3] does not cease to be itself is known popularly to be its *Prakṛti*. The purport of the *Kārikā* is that if in the case of empirical entities, which are only imagined,[4] their *nature* or *Prakṛti* does not undergo any change, then how should it be otherwise in the case of the immortal or unchanging nature regarding the Ultimate Reality, whose very *Prakṛti* is *Ajāti* or absolute non-manifestation.

[1] *Even etc.*—The purport is that if the unchangeability of the nature of a thing is noticed in ordinary experiences, then it applies

with greater force to Brahman whose changeless and immortal nature can never undergo any transformation.

[2] *Aṇimā*—There are eight superhuman powers which the *Yogis* can attain to as the result of their *Yogic* perfection. The word '*Aṇimā*' means the power of becoming as small as an atom.

[3] *Which etc.*—As the characteristics of a jar or the *jarness* of it which depends entirely upon the jar and not upon anything else.

[4] *Imagined*—According to *Advaita* Vedānta the characteristics of entities of ordinary experience which are thought of as unchanging by the dualists, are mere imagination.

जरामरणनिर्मुक्ताः सर्वे धर्माः स्वभावतः ।
जरामरणमिच्छन्तश्च्यवन्ते तन्मनीषया ॥ १० ॥

10. *All the* Jīvas *are, by their very nature, free from senility and death. They think, as it were, that they are subject to these and thus by this* very *thought they appear to deviate from their very nature.*

### Śaṅkara's Commentary

What is the basis of that *Prakṛti* whose change is imagined by the disputants? What, again, is the defect in such imagination? This is thus replied: The words 'Free from senility and death', in the text signify freedom from all changes[1] characterised by senility, death, etc. Who are thus free (from all changes)? These are all the *Jīvas*, who are, by their very nature, free from all changes. Though the *Jīvas* are such by their very nature, yet they think, as it were, that they are subject to senility and death. By such imagination[2] about their selves, like the imagination of the snake in the rope, they (appear to) deviate from the nature. This happens on account of their identification, through thinking, with senility and death. That is to say, they (appear to) fall from their real nature by this defect in their thought.

[1] *Changes*—There are six changes associated with objects in nature. They are birth, existence, growth, maturity, decay and death.

[2] *Imagination*—That the *Jīvas* are subject to birth and death is a mere imagination. These states do not exist except in the thought of the thinker. Even when the *Jīva* thinks himself to be subject to birth and death, he is, in reality, free from these changes. Such imagination cannot affect his real nature as all the water of the mirage cannot soak a grain of sand in the desert. There is no change of Reality in *Prakṛti*. If one sees any change it is due to his *Kalpanā*. The rope never becomes the snake.

कारणं यस्य वै कार्यं कारणं तस्य जायते ।
जायमानं कथमजं भिन्नं नित्यं कथं च तत् ॥ ११

11. *The disputant, according to whom the cause itself is the effect, maintains that the cause itself is born as the effect. How is it possible for the cause to be unborn if it be said to be born (as the effect)? How, again, is it said to be eternal if it be subject to modification* (i.e., *birth*)*?*

### Śaṅkara's Commentary

How is it that the *Sāṁkhyas*, who believe in the evolution of an existing cause, maintain a view which is irrational? It is thus replied by the followers of the *Vaiśeṣika* system: Those who say that the cause, that is to say, such material cause as clay, is, in itself, the effect; or in other words those disputants who assert that the cause itself changes into the effect, maintain, as a matter of fact, that the ever-existent and unborn cause, namely the *Pradhāna* etc., is born again as the effect, such as *Mahat* etc. If *Pradhāna* be born in the form of *Mahat* etc., then how can it be designated as birthless? To say that it is *unborn, i.e.*, immutable and at the same time *born, i.e.*, passing into change, involves a contradiction. Further, the *Sāṁkhyas* designate *Pradhāna* as eternal. How is it possible for *Pradhāna* to be eternal[1] if even a part of it be affected by change? In other words, ordinary experience does not furnish us with the instance of a jar, composed of parts, which, if broken in any part, can still be called permanent or immutable. The purport is that a contradiction is obvious in the statement that it is affected partly by change and at the same time it is unborn and eternal.

[1] *Eternal*—According to the *Sāṁkhya* theory, the *Pradhāna* or *Prakṛti* is composed of three parts, *viz.*, *Sattva*, *Rajas* and *Tamas*. An entity composed of parts can never be termed eternal or permanent. That which is composed of parts, must, in course of time, undergo decomposition.

कारणाद्यद्यनन्यत्वमतः कार्यमजं यदि ।
जायमानाद्धि वै कार्यात्कारणं ते कथं ध्रुवम् ॥ १२ ॥

12. *If, as you say, the cause is non-different from the effect, then the effect also must be unborn. Further, how can the cause be permanent if it be non-different from the effect which is born?*

## Śaṅkara's Commentary

This verse is meant to make the meaning of the previous one clearer. If your object be to maintain that the unborn cause is identical with the effect, then it necessarily follows that the effect also becomes equally unborn. But it[1] is certainly a contradiction to say that a thing is an effect and at the same time unborn. There is a further difficulty. In the case of identity[2] of the cause and the effect, how can, according to you, the cause, which[3] is non-different from the born effect, be permanent and immutable? It is not possible to imagine that a part of a hen is being cooked and that another part is laying eggs.

If the identity of cause and effect be maintained, then it may be asked if the cause be identical with the effect or if the effect be identical with the cause. In the former case of identity, the effect becomes unborn and in the latter case the cause becomes something born and loses its immutable and permanent character.

[1] *It etc.*—For, an effect is that which is born out of a cause.

[2] *Identity etc.*—If cause and effect be identical then how can one distinguish between the cause and the effect?

[3] *Which is etc.*—If the cause be identical with the born effect then the cause cannot be called permanent and immutable, as birth means change.

This view avoids this difficulty by denying any *act* of birth in the cause. There is only one existence, *viz.*, Brahman, which is called the cause by ignorant people whose mind is still moving in the causal plane.

अजाद्वै जायते यस्य दृष्टान्तस्तस्य नास्ति वै ।
जाताच्च जायमानस्य न व्यवस्था प्रसज्यते ॥ १३ ॥

13. *There is no illustration to support the view of him who says that the effect is born from the unborn cause. Again, if it be said that the effect is produced from a cause which is itself born then it leads to a* regressus ad infinitum.

## Śaṅkara's Commentary

Moreover, the disputant[1] who says that the effect is produced from an unborn cause, cannot furnish an illustration to support his view. In other words, it is consequently established that nothing is born from an unborn cause as there is no illustration to support this view. If,[2] on the other hand, it be contended that the effect is born from a born cause, then that cause must be born from some other born cause and so on, which position never enables us to reach a cause which is, in itself, unborn. In other words, we are faced with an infinite regress.

[1] *Disputant*—The follower of the *Sāṁkhya* system contends that such effects as *Mahat* etc., are evolved from the unborn *Pradhāna*, the cause being non-different from the effect. The *Kārikā* disproves this theory of the *Sāṁkhyas* as well as the creation theory of some Vedāntists. This theory is a matter of inference. But there is no illustration to draw the inference.

[2] *If etc.*—If the effect be produced from a born cause (*i. e.*, a cause which is the effect of some other cause), then there will be an endless regress and we shall never arrive at a cause which is, itself, unborn.

हेतोरादिः फलं येषामादिर्हेतुः फलस्य च ।
हेतोः फलस्य चानादिः कथं तैरुपवर्ण्यते ॥ १४ ॥

14. *How can they, who assert that the effect is the cause of the cause and the cause is the cause of the effect maintain the beginninglessness of both the cause and the effect?*

### Śaṅkara's Commentary

The *Śruti*, in the passage, 'When all this has, verily, become his *Ātman*' declares, from the standpoint of the Ultimate Reality, the absence of duality. From this standpoint of the Scriptural text, it is said: The cause,[1] *i.e.*, the merit (*Dharma*) and the demerit (*Adharma*), etc., has, for its cause, the effect, *viz.*, the aggregate of the body etc. Similarly, the cause,[2] *viz.*, merit and demerit etc., is the cause of the effect, *viz.*, the aggregate of the body etc. How can disputants[3] who maintain this view, *viz.*, that both the cause and the effect are with[4] beginning on account of mutual interdependence of the cause and the effect, assert that both the cause and the effect are without beginning? In other words, this position implies an inherent contradiction.[5] The *Ātman*,[6] which is eternal and immutable, can never become either the cause or the effect.

[1] *Cause etc.*—The birth in a body produces the effect, *viz.*, the merit and the demerit.

[2] *Cause etc.*—The merit and the demerit determine the birth in a body. Thus it is seen, according to this view, the cause produces the effect and the effect, in its turn, produces the cause.

[3] *Disputants*—This is the view held by the *Mīmāṁsakas*. They maintain that the endless chain of life and death, consisting of the cause and the effect, is without beginning. It is just like the begin-

ninglessness of the hen and the egg. This view is true from the relative standpoint.

[4] *With beginning*—It is because the cause has its beginning in the effect and the effect has its beginning in the cause.

[5] *Contradiction*—It is because the *Mīmāṁsakas* admitting the beginning of the cause and the effect, again assert that both are without beginning.

[6] *Ātman etc.*—The opponent may contend that the *Ātman* has become both the cause and the effect. The cause and the effect may have a beginning because both are the modifications of *Ātman*. But from the standpoint of their substratum, *viz.*, the *Ātman*, they are without beginning. This contention is baseless as the *Ātman* which is immutable, eternal and without parts cannot undergo any modification in the forms of cause and effect.

हेतोरादिः फलं येषामादिर्हेतुः फलस्य च ।
तथा जन्म भवेत्तेषां पुत्राज्जन्म पितुर्यथा । १५ ॥

15. *Those who maintain that the effect is the cause of the cause and the cause is the cause of the effect, describe, as a matter of fact, the evolution after the manner of the birth of the father from the son.*

ŚAṄKARA'S COMMENTARY

How does the contention of the opponent imply a contradiction? It is thus replied: The admission that the cause is produced from an effect, which is itself born of a cause, carries with it the contradiction which may be stated to be like the birth of the father from the son.

संभवे हेतुफलयोरेषितव्यः क्रमस्त्वया ।
युगपत्संभवे यस्मादसंबन्धो विषाणवत् ॥ १६ ।

16. *In case causality be still maintained, the order in which cause and effect succeed each other must be stated. If it be said that they appear simultaneously, then they being like the two horns of an animal, cannot be mutually related to each other.*

ŚAṄKARA'S COMMENTARY

If it be contended that the contradiction, pointed out above, cannot be valid, then the opponent should determine the order in which cause and effect succeed each other. The opponent has to show that the 'cause' which is antecedent, produces the 'effect' which is subsequent. For the following reason also, the order of 'cause' and 'effect' must be shown. For, if cause and effect arise simultaneously, then they cannot be related as the cause and the effect, as it is impossible to establish the causal relation between the two horns of a cow produced simultaneously.

This *Kārikā* refutes causality from the point of time.

फलादुत्पद्यमानस्सन्न ते हेतुः प्रसिध्यति ।
अप्रसिद्धः कथं हेतुः फलमुत्पादयिष्यति ॥ १७ ॥

17. *Your cause cannot be established if it be produced from the effect. How can the cause, which is itself not established, give birth to the effect?*

ŚAṄKARA'S COMMENTARY

How can there be no causal relation? It is thus replied: The cause[1] cannot have a definite existence if it is to be born of an effect which is, itself, yet unborn, and therefore which is non-existent like the horns of a hare. How[2] can the cause contemplated by you, which is, itself, indefinite and which is non-existent like the horns of a hare, produce an effect? Two things which are mutually dependent upon each other for their production and which are like[3] the horns of a hare, cannot be related as cause and effect or in[4] any other way.

This *Kārikā* proves that the very idea of the causal relation involves an absurdity. The contention of the opponent is this: The cause and the effect are dependent upon each other for their mutual production.

A house is built for the purpose of living. The thought of living results in the building of the house. The absurdity of this contention is thus shown: The general law of causality is that the cause is antecedent and the effect is subsequent to and dependent upon a cause. If the effect be the cause of a cause, then the cause is said to be born from something which is not yet in existence. If the cause is to be produced from a non-existent effect, then the cause itself becomes non-existent. And the cause, being itself non-existent, can but produce an effect which also is non-existent. Thus both cause and effect become non-existent like the horns of a hare. Therefore they cannot be related as cause and effect, which relation can subsist only between two existing entities.

[1] *Cause etc.*—If you say that the cause is produced from the effect (which, itself, on account of its appearing after cause, is yet non-existent), then cause cannot be established. For, in that case it is also non-existent, as it is admitted to be the product of an effect which is, itself, non-existent.

[2] *How can etc.*—If the cause itself be thus proved to be non-existent, how can it, then, produce an effect? If it cannot produce an effect, how do you call it the cause?

[3] *Like etc.*—It is because both the cause and the effect have been proved to be non-existent.

[4] *In any etc.*—Any other relation, such as that of the container and the contained, between two things which are non-existent becomes an absurdity.

यदि हेतोः फलात्सिद्धिः फलसिद्धिश्च हेतुतः ।
कतरत्पूर्वनिष्पन्नं यस्य सिद्धिरपेक्षया ॥ १८ ॥

18. *If the cause is produced from the effect and if the effect is, again, produced from the cause, which of the two is born first upon which depends the birth of the other?*

## Śaṅkara's Commentary

Though any relation between cause and effect has been found to be an impossibility, yet it may be contended by the opponent that the cause and the effect, though not causally related, yet depend upon each other for their mutual existence.

As a reply to this contention we ask: Which of the two, the cause and the effect, is antecedent to the other, upon the previous existence of which, the subsequent existence of the other is dependent?

If both the cause and the effect are mutually dependent, then how can we say that one is prior to the other? If the priority of one cannot be established, then it cannot be proved that one is dependent upon the other for its existence.

अशक्तिरपरिज्ञानं क्रमकोपोऽथ वा पुनः ।
एवं हि सर्वथा बुद्धैः अजातिः परिदीपिता ॥ १९ ॥

19. *The inability (to reply), the ignorance (about the matter) and the impossibility of (establishing) the order of succession (of the cause and the effect) clearly lead the wise to stick to their theory of absolute non-evolution* (Ajāti).

## Śaṅkara's Commentary

If you think that this[1] cannot be explained then this inability shows your ignorance, that is to say, it demonstrates that you are deluded regarding the Knowledge of Reality. Again, the order of succession, pointed out by you—that the effect comes from the cause and the cause comes from the effect—is also inconsistent.[2] Thus is shown the impropriety of the causal relation between the cause and the effect. This[3] leads the wise among the disputants, by showing the fallacy in each other's arguments, to declare, in effect, the non-evolution of things (which is our opinion).

[1] *This etc.*—That is to say, which one of the cause and the effect is antecedent and which is subsequent. It is because both are mutually dependent.

[2] *Inconsistent.*—See the previous *Kārikā*.

[3] *This etc.*—The followers of the *Sāṁkhya* as well as of the *Nyāya* and *Vaiśeṣika* systems, supporting respectively the evolution of things

from an existing and non-existing cause, indicate the fallacy in each other's arguments. It has also been demonstrated that there cannot be any order of succession of cause and effect in the evolution. Thus the disputants ultimately support the view of *Ajāti* or non-evolution of things as stated by us.

बीजाङ्कुराख्यो दृष्टान्तः सदा साध्यसमो हि सः ।
न हि साध्यसमो हेतुः सिद्धौ साध्यस्य युज्यते ॥ २० ॥

20. *The illustration of the seed and the sprout is itself a matter which is yet to be proved. The middle term (that is, the illustration) which is itself yet to be proved (to be true) cannot be used for establishing a proposition to be proved.*

## Śaṅkara's Commentary

(Objection)—We have asserted the causal relation between the cause and the effect. But you have raised mere verbal[1] difficulties to show the inconsistency in our statement and made a caricature of our standpoint by pointing out its absurdity like the birth of the father from the son or a causal relation between the two horns (of a bull) etc. We do not, for a moment, admit the production of an effect from a cause not already existent or of a cause from an effect not established.

(Reply)—What is, then, your contention?

(Objection)—We admit the causal relation as[2] in the case of the seed and the sprout.

(Reply)—To this we reply as follows: The illustration of the causal relation existing between the seed and the sprout is itself the same as the major term in my syllogism, that is to say, the[3] illustration itself is to be proved.

(Objection)—It is apparent that the causal relation of the seed and the sprout is without beginning.

(Reply)—It is not so. The beginning of all antecedents must be admitted, as is the case with the consequents. As[4] a sprout just produced from a seed is with beginning, similarly the seed also, produced from another sprout (existing in the past), by the very succession implied in the act of production, is with beginning. Therefore all antecedent sprouts as well as seeds are with beginning. As every seed and every sprout, among the seeds and the sprouts, are with beginning, so it is unreasonable to say that any one of these is without beginning. This is also equally applicable to the argument of the cause and the effect.

(Objection)--Each[5] of the series of the seeds and the sprouts is without beginning.

(Reply)–No. The unity or oneness of such series cannot be justified. Even those who maintain the beginninglessness of the seed and the sprout, do not admit the existence of a thing known as the series of the seed and the sprout apart from the seed and the sprout. Nor do they admit such a series in the case of the cause and the effect. Therefore it has been rightly asked, 'How do you assert the beginninglessness of the cause and the effect?' Other explanations being unreasonable, we have not raised any verbal difficulty. Even[6] in our ordinary experience expert logicians do not use anything, which is yet to be established, as the middle term or illustration in order to establish relation between the major and the minor terms of a syllogism. The word *Hetu* or the middle term is used here in the sense of illustration, as it is the illustration which leads to the establishment of a proposition. In the context illustration is meant and not reason.

[1] *Verbal etc.*—The opponent contends that the difficulties raised are merely verbal.

[2] *As in etc.*—It is like the production of the seed from the sprout and the *vice versa*.

[3] *The illustration etc.*—Śaṅkara contends that it is to be proved that the seed is produced from a beginningless sprout or the sprout is produced from a beginningless seed.

[4] *As a sprout etc.*—The opponent contends that the *Bīja* (seed or cause) is without beginning *(Anādi)* because he wants to make it *Aja* or beginningless. But Śaṅkara says that every *Bīja* or seed is produced and therefore every *Bīja* is with beginning. Hence the cause cannot be *Aja* or birthless.

[5] *Each etc.*—The opponent contends that there is a series of seed and there is another series of sprout. From the 'seed series' is produced the 'sprout series' and *vice versa.* Similarly, from the 'cause series' is produced the 'effect series' and *vice versa.*

[6] *Even etc.*—The illustration of the seed and the sprout has been given by the opponent to prove the beginninglessness of the cause and the effect. But Śaṅkara contends that the beginninglessness of the seed and the sprout in the illustration has not yet been proved. As a matter of fact it has been shown that both the seed and the sprout are with beginning. Hence this illustration which is itself not proved, cannot be admitted in support of the contention.

पूर्वापरापरिज्ञानम् अजातेः परिदीपकम् ।
जायमानाद्धि वै धर्मात् कथं पूर्वं न गृह्यते ॥ २१ ॥

21. *The ignorance regarding the antecedence and the subsequence of the cause and the effect clearly proves the absence of evolution or creation. If the effect* (Dharma, i.e., *the* Jīva) *has really been produced from a cause, then why can you not point out the antecedent cause?*

## Śaṅkara's Commentary

How do the wise assert the view of *Ajāti* or absolute non-evolution? It is thus replied: The[1] very fact that one does not know the antecedence and the subsequence of the cause and the effect is, in itself, the clearest indication of absolute non-evolution. If[2] the effect (*Dharma, i.e.*, the *Jīva*) be taken as produced (from a cause) then why cannot its antecedent cause be pointed out? It goes without saying that one who accepts birth as a fact must also know its antecedent cause. For, the relationship of the cause and the effect is inseparable and therefore cannot be given up. Therefore the absence of knowledge (regarding the cause) clearly indicates the fact of absolute non-evolution.

[1] *The very etc.*—The fact of birth can be said to be established if the order of the succession of cause and effect be established. In the absence of such order there cannot be any birth or evolution.

[2] *If etc.*—The idea of 'cause' cannot be thought of without the idea of 'effect' and *vice versa*. Therefore we cannot say which one is antecedent. Hence the idea of evolution *(Janma)*, *i.e.*, an antecedent cause giving birth to a subsequent effect, is due to ignorance or *Avidyā*.

स्वतो वा परतो वाऽपि न किंचिद्वस्तु जायते ।
सदसत्सदसद्वाऽपि न किंचिद्वस्तु जायते ॥ २२ ॥

22. *Nothing, whatsoever, is born either of itself or of another. Nothing is ever produced whether it be being or non-being or both being and non-being.*

## Śaṅkara's Commentary

For this reason, also, nothing whatsoever is born. That[1] which is (supposed to be) born cannot be born of itself, of another or of both. Nothing,[2] whether it be existing or non-existing, or both, is ever born. Of such an entity, birth is not possible in any manner whatsoever. Nothing[3] is born out of itself, *i.e.*, from its own form which in itself has not yet come into existence. A jar cannot be produced from the self-same jar. A thing cannot be born from another thing, which is other than itself, as a jar cannot be produced from another jar, or a piece of cloth from another piece of cloth. Similarly, a thing cannot be born both out of itself and another, as that involves a contradiction.[4] A[5] jar or a piece of cloth cannot be produced by both a jar and a piece of cloth.

(Objection)—A jar is produced from clay, and a son is born of a father.

(Reply)—Yes, the deluded use a word like 'birth' and have a notion corresponding to the word. Both the word and the notion are examined by men of discrimination who wish to ascertain whether these are true or not. After examination they come to the conclusion that things, such as a jar or a son etc., denoted by the words and signified by the notions, or mere verbal[6] expressions. The Scripture also corroborates it, saying, 'All effects are mere names and figures of speech'. If the thing is ever-existent, then it cannot be born again. The very[7] existence is the reason for non-evolution. A father[8] or clay is the illustration to support the contention. If these objects, on the other hand, be non-existent, even then they cannot be said to be produced. The very non-existence is the reason. The horns[9] of a hare are an illustration. If things be both existent and non-existent, then also, it cannot be born. For, such contradictory ideas cannot be associated with a thing. Therefore it is established that nothing whatsoever is born. Those[10] who, again, assert that the very fact of birth is born again, that the cause, the effect and the act of birth form one unity, and also that all objects have only momentary existence, maintain a view which is very far from reason. For a thing immediately after being pointed out as 'It is this', ceases to exist and consequently no memory of the thing is possible in the absence of such cognition.

There are six possible alternatives in the case of the birth of a thing. It is either born of itself, or of another, or of both. That which is born is either existing or non-existing or both. This *Kārikā* shows the absurdity of all these positions and conclusively establishes the theory of absolute non-evolution.

[1] *That etc.*—That is to say, the three alternatives are denied regarding the cause.

[2] *Nothing etc.*—In other words the three alternatives are denied regarding the effect.

[3] *Nothing etc.*—Birth always means change. If a thing produces another thing, it cannot do so without a change in itself. If it undergoes a change, it ceases to be the thing itself. Therefore a thing cannot be the cause of the same thing. A jar cannot be the cause of the very same jar.

[4] *Contradiction*—For, a cause cannot, at the same time, combine within it two contradictory aspects.

[5] *A jar etc.*—Therefore an object which is supposed to be born cannot be born from a cause which is both existing and non-existing.

[6] *Verbal etc.*—It is because the birth of a son or the production of a jar cannot be proved.

[7] *The very etc.*—Birth signifying a change would indicate that the thing, before it was born, had been non-existent. This previous non-existence cannot be reconciled with the idea of its being ever-existent.

[8] *Father etc.*—If the son or the jar be ever-existent, then they cannot be born from a father or clay.

[9] *Horns etc.*—Horns of a hare are ever non-existent. Hence no birth can be predicated of them.

[10] *Those etc.*—This is the view of the Buddhist idealists. According to them, no external objects, corresponding to our idea of them, exist. Idea alone is real. One idea gives birth to another idea. These ideas are momentary. The moment an idea is cognised as such, it vanishes giving birth to another idea. All our notions regarding the cause, the effect and the act of birth form only one unit idea. But this position is absolutely untenable. If one idea be immediately succeeded by another idea, then the antecedent idea is no longer cognised by us. In the absence of such cognition, no memory is possible. If an idea has only a momentary existence, then our very possibility of experience becomes an absurdity. If there cannot be any memory of the antecedent idea, then it is not possible to establish a causal relation between the antecedent and the subsequent ideas.

हेतुर्न जायतेऽनादेः फलं चापि स्वभावतः ।
आदिर्न विद्यते यस्य तस्य ह्यादिर्न विद्यते ॥ २३ ॥

23. *The cause cannot be produced from an effect which is without beginning, nor is the effect born of its own nature (itself). That which is without beginning is necessarily free from birth.*

## Śaṅkara's Commentary

In accepting the beginninglessness of the cause and the effect you are forced to admit the absence of birth regarding them. How is it so? The[1] cause cannot be produced from an effect, which is without beginning. In other words, you do not certainly mean that the cause is produced from an effect which is, itself, without beginning and free from birth. Nor do you[2] admit that the effect, by following its own inherent nature, (*i.e.*, without any extraneous cause) is produced from a cause which is unborn and without beginning. Therefore[3] by admitting the beginninglessness of the cause and the effect, you, verily, accept the fact of their being never produced. It is because we know from common experience that what is without beginning is also free from birth which means a beginning. Beginning is admitted of a thing which has birth, and not of a thing which has none.

[1] *The cause etc.*—The *beginningless* effect cannot produce a cause. For, otherwise it cannot be itself an effect. An effect, signifying birth, must have a beginning. Again, if the cause be produced from an effect, then the cause, itself, cannot be without beginning.

[2] *You etc.*—It is because if the effect be produced from a cause, it cannot be beginningless.

[3] *Therefore etc.*—If the cause and the effect, on account of their being never born, be ever free from birth, they cannot be cause and effect. For, the words are always associated with birth. Hence the opponent by admitting the beginninglessness of cause and effect accepts, as a matter of fact, the theory of *Ajāti* or he stultifies himself.

प्रज्ञप्तेः सनिमित्तत्वमन्यथा द्वयनाशतः ।
संक्लेशस्योपलब्धेश्च परतन्त्रास्तिता मता ॥ २४ ॥

24. *Subjective knowledge must have an objective cause; otherwise both must be non-existent. For this reason as well as that of the experience of pain, the existence of external objects, accepted by other thinkers, should be admitted.*

## Śaṅkara's Commentary

An objection is raised in order to strengthen the meaning already stated. The word *Prajñapti* in the text signifies 'knowledge', *i.e.*, the experience of such notions as that of sound etc. This (subjective) knowledge has a cause, *i.e.*, an (eternal) agent or object corresponding to it. In other words, we premise that knowledge is not merely subjective but has an object outside the perceiving subject. Cognition of sound etc., is not possible without objects. For, such experience is always produced by a cause. In[1] the absence of such (external) object, the variety and multiplicity of experiences such as sound, touch, colour, *viz.*, blue, yellow, red, etc., would not have existed. But the varieties are not non-existent, for these are directly perceived by all. Hence, because the variety of manifold experiences exist, it is necessary to admit the existence—as supported by the system of the opposite school—of external objects which are outside the ideas of the perceiving subject. The subjective knowledge has one characteristic alone, *i.e.*, it is of the very nature of illumination. It does not admit of any variety within itself. The variety of experiences of colour, such as blueness, yellowness, etc., cannot possibly be explained, by merely imagining a variety in the subjective knowledge, without admitting variety of external objects which are the substratum of these multiple colours. In other words, no variety of colour is possible in a (white) crystal without its coming in contact with such adjuncts as the external objects which possess such colours as blueness etc. For this additional reason also one is forced to admit the existence of external object—supported by the Scripture of the opposite school—an object which is external to the knowledge (of the perceiving subject): Misery[2] caused by burns etc., is experienced by all. Such pain as is caused by burns etc., would not have been felt in the absence of the fire etc., which is the cause of the burns and which exists independent of the knowledge (of the perceiving subject). But such pain is experienced by all. Hence,[3] we think that external objects do exist. It is not reasonable to conclude that such pain is caused by mere subjective knowledge. For,[4] such misery is not found elsewhere.

This *Kārikā* gives the views of the dualists who believe in the reality of external objects. They argue thus: Knowledge is not possible without the contact with an external object. Mental impressions are always created by our coming into contact with objects that lie outside of us. Besides, no variety is possible in the knowledge of the perceiving subject without a corresponding variety existing outside of it. From the experience of such knowledge as that of colour, form, etc., one must admit the existence of objects outside the perceiving mind corresponding to the subjective impressions. Again, different experiences give rise to different feelings, such as pleasant or otherwise, which also are impossible in the absence of external objects. All these arguments compel one to believe in the reality of external objects.

[1] *In etc.*—Otherwise there would be no idea of variety and objects corresponding to such ideas.

[2] *Misery etc.*—A man may create ideas, but he cannot create pain. Therefore, the pain must have an external cause.

[3] *Hence etc.*—The contention of the opponent is that there must exist causal relation between objects and our knowledge of them.

[4] *For*—That is to say, that the pain of burn is experienced only when the limb comes in contact with fire and not when it is besmeared with sandal-paste, etc. Therefore, misery, pain, etc., are not possible in the absence of a cause.

प्रज्ञप्तेः सनिमित्तत्वमिष्यते युक्तिदर्शनात् ।
निमित्तस्यानिमित्तत्वम् इष्यते भूतदर्शनात् ॥ २५ ॥

25. *From the point of view of logical reason a cause for the subjective impression must be assigned. But from the standpoint of the highest Reality or the true nature of things, we find that the (so-called) cause (of the subjective impression) is, after all, no cause.*

### Śaṅkara's Commentary

To[1] this objection, we reply as follows: We admit that you posit a cause of the subjective experience on account of such arguments as the existence of the variety (in the objective world) and because of the experience of pain. Stick for a while to your argument that reason demands that an external object should exist to produce a subjective impression.

(The opponent)—Please let us know what you (*Advaitin*) are going to say next.

(Reply)—Yes, the[2] jar etc., posited by you as the cause, that is to say, the cause of the subjective impression, are not, according to us, the external cause, the substratum (of the impression); nor are they the cause for our experiences of variety.

(Objection)—How?

(Reply)—We say so from[3] the standpoint of the true nature of Reality. When the true nature of clay is known a jar does not exist apart from the clay as exists a buffalo in entire independence of a horse. Nor does cloth exist apart from the thread in it. Similarly the threads have no existence apart from the fibres. If we thus proceed to find out the true nature of the thing, by going from one cause to another, till language or the object denoted by the language fails us, we do not still find any (final) cause.

'*Bhūtadarśanāt*' (from the true nature of the thing) may be '*Abhūtadarśanāt*' (from the unreality of the experiences). According to this interpretation, the meaning of the *Kārikā* is that we do not admit external objects as the cause on[4] account of the unreality of these (external) objects, which are as unreal as the snake seen instead of the rope. The (so-called) cause[5] ceases to be the cause as the former is due to the illusory perception of the perceiver. For,[6] it (the external world) disappears in the absence of such illusory knowledge. The man in dreamless sleep and trance (*Samādhi*) and he who has attained the highest knowledge do not experience any object outside their self as they are free[7] from such illusory cognition. An object which is cognised by a lunatic is never known as such by a sane man. Thus[8] is answered the contention regarding the causality based upon the arguments of the perception of variety and the existence of pain.

Realism which is always associated with causality is now refuted by idealism.

[1] *To etc.*—That is to say, that objection as set forth in the previous *Kārikā*.

[2] *The jar etc.*—The external jar is not the cause of our mental impression (idea) of the jar. Nor is the external jar the substratum upon which the idea of the jar is superposed.

[3] *From the etc.*—It is because from the standpoint of Ultimate Truth the external jar does not, as such, exist. That which really exists is clay (without form) which, being associated with name and form, appears as the jar. Name and form, being mere ideas of the mind, are illusory. Therefore, the jar has no real existence independent of the clay. If the opponent contends that the external objects create the subjective ideas, we ask for a cause of the external objects. The opponent cannot point out such a cause. Hence the argument of causality fails.

[4] *On account of etc.*—That is to say, no external object exists as such. What is taken as the external object is merely the idea of the perceiver. When the snake is perceived in the rope, that perception, being illusory, cannot be called the knowledge of any independent reality called snake. Similarly, the perception of the external object, being illusory, cannot point to the existence of any such object as an independent reality.

[5] *Cause etc.*—Seeking a cause for subjective ideas is due to ignorance (*Avidyā*).

[6] *For etc.*—When this ignorance, *i.e.*, the belief in causality, disappears the external world itself disappears.

[7] *Free etc.*—That is to say, they are no longer subject to the law of

causality. Hence they do not see any external world as an independent reality.

[8] *Thus etc.*—The opponent contends that external objects must exist as we are conscious of the variety of subjective impressions. Another reason for the existence of the external object is our experience of pain. The mind may create an idea, but it will not cause pain to itself. To this contention the following reply is given: We may have consciousness of variety or pain in the absence of external objects. One is conscious of the variety of objects in dream. He feels pain in dream. But the dream experiences are only the subjective impressions in the mind of the dreamer. No external object exists, at that time, which corresponds to the dream experiences. Therefore subjective impressions need not be necessarily produced by a really existing external object. There is no proof that external objects independently of the mind exist. The subjective impression of the snake in place of the rope is produced in the absence of an external snake. From the standpoint of reality, nothing exists but the Self or *Ātman*. Perception of any other existence is due to illusion. The mind, in ignorance, seeks a cause, and thereby infers an external world.

चित्तं न संस्पृशत्यर्थं नार्थाभासं तथैव च ।
अभूतो हि यतश्चार्थो नार्थाभासस्ततः पृथक् ॥ २६ ॥

26. *The mind is not related to the (external) objects. Nor are the ideas which appear as external objects, reflections upon the mind. It is so because the objects are non-existent and the ideas (which appear as external objects) are not separate from the mind.*

## Śaṅkara's Commentary

Because there are no external objects as cause, the mind does not relate itself to external objects which are supposed to be the cause of the subjective impression. Nor is the mind related to the ideas which appear as external objects, as the mind, like[1] the dream-mind, is identical with such ideas. It[2] is because the external objects such as sound etc., perceived in the waking state, are as unreal as dream-objects, for[3] reasons stated already. Another reason is that the ideas appearing as external objects are not different from the mind. It[4] is the mind alone which, as in dream, appears as external objects such as the jar etc.

[1] *Like etc.*—In dream one experiences various external objects. But it is found in the waking state that it is mind alone which appears as objects seen in dream. The mind is identical with these ideas. Therefore there cannot be any causal relation between the mind and the ideas.

[2] *It is etc.*—Therefore there cannot be any causal relation between the mind and the non-existing external objects.

[3] *For reasons etc.*—This has been treated in the second chapter of the *Kārikā* and in other places of the *Kārikā*.

[4] *It is etc.*—It is Self alone which exists. All that are perceived by the deluded as external objects are nothing but the Self. There is only non-dual *Ātman*. The duality is due to illusion.

निमित्तं न सदा चित्तं संस्पृशत्यध्वसु त्रिषु ।
अनिमित्तो विपर्यासः कथं तस्य भविष्यति ॥ २७ ॥

27. *The mind does not enter into causal relation in any of the three periods of time. How can the mind be ever subject to delusion, as there is no cause for any such delusion?*

### Śaṅkara's Commentary

(Objection)—The mind appears as the jar etc., though such objects are non-existent. Therefore there[1] must exist false knowledge. Such being the case, there must be right knowledge somewhere (in relation to, or as distinguished from, false knowledge which we point out).

(Reply)—Our reply to this contention is as follows: The mind certainly does not come in contact with a cause—an external object—in any of the three periods of time, past, present or future. If the mind had ever truly come in contact with such objects then such relation would give us an idea of true knowledge from the standpoint of Reality. And in relation to that knowledge the appearance of the jar etc., in the mind, in the absence of the jar etc., could have been termed as false knowledge. But never does the mind come in contact with an external object (which does not in reality exist). Hence how is it possible for the mind to fall into error when there is no cause for such an assumption? In other words, the mind is never subject to false knowledge. This[2] is, indeed, the very nature of the mind that it takes the forms of the jar etc., though in reality, such jar etc., which may cause the mental forms, do not at all exist.

[1] *There must etc.*—Otherwise one could not be aware of the external jar etc., which do not really exist. One cannot be aware of wrong knowledge unless one knows what right knowledge is. The opponent intends to prove the positive existence of *Avidyā* which cause illusory knowledge.

[2] *This is etc.*—This is what is known as *Avidyā* or the ignorance of the true nature of Reality. On account of this ignorance the mind, which is the same as the non-dual *Ātman, appears* to take the form of the external objects. This false knowledge is not a *correlative* of true knowledge. This false knowledge regarding the existence of the external objects is due to the ignorance of the nature of Reality. Seeking after the cause of *Avidyā* is itself the characteristic of the ignorant mind which has not yet been able to free itself from the delusion of causality.

तस्मान्न जायते चित्तं चित्तदृश्यं न जायते ।
तस्य पश्यन्ति ये जातिं खे वै पश्यन्ति ते पदम् ॥ २८ ॥

28. *Therefore neither the mind nor the objects perceived by the mind are ever born. Those who perceive such birth may as well discover the foot-prints (of the birds) in the sky.*

### Śaṅkara's Commentary

The verses of the *Kārik* from 25 to 27 give the views of a class of Buddhistic thinkers, known as the *Vijñānavādins*[1] (the subjective idealists) who thus refute the views of those who maintain the reality of external objects. The[2] Advaitic teacher (Gauḍapāda) approves of these arguments. Now he makes use of these very arguments of the *Vijñānavādins* as the ground (middle term) for refuting the conclusions of the subjective idealists. The *Kārikā* has this end in view. The subjective idealist admits that the mind, even in the absence of the (external) jar etc., takes the form of the jar etc. We also agree with this conclusion because this is in conformity with the real nature of things. In like manner, the mind, though never produced, appears to be produced and cognised as such. Therefore the mind is never produced, as is the case with the object cognised by it. The *Vijñānavādins* who affirm the production of the mind and also assert that the mind is momentary, full of pain, non-Self in nature, etc., forget that the real[3] nature of the mind can never be understood by the mind (as described by them). Thus the *Vijñānavādins* who see the production of the mind resemble those who (profess to) see in the sky foot-prints left by birds etc. In other words, the *Vijñānavādins* are more audacious than the others, *viz.*, the dualists. And the Nihilists[4] who, in spite of the perception of the visible world, assert the absolute non-existence of everything including their own experiences, are even more audacious than the *Vijñānavādins*. These Nihilists take the position of those who claim to compress the whole sky in the palms of their hands.

The three *Kārikās, viz.*, 25, 26 and 27, give the views of the Buddhist idealist who refutes those that believe in the reality of the external objects. This *Kārikā* refutes the position of the *Vijñānavādin.*

1 *Vijñānavādins*—They belong to the school of subjective idealism in the Buddhistic system of thought. According to this school, all objects are pre-existent in the subject in the form of *Vāsanās* (ideas). Cause is only a subjective idea. It does not exist as external object with which we associate it. Further, according to this school, all ideas are momentary.

2 *The Advaita etc.*—Gauḍapāda accepts the views of the *Vijñāna-*

*vādins* only in respect of the non-existence of external objects. He also agrees with the *Vijñānavādins* that the so-called external objects are nothing but the state of the mind (*cittaspandanam*).

[3] *Real nature etc.*—It is because the mind, according to the *Vijñānavādins*, is momentary. The consciousness of one moment is unrelated to that of the next moment. Such being the case, in the absence of an unchanging entity it is not possible to know the change of consciousness from one moment to another. Therefore it is absurd to assert that the mind is born every moment and that it is full of misery etc. For, there is no perceiver according to the *Vijñānavādins*, which can cognize the momentary change of consciousness as well as its painful and non-*Ātman* character.

[4] *Nihilists*—The position of the Nihilists who affirm the non-existence of everything, including the perceiver, is even more untenable. If all that exists is really a void, then there must be a perceiver of this void. Otherwise who will assert that everything is void?

अजातं जायते यस्मात् अजातिः प्रकृतिस्ततः ।
प्रकृतेरन्यथाभावो न कथंचिद्भविष्यति ॥ २९ ॥

29. *(In the opinion of the disputants) that which is unborn is said to be born. For, its very nature is to be ever unborn. It is never possible for a thing to be other than what it is.*

## Śaṅkara's Commentary

For reasons already stated it is established that Brahman is one and unborn. This verse summarises the conclusion of what has already been stated in the form of proposition. The unborn mind, which[1] is verily Brahman, is imagined by the disputants to be born. Therefore (according to them) the ever-unborn is said to be born. For, it is unborn by its very nature. It[2] is simply impossible for a thing, which is ever unborn by nature, to be anyhow born, that is to say, to be anyhow otherwise than what it is.

[1] *Which etc.*—It has been already seen that the mind is never born. Therefore the mind is Brahman, non-dual and immutable. The disputants, on account of ignorance, see the modifications and change in the mind. The very nature of the mind is that it is one and without a second, and free from change or birth.

[2] *It is etc.*—The absolute mind does not in any way undergo any change. Even through delusion the mind cannot be said to pass into birth. If it were so then it cannot be said to be unborn and unchanging in nature.

अनादेरन्तवत्त्वं च संसारस्य न सेत्स्यति ।
अनन्तता चाऽऽदिमतो मोक्षस्य न भविष्यति ॥ ३० ॥

30. *If the world be admitted to be beginningless (as some disputants assert), then it cannot be non-eternal.* Mokṣa *or liberation cannot have a beginning and be eternal.*

### Śaṅkara's Commentary

Here is another defect in the arguments of those who maintain that the *Ātman* is, in reality, subject[1] to both bondage and liberation. If the world (*i.e.*, the state of bondage of the *Ātman*) be without beginning or a definite past, then its end cannot be established by any logical reasoning. In ordinary experience, there is no instance of an object which has no beginning but has an end.

(Objection)—We[2] see a break in the beginningless continuity of the relation of the seed and the sprout.

Reply—This illustration has no validity; for,[3] the seed and the sprout do not constitute a single entity. In like manner, liberation cannot be said to have no end if it be asserted that liberation which is attained by acquisition of knowledge has a (definite) beginning. For, the jar etc., which have a beginning have also an end.

(Objection)—There[4] is no defect in our argument as

liberation, not being any substance, may be like the destruction of a jar etc.

(Reply)—In that case it will contradict your proposition that liberation has a positive existence from the standpoint of the Ultimate Reality. Further, liberation being a non-entity, like the horn of a hare cannot ever have a beginning.

This *Kārikā* gives us the reason for the statement that *Ātman* is ever-pure, ever-free and ever-existent. *Ātman,* conceived as such, is not a theological dogma, nor is it based upon the intuition of the mystic, but it is a metaphysical fact.

[1] *Subject etc.*—That is to say, the *Ātman* is bound during the state of ignorance and it becomes free with the acquisition of knowledge. Those who make this contention accept the bondage of *Ātman* as a *fact.*

[2] *We see etc.*—The opponent contends that the relation of a seed and a tree, though without beginning, is seen to come to an end when the tree dies without leaving a seed.

[3] *For the seed etc.*—The seed and sprout do not constitute a single series. Every time a new seed and a new sprout are seen to be produced. Therefore both the seed and the tree have definite beginning.

[4] *There is etc.*—The opponent contends that a non-entity results from the breaking of a jar. This non-entity has a beginning (in the breaking of the jar) but it is eternal. Liberation (*Mokṣa*) in the form of the destruction of the bondage (*bandha*), not being any substance, can be eternal like the *destruction* of a jar which, though not a substance and though with beginning, is without end. This is the contention of the opponent.

आदावन्ते च यन्नास्ति वर्तमानेऽपि तत्तथा ।
वितथैः सदृशाः सन्तोऽवितथा इव लक्षिताः ॥ ३१ ॥

31. *That which is non-existent at the beginning and in the end, is necessarily so (non-existent) in the middle. The objects we see are illusions, still they are regarded as if real.*

सप्रयोजनता तेषां स्वप्ने विप्रतिपद्यते ।
तस्मादाद्यन्तवत्त्वेन मिथ्यैव खलु ते स्मृताः ॥ ३२ ॥

32. *The serving of some purpose by them* (i.e., *the objects of waking experience*) *is contradicted in dream. Therefore they are doubtlessly recognised to be illusory* (*by the wise*) *on account of their having a beginning and an end.*

## Śaṅkara's Commentary

These two verses have been explained before in the chapter on Illusion (Chapter II. 6. 7). They are quoted here again in connection with the topics which are discussed in relation to the unreality of the universe and liberation.

The opponent may contend thus: Let the state of liberation have a beginning and an end. What is the harm in thus conceiving the state of liberation? The reply is that if a thing has a beginning and an end, it does not exist in the middle also. That is to say, it has no existence whatsoever. That we see its existence is due to our ignorance. The familiar instance is that of the mirage. The mirage has no existence prior to its vision by the deluded and it does not exist when the illusion vanishes. That we see the mirage at all is due to our ignorance. Therefore if we accept the idea of liberation as conceived by the opponent then it would be non-existent. The opponent may again contend that one cánnot quench his thirst with the water of the mirage. But liberation is conducive to our infinite happiness. The reply to this contention is that liberation as conceived by the opponent, being illusory, serves no purpose whatsoever. If liberation should have both beginning and end, then it would be like our dream or waking experiences. In the waking state a man may feel that he has enjoyed a hearty feast, but immediately after going to sleep he may experience in dream ravenous hunger. In that case the waking experiences do not serve him a lasting purpose. Any experience which has a beginning or an end is illusory from the standpoint of Reality.

सर्वे धर्मा मृषा स्वप्ने कायस्यान्तर्निदर्शनात् ।
संवृतेऽस्मिन्प्रदेशे वै भूतानां दर्शनं कुतः ॥ ३३ ॥

33. ***All objects cognised in dream are unreal, because they are seen within the body. How is it possible for things, that are perceived to exist, to be really in Brahman which is indivisible and homogeneous.***

### Śaṅkara's Commentary

This and the following verses are meant to explain in detail one of the previous *Kārikās* which states that the (so-called) cause (of the opponent) is, really speaking, no cause at all. (Ref. Verse 25, Chapt. IV.)

The purpose of the *Kārikā* is to show that Brahman, birthless and non-dual, is alone existent; for, the waking experiences, on account of their having a beginning and an end, are unreal like the dream ones. Therefore what is seen is Brahman alone. The dream objects are seen within the body; hence they are unreal as things like a mountain etc., cannot exist within the body. Similarly, all our waking experiences are supposed to be within the body (of the *Virāṭ*). Hence they are also illusory from the standpoint of Reality. The *Virāṭ* itself is in the Self (*Ātman*) which cannot, in reality, contain multiplicity. Therefore waking experiences are illusory. The dream experiences are considered illusory as time and space corresponding to such experiences do not conform to the time and space of the dreamer. In like manner waking experiences are also illusory as they, really speaking, cannot exist in the Self (*Ātman*) which is one, non-dual and homogeneous and which cannot contain any space for the existence of alien objects.

न युक्तं दर्शनं गत्वा कालस्यानियमाद्गतौ ।
प्रतिबुद्धश्च वै सर्वस्तस्मिन्देशे न विद्यते ॥ ३४ ॥

34. *It is not possible for a dreamer to go out in order to experience the (dream) objects on account of the discrepancy of the time involved in such journey. Again, on being awake, the dreamer does not find himself in the place (where he dreamed himself to be).*

### Śaṅkara's Commentary

The time and space involved in undertaking a journey and in coming back, have a definite and fixed standard in the waking state. These are seen to be reversed[1] in dream. On account of this inconsistency it can be positively said that the dreamer does not actually go out to another place during his dream experiences.

[1] *Reversed*—In dream which may last for a few minutes, a man may have experience of events which may take years to happen. Therefore the idea of time and space experienced in dream is illusory.

मित्राद्यैः सह संमन्त्र्य संबुद्धो न प्रपद्यते ।
गृहीतं चापि यत्किंचित् प्रतिबुद्धो न पश्यति ॥ ३५ ॥

35. *The dreamer on being awake, realises as illusory all the conversation he had had with friends etc., during the dream state. Further, he does not possess, in the waking state, anything which he had acquired in dream.*

### Śaṅkara's Commentary

A man, in dream, holds conversation with his friends etc. But, on being awake, he finds it all as unreal. Further, he possesses in dream gold etc., but, in the awakened state he realises all these possessions to be unreal. Though he goes to other countries in dream, he does not, in reality, make any such journey.

The conversations etc., held in dream, become unreal in the waking state. Similarly, Scriptural discussions etc., with the sages held in the waking state, are known to be illusory when one attains the Ultimate Reality. For, all beings are ever free. There is no bondage or ignorance, really speaking, which requires to be removed by religious practices. The wise man knows the study of the Scriptures etc., undertaken for the attainment of knowledge, as illusory, as dream experiences: for, *Ātman* is ever free, pure and illumined. Even eating, drinking, etc., which a knower of Truth performs, are dissociated from all ideas of subject-object relationship. Even while taking, doing, etc., he is conscious of the non-dual Brahman alone. The aim of the Scriptural study, religious practices, etc., is to de-hypnotise us from the hypnotic idea that we are not Brahman.

स्वप्ने चावस्तुकः कायः पृथगन्यस्य दर्शनात् ।
यथा कायस्तथा सर्वं चित्तदृश्यमवस्तुकम् ॥ ३६ ॥

36. *The body active in dream is unreal as the other body, quite distinct from it, is perceived. Like the body, everything, cognised by the mind, is unreal.*

## Śaṅkara's Commentary

The body, which appears to be wandering in the dream, is unreal; for, another body, quite different from it, is seen in the spot where the dreamer lies. As the body perceived in the dream is unreal, so also all that is cognised by the mind, even in the waking state, is unreal; for, all these perceived objects are mere different states of mind. The significance of this chapter is that even the waking experiences, on account of their being similar to the dream experiences, are unreal.

The body which is active in the waking state lies motionless in the bed when the dreamer perceives that he is wandering at various places. Therefore from the standpoint of the waking state, this dream body is unreal. Similarly, from the standpoint of the Ultimate Reality the body perceived in the waking state—the body which is felt to be honoured or insulted by the friends or enemies—is also unreal. It is because this body is also an idea in the mind of the perceiver. As dream objects are unreal on account of their being perceived by the mind, so also the objects of the waking experience are unreal for the very same reason. Being perceived by the mind is the common factor in both waking and dream states. Therefore the experiences of both the states bear with them the stamp of unreality.

ग्रहणाज्जागरितवत्तद्धेतुः स्वप्न इष्यते ।
तद्धेतुत्वात्तु तस्यैव सज्जागरितमिष्यते ॥ ३७ ॥

37. *As the experience (of objects) in dream is similar to the experience (of objects) in the waking state, therefore it is thought that the waking experiences are the cause of the dream-experiences. On account of this reason, the waking experiences (supposed to be the cause of the dream) appear as real to the dreamer alone (but not to others).*

## Śaṅkara's Commentary

For this reason also, the objects experienced in the waking state are unreal. The dream experiences, like the waking ones, are characterised by the subject-object relationship. On account[1] of this similarity of perception, the waking state is said to be the cause of the dream state. In other words, it is contended that the dream state is the effect of the waking one which is the cause. If that be the case, *i.e.*, if the dream be the effect of waking experiences, then the waking experiences are real to the perceiver of the dream alone (*i.e.*, who takes the dream to be real) and to no one else. The purport[2] of this *Kārikā* is that the dream appears to us real, that is to say, dream objects appear as objects of common experience and therefore real to the dreamer alone. So also the experiences of the waking state, being the cause of the dream, appear as if they were within the common experience of all and therefore real. But the objects perceived in the waking state are not the same to all. Waking experiences are verily like the dream ones.

[1] *On account etc.*—In the dream state, dream objects appear as real. To the dreamer, the dream state is the waking state. One knows the dream state to be unreal only from the waking state. As a matter of fact, we are aware of a succession of waking states alone. When we know a previous waking state to be unreal, we call it dream state. Without dream one could not know the waking state to be real. Similarly one could not know the waking state as real without the unreal dream state. We speak of the waking state as the cause of the

dream state on account of the cognition of the subject-object idea present in both the states. But, really speaking, there is no causal relation between the two states. The waking state appears real only to him who looks upon dream also as real and who seeking a cause for the dream, takes the waking state as the cause of the dream.

[2] *The purport etc.*—It may be contended that dream experience is private, its objects and actions being cognised by the dreamer and none else. But the waking experience is not private. It is universal. But this is not a fact. The dream universe has not only its suns, moons, and stars, but also its human denizens who perceive them as our fellow-beings of the waking universe do in the waking world. The distinction of private and public to mark the objects of one state from those of the other is futile. The truth is that as in the dream, the action of the mind creates the idea of a universe with the sun, the moon, friends and foes, etc., similarly, in the waking state also the mind creates the idea of a universe with all its contents.

उत्पादस्याप्रसिद्धत्वादजं सर्वमुदाहृतं ।
न च भूतादभूतस्य संभवोऽस्ति कथंचन ॥ ३८ ॥

38. *All these are known as unborn, as their creation or evolution cannot be established as a fact. It is ever impossible for the unreal to be born of the real.*

## Śaṅkara's Commentary

(Objection)—Though the waking experiences are the cause of the dream ones, still the former cannot be unreal like the latter. The dream is extremely evanescent whereas the waking experiences are seen to be permanent.

(Reply)—This[1] is true with regard to the people who do not possess discrimination. Men of discrimination do not see the production[2] or the birth of anything, as creation or evolution cannot be established as a fact. Hence all this is known in the Vedāntic books as unborn[3] (*i.e.*, non-dual Brahman). For the *Śruti* declares, 'He (the *Ātman*) is both within and without and is, at the same time, unborn'. If you contend that the illusory dream is the effect of the real waking state, we say that your contention is untenable. In our common experience, we never see a non-existing thing produced from an existing one. Such non-existing thing as the horn of a hare is never seen to be produced from any other object.

[1] *This etc.*—It is true that the time standard of the waking state does not apply to the dream state. But the standard with which the dreamer measures the time of his dream experiences seems to him perfectly consistent in the dream state.

[2] *Production etc.*—That is to say, wise men do not believe in causality.

[3] *Unborn*—That is to say, wise men see everywhere the non-dual Brahman alone which has no birth or change.

असज्जागरिते दृष्ट्वा स्वप्ने पश्यति तन्मयः ।
असत्स्वप्नेऽपि दृष्ट्वा च प्रतिबुद्धो न पश्यति ॥ ३९ ॥

39. *Being deeply impressed with the (reality of the) unreal objects which a man sees in the waking state, he sees those very things in dream as well. Moreover the unreal objects cognised in the dream are not seen again in the waking state.*

### Śaṅkara's Commentary

(Objection)—It is you who stated that the dream is the effect of the waking experience. That being the case, how do you refute causality?

(Reply)—Listen to our explanation of the causality, referred to in that instance. One perceives in the waking state objects which are unreal like the snake imagined in the rope. Being deeply impressed by such (illusory) perception, he imagines in the dream, as in the waking state, the subject-object relationship and thereby perceives (dream) objects. But though full of the unreal seen in the dream, he does[1] not see those (unreal) objects, over again, in the waking state. The reason is the absence of the imaginary subject-object relationship (one experiences in dream). The word '*ca*', 'moreover' in the text denotes that the causal relationship between the waking and the dream states is not always observed. Similarly,[2] things seen in the waking state are not, sometimes, cognised in dream. Therefore the statement that the waking condition is the cause of the dream is[3] not made from the standpoint of the Ultimate Reality.

[1] *Does not etc.*—This shows that the causal relation is not seen between the waking and the dream states.

[2] *Similarly etc.*—This is another reason to show that the causal relation does not exist between the waking and the dream states.

[3] *Is not made etc.*—Waking state is said to be the cause of the dream only from the empirical standpoint.

From the subsequent waking standpoint we call the antecedent dream state unreal. But we do not find a causal relation between the antecedent dream state and the subsequent waking one because we view it from the waking standpoint—when the dream is over. Objects seen in dream could have been seen even now in the waking state if the waking state were a part or continuation of the previous dream state.

नास्त्यसद्धेतुकमसत् सदसद्धेतुकं तथा ।
सच्च सद्धेतुकं नास्ति सद्धेतुकमसत्कुतः ॥ ४० ॥

40. *The unreal cannot have the unreal as its cause, nor can the real be produced from the unreal. The real cannot be the cause of the real. And it is much more impossible for the real to be the cause of the unreal.*

## Śaṅkara's Commentary

From the standpoint of the Ultimate Reality, things can, in no way, enter into causal relation. How? An unreal cannot be the cause of another unreal. An[1] unreal entity such as the horns of a hare, which may be said to be the cause of another unreal entity such as a castle in the air, has no existence whatsoever. Similarly,[2] an object like a jar which is perceived and which is the effect of an unreal object like the horns of the hare, is never existent. In[3] like manner, a jar which is perceived and which is the effect of another jar that also is perceived to exist, is, in itself, non-existent. And[4] lastly, how is existence possible of a real object as the cause of an unreal one? No other causal relation is possible nor can be conceived of. Hence men of knowledge find that the causal relation between any objects whatsoever is not capable of being proved.

The causal relation between the waking and the dream states has been stated from the empirical standpoint alone. But it cannot be established from the standpoint of Truth. Further, no causal relation, whatsoever, is admissible.

[1] *An unreal etc.*—This refutes the contention of the Buddhistic nihilists.

[2] *Similarly etc.*—This is the refutation of the *Nyāya* school.

[3] *In like etc.*—This refutes the *Sāṁkhya* school of causality.

[4] *And lastly etc.*—A class of *Vedāntists* hold that the ever-existent Brahman is the cause of these illusory phenomena. This is the refutation of that school of thought.

All the four systems of thought refuted above believe in causality in some form or other.

विपर्यासाद्यथा जाग्रदचिन्त्यान्भूतवत्स्पृशेत् ।
तथा स्वप्ने विपर्यासात् धर्मांस्तत्रैव पश्यति ।। ४१ ।।

41. *As one in the waking state, through false knowledge, handles, as real, objects whose nature cannot be described, similarly, in dream also, one perceives, through false knowledge, objects whose existence is possible in that condition alone.*

## Śaṅkara's Commentary

This verse intends to remove the slightest possibility of the causal relation between the waking and the dream states, though both are unreal. As in the waking state, one, through want of proper discrimination, imagines the snake seen in place of the rope as real—the nature of which, in fact, cannot be really determined—so also in dream, one, through want of discrimination, imagines as if one really perceives such objects as elephant etc. These dream objects, such as elephants, etc., are peculiar to the dream condition alone; they are not the effect of the waking experiences.

*The nature etc.*—The snake seen in place of the rope cannot be called either existent or non-existent. If it be really existent then it cannot cease to exist. And if it be really non-existent then it cannot appear as existing. This is called *Anirvacanīya* or the indescribable nature of the sense-objects.

उपलम्भात्समाचारात् अस्तिवस्तुत्ववादिनाम् ।
जातिस्तु देशिता बुद्धैः अजातेस्त्रसतां सदा ॥ ४२ ॥

42. *Wise men support causality only for the sake of those who, being afraid of absolute non-manifestation (of things), stick to the (apparent) reality of (external) objects on account of their perception (of such objects) and their faith in religious observances.*

## Śaṅkara's Commentary

Wise men, *i.e.*, the exponents of Advaita Philosophy, have, no doubt, supported causality. But they have done so only for those who have little discrimination but who are eager (to know the Truth) and who are endowed with faith. These people assert that external objects exist as real because they perceive them, and also because they cling to the observances of various duties associated with the different *Varṇas*[1] and *Āśramas*.[2] Instructions regarding causality are only meant for them as[3] a means to (some) end. Let them hold on to the idea of causality. But the students who practise disciplines in accordance with Vedānta Philosophy will, without such belief in causality, spontaneously get the knowledge[4] of Self, unborn and non-dual. Causality is declared not from the standpoint of the Ultimate Reality. These students, who[5] believe in Scriptures, and who are devoid of discrimination, fear the idea of absolute non-manifestation on account of their gross intellect, as they are afraid of the annihilation of their selves. It[6] has also been stated before that these Scriptural statements (regarding creation) are meant as a help to our higher understanding of Reality. (In reality there is no multiplicity.)

If causality be a fiction, then, it may be asked, why the Scriptures speak of Brahman as the cause of the universe. This *Kārikā* gives a reply to this question. The aim of the Scripture is to enable the students of mediocre or dull intellect to know the Supreme Reality with the help of causal arguments.

[1] *Varṇas*—That is, the four castes, *viz.*, the *Brāhmaṇa*, the *Kṣatriya*, the *Vaiśya*, and the *Śūdra*.

[2] *Āśramas*—The four stages of life, *viz.*, *Brahmacarya* (student period), *Gārhasthya* (the householder's stage), *Vānaprastha* (the period of retirement from the active duties of life) and *Saṁnyāsa* (the monastic stage).

[3] *As a means etc.*—The ordinary people on account of the perception of the apparent objects as real and also on account of their attachment to life, cannot understand the truth regarding the non-dual and changeless Brahman. They believe in the illusory idea of causality. For the benefit of such people, the wise men admit that Brahman is the cause of creation (*vide Vedānta-Sūtras*, I chapter, second aphorism). But as the cause is identical with the effect, therefore the universe is identical with Brahman. In this way, the students are taught that all that exists is Brahman. Thus by the constant study and meditation on the Scriptures, the students gradually realise the nature of Supreme Reality which is free from all change and evolution. Duality cannot be

established as the Supreme Reality either by logic or Scripture. The apparent duality is admitted from the relative standpoint.

[4] *Knowledge etc.*—This knowledge can be directly obtained by students of clear perception, following the methods given in this Upaniṣad and the *Kārikā*.

[5] *Who believe etc.*—That is to say, those who accept the literal meaning of the scriptural statements regarding creation etc.

[6] *It has etc.*—*Vide Kārikā* 3, 15.

अजातेस्त्रसतां तेषामुपलम्भाद्वियन्ति ये ।
जातिदोषा न सेत्स्यन्ति दोषोऽप्यल्पो भविष्यति ॥ ४३ ॥

43. *Those who, being afraid of the truth of absolute non-manifestation, and also on account of their perception (of phenomenal objects), do not admit* Ajāti *(absolute non-creation), are not much affected by the evil consequent on the belief in causality. The evil effect, if any, is rather insignificant.*

## Śaṅkara's Commentary

Those who on account of their perception (of the phenomenal objects) and attachment[1] to the various duties of caste and other stages of life, shrink from the non-dual and unborn *Ātman*, and believing in the existence of dual objects, go away from the Self, that is to say, pin their faith to duality—these people who are thus afraid of the truth of absolute non-manifestation, but who are endowed with faith and who stick to the path[2] of righteousness, are not[3] much affected by the evil results consequent on such belief in causality. For, they also try to follow the path of discrimination. Even if a little blemish attaches to such persons, it is insignificant, being due to their not having realised the Supreme Truth.

This shows the catholicity of Advaita Vedānta which is a sharp contrast to the narrowness of theologians. Advaita Philosophy recognises the value of different religious practices suited to diverse temperaments. The *Kārikā* further admonishes us not to find fault with others.

[1] *Attachment etc.*—See the previous *Kārikā*.

[2] *Path etc.*—That is to say, those who strictly observe the formal injunctions of religion. These people also, at last, acquire the virtue of discrimination which alone enables one to realise Truth.

[3] *Not much etc.*—The *Gītā* also says that a sincere soul which is anxious to realise Truth, surmounts all difficulties. The adherents of religions, if they are sincere and earnest, ultimately acquire those virtues which enable them to realise Truth.

उपलम्भात्समाचारान्मायाहस्ती यथोच्यते ।
उपलम्भात्समाचारादस्ति वस्तु तथोच्यते ॥ ४४ ॥

44. *As an elephant conjured up by the magician, on account of its being perceived and also on account of its answering to the behaviours (of a real animal), is said to exist, so also are objects said to exist, on account of their being perceived and also on account of their answering to our dealings with them. (In truth, the objects of sense perception are as unreal as the magician's elephant.)*

### Śaṅkara's Commentary

(Objection)—Objects answering to the features of duality do exist, on account of such evidence as our (direct) perception of them and also on account of the possibility of our dealings with them.

(Reply)—No, this objection is not valid. For, direct perception and the possibility of dealing practically with objects do not always prove the existence of objects.

(Objection)—How do you say that our contention admits of irregularity?

(Reply)—It is thus stated: The elephant conjured up by a magician, is, verily, perceived as the real elephant. Though unreal, it (the magic elephant) is called the (real) elephant, on account of its being endowed with such attributes of an elephant as the possibility of its being tied up with a rope or being climbed upon, etc. Though unreal, the magic elephant is looked upon as (a real) one. In like manner, it is said that multiple objects, pointing to duality, exist on account of their being perceived and also on account of the possibility of our dealing practically with them. Hence the two grounds, adduced above, cannot prove the existence of (external) objects establishing the fact of duality.

जात्याभासं चलाभासं वस्त्वाभासं तथैव च ।
अजाचलमवस्तुत्वं विज्ञानं शान्तमद्वयम् ॥ ४५ ॥

45. *Consciousness which appears to be born or to move or to take the form of matter, is really ever unborn, immovable and free from the character of materiality; it is all peace and non-dual.*

### Śaṅkara's Commentary

What is that entity—the Ultimate Reality—which is the substratum[1] of all false cognitions as causality (creation) etc.? It is thus replied: Though unborn it appears to be born. As for example, we say that Devadatta is born. Again it appears to move (though it is free from all motion); as we say, 'That Devadatta is going'. Further, it appears as an object in which inhere certain qualities. For instance, we say, 'That Devadatta is fair and tall'. Though from the standpoint of the Ultimate Reality, Consciousness[2] is ever unborn, immovable, and not of the character of material objects, yet it appears as a Devadatta who is born, who moves and who is known to be fair and tall. What is that entity which answers to these descriptions? It is Consciousness which, being free from birth, change, etc., is all peace and therefore non-dual.

[1] *Substratum*—From the standpoint of Reality, the *Ātman* is not even a substratum; for, nothing whatsoever exists, in relation to which

the Self can be called the substratum. The term 'Substratum' is used in connection with Ātman only from the relative standpoint.

[2] *Consciousness*—That is, Ātman.

एवं न जायते चित्तमेवं धर्मा अजाः स्मृताः ।
एवमेव विजानन्तो न पतन्ति विपर्यये ॥ ४६ ॥

46. *Thus the mind is never subject to birth or change. All beings are, thus, free from birth. Those who know (the Truth) are never subject to false knowledge.*

## Śaṅkara's Commentary

Thus, that is to say, for the reasons stated above, the mind is free from birth. Similarly the *Dharmas*, that is, the *Jīvas*, are also unborn. This is the statement of the Knowers of Brahman. The[1] word '*Dharmāḥ*' (*i.e.*, 'Selves') is metaphorically used in the plural sense, in consequence of our perception of variety which is, in reality, the appearance of the non-dual *Ātman* as different corporeal beings. Those who know the consciousness,[2] stated above, which is the essence of the Self, non-dual and free from birth etc., and accordingly, renounce the hankering after all external objects—they do not fall any more into this ocean of the darkness of *Avidyā*. The *Śruti* also says, 'Where is grief or delusion for the one that realises non-duality?'

[1] *The word etc.*—The Ultimate Reality cannot be said to be one or many. For, these predicates, being correlatives, apply to the relative world. The world '*Dharmāḥ*' has been used in the plural number to indicate that all that exists is *Ātman*. If one sees multiplicity, it is also the non-dual *Ātman*. The reflections of the sun, caught in the millions of waves and bubbles, are nothing but the reflection of the self-same sun. Similarly the same *Ātman* alone is perceived whether as objects of our waking state, or the ideas of dream or the undifferentiated consciousness of dreamless sleep.

*Consciousness*—That is, Brahman or *Ātman*.

ऋजुवक्रादिकाभासमलातस्पन्दितं यथा ।
ग्रहणग्राहकाभासं विज्ञानस्पन्दितं तथा ॥ ४७ ॥

47. *As a fire-brand, when set in motion, appears as straight, crooked, etc., so also Consciousness, when set in motion, appears as the perceiver, the perceived, and the like.*

## Śaṅkara's Commentary

In order to explain the truth regarding the Ultimate Reality already stated, it is thus said: As the common experience it is noticed that a fire-brand[1] when moved, appears straight, crooked, etc., so does Consciousness appear as the perceiver, the perceived, and the like. What is that which appears as the perceiver, the perceived, etc.? It[2] is Consciousness set in motion. There is no motion in Consciousness. It only appears to be moving. This appearance is due to *Avidyā* or ignorance. No motion is possible in Consciousness which is ever immovable. It has already been stated that Consciousness is unborn and immovable.

[1] *Fire-brand etc.* —If a fire-brand be moved swiftly it makes a circle, a straight line, or a crooked line according to the movement. When the fire-brand is moved, it does not really make any figure. In reality, there is only a point which appears as various figures.

[2] *It is etc.*—Consciousness only exists. It is ever undifferentiated. Motion in Consciousness makes it appear as the perceiver, the perceived, etc. There is no motion, really speaking, in Consciousness. The ignorant only imagine illusory subjects and objects which are the basis of our sense-perception.

अस्पन्दमानमलातमनाभासमजं यथा ।
अस्पन्दमानं विज्ञानमनाभासमजं तथा ॥ ४८ ॥

48. *As the fire-brand, when not in motion, is free from all appearances and remains changeless, similarly, Consciousness, when not in motion (imaginary action), is free from all appearances and remains changeless.*

## Śaṅkara's Commentary

As that very fire-brand, when not in motion, does not take any form, straight or crooked, etc., becomes free from all appearances and remains changeless, so also the consciousness, which appears as moving through[1] ignorance, when dissociated from the idea of motion on the disappearance of ignorance, becomes[2] free from all appearances, as those of birth etc., and remains unborn and motionless.

[1] *Through etc.*—The appearance of forms in Consciousness is due to the projecting power (*Vikṣepa-Śakti*) of *Avidyā.*

[2] *Becomes etc.*—That is to say, the Consciousness (*i.e., Ātman*) is seen as it really is. The fire-brand, when at rest, has no figure, as it is a point only. Even when moved, the fire-brand is really, nothing but a point. It only appears as a circle or straight line. Similarly, even during the state of ignorance, Consciousness always, remains what it is, *viz.*, changeless and motionless. It appears to be changing and possessing forms only on account of the ignorance of the perceiving mind.

अलाते स्पन्दमाने वै नाऽऽभासा अन्यतोभुवः ।
न ततोऽन्यत्र निस्पन्दान्नालातं प्रविशन्ति ते ॥ ४९ ॥

49. *When the fire-brand is in motion, the appearances (that are seen in it) do not come from elsewhere. When the fire-brand is not moved, the appearances do not go elsewhere from the motionless fire-brand. Further, the appearances, when the fire-brand is not moved, do not enter into the fire-brand itself.*

## Śaṅkara's Commentary

Moreover, when that very fire-brand is in motion, the appearances, straight or crooked etc., do not come to it from anywhere else outside the fire-brand. Nor do the appearances go elsewhere from the fire-brand when it is motionless. Nor, again, do the appearances enter into the fire-brand when it is motionless.

What actually exists is a point. But the mind, on account of its ignorance, sees in it various forms.

न निर्गता अलातात्ते द्रव्यत्वाभावयोगतः ।
विज्ञानेऽपि तथैव स्युराभासस्याविशेषतः ॥ ५० ॥

50. *The appearances do not emerge from the fire-brand because they are not of the nature of a substance. This also applies to Consciousness on account of the similarity of appearances (in both cases).*

ŚAṄKARA'S COMMENTARY

Moreover, those appearances do not emerge from the fire-brand as something that comes out of a house. The reason is that appearances are not of the nature of substance. The appearances have no reality. Entrance etc., can be said of a real thing but not of anything unreal. The appearance of birth etc., in the case of consciousness is exactly similar, for,[1] appearances are of the same nature in both the cases.

[1] *For etc.*—In both cases, appearances are due to the ignorance of the perceiver. Birth, death, etc., are, really speaking, illusory. They have no real existence. Therefore these are called mere appearance.

विज्ञाने स्पन्दमाने वै नाऽऽभासा अन्यतोभुवः ।
न ततोऽन्यत्र निस्पन्दान्न विज्ञानं विशन्ति ते ॥ ५१ ॥

न निर्गतास्ते विज्ञानाद्द्रव्यत्वाभावयोगतः ।
कार्यकारणताभावाद्यतोऽचिन्त्याः सदैव ते ॥ ५२ ॥

51-52. *When Consciousness is associated with the idea of activity (as in the dream and waking states), the appearances (that are seen in it) do not come from elsewhere. When Consciousness is inactive (as in deep sleep) appearances do not go elsewhere from the inactive Consciousness. Further, appear-*

*ances do not enter into it. The appearances do not emerge from Consciousness because they are not of the nature of a substance. These are always beyond our comprehension on account of their not being subject to the relation of cause and effect.*

## Śaṅkara's Commentary

How are the two appearances similar? It is thus replied: The fire-brand and Consciousness are alike in all respects. The only special feature of Consciousness is that it always remains immutable.[1] What is the cause of such appearances as birth etc., in Consciousness which is ever immutable? In[2] the absence of causality, it is not reasonable to establish the relationship of the producer and the produced (between Consciousness and appearances). The appearances, being illusory, are ever unthinkable.[3] The purport of the whole thing is this: As the fire-brand (which is merely a point) is associated with forms straight, crooked, etc., though, in reality, such crooked or straight forms are ever non-existent, so also, pure Consciousness is associated with the ideas of birth etc., though such ideas as birth etc., are ever non-existent. Hence these ideas of birth etc., associated with Consciousness are illusory.

When Consciousness is said to be active as in the waking and the dream states, the forms of birth etc., that are cognised in those states do not come from elsewhere outside Consciousness. For, such forms are not seen to exist elsewhere outside one's own consciousness. Again, when, as in deep sleep, Consciousness remains inactive, the forms of birth, death, etc., do not go elsewhere from the Consciousness in which they were perceived during the waking and the dream states. For, no one is conscious of such a happening. No one ever knows the existence of anything outside one's own consciousness. Further, when Consciousness remains inactive, as in deep sleep, the forms etc., perceived in the waking, and the dream states, do not seem to merge in Consciousness. For, Consciousness which is non-dual and beyond the ideas of time, space, etc., cannot be the cause of multiple objects existing in time and space. The objects seen in the dream and the waking states, being ever unreal, cannot be said to emerge from or merge in Consciousness.

[1] *Immutable*—Consciousness is called immutable as it is free from the idea of space and time.

[2] *In the etc.*—The idea of causality is due to *Avidyā*.

[3] *Ever unthinkable*—The ideas seen in the dream and the waking states cannot be said to be non-existent because they are perceived. Nor can they be said to exist because they are not perceived in deep sleep. Therefore it is impossible to determine their real nature. Hence they are as illusory as the snake seen in the rope.

द्रव्यं द्रव्यस्य हेतुः स्यादन्यदन्यस्य चैव हि ।
द्रव्यत्वमन्यभावो वा धर्माणां नोपपद्यते ॥ ५३ ॥

53. *Substance may be the cause of another substance. That which is not substance may be the cause of another which is not substance. But the* Jīvas *(or beings) cannot be possibly anything like substance or other than substance.*

## Śaṅkara's Commentary

It has already been established that the essence of Self is one[1] and unborn.[2] Those who imagine causal relation in *Ātman* must admit that substance may be the cause of another substance and that[3] which is other than substance may be the cause of something else which is also other than substance. But a thing itself cannot be the cause of itself. Further, we do not find in common experience a non-substance which is independently the cause of something. The selves (*i.e.*, the *Jīvas* or beings) can be called neither substance[4] nor other[5] than substance. Hence the *Jīvas* or selves cannot be the cause or effect of anything. Therefore *Ātman*, being neither substance nor other than substance, is neither the cause nor the effect of anything.

[1] *One*—That is, *Ātman* which is free from any attribute.

[2] *Unborn*—*i.e.*, *Ātman* being without parts, is not a substance.

[3] *That which etc.*—That is, an attribute such as colour or form.

[4] *Substance*—It is because a substance has always parts.

[5] *Other than etc.*—It is because a non-substance (*i.e.*, an attribute) cannot be conceived of independently of a substance.

एवं न चित्तजा धर्माश्चित्तं वापि न धर्मजम् ।
एवं हेतुफलाजातिं प्रतिशन्ति मनीषिणः ॥ ५४ ॥

54. *Thus (external) appearances (objects) are not caused by the mind nor is the mind produced by them. Hence men of discrimination hold the principle of the absolute non-evolution or negation of causality.*

## Śaṅkara's Commentary

Thus, for[1] reasons already stated, the mind is verily of the nature of the essence of the Self. External[2] objects are not caused by the mind nor is the mind the product of the external objects. That is because all (external) entities are mere appearances in Consciousness. Thus neither the (so-called) effect comes from the (so-called) cause nor the cause from the effect. In this way is reiterated the absolute non-evolution of causality. In other words, the knowers of Brahman declare the absence of causality with regard to *Ātman*.

[1] *For etc.*—The reason is that the real nature of *Ātman* is free from all modifications and not of the nature of an empirical substance.

[2] *External etc.*—The popular belief that the thought of the pot in the potter's mind is the cause of the pot and that the external pot gives rise to the idea of the pot in the mind is entirely erroneous. For the idea of causality has been proved to be an illusion.

यावद्धेतुफलावेशस्तावद्धेतुफलोद्भवः ।
क्षीणे हेतुफलावेशे नास्ति हेतुफलोद्भवः ॥ ५५ ॥

55. *As long as a man persists in the belief in causality he will find the working of cause and effect. But when attachment to causality vanishes, cause and effect become non-existent.*

### Śaṅkara's Commentary

What happens with regard to those who cling to the belief in cause and effect? In reply, it is said: As long as there is faith in causality, as long as a man thinks, 'I am the agent; these virtuous and vicious deeds belong to me. I shall enjoy the results of these actions, being born in course of time, as some being', in other words, as long as a man falsely attributes causality to *Ātman* and devotes his mind to it, cause and effect must operate for him: that is to say, the man must without intermission be subject to birth and death, which are the resalt of his attachment to the belief in causality. But when attachment to causality, due to ignorance, is destroyed by the knowledge of non-duality as described above—like the destruction of the possession of a ghost through the power of incantation, medicinal herb, etc.—then on account of the wearing away of the illusion of causality, do cause and effect cease to exist.

This *Kārikā* tells us that the chief duty of the student is to analyse the law of causality and find its illusory nature. The attainment of true knowledge solely depends upon this understanding of the causal law.

यावद्धेतुफलावेशः संसारस्तावदायतः ।
क्षीणे हेतुफलावेशे संसारं न प्रपद्यते ॥ ५६ ॥

56. *As long as there is faith in causality, the (endless) chain of birth and death will be there. When that faith is destroyed (by knowledge) birth and death become non-existent.*

## Śaṅkara's Commentary

What is the harm if the law of cause and effect continues to operate? In reply we say: As long as faith in causality is not destroyed by right knowledge, our course (of birth and death) in this world will continue. But when that faith is destroyed (by right knowledge) the world also ceases to exist for want of any other cause for its existence.

संवृत्या जायते सर्वं शाश्वतं नास्ति तेन वै ।
सद्भावेन ह्यजं सर्वमुच्छेदस्तेन नास्ति वै ॥ ५७ ॥

57. *All this is seen to be born on account of the illusion of experience (due to* Avidyā); *therefore nothing is permanent. All, again, as one with the Ultimate Reality is unborn. And therefore there is nothing like destruction.*

## Śaṅkara's Commentary

(Objection)—Nothing else verily exists except the unborn *Ātman.* Then how can you speak of the origin and destruction of the cause and the effect as well as of (the chain of birth and death constituting) the world?

(Reply)—Listen. The word *Saṁvṛti* in the text signifies the *(illusory)* experiences of the empirical world which are caused by ignorance. All this is born of this power of ignorance which brings into existence the illusory experiences of the world. For this reason, nothing is permanent in the realm of ignorance. Therefore it is said that the world, having the characteristics of origination and destruction, is spread before us (*i.e.*, the ignorant persons). But as one with the Ultimate Reality, all this is nothing but the unborn *Ātman.* Therefore, in the absence of birth, there cannot be any destruction, *viz.*, the destruction of cause or effect.

The opponent contends that if nothing but birthless and non-dual *Ātman* exists, then the statements regarding the origin and the destruction of the universe as stated in the previous *Kārikā* become irrelevant and contradictory. The reply is that there is no contradiction as the two statements are made from two different standpoints. From the standpoint of Ultimate Reality there is neither birth nor death. But from the relative standpoint, which conjures up before our vision the world of name and form, there are birth and death. Imagine a rope lying on the road. The wise man knows it as the rope alone. But the deluded person sees it as the snake and being afraid of it, takes to his heels in spite of the assurance of the wise man that it is the rope and not the snake. Now the rope and the snake are both facts from the two standpoints. The wise man sees the rope and the ignorant person sees the snake. Therefore the statement of the ignorant man does not contradict the statement of the wise one.

The ideas of birth and death are possible only from the relative standpoint. The wise man sees everything as the non-dual *Ātman*. Therefore he cannot see the possibility of destruction of anything. Comp. *Kārikā* 1, 17 and 1, 18.

धर्मा य इति जायन्ते जायन्ते ते न तत्त्वतः ।
जन्म मायोपमं तेषां सा च माया न विद्यते ॥ ५८ ॥

58. *Those* Jīvas *(entities) or beings are said to be born. But that birth which is never possible from the standpoint of Reality. Their birth is like that of an illusory object. That illusion, again, is non-existent.*

## Śaṅkara's Commentary

Those, again, who imagine the birth of the *Jīvas* and other entities, do so only through *Saṁvṛti* or the power of ignorance as stated in the preceding *Kārikā*. The *Jīvas* are seen to be born only through ignorance. But from the standpoint of the Supreme Reality no such birth is possible. This[1] (supposed) birth of the *Jīvas* through ignorance, described above, is like the birth of objects through illusion (*Māyā*).

(Opponent)—Then there must be something real known as *Māyā* or illusion?

(Reply)—It is not so. That *Māyā* or illusion is never existent. *Māyā* or illusion is the name we give to something which[2] does not (really) exist (but which is perceived).

[1] *This etc.*—The birth of *Jīvas* is exactly like the production of things by a Juggler. These things such as a mango tree or the hare produced by the Juggler do not exist. Similarly, the *Jīvas* etc., whose birth and death are seen by us in ignorance, do not exist, when the Truth is known.

[2] *Which etc.*—That is to say, *Māyā* or illusion does not exist from the standpoint of Reality.

यथा मायामयाद्बीजाज्जायते तन्मयोऽङ्कुरः ।

नासौ नित्यो न चोच्छेदी तद्वद्धर्मेषु योजना ॥ ५९ ॥

59. *The illusory sprout comes forth from the illusory seed. This illusory sprout is neither permanent nor destructible. The same applies to* Jīvas.

## Śaṅkara's Commentary

Now, is the birth of *Jīvas*, that are seen to exist, illusory? To this question, our reply is as follows: From[1] an illusory mango seed is born a mango sprout which is equally illusory. This sprout[2] is neither permanent nor destructible, simply because it does not exist. In[3] the like manner, ideas of birth and death are applied to the *Jīvas*. The purport is that from the standpoint of the Ultimate Reality, neither birth nor death is applicable to *Jīvas*.

[1] *From etc.*—This is a familiar illustration often used by the Vedāntic writers. In India, certain jugglers produce from illusory seeds illusory trees full of illusory fruits.

[2] *This sprout etc.*—Birth and death can be predicated of objects that exist. But the mango tree produced by a juggler is non-existent. Hence neither birth nor death is possible for such a mango tree.

[3] *In the etc.*—The *Jīvas*, endowed with birth and death, are seen on account of our ignorance. From the standpoint of Truth, such *Jīvas* do not exist. Hence birth and death are unreal from the standpoint of Truth. But birth and death are true, as in the case of the illusory mango tree, from the standpoint of ignorance.

नाजेषु सर्वधर्मेषु शाश्वताशाश्वताभिधा ।
यत्र वर्णा न वर्तन्ते विवेकस्तत्र नोच्यते ॥ ६० ॥

60. *The epithets of permanence or impermanence cannot be applied to unborn* Jīvas. *That which is indescribable by words cannot be discriminated (as real or unreal).*

## Śaṅkara's Commentary

From the standpoint of the Ultimate Reality, no epithet such as permanence[1] or impermanence, nor any sound corresponding to such names, can be applied to *Jīvas* (selves or beings) which are eternal, birthless, and which are always of the nature of a homogeneous consciousness. That by which an object is designated is known as '*Varṇa*' or name associated with a sound. The words fail to denote the nature of *Ātman*. It cannot be discriminated as this or that, permanent or impermanent. The *Śruti* also says, 'Whence words fall back' etc.

[1] *Permanence etc.*—Such epithets as permanence or impermance which are correlatives, are applied to the objects of the relative world.

यथा स्वप्ने द्वयाभासं चित्तं चलति मायया ।
तथा जाग्रद्द्वयाभासं चित्तं चलति मायया ॥ ६१ ॥

अद्वयं च द्वयाभासं चित्तं स्वप्ने न संशयः ।
अद्वयं च द्वयाभासं तथा जाग्रन्न संशयः ॥ ६२ ॥

61-62. *As in dream, the mind is seen to act through* Māyā *manifesting the appearance of duality, so also in the waking state the mind is seen to act, through* Māyā, *producing the appearance of duality.*

*There is no doubt that the mind which is, in fact, non-dual, appears as dual in dream; in like manner, undoubtedly, the waking state, which is non-dual, appears as dual.*

## Śaṅkara's Commentary

That pure consciousness which is non-dual (from the standpoint of the Supreme Reality) is sought to be described by words, is due to the active condition of the mind (which is due to *Avidyā*). This description (of the non-dual *Ātman* by words) has no meaning from the standpoint of the Ultimate Truth. These[1] verses have already been explained.

It may be contended that if *Ātman* cannot be described by words, why then should the scholars have taken the pains to use words to denote *Ātman*. In reply it is said that what is described by words by scholars is not the non-dual *Ātman* but a duality, perceived on account of the activity of the mind, associated with the subject-object relationship which is the characteristic of the relative plane of existence. The Ultimate Reality is the essence of everything, including ideas or descriptions.

[1] *The verses etc.—Vide* Chapter. III. 29-30.

स्वप्नदृक् प्रचरन् स्वप्ने दिक्षु वै दशसु स्थितान् ।
अण्डजान् स्वेदजान्वाऽपि जीवान् पश्यति यान् सदा ॥ ६३ ॥

63. *The whole variety of* Jīvas, *born of eggs, moisture, etc., always seen by the dreamer when he goes about (in his dream) in all ten directions (have no existence apart from the mind of the dreamer).*

ŚAṄKARA'S COMMENTARY

Here is another reason which also shows us that duality describable by words, does not exist. The beings or *Jīvas*, born[1] of eggs or moisture, which a dreamer going about in all ten directions perceives in his dream condition as existing, (have, as a matter of fact, no existence apart from the mind of the dreamer).

(Objection)—Suppose we admit this. What are you driving at?

(Reply)—Our reply is as follows:

[1] *Born of etc.*—The beings that are perceived to exist may be divided into four classes, *e.g.*, those that are born of the womb, the egg, the moisture and the soil.

स्वप्नदृक्चित्तदृश्यास्ते न विद्यन्ते ततः पृथक् ।
तथा तद्दृश्यमेवेदं स्वप्नदृक्चित्तमिष्यते ॥ ६४ ॥

64. *These (beings) which are objects of the mind of the dreamer have no existence apart from his mind. Similarly, this mind of the dreamer is admitted to be the object of perception of the dreamer only. (Therefore the mind of the dreamer is not separate from the dreamer himself).*

ŚAṄKARA'S COMMENTARY

Those[1] beings perceived by the mind of the dreamer have no existence outside the mind of the person who dreams about them. It[2] is the mind alone which imagines itself to have assumed the forms of many diversified beings. Similarly,[3] that mind of the dreamer is, again, perceived by the dreamer alone. Therefore there is no separate thing called mind which is apart from the dreamer itself.

[1] *The truth etc.*—The truth about this statement is clearly understood in the waking state.

[2] *It is etc.*—In the dream, the mind alone objectifies itself into the perceiver and the perceived.

[3] *Similarly etc.*—The mind of a man is not cognized by any other being excepting himself. The cognizing ego is also created by the mind. The ego and the non-ego come into existence together. Therefore, the charge of solipsism cannot be levelled against the Vedāntist.

चरन् जागरिते जाग्रद्दिक्षु वै दशसु स्थितान् ।
अण्डजान् स्वेदजान्वाऽपि जीवान्पश्यति यान्सदा ॥ ६५ ॥

जाग्रच्चित्तेक्षणीयास्ते न विद्यन्ते ततः पृथक् ।
तथा तद्दृश्यमेवेदं जाग्रतश्चित्तमिष्यते ॥ ६६ ॥

65-66. *The whole variety of* Jīvas, *born of eggs, moisture, etc., always seen by the waking man when he goes about (in his waking condition,) in all ten directions, is only the object of the mind of the waking man. These* Jīvas *are in no way apart from the waking mind. Similarly, the mind of the waking man is admitted to be the object of perception of the waking person only. (Therefore the mind is not separate from the perceiver).*

## Śaṅkara's Commentary

The *Jīvas*, perceived in the waking state, do not *exist* anywhere except in the mind of the perceiver, for, they are not seen independent of the mind. These *Jīvas* are similar to the *Jīvas*, perceived in the dream, which are cognized by the mind of the dreaming person alone. That mind again, having the characteristic of perception of *Jīvas* is non-different from the perceiver of the waking condition, because[1] it is seen by the perceiver, as[2] is the case with the mind which perceives the dream. The rest has already been interpreted (in the previous verses).

[1] *Because etc.*—Mind is identical with the Reality or *Ātman*. When the Reality is characterised by the perception of the subject-object idea (through ignorance), it is called the mind. And when it remains free

from any such idea, it is called *Ātman*. From the standpoint of Reality, the perceiver, the object and the instrument of perception are one. The causal relation, like the external objects, is in the mind of the perceiver.

[2] *As is the case etc.*—In dream, the dream-mind which sees objects (non-different from itself) is identical with the dreamer.

उभे ह्यन्योन्यदृश्ये ते किं तदस्तीति नोच्यते ।
लक्षणाशून्यमुभयं तन्मतेनैव गृह्यते ॥ ६७ ॥

67. *Both (the mind and the* Jīva*) are objects of perception to each other. Which then can be said to exist independent of the other? (The reply of the wise is in the negative). Both are devoid of the marks by which they could be distinguished. For, either can be cognized only through the other.*

## Śaṅkara's Commentary

Both the mind and the *Jīvas*,[1] or in other words, the mind and its modifications (which are seen as external objects) are each an object of perception to the other. In other words, one is perceived only through the other. The mind exists only in relation to the *Jīva* etc., and the *Jīva* and objects exist only in relation to the mind. Therefore they are each an object of perception to the other. Hence[2] wise men assert that nothing whatsoever, neither the mind nor its object, can be said to have any existence (if either be considered by itself) (from the standpoint of either the idealist or the realist). As in the dream the elephant as well as the mind that perceives the elephant, are not really existent, so also is the case with the mind and its objects of the waking condition. How is it so? For, both the mind and its objects have no proof of their existence (independent of each other). They are each an object of perception to the other. One cannot cognize a jar without the cognition of a jar; nor can one have a cognition of a jar without a jar. In the case of the jar and the cognition of the jar it is not possible to conceive the distinction between the instrument of knowledge and the object of knowledge.

This verse refutes the contention of the school of thought which asserts that the ego creates the non-ego.

[1] *Jīvas*—They include all objects perceived by the mind.

[2] *Hence etc.*—They exist, with relation to one another, only in the relative plane of consciousness.

The existence of the variety of objects is possible only when one object is perceived in relation to the other. Therefore the triad of 'Knower', 'Known' and 'Knowledge', mutually dependent upon one another, is possible only in the realm of ignorance.

यथा स्वप्नमयो जीवो जायते म्रियतेऽपि च ।
तथा जीवा अमी सर्वे भवन्ति न भवन्ति च ॥ ६८ ॥

तथा मायामयो जीवो जायते म्रियतेऽपि च ।
तथा जीवा अमी सर्वे भवन्ति न भवन्ति च ॥ ६९ ॥

यथा निर्मितको जीवो जायते म्रियतेऽपि वा ।
तथा जीवा अमी सर्वे भवन्ति न भवन्ति च ॥ ७० ॥

68-70. *As the dream-*Jīva *comes into being and disappears, so also all* Jīvas *(perceived in the waking condition) appear and disappear.*

*As the magician's* Jīva *comes into being and passes away, so also all* Jīvas *(perceived in the waking condition) appear and disappear.*

*As the artificial* Jīva *(brought into existence by incantation, medicinal herb, etc.) comes into being and passes away, so also all the* Jīvas *(perceived in the waking condition) appear and disappear.*

ŚAṄKARA'S COMMENTARY

The 'magician's *Jīva*' means that which is conjured up before our vision by the feat of a magician. The 'artificial *Jīva*' is that which is brought into existence by means of incantation , medicinal herb, etc.

As the *Jīvas* born of egg etc., and created in dream, are seen to come into existence and then to pass away, so also the *Jīvas* such as human beings etc., seen in the waking state, though really non-existent (appear to come into existence and then pass away). These[1] are merely the imagination of the mind.

It may be contended that if the *Jīvas* perceived in the waking state be unreal, then their birth and death, which are objects of common experience, become an impossibility. This *Kārikā* says in reply that as in the case of dream-beings etc., really non-existent birth and death are possible, so also the appearance of birth etc., is possible in the case of beings that are perceived in the waking state.

[1] *There are etc.*—In other words, the *Jīvas*, perceived in the waking state, with all concomitant appearance of birth, death, etc., are mere results of the objectifying tendency of the mind, and nothing more.

न कश्चिज्जायते जीवः संभवोऽस्य न विद्यते ।
एतत्तदुत्तमं सत्यं यत्र किंचिन्न जायते ॥ ७१ ॥

71. *No kind of* Jīva *is ever born nor is there any cause for any such birth. The Ultimate Truth is that nothing whatsoever is born.*

ŚAṄKARA'S COMMENTARY

It has already been stated that the appearances of birth, death, etc., of the *Jīvas* are possible only in the empirical plane, as in the case with the dream-beings. But the Ultimate Truth is that no *Jīva* is ever born. The rest has already been stated.

This is the repetition of the last verse of the third chapter of the *Kārikā*.

चित्तस्पंदितमेवेदं ग्राह्यग्राहकवद्द्वयम् ।
चित्तं निर्विषयं नित्यमसंगं तेन कीर्तितम् ॥ ७२ ॥

72. *This perceived world of duality, characterised by the subject-object relationship, is verily an act of the mind. The mind, again, (from the standpoint of Reality) is without touch with any object (as it is of the nature of* Ātman*). Hence it is declared to be eternal and unattached.*

## Śaṅkara's Commentary

The whole world of duality consisting of the subject and the object is, verily, an act of the mind. But from the standpoint of the Ultimate Reality, the mind, which is verily *Ātman*, is[1] unrelated to any object. On account of the absence of relation (with any object), the mind is declared as eternal and unattached. The *Śruti* also says, 'The *Puruṣa* is always free from relation'. That which perceives objects outside of it, is related to such objects. But the mind, having no such external object, is free from all relations.

[1] *Is unrelated etc.*—The objects and their relation with the mind are perceived only in the state of ignorance. Even when the ignorant person perceived the mind to be associated with the subject-object relationship, the mind, truly speaking, is non-dual, unattached and absolute.

The mind is, really, free from all ideas of the subject-object relationship. The idea of the object is superimposed upon the mind through ignorance. These objects have no existence apart from the mind. This has been already established by the dream-analogy. Therefore from the standpoint of the Ultimate Reality, the mind is ever unrelated to objects, as such objects do not exist. Hence mind is *Ātman* or Reality.

योऽस्ति कल्पितसंवृत्या परमार्थेन नास्त्यसौ ।
परतन्त्राभिसंवृत्या स्यान्नास्ति परमार्थतः ॥ ७३ ॥

73. *That which exists on the strength of the illusory experiences does not, really speaking, exist. That which, again, is said to exist on the strength of the views supported by the other schools of thought, does not, really speaking, exist.*

## Śaṅkara's Commentary

(Objection)—It has been said that the mind is free from the relation with any objects, as such objects do not exist. But this non-attachment regarding the mind cannot be maintained inasmuch as objects in the forms of the teacher, the Scripture and the pupil exist.

(Reply)—There is no such defect in our contention.

(Objection)—How?

(Reply)—The[1] existence of such objects as Scripture etc., is due to the empirical experience which is illusory. The empirical knowledge is respect of Scripture, teacher and taught is illusory and imagined only as a means to the realisation of the Ultimate Reality. Therefore Scripture etc., which exist only on the strength of illusory empirical experiences, have no real existence. It has already been said that duality vanishes when the Ultimate Reality is known. Again, the[2] objects (which appear to come into existence through the illusory experiences), supported by other schools of thought as existent, do not, when analysed from the standpoiut of the Ultimate Reality, verily exist. Hence it has been rightly said in the previous *Kārikā* that the mind is unattached.

[1] *The existence etc.*—That is to say, the Scripture, the teacher and the taught have meaning only in the state of ignorance. The purpose of these ideas is to help the ignorant person to realize Truth. Compare with the *Kārikā* 28 in the *Āgama Prakaraṇa*.

[2] *The objects etc.*—The *Vaiśeṣika* school of thought maintains the existence of Six Categories. But these categories are non-existent from the standpoint of the Ultimate Reality. These are perceived to exist only in the plane of our empirical experiences.

अजः कल्पितसंवृत्या परमार्थेन नाप्यजः ।
परतन्त्राभिनिष्पत्त्या संवृत्या जायते तु सः ॥ ७४ ॥

74. Ātman *is called unborn* (Aja) *from the standpoint of the illusory empirical experiences. It is, truly speaking, not even unborn. That unborn* Ātman *appears to be born from the standpoint of the belief of the other schools of thought.*

### Śaṅkara's Commentary

(Objection)—If Scriptural teaching etc., were illusory, then the birthlessness of *Ātman*, as taught by Scripture, is also due to illusory imagination.

(Reply)—This is, indeed, true, *Ātman* is said to be unborn only in relation to illusory empirical experiences which comprehend ideas of Scripture, teacher and taught. From[1] the standpoint of the Ultimate Reality, *Ātman* cannot be said to be even. *Ātman*[2] which is said to be unborn only as against the conclusion of those schools (which maintain that *Ātman* comes into existence), appears to be born to the ignorant. Therefore, the notion (based upon illusion) that *Ātman* is unborn has no bearing on the Ultimate Reality.

[1] *From etc.*—The idea of birthlessness is the correlative of the idea of birth. Hence both the ideas belong to the realm of ignorance. *Ātman*, as it really is, cannot be described either as born or unborn. Nothing can be predicated of *Ātman* from the standpoint of the Ultimate Reality.

[2] *Ātman etc.*—The Sāṁkhya School of Thought, believing in causality, asserts the birth of *Ātman*. As against the conclusion, it is maintained that *Ātman* is unborn *(Aja)*. This assertion regarding the birthlessness of *Ātman* is also due to *Avidyā* inasmuch as it aims at the refutation of the opposite theory. The theory of *Ātman* being ever unborn is based upon the illusory idea regarding its birth. It may be contended that the birthlessness of *Ātman* is not an illusory idea but truth. In reply it is that the predicate of birthlessness cannot have any application with regard to the Ultimate Reality. *Ātman* is

considered to be unborn only from the standpoint of an illusion that it is born. Hence, being correlative of an illusion, the birthlessness of *Ātman* also becomes illusory. The real nature of *Ātman* cannot be determined by any instrument of knowledge which has its applicability only in the relative plane.

अभूताभिनिवेशोऽस्ति द्वयं तत्र न विद्यते ।
द्वयाभावं स बुद्ध्वैव निर्निमित्तो न जायते ॥ ७५ ॥

75. *Man has mere persistent belief in the reality of the unreal (which is duality). There is no duality (corresponding to such belief). One who has realised the absence of duality is never born again as there remains, no longer, any cause (for such birth).*

ŚAṄKARA'S COMMENTARY

As objects are, really speaking, non-existent, therefore people who believe in their existence have, in fact, attachment for duality which is unreal. It is a mere belief in the (existence of) objects which (really speaking) do not exist. There is no duality. The cause of birth is this attachment. Therefore one who has realised the unreality of duality is never born again as he is free from the cause (of birth), *viz.*, attachment to the illusory duality.

यदा न लभते हेतूनुत्तमाधममध्यमान् ।
तदा न जायते चित्तं हेत्वभावे फलं कुतः ॥ ७६ ॥

76. *When the mind does not find any cause superior, inferior or middling, it becomes free from birth. How can there be an effect without a cause?*

ŚAṄKARA'S COMMENTARY

The superior cause consists of those *Dharmas* (*i.e.*, duties of life), wholly virtuous, which are prescribed according to different castes and stages of life, and which when performed without any attachment to the result, enable one to attain to the position of gods etc. The middling cause consists of those duties, mixed with certain irreligious practices the observance of which enables one to attain to the position of man etc. The inferior cause consists of those particular tendencies, characterised by irreligious practices alone, which lead one to the position of lower creatures, such as beasts, birds, etc. When the mind realising the essence of Self which is one and without a second and which is free from all (illusory) imaginations, does not find the existence of any of the causes, superior, inferior or middling, all[1] imagined through ignorance—like a man of discrimination not seeing any dirt which a child sees in the sky—then it does not undergo any birth, *i.e.*, it does not objectify itself as god, man or beast, which are the effects of their respective causes (enumerated above). No effect can be produced in the absence of a cause, as sprouts cannot come forth in the absence of the seed.

[1] *All etc.*—All beings from the angel to the beast and the bird belong to the realm of ignorance.

अनिमित्तस्य चित्तस्य याऽनुत्पत्तिः समाऽद्वया ।
अजातस्यैव सर्वस्य चित्तदृश्यं हि तद्यतः ॥ ७७ ॥

77. *The non evolution* (i. e., *the state of knowledge*) *of the mind, which is unborn and free from causal relation, is absolute and constant. Everything else is also equally unborn.* (*So what is true of the mind is true of everything else as well.*) *For, all duality is merely an objectification of the mind.*

## Śaṅkara's Commentary

It has already been stated that in the absence of a cause, the mind is not subject to birth. But what is the nature of that non-evolution of the mind? It is thus replied: The causes of birth are meritorious actions and their opposite.

The state of absolute non-manifestation of the mind—known as liberation (knowledge) and free from causality[1] on account of the realisation of the Supreme—is[2] always constant under all conditions and absolute, that is, ever non-dual. Even[3] before the attainment of knowledge, the mind always remains non-manifest and non-dual. Even prior to the realisation of the highest knowledge the idea of duality (*i.e.*, the subject and the object) and the idea of birth are merely an objectification of the mind. Hence the non-evolution of the mind which is always[4] free from change or birth is constant and absolute. In other words, it cannot be said that this non-evolution or liberation sometimes exists and sometimes disappears. It is always the same and changeless.

It may be contended from the previous *Kārikā* that liberation depends upon the external factor of time. This contention is answered in this verse.

[1] *Which etc.*—The causes of birth, in the form of meritorious and vicious deeds, are seen to exist only during the state of ignorance.

[2] *Is always etc.*—All duality, due to the objectification of the mind, is unreal. There is no cause for the mind which is absolute, eternal, immutable and all-sufficient, to pass into birth. Therefore from the standpoint of Reality, the mind or *Jīva* is always liberated. He is ever free from bondage which is non-existent.

[3] *Even before etc.*—It may be objected that liberation is possible only during the state of knowledge, while the *Jīva* is bound during the state of ignorance. In reply it is said that from the standpoint of Reality ignorance does not exist. Even when a man looks upon himself as subject to birth and death and living in the plane of ignorance, he is, really speaking, *Ātman* free and non-dual. Even when the rope is seen to be the snake by the ignorant mind, it is nothing but the rope. Similarly *Ātman* never deviates from his real nature though he appears as *Jīva* during ignorance. The idea of birth, death, etc., is mere unreal imagination.

[4] *Always*—That is to say, the mind is really free from birth, etc., even when the ignorant persons see it coming into existence and again disappearing.

बुद्ध्वाऽनिमित्ततां सत्यां हेतुं पृथगनाप्नुवन् ।
वीतशोकं तथा काममभयं पदमश्नुते ॥ ७८ ॥

78. *Having (thus) realised the absence of causality as the Ultimate Truth, and also not finding any other cause (for birth), one attainns to that (the state of liberation) which is free from grief, desire and fear.*

## Śaṅkara's Commentary

Through[1] the reasoning indicated above, one knows the absence of duality, which is the cause of birth and thus realises absolute non-causation as the Ultimate Truth. Further, he[2] does not see the reality of anything else as cause, such as religious merit etc., which may enable one to attain to the position of gods etc. Thus freeing himself from all desires, he attains to the highest state, *i.e.*, liberation (knowledge) which is free from desire, grief, ignorance and fear. That is to say, he no longer becomes subject to birth and death.

[1] *Through etc.*—All dual objects are illusory like dream objects on account of their being perceived. See *Kārikā* 4, Chapter II.

[2] *He etc.*—The meritorious or vicious deeds as well as gods, men or birds and beasts which are the results of these actions, belong to the realm of ignorance.

अभूताभिनिवेशाद्धि सदृशे तत्प्रवर्तते ।
वस्त्वभावं स बुद्ध्वैव निःसङ्गं विनिवर्तते ॥ ७९ ॥

79. *On account of attachment to the unreal objects, the mind runs after such objects. But it comes back (to its own pure state) when it becomes unattached (to objects) realising their unreality.*

ŚAṄKARA'S COMMENTARY

Attachment to the unreal (objects) is due to the firm belief that duality exists, though in reality such duality is ever non-existent. On[1] account of such attachment which is of the nature of delusion caused by ignorance, the mind runs after objects corresponding to those desires. But when a man knows the unreality[2] of all duality of objects, then he becomes indifferent to them and turns away his mind from the unreal (objects) to which he feels attached.

[1] *On account etc.*—It is desire, due to ignorance, that creates objects around us.

[2] *Unreality etc.*—The only way to become detached from the world is to know its unreal nature by following the Vedāntic method of reasoning. The Yogic method of mechanical concentration may make the mind oblivious of the world for the time being, but when that concentration is relaxed, the world with its objects again appears as before. Vedāntic Knowledge alone convinces one of the illusory nature of the world.

निवृत्तस्याप्रवृत्तस्य निश्चला हि तदा स्थितिः ।
विषयः स हि बुद्धानां तत्साम्यमजमद्वयम् ॥ ८० ॥

80. *The mind, thus freed from attachment* (*to all external objects*) *and undistracted* (*by fresh objects*) *attains to its state of Immutability. Being actually realised by the wise, it is undifferentiated, birthless and non-dual.*

ŚAṄKARA'S COMMENTARY

When the mind is withdrawn from all duality of objects, and when it does not attach itself to any objects—as no objects exist—then the mind attains to the state of immutability which[1] is of the same nature as Brahman. This[2] realisation of the mind as Brahman is characterised by the mass of unique non-dual consciousness. As that condition of the mind is[3] known, (only) by the wise who have known the Ultimate Reality, that state is supreme and undifferentiated, birthless and non-dual.

[1] *Which is etc.*—The mind free from relativity and objectification is Brahman.

[2] *This etc.*—The mind free from the subject-object relationship has the same characteristic as Brahman.

[3] *Is known etc.*—This state of the mind, which is the highest Reality, can be known with the help of reasoning. Scripture, which also belongs to the realm of relativity, cannot describe Brahman or the Supreme Reality.

अजमनिद्रमस्वप्नं प्रभातं भवति स्वयम् ।
सकृद्विभातो ह्येवैष धर्मो धातुस्वभावतः ॥ ८१ ॥

81. *(Reality which is) free from birth, and (which is) free from sleep and dream, reveals itself by itself. For, this* Dharma (*i.e.*, Ātman) *is from its very nature ever-luminous.*

### Śaṅkara's Commentary

The nature of that which is realisable by the wise is again described: It (*Ātman*) reveals itself by itself. It does not depend for its revelation upon any external[1] light, such as the sun etc. Self-luminosity[2] is its very nature. It is ever-luminous. This is the inherent characteristic of the *Dharma*, known as *Ātman*.

[1] *External etc.*—*Ātman* itself is the substratum of everything. Therefore it cannot be dependent upon anything else.

[2] *Self-luminosity etc.*—*Ātman* is called self-luminous as, in the state of deep sleep, the real nature of *Ātman* is revealed though all external instruments such as the sense-organs, the mind, etc., then remain inactive.

The text characterises *Ātman* as free from dream and sleep. Dream indicates the wrong apprehension of truth while sleep stands for its non-apprehension. The waking state is omitted as because either it is included in the dream state or it stands for the state of knowledge.

सुखमाव्रियते नित्यं दुःखं विव्रियते सदा ।
यस्य कस्य च धर्मस्य ग्रहेण भगवानसौ ॥ ८२ ॥

82. *On account of the mind apprehending single objects, the Bliss* (i.e., *the real essence of the Self*) *always remains concealed and misery comes to the surface. Therefore the ever-effulgent Lord* (*is not realised though taught again and again by Scriptures and teachers*).

## Śaṅkara's Commentary

How is it that the people, at large, do not realise *Ātman*, which is the Supreme Reality, though It is again and again thus explained? To this the following reply is given: On[1] account of the mind apprehending through attachment, single objects of the world of duality, the blissful nature of *Ātman* is easily covered. The reason for this concealment is only the perception of duality. There is no other cause for it. Moreover, misery[2] is brought to the surface. The knowledge of the Supreme Reality is extremely hard to attain. The Lord, the non-dual *Ātman*, the effulgent Being, though again and again taught by the Vedānta Scriptures and the teachers, is not therefore comprehended. The *Śruti* also says, 'One who speaks of *Ātman* is looked upon with wonder and he who has attained and who has realised it, is equally an object of wonder'.

[1] *On account of etc.*—That is to say, people on account of their prejudices associate *Ātman* with various illusory ideas. *Ātman* is free from all *ideas (Kalpanā)*. See next *Kārikā*.

[2] *Misery*—In reality there is no misery. Bliss alone, which is the characteristic of *Ātman*, exists. But misery is experienced when the Blissful *Ātman* is not known.

अस्ति नास्त्यस्ति नास्तीति नास्ति नास्तीति वा पुनः ।
चलस्थिरोभयाभावैरावृणोत्येव बालिशः ॥ ८३ ॥

83. *Childish persons verily cover It (fail to know It) by predicating of It such attributes as existence, non-existence, existence and non-existence and absolute non-existence, derived respectively from their notion of change, immovability, combination of both and absolute negation.*

## Śaṅkara's Commentary

Attachment of the learned to such predicates[1] as existence, non-existence, etc., serves verily as a veil between them and the Supreme Reality. What wonder is there that childish persons on account of their undeveloped intellect are unable to grasp *Ātman!* This *Kārikā* brings out the aforesaid idea. Some[2] disputant asserts that *Ātman* exists. Another[3] disputant, *viz.*, the Buddhist, says that it is non-existent. A third[4] disputant, the Jaina, who is a pseudo-nihilist, believing in both the existence and non-existence of Self, proclaims that *Ātman* both exists and does not exist. The[5] absolute nihilist says that nothing exists at all. He[6] who predicates existence of *Ātman* associates it with changeability in order to make it distinct from such impermanent objects as a jar etc. The[7] theory that *Ātman* is non-existent, *i.e.*, inactive, is held on account of its undifferentiated nature. It[8] is called both existent and non-existent on account of its being subject to both changeability and immutability. Non-existence is predicated of *Ātman* on account of everything ending in absolute negation or void. All the four classes of disputants, mentioned above, asserting existence, non-existence, existence and non-existence, and total non-existence (about *Ātman*), derived respectively from their notion of changeability, immutability, combination of both and total negation, reduce themselves to the position of the childish, devoid of all discrimination; and by associating *Ātman* with all these illusory ideas (*Kalpanā*) cover Its[9] real nature. If these (so-called) learned men act as veritable children on account of their ignorance of Ultimate Reality, what is to be said regarding those who are, by nature, unenlightened!

[1] *Predicates etc.*—These predicates of *Ātman* are due to illusory ideas *(Kalpanā)* regarding its real nature.

[2] *Some disputant*—This refers to the follower of the *Vaiśeṣika* theory. He asserts that there is an *Ātman* which is separate from the body, sense-organ, *Prāṇa*, etc. It is the knower and enjoyer of misery and happiness.

[3] *Another etc.*—This refers to the followers of Subjective idealism among the Buddhists known as *Kṣaṇika Vijñānavādins*. According to them *Ātman*, though separate from body etc., is identical with Buddhi or intellect. It is not permanent. Our consciousness which disappears after only a moment's existence is the only reality. Any reality, in the sense of a permanent entity, is non-existent.

[4] *The third etc.*—This refers to the followers of the *Jaina* school of thought. According to this school, *Ātman* is both existent and non-existent. Though *Ātman* is separate from the body, yet it has the same size as the body. It exists as long as the body exists and it is destroyed with the destruction of the body.

[5] *The Absolute etc.*—This refers to the extreme school of Buddhism known as the Nihilistic school. According to the follower of this theory, there is no permanent Reality like *Ātman*. All things end in destruction. Therefore absolute negation is the Highest Truth. The word 'non-existence' has been repeated in the verse in order to show the determined belief of the nihilist in his own opinion.

[6] *He who etc.*—According to the *Vaiśeṣika* theory the nature of *Ātman* is changeable as it, at different times, becomes subject to happiness, misery, desire, knowledge, etc. *Ātman* is designated as existent in order to distinguish it from all objects of an impermanent nature, such as a pot etc.

[7] *The theory etc.*—The Subjective idealist asserts that *Ātman* has a momentary existence, and as having existed only for a moment, it cannot be subject to any change or modification.

[8] *It is etc.*—The *Jaina* school predicates both existence and non-existence of *Ātman* as it partakes of the nature of both.

[9] *Its real nature.*—The real nature of *Ātman* is that it is free from all ideas or *Kalpanā*. People clinging to their pet theories, on account of their false attachment, cannot know the real nature of *Ātman*.

कोटचश्चतस्र एतास्तु ग्रहैर्यासां सदाऽऽवृतः ।
भगवानाभिरस्पृष्टो येन दृष्टः स सर्वदृक् ॥ ८४ ॥

84. *These are the four alternative theories regarding (the nature of)* Ātman, *on account of attachment to which It always remains covered (from one's view). He who has known that* Ātman *is ever-untouched by any of these (predicates) indeed sees all.*

ŚAṄKARA'S COMMENTARY

What is the nature of the essence, *i.e.*, the Ultimate Reality, by knowing which people are purged of their stupidity and are really made to attain to wisdom? It is thus replied: There are four alternate theories regarding *Ātman* such as, It exists, It does not exists, etc., mentioned in the works of those who are fond of disputations. The *Ātman* always remains covered and hidden from these vain talkers on account of their attachment to their theories. The thoughtful person who has realised the *Ātman*, known only by the (correct understanding of) Upaniṣads, as ever-untouched by any of the four alternative predicates such as It exists, It does not exist etc., is the seer[1] of all, the omniscient and the real knower of the Ultimate Reality.

[1] *Seer of all*—All that exists is *Ātman*. Therefore one who knows *Ātman* knows all. There remains nothing else to be known by him.

प्राप्य सर्वज्ञतां कृत्स्नां ब्राह्मण्यं पदमद्वयम् ।
अनापन्नादिमध्यान्तं किमतः परमीहते ॥ ८५ ॥

85. *What else remains for him to be desired when he has attained to the state of the* Brāhmaṇa—*a state of complete omniscience, non-duality and a state which is without beginning, end or middle?*

## Śaṅkara's Commentary

The[1] state of the *Brāhmaṇa* signifies the state in which one is established in Brahman. The *Śruti* says, 'This is the eternal[2] glory of the *Brāhmaṇa*'. That state of *Brāhmaṇa* is free from beginning, end or middle. That is to say, that state of non-duality is free from the (illusory ideas of) creation, preservation and destruction. Having obtained the whole[3] of omniscience, described[4] above, *i.e.*, the state of *Brāhmaṇa*, a non-dual state without beginning, end or middle, which is the same as the realisation of Self, the *summum bonum* of existence—what else remains for him to be desired? In other words, all other strivings become useless for him. It is thus said in *Gītā*, 'He has nothing to gain by the activities (of the relative world)'.

The contention of the opponent that even a Knower of Brahman should observe the ritualistic duties of daily life is refuted by this *Kārikā*.

[1] *The state etc.*—He alone is the real *Brāhmaṇa* who has directly realised himself as Brahman.

[2] *Eternal glory*—This is to say, this state is free from all modifications and changes, such as birth, death, etc.

[3] *Whole etc.*—Having realised that state one becomes totally omniscient. There is nothing else for him to know. It is because that state is the very essence of knowledge itself.

[4] *Described above*—That is to say, Brahman is free from the four attributes or predicates referred to in *Kārikā* 83.

विप्राणां विनयो ह्येष शमः प्राकृत उच्यते ।
दमः प्रकृतिदान्तत्वादेवं विद्वाञ्शमं व्रजेत् ॥ ८६ ॥

86. *This* (i.e., *the realisation of Brahman*) *is the humility natural to the* Brāhmaṇas. *Their tranquillity* (*of mind*) *is also declared to be spontaneous* (*by men of discrimination*). *They are*

*said to have attained to the state of sense-control (not through any artificial method as it comes quite natural to them). He who thus realises Brahman which is all-peace, himself becomes peaceful and tranquil.*

## Śaṅkara's Commentary

The humility of the *Brāhmaṇas* which is due to their realisation of their identity with the Self, is quite natural This is (the real significance of) his humility. The tranquillity (of the mind which the Knowers of Brahman enjoy) is also natural and not induced by any artificial[1] means. Brahman is all-peace and tranquillity. Hence the *Brāhmaṇas* are said to have controlled their sense-organs (from pursuing the external objects). This is also the cause of the tranquillity of their nature. Having realised Brahman which is, by nature, all-peace the wise man attains to peace which is the characteristic of Brahman. That is to say, he becomes identical with Brahman.

It has been stated in the previous *Kārikā* that the Knower of Brahman need no longer perform the daily ritualistic duties which are obligatory for ignorant persons. This *Kārikā* states that he need not undergo any *Yogic* or other practices in order to acquire humility, control of the senses and tranquillity of the mind. One who is established in Brahman, non-dual and all-peace, naturally and spontaneously acquires these virtues. The wise man realises that Brahman alone exists. Therefore his mind does not run after external objects, simply because they are non-existent for him. Realising Brahman everywhere, he does not show arrogance. Peace and tranquillity are quite natural for him. *Yoga* prescribes various artificial disciplines for acquiring these virtues. But he who clings to the *Yogic* practices, must be always on the alert lest his mind should be diverted to external objects. The Vedāntic method, depending upon discrimination, reveals everything as Brahman. Therefore for a *Jñānī* these virtues are quite spontaneous.

[1] *Artificial etc.*—That is to say, the *Yogic* methods.

सवस्तु सोपलम्भं च द्वयं लौकिकमिष्यते ।
अवस्तु सोपलम्भं च शुद्धं लौकिकमिष्यते ॥ ८७ ॥

87. *(Vedānta) recognises the ordinary (empirical) state of waking in which duality, consisting of objects and ideas of coming in contact with them, is known. It further recognises another more subtle state (*i.e., *the dream common to all) in which is experienced duality, consisting of the idea of coming in contact with the objects, though such objects do not exist.*

## Śaṅkara's Commentary

We have so far, come to the following conclusions: The theories of mere disputants contradicting one another, are the causes of our existence in the relative (*Saṁsāra*) world. Further these theories are characterised by partiality and aversion. Therefore these are merely false, as already shown by reasoning. On the other hand the philosophy of *Advaita* alone gives us true knowledge, as—being free from the four alternative predicates referred to above—it is untouched by partiality and aversion and is all-peace by its very nature.

Now the following topic is introduced as an explanation of the Vedāntic method of arriving at truth. The word '*Savastu*' in the text implies objects that are perceived in our empirical experiences. Similarly, the word '*Sopalambha*' in the text implies the idea of one's coming in contact with such objects. This constitutes the world of duality, common to all human beings and known as the waking state which is characterised by the subject-object relationship and which alone is the sphere of all our dealings including[1] the Scriptural etc. The waking[2] state, thus characterised, is admitted in the Vedānta Scriptures. There is another state which lacks the experiences (of the waking state) caused by external sense-organs. But[3] there exists in that state the idea of coming in contact with objects, though such objects are absent. This is admitted (in the Vedāntas) as the dream state, which is again common to all, and different from and subtler than the gross state of waking.

The nature of Ultimate Reality has been hinted at by the refutation of the theories hostile to the *Advaita Philosophy*. Now is given the *Advaita* method of arriving at Truth which consists in the analysis and co-ordination of the experiences of the three states, *viz.*, waking, dream and deep sleep.

[1] *Including etc.*—The Scriptures, limited to the sphere of duality, have no application to *Ātman*.

[2] *The waking etc.*—Vedānta admits the waking state as real to long as ignorance lasts, and further points out that the analysis of the experiences of this state together with those of the two other states leads us, indirectly, to the realisation of *Ātman*.

[3] *But etc.*—Though the objects experienced in dream exist so long as the dream lasts, they are found to be non-existing from the waking standpoint. The internality and the externality of perceptions in the dream and the waking states are mere creations of the mind.

When we look at the objects from the waking standpoint alone we think them to be real. When the same objects seen in the dream are judged from the waking standpoint we know them to be mere ideas of the mind. And analysis of deep sleep, in co-ordination with the experiences of the dream and the waking states, convinces us that everything is mind or Brahman. This is the Vedāntic method. The following verse gives a fuller explanation.

अवस्त्वनुपलम्भं च लोकोत्तरमिति स्मृतम् ।
ज्ञानं ज्ञेयं च विज्ञेयं सदा बुद्धैः प्रकीर्तितम् ॥ ॥ ८८ ॥

88. *There is another state (admitted by the wise) which is free from contact with (external) objects and altogether free from the idea of coming in contact with objects. This state is beyond all empirical experiences. The wise always describe the three,* viz., *Knowledge, Knowledge of objects and the Knowable as the Supreme Reality (which is ultimately knowable).*

## Śaṅkara's Commentary

The state in which one neither perceives any object[1] nor possesses the idea[2] of coming in contact with such object—a state free from the relationship of subject and object—is called the highest state, which is beyond all empirical experiences. All empirical experiences consist of the subject-object relationship. This state is free from all such relationship and is the seed of future experiences. This[3] is known as the state of deep sleep. That alone is called knowledge which is the realisation of essence, *i.e.*, the Supreme Reality, as well as the means to do so, *viz.*, the analysis of the states of gross experience, subtle experience and the condition beyond all experiences. The[4] three states, mentioned above, are the objects of knowledge; for, there cannot be anything knowable besides these three states. All entities falsely imagined by the different schools of the disputants are included in these three states. That which is to be ultimately known is the truth regarding the Supreme Reality, known as *Turīya*, *i.e.*, the knowledge of Self, non-dual and unborn. The illumined ones, *i.e.*, those who have seen the Supreme Reality have described these features (topics) ranging from the objects of gross experience to the Supremely Knowable Self.

[1] *Object etc.*—That is to say, the waking state.

[2] *The idea etc.*—*i.e.*, the dream state in which one, in the absence of external objects, seems to perceive such objects.

[3] *This is etc.*—In deep sleep one does not perceive any object, gross or subtle. There is no experience in deep sleep which when judged from the causal standpoint, consists of mental modification—as in the dream—due to the perception of external objects in the waking state. Deep sleep is further characterised by the total absence of the subject-object relationship. In deep sleep there exists one's real self. It has been characterised as containing the seeds of the two other states, only from the causal standpoint. Again it is from the relative standpoint

that *Turīya*, the witness of three states, is mentioned as the state of the Ultimate Knowledge.

[4] *The three etc.*—All experiences are limited to the three states. Therefore the Truth discovered by the study of the three states is the Supreme Reality.

Therefore the Vedāntic mothod of arriving at Reality is the co-ordinated study of the three states. All experiences are confined to the limits of three states.

ज्ञाने च त्रिविधे ज्ञेये क्रमेण विदिते स्वयम् ।
सर्वज्ञता हि सर्वत्र भवतीह महाधियः ॥ ८९ ॥

89. *Knowledge and the threefold knowable being known, one after another, the knower possessed of the highest reason spontaneously attains to the state of knowledge everywhere and in all things in this very life.*

### Śaṅkara's Commentary

The word *Jñānam* signifies knowledge by which one grasps the significance of the three states. The word '*Jñeya*' or knowable, signifies the three states which should be known. The first (knowable) consists of the gross state[1] of empirical experience. Then comes the state of subtle[2] experience in which the first state loses itself, *i.e.*, merges. And last comes deep sleep which is beyond all empirical experiences (gross or subtle) which results in the absence of the two previous states, *i.e.*, in which the two previous states merge. By the knowledge of these three one after[3] the other, and consequently, by the negation of the three states the *Turīya*,[4] non-dual, birthless and fearless, which alone is the Supreme Reality, is realised. Thus the knower (possessed of the highest power of discrimination) attains in this[5] very life the state of omniscience[6] which is identical with the knowledge of Self. He is called *Mahādhīḥ*[7] or the man of the highest intellect as he has understood that which transcends all human experiences. His omniscience is constant and remains undiminished. For, the knowledge of Self once realised remains as such for ever. This is[8] because the knowledge of the knower of the Supreme Reality does not appear and disappear like that of mere vain disputants.

The scriptural statements that the *Ātman* being known, everything else is known, is explained in the *Kārikā*.

[1] *Gross state etc.*—That is, the waking state.

[2] *Subtle etc.*—That is, the dream state.

[3] *One after etc.*—That is to say, by knowing that the waking state merges in the dream, and both the states merge in deep sleep.

[4] *Turīya*—Turīya is conceived to be transcendental from the relative standpoint.

[5] *In this etc.*—One need not wait for death or the other world for the realisation of the Ultimate Truth.

[6] *Omniscience.*—It is *Ātman* alone which appears as the three states. Therefore when *Ātman* is realised, all objects included in the three states are known.

[7] *Mahādhīḥ*—The Knower of Truth is designated as the possessor of the highest intellect (*buddhi*); for, the keenest intellect alone can know *Ātman*.

[8] *This is etc.*—The appearance and disappearance of knowledge, which is often noticed in our empirical experience, is due to the ignorance of the real nature of the Self. As the *Jñānī* is free from ignorance, his knowledge is constant.

This *Kārikā* further elaborates the *Advaita* method of realising Self. To the man of the grossest intellect the object appears to be extraordinary. To the man of better discrimination, the object appears to be a mere idea or modification of the mind. The *Jñānī* sees only the mind, undifferentiated, changeless and non-dual in whatever manner the objects appear. That which appears as ideas, associated with the relationship of subject and object, is known to the *Jñānī* as mere non-dual mind or *Ātman*. This is better explained in the light of the three states. The gross external objects perceived in the waking state are known to be ideas—as in dream. And the ideas of dream are known to be pure mind, non-dual and unchanging, as in deep sleep ideas disappear in the mind. This is the meaning of the merging of the previous state of waking in the subsequent state of dream and the ultimate merging of both states in deep sleep, which includes all the states. This method has been explained in the second *Mantra* of the Upaniṣad with reference to *AUM*. '*A*' which stands for the waking experiences as merged in '*U*' which signifies dream state. '*A*' and '*U*' are merged into '*M*' which indicates deep sleep. All thc three states merge in *Turīya* which is *Ātman*. From the absolute standpoint the undifferentiated mind, free from the subject-object relationship, in the Highest Reality. One who knows these becomes omniscient. He sees everywhere the non-dual *Ātman* alone. That which appears to others as name, form, object or idea, is realised by a *Jñānī* to be Self alone. *Ātman* alone exists.

हेयज्ञेयाप्यपाक्यानि विज्ञेयान्यग्रयाणतः ।
तेषामन्यत्र विज्ञेयादुपलम्भस्त्रिषु स्मृतः ॥ ९० ॥

90. *The four things to be known first are: the thing to be avoided, the objects to be realised, the things to be attained (by practice) and the thoughts to be rendered ineffective. Among these four, the three things, excepting what is to be realised*, viz., *the Supreme Reality, exist only as imagination.*

ŚAṄKARA'S COMMENTARY

There may arise a doubt that the three states of empirical experience may constitute the Ultimate Reality on account of their being pointed out[1] as things to be *gradually known*. In order to remove this doubt it is said, the '*Heyas*' or things to be avoided are the three states of empirical experience, *viz.*, the waking, the dream and the deep sleep. These do not exist in *Ātman* just as the snake is not present in the rope. Therefore they should be avoided. The *Jñeya*, *i.e.*, the thing to be known, in this text refers to the knowledge of the Ultimate Reality, free from the four[2] alternative theories described before. The things to be acquired are the accessories of spiritual realisation, *viz.*, wisdom,[3] childlike[4] innocence and silence.[5] These virtues are practised by the sages after they have renounced the threefold[6] desires. The word '*Pākyāni*' in the text signifies the latent[7] impressions which in due course attain maturity, *viz.*, such blemishes as attachment, aversion, delusion, etc. These are known as *Kaṣāya* or the passions that hide the real nature of the soul. As[8] a means to their realisation of the Supreme Reality, sages should first of all be acquainted with these four things, *viz.*, the thing to be avoided, the thing to be realised, the thing to be acquired and the thing to be rendered ineffective. These, however, with the exception of the thing to be known—that is to say, with the exception of the non-dual Brahman alone, the essence of the Ultimate Reality, that should be realised—are perceived[9] on account of our imagination. This is the conclusion of the Knowers of Brahman with regard to the three things, *viz.*, those to be avoided, acquired, and those that are (awaiting maturity and therefore) to be made ineffective. In other words, these three do not exist from the standpoint of the Ultimate Reality.

[1] *Pointed out etc.*—Compare *Kārikās* 88 and 89 (Chapter 4).

[2] *Four etc.*—Compare *Kārikā* 83 (Chapter 4).

[3] *Wisdom*—This wisdom consists of the intellectual capacity to know that the non-dual Brahman alone is the objective of the Vedānta Scriptures.

[4] *Childlike etc.*—That is to say, freedom from egoism, vanity, etc.

[5] *Silence*—It means that intense concentration on Brahman which makes one avoid all vain talk.

[6] *Threefold etc.*—That is, the desires for children, for wealth and for heavenly felicity.

[7] *Latent etc.*—An ignorant man cherishes many vices, such as attachment, hatred, delusion, etc. These are known in Vedānta as *Kaṣāya*. Among those vices, the effect of past work and thought, some are bearing fruits which are seen in our daily activities. But others are mere tendencies and latent impressions waiting for favourable conditions to manifest themselves. These latent impressions are known as '*Pākya*'. These should be destroyed by discrimination.

[8] *As a means etc.*—The seeker after Truth should know the nature of the three things to be avoided, etc., because it helps him in his spiritual progress.

[9] *Are perceived*—From the standpoint of the Ultimate Reality, Brahman alone exists. Duality is perceived on account of illusion. Therefore these three things are perceived to exist only on the plane of ignorance. And this is due to ignorance. On the acquisition of knowledge one understands that there is nothing to be avoided or shunned as Brahman alone exists (everywhere).

प्रकृत्याऽऽकाशवज्ज्ञेयाः सर्वे धर्मा अनादयः ।
विद्यते न हि नानात्वं तेषां क्वचन किंचन ॥ ९१ ॥

91. *All* Dharmas *(entities) are, by their very nature, beginningless and unattached like the* Ākāśa. *There is not the slightest variety in them, in any way, at any time.*

## Śaṅkara's Commentary

Those who seek liberation should regard, from the standpoint of the Ultimate Reality, all *Jīvas*, as by their very nature without beginning, *i.e.*, eternal, and, like *Ākāśa*, subtle, free from all blemish and all-pervading. The plural number used with regard to the '*Jīvas*' may suggest multiplicity. The second line of the *Kārikā* is meant to remove[1] any such apprehension. There is no multiplicity in the *Jīvas* even[2] in the slightest degree and under any condition.

[1] *To remove etc.*—The plural number is used in consideration of the multiplicity of *Jīvas* seen from the empirical standpoint. Even though an ignorant person sees multiplicity of embodied beings yet, in reality, there exists nothing but non-dual *Ātman*.

[2] *Even etc.*—It is because the apparent multiplicity is due to the obsession of the imaginary time and space as well as causal relation. As *Ātman* is ever free from time, space and causal relation, therefore no idea of multiplicity can ever be applied to *Ātman*.

आदिबुद्धाः प्रकृत्यैव सर्वे धर्माः सुनिश्चिताः ।
यस्यैवं भवति क्षान्तिः सोऽमृतत्वाय कल्पते ॥ ९२ ॥

92. *All* Jīvas *are, by their very nature, illumined from the very beginning and they are ever immutable in their nature. He who, having known this, rests without (sees the needlessness of) seeking further knowledge, is alone capable of realising the Highest Truth.*

ŚAṄKARA'S COMMENTARY

Even the knowableness attributed to the *Jīvas* is also due to the illusion of empirical experiences. It cannot be applied from the standpoint of the Supreme Reality. This idea is explained in this text. The *Jīvas* are illumined, by their very nature, from the very beginning. That is to say, all the *Jīvas*, like the sun which is of the very nature of eternal light, are ever illumined. No effort need be made to define their nature, as the nature of the *Jīva* is, from the very beginning, well determined.[1] It cannot be subject to any such doubt as, 'The *Jīva* may be like this or like that'. The seeker of liberation who in the manner above described, does not stand in need of anything else to make this knowledge certain to himself or others—just as the sun, by nature ever illumined, is never in need of any light from itself or others—who thus always rests[2] without forming ideas of duality regarding any further knowledge of his own self, becomes capable of realising the Ultimate Reality.

[1] *Well determined—i.e.*, all *Jīvas* are, by their very nature, ever free, pure and illumined.

[2] *Rests etc.*—That is to say, no duty nor any moral imperative can be applied to the non-dual *Ātman*.

आदिशान्ता ह्यनुत्पन्नाः प्रकृत्यैव सुनिर्वृताः ।
सर्वे धर्माः समाभिन्ना अजं साम्यं विशारदम् ॥ ९३ ॥

93. *All* Dharmas *or* Jīvas *are from the very beginning and by their very nature, all peace, unborn and completely free. They are characterised by sameness and are non-separate from one another. Therefore the* Jīvas *are* Ātman *unborn, always established in 'sameness' and 'purity' itself.*

### Śaṅkara's Commentary

Similarly, there is no room for any effort to make *Ātman* peaceful, for, all *Jīvas* are, by their very nature, eternally peaceful, unborn and of the nature of eternal freedom. All *Jīvas* are further of the same nature and non-separate from one another. They being *Ātman* in their very essence, ever pure, unborn and established in sameness, therefore the effort of attaining to liberation is meaningless. For, if something is accompanied with regard to an entity which is always of the same nature, it does not make any change in the thing itself.

The previous *Kārikā* stated the condition which alone makes one capable of attaining to liberation. But this liberation is not something external or foreign to be achieved or acquired. The Self is, by its very nature, ever free and illumined. It has never been covered with a veil. Therefore one who understands the real import of *Advaita* Vedānta, realises himself as ever pure, free and illumined and automatically ceases from making efforts at gaining further knowledge.

वैशारद्यं तु वै नास्ति भेदे विचरतां सदा ।
भेदनिम्नाः पृथग्वादास्तस्मात्ते कृपणाः स्मृताः ॥ ९४ ॥

94. *Those who always rely on (attach themselves to) separateness can never realise the innate purity of the Self. Therefore those who are drowned in the idea of separateness and who assert the separateness of (entities) are called narrow-minded.*

### Śaṅkara's Commentary

Those who have realised the truth regarding the Ultimate Reality as described above, are alone free from narrowness. Others are verily narrow-minded. This is thus described in this verse. 'Drowned in the idea of separation' means those who stick to the idea of separation, that is to say, those who confine themselves to the multiplicity of phenomenal experiences. Who are they? They are those who assert that the multiplicity of objects exists, i.e., the dualists. They are called 'narrow-minded' as they never realise the natural purity of *Ātman* on account of their ever-dwelling on the thought of multiplicity, *i.e.*, on account of their taking as real the duality of experiences imagined through ignorance. Therefore it has been truly said that these people are narrow-minded.

Compare 'Who ever, O Gārgī, without knowing that *Akṣara* (the Imperishable), offers oblations in this world, sacrifices, and performs penance for a thousand years, his work will have an end. Whatsoever, O Gārgī, without knowing this *Akṣara*, departs this world, he is *narrow-minded*. But he, O Gārgī, who departs this world, knowing this *Akṣara*, is a *Brāhmaṇa*' (*Bṛ. Up*. 3. 8. 10).

अजे साम्ये तु ये केचिद्भविष्यन्ति सुनिश्चिताः ।
ते हि लोके महाज्ञानास्तच्च लोको न गाहते ॥ ९५ ॥

95. *They alone are said to be of the highest wisdom who are firm in their conviction of the Self, unborn and ever the same. This, ordinary men cannot understand.*

### Śaṅkara's Commentary

That this knowledge of the Supreme Reality is incapable of being understood by the poor intellect, by the unwise,[1] *i.e.*, by persons of small intellect who are[2] outside the knowledge of Vedānta—is thus explained in this verse. Those few, even though[3] they may be women or others, who are firm in their conviction of the nature of Ultimate Reality, unborn and undivided, are alone possessors of the highest wisdom. They alone know the essence of Reality. Others,[4] *i.e.*, persons of ordinary intellect, cannot understand their ways, that is to to say, the Supreme Reality realised by the wise. It is said in the *Smṛti*, 'Even the gods[5] feel puzzled while trying to follow in the footsteps of those who leave no track behind, of those who realise themselves in all beings and who are always devoted to the welfare of all. They leave[6] no track behind like the birds flying through the sky'.

[1] *The unwise*—That is, men devoid of discrimination.

[2] *Who are etc.*—The Vedānta Scriptures alone can illumine us regarding the real nature of the Self. But the real meaning of the Vedānta can be understood only through reason.

[3] *Even through*—Women and *Śūdras* were interdicted from the study of the Upaniṣads though it was conceded that they could attain to the highest knowledge through *Smṛti*. This was the tradition in India during post-Upaniṣadic age. But in the age of the Upaniṣads, women were certainly not precluded from seeking or attaining the highest knowledge. Many inspiring portions of the Vedas were composed by women.

[4] *Others etc.*—Ordinary people cannot appreciate the life and activities of the truly wise because the former do not understand the truth about, and believe in Brahman and the phenomenal world.

[5] *Gods*—That is to say, the beings that are said to move in a higher plane of existence. They also stand stupefied before the Knowers of Brahman as the former have not yet transcended the realm of duality.

[6] *They leave etc.*—The wise, on account of their realisation of the non-dual *Ātman*, never manifest by way of advertisement, any supernatural characteristics by which the ordinary men could mark their greatness. The life of the truly wise is perfectly natural though their angle of vision is totally different from that of the ordinary folk. Hence no one except those who have similar wisdom can understand the nature of the wise.

अजेष्वजमसंक्रान्तं धर्मेषु ज्ञानमिष्यते ।
यतो न क्रमते ज्ञानमसंगं तेन कीर्तितम् ॥ ९६ ॥

96. *Knowledge (consciousness), the essence of the* Jīvas *(who are unborn), is admitted to be itself unborn and unrelated (to any external object). This knowledge is proclaimed to be unconditioned as it is not related to any other object (which, really speaking, does not exist).*

### Śaṅkara's Commentary

What constitutes the highest wisdom (*i.e.*, the wisdom of the knower of the non-dual *Ātman*)? This is thus explained: Knowledge which constitutes the essence of the *Dharmas* (*Jīvas*), unborn, immutable and identical with *Ātman*, is also admitted to be unborn[1] and immutable. It is just like the light and the heat belonging to the sun. Knowledge, being ever unrelated to other[2] objects, is said to be unborn. As knowledge is, thus, unrelated to other objects, it is like the *Ākāśa*, called unconditioned or absolute.

[1] *Unborn etc.*—This refutes theory of the *Nyāya* realists who say that knowledge is an attribute of *Ātman* and arises only by the contact of the mind with an external object. It has already been pointed out that the appearance of external objects is due to illusion. But consciousness (*Ātman*) does not cease to exist in the absence of objects as in *Yoga-Samādhi* or deep-sleep. Therefore the real nature of knowledge is that is is unborn and unattached. From the standpoint of Reality the *Jīva* is identical with consciousness like the identity of the sun with its heat and light.

[2] *Other objects*—It is because such objects do not, from the standpoint of Reality, exist.

अणुमात्रेऽपि वैधर्म्ये जायमानेऽविपश्चितः ।
असंगता सदा नास्ति किमुताऽऽवरणच्युतिः ॥ ९७ ॥

97. *The slightest idea of variety (in* Ātman) *entertained by the ignorant bars their approach to the unconditioned. The destruction of the veil (covering the real nature of* Ātman) *is out of the question.*

ŚAṄKARA'S COMMENTARY

If persons, through ignorance, think—as those who differ from us assert—that as entity (*i.e., Jīva* or Ātman) does undergo the slightest change, either subjectively or objectively, then such ignorant persons can never realise the ever-unrelatedness (of *Ātman*),[1] Therefore[2] it goes without saying that there cannot be any destruction of bondage (that is supposed to keep the *Jīva* bound to the world).

Accordingly the Ultimate Reality is immutable and non-dual Self. Knowledge is ever unrelated to objects as they do not, as such, exist. The view of the opponent regarding the separate existence of objects cannot be upheld as it contradicts the unrelated nature of *Ātman* which is admitted by all schools of thought.

[1] *Ātman etc.*—If the birth or production of an object be admitted, knowledge must be related to it. Otherwise one cannot know its birth. In that case the absolute and unrelated nature of knewledge cannot be maintained.

[2] *Therefore etc.*—If it be contended that knowledge is produced or if it be said that knowledge (Consciousness or *Ātman*) is not birthless by nature, then one cannot speak of liberation or the destruction of bondage, as there is no guarantee of the liberation being permanent.

अलब्धावरणाः सर्वे धर्माः प्रकृतिनिर्मलाः।
आदौ बुद्धास्तथा मुक्ता बुध्यन्त इति नायकाः ॥ ९८ ॥

98. *All* Dharmas (*i.e.,* Jīvas) *are ever free from bondage and pure by nature. They are ever illumined and liberated from the very beginning. Still the wise speak of the* Jīvas *as capable of knowing ('the Ultimate Truth').*

## Śaṅkara's Commentary

(Objection)—It has been stated in the previous *Kārikā* that (according to the view of the ignorant) the destruction of the veil covering the real nature of *Ātman* is not possible. This is a (tacit) admission by the Vedāntist that the (real) nature of the *Jīvas* is covered by a veil.

(Reply)—It[1] is not so. The *Jīvas*[2] are never subject to any veil or bondage imposed by ignorance. That is to say, they are ever free from any bondage (which does not at all exist). They are pure by nature; illumined and free from the very beginning as it is said that they are of the nature of eternal purity, knowledge and freedom. If so, why are *Jīvas* described as capable of *knowing* (the Ultimate Reality) by teachers who are competent to know the Truth, *i.e.*, those who are endowed with the power of discrimination? The reply is that it[3] is like speaking about the sun as *shining* though the very nature of the sun is all-light, or speaking about the hill, which is ever free from any motion, as always *standing*.

[1] *It etc.*—People imagine that they can remove the veil of *Ātman* by knowledge. This is also due to *Avidyā* or ignorance.

[2] *The Jīvas etc.*—If a man has got the idea of veil or impurity, then he is bound. But in the absence of such idea he is free. *Ātman* has no veil. One speaks of veil, bondage, etc., only from the causal standpoint. This position is the most difficult to be correctly understood inasmuch as for the generality of men, causation is a fact, therefore the veil or bondage of *Ātman* is also a fact. But from the standpoint of the Ultimate Truth, there is no causality and therefore no veil, bondage or ignorance.

[3] *It is like etc.*—One speaks of the rising and the shining of the sun though the sun, inasmuch as it is always of the nature of light, cannot be said to rise or shine at any particular moment. Similarly one describes the hill is standing, which correctly speaking is only a correlative of motion. Nevertheless, though the hill never moves, yet it is described as standing. As the ideas of rising, shinning, etc.,

associated with the sun or the ideas of standing etc., attributed to the hill do not effect their real nature, so also the idea of 'knowability' ascribed to the *Jīva*, which is all-knowledge by nature, does not affect it in any way.

क्रमते न हि बुद्धस्य ज्ञानं धर्मेषु तापि (यि) नः ।
सर्वे धर्मास्तथा ज्ञानं नैतद्बुद्धेन भाषितम् ॥ ९९ ॥

99. *The knowledge of the wise one, who is all-light, is ever untouched by objects. All the entities as well as knowledge (which are non-different) are also ever-untouched by any object. This is not the view of the Buddha.*

## Śaṅkara's Commentary

The knowledge of the wise man, that is to say, of the one who has attained to the Supreme Reality, is ever unrelated to other[1] objects or *Jīvas*. This knowledge is always centred in or is identical with *Jīva* (*i.e.*, *Ātman*) like the sun and its light. The word '*Tāyī*', '*All*-light', in the text signifies that which is all-pervasive like *Ākāśa* or, it may mean that which is adorable or all-knowledge. All entities, *i.e.*, *Jīvas* (beings like so many Ātmans) are as unattached as the *Ākāśa*, and ever-unrelated to anything else. Knowledge (*Jñāna*) which has been compared to *Ākāśa* in the beginning[2] of this chapter is non-different from the knowledge of the wise one who is all-light. Therefore the *Ākāśa* like knowledge of the wise does not relate itself to any other object. This is also the essence of the *Dharmas* or all entities. The essence of all the entities is the essence of Brahman, and is, like *Ākāśa*, immutable, changeless, free from parts, permanent, one and without a second, unattached, non-cognizable, unthinkable and beyond hunger and thirst. The *Śruti* also says, 'The knowledge (characteristic) of the seer is never absent'. This knowledge regarding the Ultimate Reality, non-dual and characterised by the absence of perceiver, perception and the perceived, is not the same as that declared by the Buddha.[3] The view[4] of the Buddha, which rejects the existence of external objects and asserts the existence of ideas alone, is said to be similar to or very near the truth of non-dual *Ātman*. But this knowledge of non-duality which is the Ultimate Reality can be attained through Vedānta alone.

[1] *Other etc.*—It is because objects or *Jīvas*, different from knowledge or *Ātman*, do not exist.

[2] *Beginning etc.*—Compare the first verse of the fourth chapter.

[3] *Buddha*—The reference is to the views held by the Buddhist idealists.

[4] *The view etc.*—Metaphysically speaking, Buddhistic philosophy is nearest to Advaita Vedānta in its dialectics.

दुर्दर्शमतिगम्भीरमजं साम्यं विशारदम् ।
बुद्ध्वा पदमनानात्वं नमस्कुर्मो यथाबलम् ॥ १०० ॥

100. *Having realised that condition* (i.e., *the knowledge of the Supreme Reality*) *which is extremely difficult to be grasped, profound, birthless, always the same, all-light, and free from multiplicity, we salute It as best as we can.*

### Śaṅkara's Commentary

The treatise is now completed. This Salutation is made with a view to extol the knowledge of the Supreme Reality. It[1] is extremely difficult to understand it. In other words, it is difficult of comprehension as it is not related to any of the four[2] possible predicates, such as existence, non-existence, etc. It is profound, that is, very deep like a great ocean. People[3] devoid of discrimination cannot fathom it. This knowledge (*Jñāna*) is, further, birthless, always the same and all-light. Having attained this knowledge which is free from multiplicity, having[4] become one with it, we salute it. Though[5] this absolute knowledge cannot be subjected to any relative treatment (such as, salutation etc.) yet we view it from the relative standpoint and adore it to[6] the best of our ability.

[1] *It is etc.*—It is because the knowledge of the non-dual *Ātman* is not possible by direct perception through the instrumentality of the sense-organs.

[2] *Four etc.*—Reference—*Kārikā* 83, Chapter IV.

[3] *People etc.*—This knowledge of *Ātman* can be attained only through discrimination by which one can negate what is ignorance. Then the knowledge of Self reveals itself.

[4] *Having etc.*—The knowledge of *Ātman* enables one to realise one's identity with It.

[5] *Though etc.*—Salutation always implies duality and is possible only from the relative standpoint. The author, being full of human love and gratitude to the knowledge that enabled him to realise the Supreme Reality, drags it, as it were, to the relative plane by imagining it as a Person or Teacher and then adores it by saluting it, to set an example to the ignorance.

[6] *To the best etc.*—No salutation is possible with regard to the non-dual *Ātman* because the knower of *Ātman* is one with *Ātman* Itself. This salutation is made from the relative standpoint.

Here ends Śrī Gauḍapāda's *Māṇḍūkya Upaniṣad Kārikā* with the Commentary of Śrī Śaṅkara.

Aum Peace! Peace! Peace!

## The Concluding Salutation by Śrī Śaṅkarācārya.

अजमपि जनियोगं प्रापदैश्वर्ययोगा-
दगति च गतिमत्तां प्रापदेकं ह्यनेकम् ।
विविधविषयधर्मग्राहिमुग्धेक्षणानां
प्रणतभयविहन्तृ ब्रह्म यत्तन्नतोऽस्मि ॥ १ ॥

I bow to that Brahman, destroyer of all fear of those who take shelter under It,—which, though unborn, appears to be associated with birth through Its (inscrutable and indescribable) power (of knowledge and activity); which though ever at rest, appears to be moving; and which, though non-dual, appears to have assumed multifarious forms to those whose vision is deluded by the perception of endless objects and their attributes.

प्रज्ञावैशाखवेधक्षुभितजलनिधेर्वेदनाम्नोऽन्तरस्थं
भूतान्यालोक्य मग्नान्यविरतजननग्राहघोरे समुद्रे ।
कारुण्यादुद्दधारामृतमिदममरैर्दुर्लभं भूतहेतो-
र्यस्तं पूज्याभिपूज्यं परमगुरुममुं पादपातैर्नतोऽस्मि ॥ २ ॥

I prostrate to the feet of that Great Teacher, the most adored among the adorable, who—out of sheer compassion for the beings drowned in the deep ocean of the world, infested with the terrible sharks of incessant births (and deaths)—rescued, for the benefit of all, this nectar, hardly obtainable even by the gods, from the innermost depths of the ocean of the Vedas by churning it with the (churning) rod of his illumined reason.

यत्प्रज्ञालोकभासा प्रतिहतिमगमत्स्वान्तमोहान्धकारो
मज्जोन्मज्जच्च घोरे ह्यसकृदुपजनोदन्वति त्रासने मे ।
यत्पादावाश्रितानां श्रुतिशमविनयप्राप्तिरग्र्या ह्यमोघा
तत्पादौ पावनीयौ भवभयविनुदौ सर्वभावैर्नमस्ये ॥ ३ ॥

I make obeisance with my whole being to those holy feet—the dispellers of the fear of this chain of births and deaths—of my great teacher who, through the light of his illumined reason, destroyed the darkness of delusion enveloping my mind; who destroyed for ever my (notions of) appearance and disappearance in this terrible ocean of innumerable births and deaths; and who makes all others also that take shelter at his feet, attain to the unfailing knowledge of Scriptures, peace and the state of perfect non-differentiation.

Aum Peace! Peace! Peace!

# INDEX

## TO FIRST LINES OF KĀRIKĀS


| | Ch. | Verse |
|---|---|---|
| **अ** | | |
| अकल्पकमजं ज्ञानम् | III | 33 |
| अकारो नयते विश्वम् | I | 23 |
| अजमनिद्रमस्वप्नम् | III | 36 |
| ,, ,, | IV | 81 |
| अजातस्यैव धर्मस्य | IV | 6 |
| अजातस्यैव भावस्य | III | 20 |
| अजातेस्त्रसतां तेषाम् | IV | 43 |
| अजातं जायते यस्मात् | IV | 29 |
| अजाद्वै जायते यस्य | IV | 13 |
| अजेष्वजमसंक्रान्तम् | IV | 96 |
| अजे साम्ये तु ये केचित् | IV | 95 |
| अजः कल्पितसंवृत्या | IV | 74 |
| अणुमात्रेऽपि वैधर्म्ये | IV | 97 |
| अतो वक्ष्याम्यकार्पण्यम् | III | 2 |
| अदीर्घत्वाच्च कालस्य | II | 2 |
| अद्वयं च द्वयाभासम् | III | 30 |
| ,, ,, | IV | 62 |
| अद्वैतं परमार्थो हि | III | 18 |
| अनादिमायया सुप्तः | I | 16 |
| अनादेरन्तवत्वं च | IV | 30 |
| अनिमित्तस्य चित्तस्य | IV | 77 |
| अनिश्चिता यथा रज्जुः | II | 17 |
| अन्तःस्थानात्तु भेदानाम् | II | 4 |
| अन्यथा गृह्णतः स्वप्नः | I | 15 |
| अपूर्वं स्थानिधर्मो हि | II | 8 |
| अभावश्च रथादीनाम् | II | 3 |
| अभूताभिनिवेशाद्धि | IV | 79 |
| अभूताभिनिवेशोऽस्ति | IV | 75 |
| अमात्रोऽनन्तमात्रश्च | I | 29 |
| अलब्धावरणाः सर्वे | IV | 98 |
| अलाते स्पन्दमाने वै | IV | 49 |
| अव्यक्ता एव येऽन्तस्तु | II | 15 |
| अवस्त्वनुपलम्भं च | IV | 88 |
| अशक्तिरपरिज्ञानम् | IV | 19 |
| असज्जागरिते दृष्ट्वा | IV | 39 |
| असतो मायया जन्म | III | 28 |
| अस्ति नास्त्यस्ति नास्तीति | IV | 83 |
| अस्पन्दमानमलातम् | IV | 48 |
| अस्पर्शयोगो वै नाम | III | 39 |
| ,, ,, | IV | 2 |
| **आ** | | |
| आत्मसत्यानुबोधेन | III | 32 |
| आत्मा ह्याकाशवज्जीवैः | III | 3 |
| आदावन्ते च यन्नास्ति | II | 6 |
| ,, ,, | IV | 31 |

| | Ch. | Verse |
|---|---|---|
| आदिबुद्धाः प्रकृत्यैव | IV | 92 |
| आदिशान्ता ह्यनुत्पन्नाः | IV | 93 |
| आश्रमास्त्रिविधा हीन | III | 16 |
| **इ** | | |
| इच्छामात्रं प्रभोः सृष्टिः | I | 8 |
| **उ** | | |
| उत्पादस्याप्रसिद्धत्वात् | IV | 38 |
| उत्सेक उदधेर्यद्वत् | III | 41 |
| उपलम्भात्समाचारात् | IV | 42 |
| ,, ,, | IV | 44 |
| उपायेन निगृह्णीयात् | III | 42 |
| उपासनाश्रितो धर्मः | III | 1 |
| उभयोरपि वैतथ्यम् | II | 11 |
| उभे ह्यन्योन्यदृश्ये ते | IV | 67 |
| **ऋ** | | |
| ऋजुवक्रादिकाभासम् | IV | 47 |
| **ए** | | |
| एतैरेषोऽपृथग्भावैः | II | 30 |
| एवं न चित्तजा धर्माः | IV | 54 |
| एवं न जायते चित्तम् | IV | 46 |
| **ओ** | | |
| ओंकारं पादशो विद्यात् | I | 24 |
| **क** | | |
| कल्पयत्यात्मनाऽऽत्मानम् | II | 12 |
| कारणाद्यद्यनन्यत्वम् | IV | 12 |
| कारणं यस्य वै कार्यम् | IV | 11 |
| कार्यकारणबद्धौ तौ | I | 11 |
| काल इति कालविदः | II | 24 |
| कोटयश्चतस्र एतास्तु | IV | 84 |
| क्रमते न हि बुद्धस्य | IV | 99 |
| **ख** | | |
| ख्याप्यमानामजातिं तैः | IV | 5 |
| **ग** | | |
| ग्रहणाज्जागरितवत् | IV | 37 |
| ग्रहो न तत्र नोत्सर्गः | III | 38 |
| **घ** | | |
| घटादिषु प्रलीनेषु | III | 4 |
| **च** | | |
| चरन् जागरिते जाग्रत् | IV | 65 |
| चित्तकाला हि येऽन्तस्तु | II | 14 |
| चित्तं न संस्पृशत्यर्थम् | IV | 26 |
| चित्तस्पन्दितमेवेदम् | IV | 72 |
| **ज** | | |
| जरामरणनिर्मुक्ताः | IV | 10 |
| जाग्रच्चित्तेक्षणीयास्ते | IV | 66 |
| जाग्रद्वृत्तावपि त्वन्तः | II | 10 |
| जात्याभासं चलाभासम् | IV | 45 |
| जीवं कल्पयते पूर्वम् | II | 16 |
| जीवात्मनोरनन्यत्वम् | III | 13 |
| जीवात्मनोः पृथक्त्वं यत् | III | 14 |

| | Ch. | Verse |
|---|---|---|
| **त** | | |
| तत्वमाध्यात्मिकं दृष्ट्वा | II | 38 |
| तस्मादेवं विदित्वैनम् | II | 36 |
| तस्मान्न जायते चित्तम् | IV | 28 |
| तैजसस्योत्वविज्ञाने | I | 20 |
| त्रिषु धामसु यत्तुल्यम् | I | 22 |
| त्रिषु धामसु यद्भोज्यम् | I | 5 |
| **द** | | |
| दक्षिणाक्षिमुखे विश्वः | I | 2 |
| दुःखं सर्वमनुस्मृत्य | III | 43 |
| दुर्दर्शमतिगम्भीरम् | IV | 100 |
| द्रव्यं द्रव्यस्य हेतुः स्यात् | IV | 53 |
| द्वयोर्द्वयोर्मधुज्ञाने | III | 12 |
| द्वैतस्याग्रहणं तुल्यम् | I | 13 |
| **ध** | | |
| धर्मा य इति जायन्ते | IV | 58 |
| **न** | | |
| न कश्चिज्जायते जीवः | III | 48 |
| ,, ,, | IV | 71 |
| न निर्गता अलातात्ते | IV | 50 |
| न निर्गतास्ते विज्ञानात् | IV | 52 |
| न निरोधो न चोत्पत्तिः | II | 32 |
| न भवत्यमृतं मर्त्यम् | III | 21 |
| ,, ,, | IV | 7 |
| न युक्तं दर्शनं गत्वा | IV | 34 |
| नाऽऽकाशस्य घटाकाशः | III | 7 |
| नाजेषु सर्वधर्मेषु | IV | 60 |
| नात्मभावेन नानेदं | II | 34 |
| नात्मानं न परांश्चैव | I | 12 |
| नास्त्यसद्धेतुकमसत् | IV | 40 |
| नाऽऽस्वादयेत्सुखं तत्र | III | 45 |
| निगृहीतस्य मनसः | III | 34 |
| निमित्तं न सदा चित्तम् | IV | 27 |
| निवृत्तस्याप्रवृत्तस्य | IV | 80 |
| निवृत्तेः सर्वदुःखानाम् | I | 10 |
| निश्चितायां यथा रज्ज्वाम् | II | 18 |
| निस्तुतिर्निर्नमस्कारः | II | 37 |
| नेह नानेति चाम्नायात् | III | 24 |
| **प** | | |
| पञ्चविंशक इत्येके | II | 26 |
| पादा इति पादविदः | II | 21 |
| पूर्वापरापरिज्ञानम् | IV | 21 |
| प्राकृत्याकाशवज्ज्ञेयः | IV | 91 |
| प्रणवो ह्यपरं ब्रह्म | I | 26 |
| प्रणवं हीश्वरं विद्यात् | I | 28 |
| प्रपञ्चो यदि विद्येत | I | 17 |
| प्रभवः सर्वभावानाम् | I | 6 |
| प्रज्ञप्तेः सनिमित्तत्त्वम् | IV | 24 |
| ,, ,, | IV | 25 |
| प्राण इति प्राणविदः | II | 20 |

| | Ch. | Verse |
|---|---|---|
| प्राणादिभिरनन्तैश्च | II | 19 |
| प्राप्य सर्वज्ञतां कृत्स्नाम् | IV | 85 |
| **फ** | | |
| फलादुत्पद्यमानस्सन् | IV | 17 |
| **ब** | | |
| बहिष्प्रज्ञो विभुर्विश्वः | I | 1 |
| बीज़ाङ्कुराख्यो दृष्टांतः | IV | 20 |
| बुद्ध्वाऽनिमित्ततां सत्याम् | IV | 78 |
| **भ** | | |
| भावैरसद्भिरेवायम् | II | 33 |
| भूततोऽभूततो वाऽपि | III | 23 |
| भूतं न जायते किञ्चित् | IV | 4 |
| भूतस्य जातिमिच्छन्ति | IV | 3 |
| भोगार्थं सृष्टिरित्यन्ये | I | 9 |
| **म** | | |
| मकारभावे प्राज्ञस्य | I | 21 |
| मन इति मनोविदः | II | 25 |
| मनसो निग्रहायात्तम् | III | 40 |
| मनो दृश्यमिदं द्वैतम् | III | 31 |
| मरणे संभवे चैव | III | 9 |
| मायया भिद्यते ह्येतत् | III | 19 |
| मित्राद्यैः सह संमन्त्र्य | IV | 35 |
| मृल्लोहविस्फुलिङ्गाद्यैः | III | 15 |
| **य** | | |
| यथा निर्मितको जीवः | IV | 70 |
| यथा भवति बालानाम् | III | 8 |
| यथा मायामयाद्बीजात् | IV | 59 |
| यथा मायामयो जीवः | IV | 69 |
| यथा स्वप्नमयो जीवः | IV | 68 |
| यथा स्वप्ने द्वयाभासम् | III | 29 |
| ,, ,, | IV | 61 |
| यथैकस्मिन्घटाकाशे | III | 5 |
| यदा न लभते हेतून् | IV | 76 |
| यदा न लीयते चित्तम् | III | 46 |
| यदि हेतोः फलात्सिद्धिः | IV | 18 |
| यं भावं दर्शयेद्यस्य | II | 29 |
| यावद्धेतुफलावेशः | IV | 55 |
| ,, ,, | IV | 56 |
| युञ्जीत प्रणवे चेतः | I | 25 |
| योऽस्ति कल्पितसंवृत्या | IV | 73 |
| **र** | | |
| रसादयो हि ये कोशाः | III | 11 |
| रूपकार्यसमाख्याश्च | III | 6 |
| **ल** | | |
| लये संबोधयेच्चित्तम् | III | 44 |
| लीयते हि सुषुप्ते तत् | III | 35 |
| लोकाँल्लोकविदः प्राहुः | II | 27 |
| **व** | | |
| विकरोत्यपरान्भावान् | II | 13 |
| विकल्पो विनिवर्तेत | I | 18 |
| विपर्यासाद्यथा जाग्रत् | IV | 41 |
| विप्राणां विनयो ह्येषः | IV | 86 |

| | Ch. | Verse |
|---|---|---|
| विभूतिं प्रसवं त्वन्ये | I | 7 |
| विश्वस्यात्वविवक्षायाम् | I | 19 |
| विश्वो हि स्थूलभुङ्नित्यम् | I | 3 |
| विज्ञाने स्पन्दमाने वै | IV | 51 |
| वीतरागभयक्रोधैः | II | 35 |
| वेदा इति वेदविदः | II | 22 |
| वैतथ्यं सर्वभावानाम् | II | 1 |
| वैशारद्यं तु वै नास्ति | IV | 94 |
| **स** | | |
| स एष नेति नेतीति | III | 26 |
| सतो हि मायया जन्म | III | 27 |
| सप्रयोजनता तेषाम् | II | 7 |
| ,, ,, | IV | 32 |
| संघाताः स्वप्नवत्सर्वे | III | 10 |
| संभवे हेतुफलयोः | IV | 16 |
| संभूतेरपवादाच्च | III | 25 |
| संवृत्या जायते सर्वम् | IV | 57 |
| सर्वस्य प्रणवो ह्यादिः | I | 27 |
| सर्वाभिलाषविगतः | III | 37 |
| सर्वे धर्मा मृषा स्वप्ने | IV | 33 |
| सवस्तु सोपलम्भं च | IV | 87 |
| सांसिद्धिकी स्वाभाविकी | IV | 9 |
| सुखमाव्रियते नित्यम् | IV | 82 |

| | Ch. | Veres |
|---|---|---|
| सूक्ष्म इति सूक्ष्मविदः | II | 23 |
| सृष्टिरिति सृष्टिविदः | II | 28 |
| स्थूलं तर्पयते विश्वं | I | 4 |
| स्वतो वा परतो वापि | IV | 22 |
| स्वप्नजागरितस्थाने | II | 5 |
| स्वप्नदृक्चित्तदृश्यास्ते | IV | 64 |
| स्वप्नदृक्प्रचरन् स्वप्ने | IV | 63 |
| स्वप्ननिद्रायुतावाद्यौ | I | 14 |
| स्वप्नमाये यथादृष्टे | II | 31 |
| स्वप्नवृत्तावपि त्वन्तः | II | 9 |
| स्वप्ने चावस्तुकः कायः | IV | 36 |
| स्वभावेनामृतो यस्य | III | 22 |
| ,, ,, | IV | 8 |
| स्वसिद्धान्तव्यवस्थासु | III | 17 |
| स्वस्थं शान्तं सनिर्वाणम् | III | 47 |
| **ह** | | |
| हेतुर्न जायतेऽनादेः | IV | 23 |
| हेतोरादिः फलं येषाम् | IV | 14 |
| ,, ,, | IV | 15 |
| हेयज्ञेयाप्यपाक्यानि | IV | 90 |
| **ज्ञ** | | |
| ज्ञाने च त्रिविधे ज्ञेये | IV | 89 |
| ज्ञानेनाऽकाशकल्पेन | IV | 1 |